To David

a Superb ph[...]

my admira[...] [...]gamm[...]

Ed Zigler

The Hidden History
of Head Start

Development at Risk Series

Series Editor
Jacob A. Burack

The Hidden History of Head Start
Edward Zigler and Sally J. Styfco

The Hidden History of Head Start

EDWARD ZIGLER

SALLY J. STYFCO

UNIVERSITY PRESS

2010

OXFORD
UNIVERSITY PRESS

Oxford University Press, Inc., publishes works that further
Oxford University's objective of excellence
in research, scholarship, and education.

Oxford   New York
Auckland   Cape Town   Dar es Salaam   Hong Kong   Karachi
Kuala Lumpur   Madrid   Melbourne   Mexico City   Nairobi
New Delhi   Shanghai   Taipei   Toronto

With offices in
Argentina   Austria   Brazil   Chile   Czech Republic   France   Greece
Guatemala   Hungary   Italy   Japan   Poland   Portugal   Singapore
South Korea   Switzerland   Thailand   Turkey   Ukraine   Vietnam

Library of Congress Cataloging-in-Publication Data

Zigler, Edward, 1930–
The hidden history of head start / Edward Zigler, Sally J. Styfco.
p.   cm. — (Development at risk series)
Includes bibliographical references.
ISBN 978-0-19-539376-7
1. Head Start Program (U.S.)—History.   2. Early childhood
education—United States—History.   I. Styfco, Sally J.   II. Title.
LC4091.Z55 2010
372.210973—dc22
2009034602

1   3   5   7   9   8   6   4   2

Printed in the United States of America
on acid-free paper

We dedicate this book to Sargent Shriver,
the first father of Head Start.

Acknowledgments

To uncover some of Head Start's hidden and/or forgotten history, I interviewed many old friends and colleagues who were closely involved in the behind-the-scenes details. They include Richard Darlington, Carolyn Harmon, Ron Herndon, Irving Lazar, John Meier, Clennie Murphy, Peggy Pizzo, Julius Richmond, Jule Sugarman, and Shep White. Also helpful in filling in the blanks were Ben Allen, Jeanne Brooks-Gunn, Lois-Ellin Datta, Ruth Hubbell McKey, John Merrow, Joan Ohl, Bob Patricelli, Gregg Powell, and Larry Schweinhart. For one of my earlier books on Head Start, Susan Muenchow interviewed scores of people, many of whom are no longer here to tell their stories. Some of the quotes I use are taken from these interviews, and I am therefore grateful to Susan for her contributions to this book. I also thank Leigh Esparo and Rebecca Sullivan for their hard secretarial work.

The book was made possible through the financial support of the Smith Richardson Foundation, the William T. Grant Foundation, the Foundation for Child Development, and the A. L. Mailman Family Foundation.

Preface

The genesis of this and earlier books my colleagues and I have written about our nation's Head Start program can be traced to a conversation I had with Pat Moynihan in the Nixon White House in 1971. Moynihan was then serving as domestic counselor to the president, and I was a Nixon appointee heading a new federal agency, the Office of Child Development (OCD), which evolved into the current Administration on Children, Youth and Families. OCD was the agency responsible for managing the Head Start program. Pat (a sociologist) and I (a child psychologist) were both scholars and had been friends since he taught at Wesleyan, a short distance from my own academic home at Yale.

Moynihan was very upset and needed someone with whom he could ventilate. He rushed at me and said, "Ed, you're not going to believe this!" Evidently he had searched all the libraries and resources available to the federal government and was unable to find even a single pamphlet on the Civilian Conservation Corps (CCC), a Roosevelt New Deal program that provided education and jobs to older adolescents and young adults during the Great Depression of the 1930s. This program had similarities to the Job Corps program then being launched by the Office of Economic Opportunity. I joined Moynihan in scholarly ire that such primary resources had vanished and with them the recorded history of the CCC.

I had served on Head Start's planning committee and at the time was the federal official in charge of the program. I promised Moynihan that this fate of being forgotten would never befall Head Start and that I would do my best to document its story. Neither of us had an inkling that Head Start would become such a milestone program or that it would generate an entire literature incrementally constructed by historians, social scientists, and policy analysts. This book is therefore not a complete history of Head Start or its very programmatic roots. Excellent historical accounts can be found in Vinovskis's (2005) detailed book about Head Start in the Kennedy and Johnson administrations and the broader history by Harold and Pamela Silver (1991). Two revisionist histories were compiled by Lynda Ames and Jeanne Ellsworth (1997; Ellsworth & Ames, 1998). I myself have produced two earlier records, one co-edited with Jeanette Valentine (1997) and the other written with Susan Munchow (1992).

What, then, is there left to say? Surprisingly, a great deal. As one who has great respect for the power of history to teach us, it troubles me that many key aspects of Head Start's past remain untold or are widely misunderstood. For example, Head Start is typically described as an antipoverty program or a school-readiness program. When it began, however, some thought it could be an effort to reduce mental retardation. President Johnson's chief in the War on Poverty, Sargent Shriver, himself leaned this way, seizing premature research findings to champion Head Start's capacity to raise children's IQs—the ultimate benchmark as to whether or not a child is retarded.

In the same vein, few are aware that Head Start had two dissimilar sets of roots in the Office of Economic Opportunity (OEO). The planning committee was totally unaware that a plan quite different than the one they recommended had already been produced within OEO's Community Action Program (Kuntz, 1998). Head Start, which was housed in OEO, attempted to straddle both sets of roots for the first 5 years of its existence. This ended in the early 1970s, when program administrators fully embraced the single goal of the planning committee, namely optimizing children's total development.

There are many other gaps in the Head Start chronicles. Although all histories report how the 1969 Westinghouse report almost destroyed Head Start, the redeeming importance of the later Cornell Consortium has never been sufficiently recognized. Nor has the fact that two of Head Start's greatest scholarly heroes played roles in its near destruction. Although the Nixon White House plan to dismantle the program over a 3-year period has been mentioned, just how far along this plan was is still unknown. Further, key events in Head Start's later years, from President Reagan to George W. Bush, have yet to be summarized. The purpose of this book, then, is to present a brief, accessible account of often overlooked details of Head Start's history extending to recent times. To make the story coherent, we will have to retell some key events that have already been reported about Head Start's amazing past.

My vantage point is that of an insider, my story based on personal experience stored in near and distant memory. (Others' recollections may not always coincide with mine.) My life has been closely involved with Head Start since, at the age of 35, I became the youngest member of the planning committee in 1965. I took a leave from academia from 1970–1972 to serve as the federal official responsible for the program. Today, at the age of 79, I am still very active in Head Start matters. I have been a consultant on Head Start to every administration (both Republican and Democrat) since the early 1970s, and I continue to advise cabinet-rank officers and congressional committees responsible for overseeing Head Start. I surmise the reason for my long-term commitment is that during these four decades, Head Start changed me. It certainly changed my scholarly field of human development, and I played a role in changing Head Start. Some have vilified me for the changes I made, while others have extolled me for keeping Head Start alive and trying to make it better.

This discussion brings up a sensitive issue that proves the need for this "hidden" history. I have often been called the "father" of Head Start, but this claim is untrue. In fact, the Head Start history I wrote with Susan Muenchow in 1992 was dedicated to Sargent Shriver, Robert Cooke, Julius Richmond, and Jule Sugarman as the four individuals who "made Head Start happen." We listed them in the order of their importance in creating Head Start. Sargent Shriver, to whom this book is dedicated, is unquestionably the real father of Head Start. He selected Cooke to be chairman of the planning committee, named Richmond as the program's first director, and hired Sugarman to be the day-to-day administrative leader. These facts are pretty clear, so how did I get into competition for the title of "father"?

The misnomer simply will not go away. For example, in a recent article in the *Washington Post*, the reporter wrote that I was "frequently referred to as the father of Head Start." A complaining letter to the editor was sent by an individual who had been in OEO's Community Action Program (CAP) asserting that I wasn't even present at Head Start's beginning. This is also true. Head Start was first born in the CAP and had a second birth in response to the vision of the planning committee. As explained in the early chapters of this book, trying to crosswalk both of these visions caused both Head Start and CAP to experience a lot of grief during the first few years of their existence.

The *Washington Post* experience reminded me of an incident many years ago. While eating dinner, I was watching a national newscast and probably rolled my eyes when the anchor referred to me as the father of Head Start. No more than 30 seconds later, the phone rang. It was Sarge Shriver. He told me that he didn't mind, but that his wife Eunice (a close friend of mine for many years) was very upset that he wasn't getting due credit. (Sarge had my sympathy since I remembered his son, Tim, once pointing out that what his father and his uncle, Senator Ted Kennedy, had in common was that both were intimidated by

Eunice.) Sarge concluded the conversation by saying, "You have to do something about this." I hung up the phone upset, not knowing exactly what to do.

I don't know why I am frequently referred to in this way. I could guess I received this undeserved honor because I am the only individual whose name has been associated with Head Start throughout its existence, beginning with the planning committee. Another explanation is contained in the inscription of an award I received from the Department of Health and Human Services at Head Start's Third National Research Conference in 1996. It reads in part:

> Head Start was fortunate. In the 31 years of its existence, it has always had fatherly love, guidance and support through Edward Zigler. He was not only there for Head Start's conception, but he helped with the birth, and was always there during the years it was growing up. As the good father he is, Ed was there to praise Head Start when it did well, protect, nourish, and encourage it during dangerous times, and admonish and correct it, when he felt it could do better. But whatever the fatherly task might be, it was always undertaken with unwavering and unconditional love.
>
> And finally, after the child had reached full maturity, he was proudly there to assist with the birth of, and to welcome the new generation, Early Head Start.
>
> And so, in recognition and gratitude for a father's strength, guidance, and support, you are presented with this plaque on behalf of Head Start and all the conference attendees.
>
> It reads: "To Edward Zigler, Ph.D., the true 'father' of Head Start. You have raised this child well."

As I said, I believe Sarge is Head Start's "true" father, but perhaps there is room for both of us. In my field of study, we make a distinction between the "biological" father who conceives a child, and the "psychological" father who raises the child. Sarge Shriver is the "biological" or real father of Head Start, whereas the Head Start community has viewed me as its psychological father.

My selection of Sally Styfco to co-author this book was both an easy and logical choice. Sally has worked with me as a collaborator for over 40 years. She has co-edited two books on Head Start with me. She too has been very close to Head Start for many years in her role as Director of the Head Start Unit at Yale's Edward Zigler Center in Child Development and Social Policy. Finally, Sally is a superb writer as well as editor who takes my prolix writing and penchant for scientific jargon and turns it into concise and readable prose.

Although we each have invested relatively equal amounts of work into preparing this book, we have chosen to use the first person when relating

Zigler's recollections and first-hand experiences. This was done not only to ease readability but, because part of the story conveys the inner workings of Washington, to add depth to my harsh introduction to the politics that were just as much in charge of Head Start as I was when I ran OCD. At times we speak in the plural when explaining our collective interpretations and opinions.

Edward Zigler, Ph.D.
New Haven, CT
May 2009

Contents

The Hidden History
of Head Start

I

The Predawn of Head Start

Beginnings of Early Childhood Intervention

Elements of the philosophy underlying Head Start's conception and design can be gleaned from a sampling of its historical forebearers. Efforts to help poor children's early learning can be traced back at least to the seventeenth century and Comenius's "school of the mother's knee" (Towns, 1975). In the early nineteenth century when the industrial revolution got underway, British social reformers established infant schools for disadvantaged young children in factory towns and large cities (Vinovskis, 1999). Their purpose was only partly to provide child care for youngsters whose mothers worked long hours in the factories. Many of these programs were designed to provide moral and character training so the children would grow up to be honest and hard-working (Cahan, 1989). The movement spread to the United States in the 1820s, when religious and civic groups established infant schools for children from poor families. The curricula were mainly religious and moral, although lessons in hygiene and early academics were sometimes offered.

More affluent families took note of the early educational opportunities being provided to the children of the poor and wanted their own children to have access to preschool. In Boston and other progressive cities, private infant schools were opened to meet this desire. The schools focused mainly on early enrichment rather than moral training, which higher-income families were presumed to teach at home (Cahan, 1989).

Infant schools in America generally served children from about 18 months to 4 years old. By 1840, 40% of all 3-year-olds in Massachusetts were enrolled in an infant school or, by this time, attended regular public or private school (Vinovskis, 1999). This venue of early schooling, however, was short-lived. The demise of the infant schools was precipitated by a paper written in 1833 by a prominent physician, Amariah Brigham, who argued that "overstimulating a child's mind deprived the developing brain of the energy necessary for growth and eventually resulted in an enfeebled mind," dooming children educated too early "to insanity in later life" (Vinovskis, 1999, pp. 71–72). Donations to the schools abruptly ceased, and the social order returned to the premise that young children are best raised by their mothers at home.

Poor mothers, of course, still needed to work after the infant schools closed and left them without a source of child care. Eventually the welfare system was built to enable them to remain at home with their children. When Head Start began, parents were invited to participate in their children's classrooms, which helped it dodge century-old criticisms that young children belong at their mother's side. Although the main premise of the infant schools had been discredited by the time Head Start and other modern early childhood intervention programs were launched, their legacy was a belief that teaching preschool children is beneficial and can have a salutary effect on their later development. Yet, reminiscent of the naysayers of the nineteenth century, prominent scholars of today still argue that unless the education program is developmentally appropriate and geared to the capacities of preschool children, institutionalized schooling for this age group can be counterproductive.

Seeds of Head Start can also be found in other programs dating back to the early 1900s. In England, Margaret McMillan founded the "open-air nursery" for deprived children living in slums. Services focused on health as well as education (Condry, 1983), content reminiscent of Head Start's comprehensive services. In Rome, Maria Montessori founded the Casa di Bambini in the basement of a slum apartment house (Condry, 1983). Montessori attempted to improve deprived children's cognitive abilities with a curriculum she developed that emphasized spontaneous learning and sensory training rather than didactic teaching. In addition to education and child care, medical attention was provided. The children's mothers were required to attend the "children's house" once a week (Ross, 1997), an early instance of parent involvement. Montessori schools still exist across America, and her preschool curriculum is in use in some Head Start centers.

Perhaps Head Start's closest predecessor was America's nursery school movement, which is typically traced back to 1929 with the birth of the National Association for Nursery Education. (NANE later became today's National Association for the Education of Young Children, or NAEYC.) Like the Head Start Planning Committee, NANE's infrastructure included some leading developmental thinkers such as Arnold Gesell and Lois Stolz. Thus, developmental scientists and nursery school educators had already been allies for decades before Head Start, when they once again collaborated in the hope of facilitating poor children's development. Their collaboration was facilitated by a major initiative by foundations that funded a number of university-based child research settings, with most containing a nursery school component. Yale's own Child Study Center dates back to this time.

Beatty states the hope of the nursery school movement was that "child-development research conducted in special university-affiliated institutes and campus nursery schools would generate useful information about child-rearing" (2001, p. 176). Indeed, the scientific insights gathered in these schools were passed on to mothers via parent education activities, and the nurseries were often used as "practice grounds" for young women. The nursery school movement certified the value of preschool for children by the child development science existing at the time. As long ago as 1931, George Stoddard, Director of the Iowa Child Welfare Research Station, concluded "hypothesis, theory, observation, and experiment all seem to point . . . to a strong need for organized, professional . . . education for children, three or four years below the conventional primary age" (quoted in Beatty 2001, p. 176). This message was delivered mainly to well-educated, middle- and upper-class parents, who were the primary clients of the university schools. "In short, the nursery school persisted as a track for affluent parents and their children" (Cahan, 1989, p. 32).

For the planners of Head Start, it was not a huge leap to believe that poor children from educationally deprived homes would profit even more from nursery school experience than wealthier children whose home life already provided enriched interactions with the environment. Indeed, educators and scientists from affiliated schools in the 1940s were arguing that "nursery schools were good things for the economically underprivileged" (in Beatty 2001, 177). The challenge for Head Start's planners was how to modify the typical nursery school program delivered to children from wealthy homes to meet the unique needs of children and their families living in poverty.

Sargent Shriver noted the historic debt he owed to the kindergarten movement, which also predated Head Start. (As noted in the preface and detailed in Chapter 2, Shriver conceived the idea of a preschool program for poor children that blossomed into Head Start.) The concept of kindergarten (a children's garden) was brought to America by Margaretta Schurz in the mid–nineteenth century. Initially opened to children of the wealthy, philanthropists picked up the idea and offered kindergarten to poor children to help them develop the basic skills they would need in school (Ross, 1997). Eventually kindergarten became an integrated part of public school systems, but it was not universally available. By the time Head Start opened in 1965, only 42% of 5-year-olds were in kindergarten (Vinovskis, 2005), and they tended to be from the middle class (Rioux, 1967). For a complete history of preschool programs in America, including the nursery school movement, the reader is referred to the excellent works by Barbara Beatty (1995, 2001).

Experimental Interventions in America

Despite the long history of intervention programs for poor children prior to Head Start, most were run by charities, social reformers, individuals, and private groups with a mission or calling. The growing child study movement did not infiltrate these programs to the point that practice could be linked to child out-comes. In other words, little was known about the effectiveness of the programs or even about the dynamics of what went on in them on a day-to-day basis. When the planners met to design Head Start, they had very little scientific evidence to guide them. If they were to build a program to prepare poor children for school, they needed to know more about poor children's needs and about practices effective in meeting them. They turned therefore to a handful of experimental interventions that were publishing early findings in the scientific literature.

One experimental project that became very important because it captivated Sargent Shriver was the Early Training Project (Gray and Klaus, 1970; Klaus and Gray, 1968). The program was created by Susan Gray and Rupert Klaus, who were at the George Peabody College for Teachers in Nashville. Significantly, Peabody, which later became part of Vanderbilt University, was something of a mecca for research on mental retardation. The preschoolers chosen for the Early Training Project, however, were not retarded. Rather, they were at risk for "progressive retardation" in their school performance. This term captured the common observation that poor children often begin school behind in language and social skills so are unable to keep up with the curricula and fall further behind as they progress through school.

The 88 participants were from extremely poor inner-city homes headed by parents with weak educational and occupational status. All of the children were black, and because schools in Tennessee were still segregated, most later attended all-black elementary schools. The children were randomly assigned to four groups, two of which were controls and did not receive intervention. One of the treatment groups attended half-day preschool for 10 weeks during the summer before they entered elementary school. The program continued the following two summers. During the rest of the year, weekly home visits were made. The second treatment group had the same intervention but for two summers and 2 years of home visiting. The classroom curriculum was designed to foster those attitudes and aptitudes that contribute to academic success. The home visits were intended to teach parents to be active participants in their child's learning and to raise their expectations for the child's achievements and future.

The results showed that the children's IQ scores increased after the first summer, then leveled off, and eventually declined slightly once the intervention was over. The control groups also showed an increase in IQ when the children started elementary school but then had a small but consistent decline (evidence of "progressive retardation"). Three years after the intervention was over, the IQs of the treatment groups remained significantly higher. Achievement test scores followed roughly the same pattern, but the early advantage of the treatment groups disappeared by the end of fourth grade, a loss the researchers ascribed to the failure of the schools the children attended to build on their early success and the fact that 2 to 3 years of home visits were not enough to change the home environment's contribution to school performance.

The scientific significance of the Early Training Project is that it was one of the earliest to demonstrate, in a random assignment design (now considered the gold standard for research), that early enrichment and parental involvement can boost the intellectual performance of children at risk of school failure. Another contribution is that it disproved the notion that brief intervention could forever change the life of a poor child. An initial pilot program, conducted for one summer alone, had shown that children's gains were lost after a year in school. That experience led the researchers to design the longer intervention.

The project also came to be very important to social policy decisions. Sargent Shriver had visited the program as part of his work with the family's Kennedy Foundation, which funded the experiment. He was amazed with the findings of increased IQ test scores. "Being of an era when we thought you were born with an IQ just as you are born with blue eyes, that fact really impressed me and stuck in my head" (quoted in Zigler and Muenchow, 1992, p. 5). Shriver thought that if intensive efforts were able to raise the IQs of "retarded" children, a similar program might achieve comparable results with children who were of normal intelligence but who were poor and unlikely to do well in school. Although he was wrong about the children in the Early Training Project having initial IQs in the retarded range, he took home the correct message: that early intervention can indeed improve the cognitive functioning and school performance of poor children. (Shriver was not the only one to confuse poverty with retardation. Because Gray's project was conducted at Peabody, which was famous for mental retardation research, many scholars simply assumed the participants were retarded.)

Another experimental effort that gained prominence because it attracted a great deal of media attention was developed by Martin and Cynthia Deutsch at New York University. The Institute for Developmental Studies (IDS) Early Enrichment Program was an attempt to alter the life trajectory of minority children living in the Harlem neighborhood of New York City. The short-term goal was to arrest the "cumulative deficit" observed in disadvantaged children as they progress through school by teaching them the concepts and skills they need when they begin formal education. Over the long term, the program aimed to develop communication skills, approaches to learning, motivation, and healthy self-perception that would continue to benefit the children's performance in later schooling and in adult life (Jordan, Grallo, Deutsch, & Deutsch, 1985). The project was thus a concerted attempt to test the power of the environment to enhance cognitive growth and life adjustment.

After several years of pilot testing, each year between about 1963 and 1969 a new group of preschoolers was enrolled, resulting in seven waves of classes totaling 483 children and over 800 children in various control groups. Participants had to be in the lower socioeconomic class and could have no serious physical, emotional, or behavioral problems. Both children and parents had to be English speaking. These rather rigid selection criteria could have resulted in a sample not quite representative of the poor population. Further, the sample was "self-selected" because parents voluntarily signed up their children, limitations that were acknowledged by the researchers (Deutsch et al., 1983).

Preschool was generally held in the neighborhood schools the children would later attend. The enrichment curricula continued through third grade. Teachers and assistants at each grade level received frequent training from specialists and supervisors. Educators made home visits to engage parents in their children's learning, and social workers and community aides helped families with problems relating to housing, medical needs, and other concerns. Because many of the children arrived at school hungry, a school breakfast program was launched.

Early results were modest—about a 3 point increase in IQ after the preschool year—but the control group had *dropped* 6 points. During kindergarten, the IQ disparity between the program and control groups had widened to 12 points (Stendler-Lavatelli, 1968). (Later waves showed even larger IQ increases for program students and larger distances from controls.) The hype surrounding the IDS, however, took on a life of its own. Mrs. Lyndon Johnson visited the program, and Martin Deutsch brought 20 of his students to Washington, DC to show off their abilities (Grotberg, 1983). Charles Silberman wrote in *Harpers Magazine*, "Kindergarten teachers who receive youngsters exposed to even as little as six months of Deutsch's experimental program are almost speechless with enthusiasm. In all their years of teaching, they say, they have never had slum youngsters enter as well-equipped intellectually, as alert, as interested, or as well-behaved" (quoted in Vinovskis, 2005, p. 50).

The Deutsches' work was used extensively by the Johnson administration and Congress in their decision to mount a national preschool program (Vinovskis, 2005). The Deutsches, however, were not so sanguine. The IDS program was not only very comprehensive, but it was extensive, designed to last a full 5 years for each child. The researchers were obviously not naive enough to think that a brief intervention could permanently alter the life course of a child raised in stark poverty. Martin Deutsch was outspoken with his belief that the education establishment was failing low-income children (Deutsch, 1967; Silver and Silver, 1991), which is another reason why he brought the IDS curriculum into the primary grades and emphasized teacher training. In fact, when Deutsch was appointed to Head Start's national advisory commission, he expressed that he was "suspicious of intentions to train teachers for two to four weeks, and to achieve literacy for Head Start children in a crash summer programme." He was promptly asked to resign: "They wanted to allow the public image that a miracle cure was possible . . . I said it just won't work" (Silver and Silver, 1991, p. 86). He also argued that Head Start was being run much too cheaply to make meaningful upgrades in the poor child's environment, particularly the elementary school environment.

Deutsch was right on all counts, of course, but his judgments were before their time. The value of high-quality, extended intervention services for children living in poverty would not be widely recognized for decades by a society in search of a silver bullet. Other legacies of the IDS include the use of classroom aides, now common in early childhood classrooms, as are school breakfast programs in low-income schools (Deutsch et al., 1983).

Another pre-Head Start experiment is notable both because it exemplifies the private sector's involvement in early education and antipoverty initiatives and because it operated in New Haven, CT. This being my home base, I had close ties with the program that I freely shared with other members of the planning committee. Continuing a long tradition of philanthropic support for young children living in poverty (see Cahan, 1989), the Ford Foundation funded the New Haven Prekindergarten Program as part of its Gray Areas agenda. In its larger Great Cities effort, the Foundation had learned that its school improvement efforts were inadequate without addressing the problems students encountered outside of school (Magat, 1979). It then chose to work with a few selected cities where government and community agencies were committed to partnering at all levels to improve the whole of urban life.

The New Haven Prekindergarten opened in 1963 in the public schools. The program was coordinated and run by Jeannette Galambos Stone and others involved in early childhood education and community planning. The effort was initially "aimed to test the validity of traditional nursery school education for children of the poor" (Stone, 1997, p. 163). Based on their experience with the New Haven trial, Stone and Marjorie Graham Janis were asked to develop curriculum guidelines for the national Head Start office shortly before the program launched. They wrote broad goals encompassing social, emotional, physical, and intellectual development to be achieved through a flexible teaching style that worked with children's natural curiosity and creativity.

In 1965, the New Haven Prekindergarten became one of the nation's new Head Start centers. By this time, War on Poverty programs were coming on board, and the Gray Areas projects could be phased out. The Ford Foundation's mission in the undertaking was being achieved. The Gray Areas program had become "the working model of the federal government's Great Society programs" (Magat, 1979, p. 121). An adjunct to that mission was to develop a research base and political dialogue on meeting the needs of young poor children (Silver and Silver, 1991). To this end, the Foundation had supported the Deutsches' IDS program, which made it interested enough in early schooling to branch out to places like New Haven. Now, the dialogue was sprouting vigorously.

Another experiment that deserves mention here is the Children's Center in Syracuse, New York. Though the program was young and evolving when Head Start's planners met, its founders were Bettye Caldwell, a huge name in child development, and Julius Richmond, the prominent pediatrician who was to become Head Start's first director and my lifelong mentor. The Center was a child care and preschool setting for children from about 6 months to 5 years of age. It was designed as a research and demonstration facility to provide an enriched environment "to forestall the verbal and motivational deficit which can be observed on the first day of formal schooling" and carries throughout a poor child's academic career (Caldwell and Richmond, 1968, p. 328). Unsurprisingly, there was a heavy concentration on health care, but the researchers also developed a progressive curriculum to foster cognitive and socioemotional development as well as a social services component to address the needs of participating families.

Other elements of the Children's Center design were both innovative and prescient. For one, the program was socioeconomically integrated, enrolling both middle- and low-income families. Classes were originally scheduled for the full day, but soon the more typical half-day attendance was permitted for those children whose families had a preference. The inclusion of infants and toddlers was a very big step at the time, when the Child Welfare League of America was arguing against out-of-home care for very young children. The professional reputations of Caldwell and Richmond enabled them to embark on such a controversial path that would have been nixed for scientists of lesser stature. In fact, in 1969 when the Syracuse Family Development Research Program serving families from the prenatal period to elementary school age opened, the developers cited the reputation of the Children's Center as facilitative to their start-up (Lally et al., 1988). (It deserves note that Caldwell and Richmond were themselves concerned that their center-based care might disrupt attachment behavior and family relationships and were careful to build in "emotional safeguards" and assessments of socioemotional tags and development to be sure the program did no harm.)

Richmond carried lessons from the Children's Center to planning the day-to-day operations of Head Start. When he arrived in Washington, he immediately rejected plans to have one teacher in a class of 30 students, revising the ratio to one teacher and two aides per 15 students. He also steered health services toward assessment instead of treatment, fearing that communities would find it too easy to let Head Start pay for health costs so they could use their own funds for other purposes (Richmond, 1997).

There were of course many other small experiments that made their way into the planners' deliberations. One was the now famous High/Scope Perry Preschool (discussed later), which was then a tiny project in the small Michigan city of Ypsilanti. Those projects mentioned here carried perhaps a bit more weight than the others. Still, the ongoing research had not yet produced a sturdy body of findings generalizable to an immense national program. The planners were essentially entering uncharted waters guided only by the dim and scattered lights of these novel field tests.

Input from the Mental Retardation Field

None of the projects described above was mounted for the explicit purpose of reversing the developmental delays associated with mental retardation. Rather, most were attempts to ward off the incremental learning failures that were the common fate of children who started off school so far behind in knowledge and skills that they never caught up. Nonetheless, an important strand running in the background of Head Start's planning was the grand idea of reducing if not eliminating the incidence of mental retardation. Never mind that Head Start was to be an intervention program for young children whose developmental opportunities were affected by low income, *not* low intelligence. The field of mental retardation was in a somewhat euphoric state at the time, and some of its participants were also involved in conceptualizing Head Start.

We have already alluded to the close ties Sargent Shriver had with the Joseph P. Kennedy, Jr. Foundation, the organization started by his in-laws to provide leadership in the field of mental retardation and service to affected people and their families. For decades before her death in 2009, his wife, Eunice Kennedy Shriver, was the Foundation's executive vice president. (In 1962, she began a camp for children with intellectual disabilities at their home in Maryland, an effort that grew to become the Special Olympics [Special Olympics, 2007].) Although the Foundation was named for her brother, a Kennedy son who was killed in World War II, its mission was inspired by her sister Rosemary, who arguably had mild retardation until a frontal lobotomy left her severely mentally disabled. The Foundation's lead scientific advisor was Dr. Robert Cooke, the family pediatrician and later chairman of the Head Start planning committee.

With Cooke as the point person, President John Kennedy established the National Institute of Child Health and Human Development (NICHD), with a division devoted to mental retardation. He had initially wanted to start an institute on mental retardation, parallel to other of our nation's Institutes of Health such as the National Cancer or Eye Institutes. I had been studying mental retardation since 1955 and had become something of a protégé of Eunice Shriver, so I was invited into the discussion. Dr. Cooke and I argued against the idea, pointing out that mental retardation is not a disease or body organ such as those after which the various institutes are named. A presidential task force Cooke chaired built our case that the best way to understand mental retardation is to heighten our understanding of human development in general. Not only did NICHD became a funding source for research on birth defects and mental retardation, but it "became the first NIH Institute to focus on the entire life process, rather than on a specific disease or illness" (NICHD, 2007, p. 2). This solution enabled the president to have his special concern addressed in a way acceptable to scientists, many of whom thought research money was better spent on causes more worthy and less intractable than mental retardation.

My work in the mental retardation field is actually what brought the invitation to join the Head Start planning committee. Back then I was an impudent young scientist who was challenging the most revered thinkers and most accepted theories in mental retardation. I began studying the behavior of children with mental retardation when I was a graduate student in the mid-1950s. At the time, it was widely believed that individuals with mental retardation behaved the way they did because of the retardation. In other words, their performance was dictated by their low intelligence, which swamped all other factors that might have a bearing on behavior. For example, it was common practice at the time to compare children with mental retardation residing in institutions with children of normal intellect living at home. Any differences discovered between the two groups were attributed to retardation rather than to the effects of the institutional environment. This was in spite of the fact that a prominent sociologist, Goffman (1961), had studied what he called "total institutions" and demonstrated just how deleterious it was to experience institutional care regardless of intelligence level. In support of the importance of life experiences independent of cognitive ability, I found that individuals of normal intellect who were residing in orphanages behaved in much the same way as individuals of retarded intellect living in large state institutions. Obviously, something more than IQ scores was responsible.

I then began to study the frequently documented phenomenon known as the mental age (MA) deficit; MA refers to an individual's absolute level of cognitive functioning. Thus a 10-year-old child with a perfectly average IQ of 100 has an MA of 10, whereas a 10-year-old with an IQ of 60 has an MA of 6—roughly the intellectual functioning of the average 6-year-old. The MA deficit refers to the observation that individuals with cultural–familial retardation (the type not caused by organic factors) often perform at a level beneath that predicted by their MA. As I was to find later with poor children of normal intellect, these children were not using the intelligence they possessed. What experiences did they have that attenuated their everyday performance? One obvious experience was social deprivation. I constructed a scale to measure the amount of social deprivation a child had suffered and found the scores were correlated with how long the child would play a perseverative, tedious game (repeatedly dropping a marble into a hole) administered by a friendly adult. It took me some time to unravel this mystery, but then it became perfectly clear. Deprived children do not get enough attention, praise, and social support. They are therefore willing to play a really boring game for as long as they can because they relish the social reinforcement.

I then began to look for other experiential factors that might also affect performance levels. I found that children who had suffered negative effects (e.g., too little emotional support, physical abuse) at the hands of adults important to them became wary of adults in general and reluctant to interact with them. This response can be detrimental when the adult is a teacher or therapist, for example. Another common event for children with IQs in the retarded range is frequent failure, beginning when they cannot do what is expected at their age. Much research has now indicated that such encounters can motivate children to avoid failure rather than to achieve success. They also come to rely on cues from others instead of trusting their own reasoning and memory in solving problems, a cognitive style called outerdirectedness.

In my studies I compared the behavior of retarded children and low- and middle-income children of normal intellect, with all three groups being at exactly the same level of cognitive functioning (MA). The poor children behaved similarly to the retarded sample, with both groups differing markedly from the middle-class children. What defeats low-income children? As a result of their frequent failure experiences, they develop a low expectancy of success and a negative self-image. I then manipulated the number of success and failure experiences each child had. I discovered that following success experiences, retarded as well as poor children performed much like middle-class children, whereas middle-class children behaved more like children with retardation following failure experiences.

Dr. Cooke also believed strongly that a child's daily experiences have a lot to do with performance. He thought that poor children encountered so much failure that their learning suffered. He had heard me speak on the impact of failure experiences on retarded children, which is why he thought of me when he was assembling Head Start's planning committee. In fact, Cooke's nomination for the name of the program that would later become Head Start was "Project Success."

Cooke and Zigler were not the only members of the planning committee involved in mental retardation. Several others were well versed in the retardation literature. Indeed, a key member and the committee's most famous child psychologist was Urie Bronfenbrenner, who was raised on the grounds of Letchworth Village, a residential institution for individuals with mental retardation in New York State. He lived there because his father was a physician at the facility. There he claimed that he saw nonretarded children who were mistakenly placed in the institution come to behave like the residents who did have retardation. He purported that these children adopted more normal behavior when placed in a more normal environment, that is, working in the Bronfenbrenner home.

Undercurrents from the Nature–Nurture Debate

Having Head Start designers who were also experts in mental retardation would not have meant anything if it weren't for some rather extreme positions beginning to dominate the field and generating a lot of publicity. Scientists were (and still are) engaged in heated arguments concerning the relative roles of heredity and experience in determining an individual's intelligence. In the nineteenth century, Sir Francis Galton and the English workers who followed him (e.g., from Sir Cyril Burt to Hans Eysenck) stressed heredity. The environmental emphasis can be traced back at least to Alfred Binet, creator of the first widely used intelligence test. He developed the concept of "mental orthopedics," the notion that the intellect could be improved through proper training experiences. The nature of such training was probed by French thinkers such as Jean Itard and Edouard Seguin.

Although Binet and his followers came down on the nurture side of the controversy, when his intelligence test was brought to America in the early part of the twentieth century the predominant view was that intelligence was determined by genes. A common definition of intelligence in the pre–World War II era was "by intelligence, the psychologist understands inborn, all-around, intellectual ability. It is inherited, or at least innate, not due to teaching or training" (Burt, Jones, Miller, and Moody, quoted in Condry, 1983, pp. 3–4). This hereditarian emphasis is exemplified by the work of the famous American scientist Arnold Gesell, who advanced the maturational view of human development. Gesell's theories followed a predeterministic approach in which the characteristics of the adult were thought to be present at birth. Development then is merely an unfolding process, much as the rosebud flowers petal by petal into a full rose. The Gesell Institute still occupies space in my office building at Yale, although it is not part of the university. While the group's focus has switched to assessing developmental readiness for school and identifying developmentally appropriate curricula, there is still a display of some of the thousands of photographs Gesell took to chart normal child development unfolding and the antique equipment he invented to produce heavy glass slides of his subjects.

If intelligence is determined only by genes, then efforts to raise IQ are destined to be fruitless. At least they were thought to be fruitless until the famous Iowa studies began around the 1930s. These studies (some of which are described by Condry, 1983) appeared to demonstrate that just transferring a child from a socially depriving institution to a more stimulating environment resulted in a higher IQ score. Particularly relevant to Head Start were the findings of one study that orphans who attended a model nursery school showed IQ gains, whereas those who experienced the regular orphanage fare lost IQ points. The Iowa studies were so replete with methodological flaws that perhaps more pages of critiques were written about them than were filled by the research itself (e.g., McNemar, 1940; Spitz, 1986; Zigler and Cascione, 1977). Yet they gave root to the idea that mental retardation might be ameliorated by proper environmental stimulants.

By the 1960s and early 1970s, American psychology had cast aside heredity and adopted the opposite position—extreme environmentalism. The leading champion of this view was the prominent psychologist, Joe McVicker Hunt of the University of Illinois. His message was expressed in his powerful book, *Intelligence and Experience* (1961). Building on the theoretical work of Piaget and on the animal research of Riesen and Hebb, Hunt argued that intelligence was determined mainly by the child's experiences. The book was a bombshell in its total refutation of the conventional wisdom of many decades, namely the equally extreme view that intelligence is solely the product of genes.

Hunt's influence was great indeed. He chaired a presidential advisory committee for President Johnson. He wrote an article for the *Reader's Digest* that was marketed with a prominent flyer on the cover reading, "How to Raise Your Child's IQ by 20 Points." This was supposed to be accomplished through a few changes in parents' child-rearing practices. Twenty points was actually small change to Hunt. Although more moderate thinkers such as Hebb (another champion of the power of the environment), Cronbach, and Zigler all estimated the reaction range of intelligence to be about 20 points or less, Hunt argued until his death that the reaction range of intelligence was 100 points. (The reaction range is the amount a given individual's IQ could be expected to fluctuate depending on whether he or she is raised in a good or bad environment.) Indeed, Hunt reported an intervention he conducted with infants that resulted in a 70 point increase in their development quotients (analogous to the IQ assessed in older children).

I knew Hunt well and spent the 1960s debating him on a variety of podiums across the nation. In my opinion, Hunt's ideas burdened social policy efforts like Head Start with two erroneous views: (1) how easy it is to raise IQ scores, and (2) the most important part of human development is cognitive development. (This view is readily seen in the way the George W. Bush administration has managed Head Start, a topic we cover in Chapter 12.) I have always preferred the "whole-child" approach, in which the child's physical, emotional, and social development are treated to be just as important as cognition. These domains do not occupy separate gated communities in the brain. Rather, optimal development in one sphere is inextricably linked to healthy development in the others.

The dream of easy ways to raise intelligence was just too tantalizing to succumb to "wet blankets" like me. Hunt's work and the conventional wisdom of the period suggested that the early years of life were the most promising time to mount IQ-boosting interventions. However, this idea was not nailed down until Benjamin Bloom of the University of Chicago published the influential book, *Stability and Change in Human Characteristics* (1964). Bloom emphasized what parents can see with their naked eye, namely that the first 4 years of life are a period of very rapid physical and cognitive growth. He argued that during such periods of rapid change the child is most susceptible to intervention. This book gave rise to the worn-out phrase, "Half the child's learning is over by the age of four." Indeed, members of congress picked up this statement and were still using it in the 1970s. Some scientists, myself included, made speeches and wrote articles refuting both Hunt's views and the logic of Bloom's argument, but we were no match for *Reader's Digest* covers and newspaper headlines.

What is frightening is that now, in the twenty-first century, we are close to making the same errors that plagued the 1960s. I am referring to the much-publicized work on early brain development showing that 90% of brain growth is completed by the age of 3. To laypersons, the brain means intelligence. The publicity has created a boom market in Mozart tapes, Baby Einstein programs, and hundreds of supposedly brain-building toys and other products (Kantrowitz, 2007)—all echoes of the crib mobiles and talking typewriters of the 1960s and 1970s. The fact is that the brain keeps developing and pruning connections (synapses) until we die, even though much of this activity occurs in the early years of life. Further, the brain also mediates emotional, social, and all other functions, and these domains are interconnected in the central nervous system. Trying to focus on the cognitive system exclusively would be like ignoring the vowels in the English language.

Mental Retardation and Wishful Thinking

While Hunt's and Bloom's notions seemed to address the mass market of children born with perfectly normal IQs, environmentalism was also invading the fields of mental retardation and early intervention for poor children. Preceding Head Start by 3 years, the first proposal for a public compensatory education program came from the President's Panel (later called Committee) on Mental Retardation (PCMR) in 1962.

The PCMR report married the prevailing cultural-deprivation stereotype with New Frontier liberalism and developed a plan that was environmental, intellectually oriented, and highly idealistic. It proposed widespread establishment of nursery centers in disadvantaged communities. Unlike Head Start, these centers would not be concerned with health and nutrition. They would be designed to foster "the specific development of the attitudes and aptitudes which middle-class culture characteristically develops in children, and which contributes in large measure to the academic and vocational success of such children" (quoted in Zigler and Anderson, 1997, p. 12).

These centers were to be attached to all public housing projects and all public schools in impoverished neighborhoods. Note the naked classism here—the stereotypical view of the poor as inherently defective and their culture as so inferior that their children, and only their children, need remedial services.

The panel went on to claim that such compensatory education programs could reduce mental retardation by 50%. This proposal was clearly directed at the large number of individuals with cultural–familial (generally mild) retardation who are predominantly born into the lower socioeconomic classes. A later PCMR report, equally foolish and idealistic, proposed cutting by half the incidence of individuals with organic (physiologic, generally more severe) retardation through improved health care.

The enthusiasm for raising intelligence was so great that even the distinguished scientists on the panel did not seem to realize the absurdity of imbuing an untried social program with the power of eradicating fully half of mental retardation, a problem probably as old as civilization itself. Indeed, when I served on the PCMR, some members became intrigued with newspaper accounts of an early intervention effort described in the press as the "Miracle in Milwaukee" (Haywood, 1970). This was an intensive stimulation program for infants at very high risk of mental retardation. (Their mothers were retarded.) Supposedly, after 4 years of intervention the children surpassed even normal IQs and scored in the intellectually superior range. Some panelists wanted to include the reported findings in the official PCMR report. I complained that there had not been a single published, empirical paper with peer review that ever came out of this project and that a group of scientists should not be placing such credence on unconfirmed press releases. A vote was taken, and the Milwaukee study was voted out of the report.

That naive environmentalism had spun out of control was evident at an international conference in 1968 sponsored by the National Institute of Mental Health and held at Peabody College (Haywood, 1970). A letter of good wishes was sent to the participants by President Johnson. Using the incidence rates at the time for cultural–familial retardation, the president stated, "We have come to recognize that up to three-quarters of the mental retardation in this nation is associated with conditions of life that blunt and cripple the development of human intelligence" (Haywood, 1970, p. vi). He went on to state his administration had begun an attack on these conditions through the War on Poverty programs as well as newly mounted health and education efforts. One that Johnson took great pride in was Title I of the 1965 Elementary and Secondary Education Act, which provided (and still provides) compensatory education for children living in poverty.

The chairman of this conference on "social–cultural" aspects of mental retardation was Carl Haywood, who expressed his intellectual indebtedness to his mentor, Joe Hunt. Indeed, the opening session was chaired by my standard antagonist of the 1960s, Joe Hunt himself. The core paper was presented by a younger worker, Ina Uzgiris, who was also a Hunt student. Uzgiris reviewed the literature concerning environmental influences on the development of intelligence. Two more senior workers in the field of mental retardation were discussants of this paper. One was Boyd McCandless, a member of the group who produced the frequently debated Iowa studies. Unsurprisingly, McCandless wholeheartedly endorsed Uzgiris's environmental position. I was the other discussant. I attacked the overemphasis on the role of environment, documented the many weaknesses of the Iowa studies, and argued that both nature and nurture interact to determine intelligence (Zigler, 1970). Walking to lunch after the opening panel, I happened to be directly behind Haywood, who was with a very distinguished invitee from Europe. The European remarked to Haywood that I took a quite different position from all the other panel members and wondered why. Haywood responded by saying, "Zigler is America's *enfant terrible.*"

The environmental bias in the mental retardation field lasted a long time. For example, in the early 1980s the Kennedy Foundation and PCMR sent a group of scholars (led by Cooke with Zigler in tow) to Sweden to examine data indicating that the prevalence of mild mental retardation (IQs between approximately 50 and 70) was markedly lower than that found in the United States. Fitting their optimistic and can-do style, the Kennedy people embraced an environmental explanation. They were advancing the hypothesis that the many social programs mounted in Sweden to assist individuals with mental retardation resulted in the prevention or amelioration of a large number of cases that in America would have been placed in the mentally retarded category. Alas, through some careful digging it was discovered that the Swedish prevalence of mild mental retardation was actually very similar to that found in the United States and other countries (Zigler and Hodapp, 1986).

Facts were not enough to keep rampant environmentalism from overtaking the discipline. Even the diagnosis, "cultural–familial retardation," was deemed a misnomer because it included hereditary ("familial") factors. The term was replaced with "mental retardation due to social disadvantage," or psychosocial retardation for short. The shift in terminology was a bold denial of the importance of heredity in intellectual development.

A Balanced Approach

The view that intelligence is completely determined by genes was wrong, as was the counterview that genes have nothing to do with cognition. As is the case with most polar positions, the truth typically lies somewhere in between. Each person is born with many genes for the trait of intelligence, and, beginning in utero, these genes encounter environments that influence how they will be expressed (the person's IQ). If essential nutrients or opportunities to learn are absent, IQ might end up being at the low end of genetic potential (or at the high end, if exposed to a superior environment). As noted above, the reaction range for intelligence is neither zero as the hereditarians claim, nor is it limitless as Hunt enticed. A more defensible position is that two identical twins having the exact same genotype will have IQ scores approximately 20 points apart (a reaction range of 20) if one twin encounters the best possible environment and the other encounters a terrible environment. Confronted with this nature–nurture interaction, many people nevertheless want to know which is more important, nature or nurture. Asking this question is analogous to asking what is more important in water (H_2O), hydrogen or oxygen?

The way the nature–nurture question is framed and answered has a tremendous impact on the treatment of individuals with mental retardation and on early intervention efforts for children born into poverty. For example, when I was a graduate student a major theoretical formulation to explain the behavior of retarded persons was advanced by a stellar figure in American psychology, Kurt Lewin. Research by Lewin and his students convinced them that individuals with mental retardation had an inherent cognitive rigidity. During the 1950s and 1960s, other major workers described other inherent deficits from which individuals with retardation presumably suffered. Thus we can see in the mental retardation field an analog to the deficit approach that was to be advanced about poor children in the 1960s—that something is "wrong" with them.

Lewin's formulation had a real impact on the everyday lives of individuals with mental retardation. His work suggested that because of their rigid cognitive structure, people with retardation would be good at perseverative tasks. This reasoning led to the opening of sheltered workshops where clients with retardation were given repetitive jobs to perform. Further, clinicians were very reluctant to employ psychotherapy with individuals with mental retardation because their cognitive rigidity would be a barrier to improvement, which was believed to demand "psychological movement." Similar pessimism was noted by Skeels, who described how when he began the Iowa studies, "It was believed that knowing a child's mental level facilitated planning for his future" (1966, p. 1) because nothing could be done to adjust that level.

While denial that the environment has anything to do with intelligence or learning obviously limits attempts to help people with mental retardation or those who fit some profile of future school failure, denying that genes have anything to do with intelligence creates false hopes and, inevitably, disappointment. This is exactly what happened when reports of early interventions showed that initial gains in IQ scores appeared to fade away as time went by. Such losses convinced Jensen to write in his famous monograph that "Compensatory education has been tried and it apparently has failed" (1969, p. 2). His position on the fixed nature of intelligence was echoed decades later in the hot-selling book, *The Bell Curve* (Herrnstein and Murray, 1994). Bolstering such opinions on the importance of heredity and the impotence of the environment in determining intelligence is the fact that although many efforts have been made to raise the IQ scores of children with mental retardation, not one has resulted in success. The most realistic explanation is that although environmental inputs can modify intellectual functioning to an extent, they cannot completely override the contributions of inheritance.

Hopefully this discussion clarifies why the hype about eliminating mental retardation was baseless. Genes are important, and there is no way to add more genes for intelligence to a child's biological makeup. But the environment is important too, and, unlike the genetic substrate, there *are* ways to alter the environment so it is more conducive to cognitive development. Factors bestowed by the environment such as frequent failure, social deprivation, and low aspirations can attenuate learning and everyday social competence not just in children with retardation but in any child who has the same type of incessant experiences. Many children raised in poverty fit that description. The goal of intervention, then, is not to add more IQ points but to enable children to overcome these motivational deterrents and use the intelligence they possess. To a child with mild retardation, a supportive environment can mean the difference between helplessness and relative self-sufficiency. For a child raised in poverty, intervention can likewise make the difference between underperformance and realizing his or her full intellectual potential. This goal is not as glamorous as making every child with retardation achieve normal intellect and every normal child become brilliant, but it is worthy and much more achievable.

Confounding Poverty and Mental Retardation

Everyone involved in Head Start's planning was aware that this was to be a program for poor children, *not* children with mental retardation. Unfortunately, with high-profile names like Shriver, Cooke, Zigler, and several others associated with the mental retardation field, their participation in Head Start created a subtle link in people's minds between poverty and developmental disabilities. Of course, these planners were just a small part of the reason that the fields of mental retardation and preschool intervention for children living in poverty became so theoretically intertwined. Given the thinking in the two fields at the time, this development was probably inevitable. Both fields were wedded to an environmental emphasis and discounted the importance of heredity in human development. Yet neither Cooke nor Zigler believed that intelligence could be raised dramatically. Shriver vacillated, although at times his speech writers got carried away with the idea.

The confusion between the goals of alleviating mental retardation and preparing poor children for school is obvious in an attack on Head Start by a noted English couple who were experts in the field of mental retardation. Ann and Alan Clarke (1977) took issue with the PCMR that the incidence of mild mental retardation could be reduced by 50% by the end of the twentieth century through such activities as early intervention. In attacking this miraculous claim, they attacked Head Start with the erroneous assumption that the program's primary goal was to reduce mental retardation. In a rebuttal, Zigler and Cascione (1977) concurred that the 50% goal was highly unlikely. To achieve it, we would have to repeal the biological law of human variability and believe everyone should be the same. Our rebuttal was titled, "Head Start Has Little to Do with Mental Retardation," and I wish it could have been printed in neon lights.

Although cultural–familial retardation tends to occur in the lower socio-economic class, the vast majority of children living below the poverty line do not have IQs in the mental retardation range. A child would have to experience extreme poverty and live in abysmal conditions for a long time before his or her intellectual development would be stymied so much to fall into the retarded range (Zigler and Hodapp, 1986). The fact is children growing up in poor families exhibit every level of intelligence, from limited to brilliant. I know former Head Start participants who are now serving in Congress. At least two graduate students in the Psychology Department at Yale told me they once attended Head Start. At the program's 40-year celebration, I met a Head Start graduate who has both MD and PhD degrees; I myself grew up in a poor family during the Great Depression. Head Start hadn't been invented yet, but no one ever assumed I was retarded just because I was poor.

Although Head Start was not mounted to raise intelligence, it suffered by association with those efforts that were. The greatest negative consequence of those early intervention programs directed at improving intelligence is that they led to stigmatizing the poor as stupid. Such thinking is counterproductive if the goal is to improve poor children's academic success. For example, we underassess the abilities of poor children and lower our expectations of what they can accomplish. According to studies of the "Pygmalion effect" (Rosenthal and Jacobson, 1968), low expectations can become self-fulfilling prophecies—the child who is expected to perform poorly does exactly that. Although we have many criticisms of President George W. Bush's No Child Left Behind effort, we approve of its mandate to hold high expectations of all children.

The confounding of low intelligence and poverty still has serious ramifications beyond low expectations. Consider the two most widely cited early intervention programs, the Abecedarian Project and the High/Scope Perry Preschool program. Although only Abecedarian reported sustained increases in IQ scores, participants of both interventions grew up to be more educated and socially adapted than controls, who were more likely to drop out of school, get arrested, and rely on welfare support. What is completely overlooked is that children were initially selected for these programs because they were at risk for mild mental retardation. Thus they were not representative of children growing up in poverty, who have a wide range of intellectual abilities.

The selection of children atypical of the poor population in these model programs appears to have been lost in the mist of history. Today, leading economists, including a Nobel laureate, are doing cost–benefit analyses (calculating the value of the benefits a program has to the participants and to society compared to the program's cost) and concluding that preschool programs can result in annual returns of about 18%. Decision makers are anxious to achieve such compounded returns and are supporting Head Start expansion and universal preschool as the solution to all our nation's shortcomings in education, labor force training, and global competitiveness.

While we are strongly in favor of universal preschool, it should not be justified on the basis of outcomes of two tiny intervention programs that served children hardly representative of the poor population. Economic analyses that rely on the Abecedarian and Perry projects are misleading and can ultimately undermine the cause they are supporting. Just as pessimism set in when mental retardation was not obliterated, and just as early intervention was threatened when initial IQ gains appeared to deflate, universal preschool can lose public backing if the promised returns fall short of grand expectations.

In hindsight, those of us involved in both mental retardation and planning Head Start should have been more aggressive in rejecting the association between economic poverty and intellectual poverty. Head Start children do have many problems that get in the way of their using their intelligence fully. These problems do not include a scarcity of IQ points but poor health, inadequate housing, troubled neighborhoods, unsavory role models, and above all few financial resources. In the early 1970s, it was mandated that 10% of Head Start slots be reserved for children with disabilities. Even after the active recruitment of this population, only 6% of the children in Head Start had diagnoses of mental retardation (Zigler and Cascione, 1977). It is worth remembering that at the turn of the nineteenth century, New York City's eastside slums produced their share of gangsters as well as many of our nation's most renowned intellectuals. A major purpose of Head Start is to increase the likelihood that poor children follow a positive rather than a negative growth trajectory, that they become good students instead of gangsters. This goal is similar to that of the earliest interventions discussed at the beginning of this chapter and remains a worthy endeavor.

2

The Two Roots of Head Start

Head Start was born as the civil rights revolution was taking place, an era of great social turbulence and upheaval in the United States. It followed a period of relative complacency as the benefits of a strong economy spread across the nation. John Kenneth Galbraith's (1958) classic book, *The Affluent Society*, described America as a place where basic needs were more likely to be met than consumer wants, redefining the meaning of poverty. His was an economic treatise decrying the lack of investment in social capital in favor of investments in producing consumer goods and in advertising to convince people to buy them. While Galbraith acknowledged the existence of true poverty, its reality had to be rediscovered in a nation where the majority was relatively economically secure.

A reawakening was stirred by Michael Harrington's (1962) book, *The Other America*, in which he vividly depicted the struggles of poor Americans living in pockets across rural, suburban, and city landscapes. The effect was to raise a sense of guilt that so many had so little in this land of plenty. Although it is unknown whether the book or its many reviews were read by President John F. Kennedy, he personally had been shocked by the low standard of living and lack of educational opportunities he saw while campaigning in the Appalachians in West Virginia (Silver and Silver, 1991). He began to formulate ideas for programs and services to alleviate poverty, notably by emphasizing education and vocational training. Kennedy's assassination put Lyndon Johnson in charge, and poverty could not have found a more sympathetic advocate.

Johnson was a populist, raised in the poor hill country of Texas. He had graduated from Southwest Texas State Teachers College and became a teacher during the days when the profession was neither highly regarded nor well paid. Throughout his life Johnson had a profound respect for the power of education, instilled by his learned mother (Woods, 2006). He once stated, "If it weren't for education, I'd still be looking at the southern end of a northbound mule" (Zigler and Muenchow, 1992, p. 26). Johnson not only strongly agreed with the American ethos that education was the ticket to upward social mobility, but he believed its benefit was almost limitless.

The Kennedy administration's efforts to mount an antipoverty campaign were thus inherently appealing to President Johnson, who was also eager to be viewed as continuing Kennedy's legacy. As Vinovskis notes, "Rather than proceeding slowly, and building on the scattered but promising existing programs, Johnson announced a massive War on Poverty and pledged to win it" (2005, p. 147). Further, President Johnson saw himself in the tradition of both Franklin Delano Roosevelt and his own mentor, Sam Rayburn, a strong Roosevelt supporter and one-time Speaker of the House. With this inspiration, Johnson would not only conquer poverty but would create a "Great Society":

> in our time we have the opportunity to move not only toward the rich
> society and the powerful society, but upward to the Great Society. The
> Great Society rests on abundance and liberty for all. It demands an end
> to poverty and racial injustice. . . . But that is just the beginning. The
> Great Society is a place where every child can find knowledge to enrich
> his mind and to enlarge his talents. . . . (quoted in Silver and Silver,
> 1991, p. 73)

To President Johnson, his Great Society was a fully appropriate descendant of FDR's New Deal. Although President Kennedy initiated many of the ideas and plans later championed by Johnson, the young president didn't have Johnson's unequaled power in propelling his legislative initiatives through Congress.

Details of the War on Poverty are well recorded, so we will not dwell on them here. One lesser-known fact of interest is that the term "War on Poverty" was the title of a book by then Senator Hubert Humphrey (1964), who became Johnson's vice president. Humphrey decried the horrific poverty existing in parts of the nation and called for greater government involvement and reprioritizing of federal spending choices. The war was officially launched with the passage of the Economic Opportunity Act of 1964. The act legislated education and work-training programs and dedicated efforts to combat rural poverty. The most controversial title was community action, which granted "maximum feasible participation" of the poor in shaping local responses to poverty. The intention was to give previously disenfranchised poor citizens a voice in their communities and in the programs designed to serve them. In some places, however, community *action* turned into *activism*, with some militant players making extravagant demands and attempting to overthrow the political system. We will have more to say on the activities and perceptions of community action later.

The antipoverty agenda was run from the new Office of Economic Opportunity (OEO), which housed programs such as the Job Corps and the Community Action Program (CAP), created to assist localities in their efforts to eliminate poverty and its causes. Sargent Shriver, who at the time headed the Peace Corps, was appointed the director of OEO. He insisted on keeping his Peace Corps responsibilities, so he ran both efforts simultaneously—a fact that epitomizes his management style. Sarge was an enthusiastic leader, but he was always doing a million things at once. In a huge undertaking like combating poverty, he had so many ideas and ran them by so many people that he couldn't keep track of what the plans were or to whom he had delegated them.

Shriver (1997) recalls that OEO had been up and running for several months before statistical analyses were completed that showed over half of the poor population was under the age of 16. He realized there was no way the nation could win its war against poverty without doing something for 50% of the target population. The Economic Opportunity Act specifically prohibited grants to primary and secondary schools (Silver and Silver, 1991), which is odd in that education was to be a major weapon in the War on Poverty arsenal. The law did permit funding for nursery schools for poor children, although the policy was merely mentioned in a phrase and was not detailed.

As a result of his Kennedy Foundation activities centering on mental retardation, Shriver was familiar with Gray's preschool intervention program in Nashville (described in Chapter 1) and was impressed by the rise in IQs of participating children. The Kennedy Foundation was also supporting the work of Philip Dodge, who was demonstrating that better nutrition was related to improvements in mental functioning. Another approach the Foundation was exploring was efforts in parent education (which became a key feature of the Head Start program). With all of these data in mind, Shriver began to entertain the notion of mounting a preschool program to help prepare children for elementary school.

Prior to his days in Washington, Shriver served as president of the Board of Education in Chicago. He was well aware that many poor children started school far behind more affluent children in academic and social skills. He admits, "I had a bias in favor of education, and originally I had thought of Head Start as an educational program" (1997, p. 59). Shriver notes that Head Start was not the only OEO program with an educational emphasis. Other efforts included a college preparation program for low-income adolescents called Upward Bound as well as the Federal Work–Study program—both of which still exist today.

Given President Johnson's high regard for the power of education, he was extremely receptive to Shriver's plan for a preschool for children of the poor. His wife, Lady Bird, was also enamored with the idea of a program that could improve the life chances of poor children. Long before any formal planning took place, Lady Bird invited the famous child psychologist Urie Bronfenbrenner (later a member of the Head Start planning committee) to the White House, where he discussed the value of early childhood intervention. As Vinovskis (2005) documents, Bronfenbrenner also testified before Congress on the value of preschool and as a result mobilized the support of House Republicans.

The idea of mounting a preschool program under the War on Poverty appeared to be a winner. Not only did it gain praise from most people to whom Shriver spoke, but serving young children was more palatable to local officials than supporting community activists. Hearing about some unsavory deeds of these activists and unwilling to yield power to the poor, many communities were refusing to accept CAP funds. Shriver was faced with the possibility of an embarrassing surplus in his war chest and had to find a way to spend it or risk losing it. Small children could not be blamed for being lazy or unemployed, and they posed no threat to the power of elected officials. Thus, initiating a preschool program would not only move along the goals of the War on Poverty but might win over some reluctant warriors.

True to Shriver's eccentric way of getting things done, he began planning for the preschool program through multiple channels. He talked with friends, academics, and education officials. He told his staff at CAP to work up a design. He asked a friend and advisor at the Kennedy Foundation, pediatrician Dr. Robert Cooke, to assemble a planning committee. Both the formal committee and CAP acted independently, each only vaguely aware of what the other was doing.

I knew Shriver as a charismatic and inspiring leader. However, I have to agree with the historian Vinovskis's conclusion that Shriver was "not a disciplined administrator . . . and his lack of management skills contributed to the administration's difficulties in organizing, implementing, and evaluating the complex and controversial War on Poverty" (2005, p. 147). Of course, more than strong leadership was required to implement so many large-scale, brand new programs that had never been tried or assessed, either for their practicality or their efficacy. We concur with Vinovskis's analysis of the War on Poverty: "This bold and ambitious goal captured the public's imagination, but the federal government lacked the funds and knowledge to achieve its lofty objectives" (2005, p. 147).

Not only was the speed too great and the existing capability and considerable sums of money too little, but the entire War on Poverty reeked of overoptimism. During the birth of OEO, I remember watching *Meet the Press* one Sunday morning and heard Shriver promise the nation that poverty would be eliminated in America within 10 years. (Forty-something years later, the United States has a larger percentage of children living in poverty than most advanced industrialized nations in the world [OECD, 2009].)

While economists and decision makers had become very concerned about poverty, in the 1960s we had few scientific studies that could teach us just how detrimental the phenomenon of growing up in poverty is to normal human development. There is no way that a short preschool program could offset the harm caused by experiencing poverty in the early years of life and create the school readiness and life success that was being promised by the nation's leaders. Nonetheless, it is necessary to be optimistic if the goal is to help children succeed. President Johnson and Shriver's enthusiasm for attacking poverty led to action and change. Although they did not accomplish their mission, it was not for lack of trying.

The Head Start Planning Committee

Shriver either forgot he had asked CAP staffers to write a plan for the new preschool program or was unimpressed with the result. Both possibilities could explain why the CAP plan was never mentioned in his 761-page biography (Stossel, 2004). Instead he turned to some trusted advisors to assemble a committee of experts in child development, who in turn would develop his idea of a preschool into a workable program. The selection committee of course included Dr. Robert Cooke, a brilliant pediatrician whose advice the Shrivers had come to trust in both private and policy decisions. Also involved were Richard Boone, a Justice Department official credited with coining the term, "maximum feasible participation" of the poor; Jule Sugarman, who would become executive secretary of the planning committee and later be assigned with the details of launching the new program; and Dr. Edward Davens, deputy director of health for the state of Maryland and an eventual member of the planning committee.

The authority of medical professionals in choosing Head Start's planners might seem unlikely given Shriver's admission that he originally thought of Head Start as an education program. Unsurprisingly, the medical field was well represented among those selected to join the planning committee. Dr. Cooke had received his undergraduate and MD degrees from Yale University, where he was a faculty member until 1956 when he left to become chair of pediatrics at Johns Hopkins University in Baltimore. (I did not arrive at Yale until 1959, so our paths did not cross until later.) Like Cooke, Dr. Davens was also a pediatrician and an expert in mental retardation. Dr. E. Perry Crump was likewise a pediatrician, bringing the total such specialists to three. Dr. Reginal Lourie, one of America's truly great child psychiatrists and a member of the President's Panel on Mental Retardation, also joined. Another member was Dr. Myron Wegman, dean of the University of Michigan School of Public Health. Mary Kneedler was a public health nurse who later founded Western Carolina University's Kneedler Child Development Center, now managed by none other than Head Start. With roughly half of the seats on the planning committee held by medical professionals, it was clear the new Head Start program would have a strong focus on child health.

Three psychologists were also named. The most famous was Urie Bronfenbrenner, who was beginning to formulate his bio-ecological model of human development. At the time, psychologists typically believed parents (especially mothers) were the cause of all manner of children's problems. The solution was to entrust the child to a professional to "fix." Bronfenbrenner believed that child development is influenced not only by parents but by the community where the child lives, by state and national social policies, and by happenings across the globe. He argued that to be effective, intervention must target not only the child but each of these systems that ultimately impacts the child's life course.

Another member was Mamie Clark, a clinical child psychologist who, as a team with her spouse Kenneth Clark, was noted for work on racial inequities as well as mental retardation. I was the third psychologist and the youngest member of the group. As explained in Chapter 1, Cooke took note of my work on the motivational aspects of mental retardation and especially on the consequences of repeated failure. In addition to developmental insights, the psychologists on the committee were trained in the scientific/research tradition and were able to add that perspective to the group's deliberations.

Planning for a school-readiness program of course demanded the input of early childhood educators. There were only two on the committee, but they were powerhouses of knowledge and expertise. One was James Hymes, Jr., a professor of education at the University of Maryland and once president of the National Association for the Education of Young Children (NAEYC). He had been a specialist in early education since the 1930s and had mounted child care programs during World War II under the Lanham Act. The other was John Niemeyer, President of Bank Street College—a mecca for early childhood education—and a phenomenal administrator. A third educator was not a specialist in early childhood but was a known professional leader. He was George Brain, the superintendent of schools in Baltimore.

A lone representative of the social work profession was Mitchell Ginsberg, who was Commissioner of Social Services for New York City. Rounding out the planning committee was Jacqueline Wexler, one of the few members who didn't have ties to Cooke through the President's Panel on Mental Retardation or by virtue of working in Baltimore, Cooke's home base at Johns Hopkins. I don't remember her academic credentials, but I do recall that she had worked on an educational task force for the Peace Corps and later became president of Roman Catholic Webster College, and that she was very smart. She was also a nun. Shriver was a devout Catholic, and many of the groups and advisory boards he convened contained a priest or other representative of his faith. Perhaps he was trying to inject God's blessing into the efforts, or perhaps raise the fear of God in the participants so they would do the right thing. Sister Jacqueline raised the fear of God in me. Maybe because I was meeting so many new faces when I joined the committee, or because I was a bit intimidated (being a young Jewish man who had never worked closely with a nun before), I never could remember her name. I therefore kept referring to her as "the good sister," thinking I was being cleverly polite and respectful. Eventually Sister Jacqueline caught on and said, "Ed, if you call me 'the good sister' one more time, I'm going to kick you in your ankle." I didn't forget her name again.

Bob Cooke was the perfect chairman of the planning committee and ran the meetings in a way that everyone felt free to say what was on his or her mind. Without this climate, we could never have accomplished our charge. In the 1960s, interdisciplinary work was rare. The scholars, professionals, and practitioners in the group were simply not used to straying from their defined fields and initially were somewhat ignorant of what people in other disciplines could possibly contribute to the task. That attitude changed during our first meeting, and, under Cooke's skillful guidance, we quickly became a team. Believe it or not, we only met eight times beginning in January 1965. Yet many of us became lifelong friends.

Initially, our project didn't have a name. It was tentatively called the "kiddie korps," perhaps to imitate the sound of the popular Peace Corps or the new Job Corps. Getting poor people into jobs was a thrust of the War on Poverty, which is likely why Judah Drob was called over from the Labor Department to work on some OEO initiatives. Drob is the hero who suggested the name, "Head Start." It was enthusiastically accepted. I still wonder if any self-respecting parent, poor or not, would have sent her or his child to a program called the "kiddie korps."

Overcoming the Deficit Stereotype

The planners' first order of business was to determine what children living in poverty need to get ready for school. This seemingly practical task immediately became a theoretical one in which we had to think about whether poverty was a cause or an effect of individual attributes. The language of the 1960s emphasized the inadequacies of the poor. People lacked money because they were lazy, unintelligent, or immoral. Three years before the birth of Head Start the book, *The Culturally Deprived Child*, by Frank Riessman (1962) was published. Unfortunately, the title of this book had an impact that was in total opposition to its purpose, which was to demonstrate the strengths of children living in poverty. (Riessman became aware that his poor choice of words fed the position he was arguing against. He wrote a second book in 1976 entitled, *The Inner-City Child*, in which he pointed out how inappropriate the first title was and again tried to debunk myths about "what is wrong" with poor children.)

The notion of cultural deprivation carried the implicit assumption that the culture of the poor was inferior to that of the middle class—as if the latter were the *only* culture, and poor people didn't have it. Yet sociologists have shown that no human group can exist without a culture. All cultures must have positive features for the members to stay together and the group to continue. The problem was that in the 1960s many failed to distinguish between the environment or conditions of life of a group and its culture. The culture actually evolves as a means to cope with the environmental conditions that confront the group. Thus, "culture" includes traditions, values, mores, and adjustment mechanisms that members pass on as tools of survival and identity.

In addition to the cultural deprivation issue, Head Start's planners had to confront the black–white issue. Because such a high prevalence of the poor were black, the deficit model was quickly transposed to the view that blacks were inherently inferior compared to whites. Compounding the error was confusion between race and social class. Laypeople often use the terms poor and black (and more recently Hispanic) as synonymous, but academics have been just as guilty. Over the years too many studies have compared the performance of poor black children with that of middle-class white children, and, when differences were discovered, they were attributed to the child's race. Some years ago my colleagues and I conducted a large study that involved lower- and middle-class blacks as well as whites (Yando, Seitz, and Zigler, 1979). Our findings were clear and probably still hold today. We discovered that social class has a much greater effect than race on the child's behavior across many different tasks.

The planners did have to face the fact that the culture in which poor children of whatever race lived sometimes got in the way of their succeeding in schools built on middle-class expectations. For example, all teachers and testers have encountered the ubiquitous "I don't know" phenomenon when working with poor children. As Riessman explained, a child can escape an unfamiliar demand or a strange and somewhat threatening test situation by simply saying, "I don't know." This response may not reflect ignorance but the child's desire to disengage.

I will never forget the White House occasion when the honorary chairperson of Head Start, Lady Bird Johnson, first announced the program to the nation. In her address, which I'm sure some staffer wrote, she spoke of the tragedy that children of the poor were so deprived they often started school without even knowing their own names. I was very fond of Mrs. Johnson, whose heart sincerely went out to the poor. However, at that moment I could have strangled her speech writer. Kindergarten was not widely available in 1965, so children typically began school at the age of six. Does the reader know any children aged six (or two, for that matter) who do not know their names? A child of six who doesn't know his or her name would have to be severely retarded, although even children in that IQ group typically respond to their names. Perhaps the invisible staffer was familiar with Martin Deutch's preschool intervention where the curricula combined cognitive and social–emotional features and emphasized using the child's name again and again.

Being an experimentalist by nature, I returned to New Haven and conducted a small study in the Ford Foundation preschools for children in poverty that a friend of mine directed. I asked her to train the teachers to ask the children their names on the first day of preschool and to record their responses. If a child said, "I don't know," the teacher was to say, "It must be scary to have someone you don't know very well ask you your name, and you're probably wondering why I need to know your name. A little later we're going to have juice and cookies. If I don't know your name, I won't be able to call you, and I don't want you to miss out on juice and cookies." With this simple manipulation, all but one of the handful of children who said they didn't know their names immediately remembered them. There was one hold-out who proved to be a lesson for all of us. This little girl was not about to reveal her name even though the teacher didn't give up and kept pressing her. (Although my experiment was over, it must have been hard to run group activities with one nameless student.) One day an older child came to pick up this little girl, and the teacher asked her the younger child's name. Sensing the trick, the younger heroine shouted, "Don't tell her!" For some reason this had become a battle of wills between child and adult, and the child simply wasn't going to lose.

Thinking about it, the reluctance to tell one's name to a relative stranger is not uncommon in poor communities, particularly minority communities. This seeming paranoia may have some justification. Revealing one's name could have something to do with stopping the welfare check or an encounter with the police. Even today, residents of inner-city neighborhoods are undercounted in the census because they refuse to talk to census takers.

The "I don't know" syndrome can obviously affect a child's performance on an intelligence or achievement test. Riessman wrote that the poor child has a "hidden IQ." Although many would like to believe that an IQ test score is an inexorable readout of a child's intellectual capacity, it really is a measure of the child's responses to a set of boring questions presented by a relatively disinterested examiner. These questions are often introduced with, "We are going to play some games today," followed by many strange activities, few of which are game-like. Few scholars have looked into *why* a young child not yet adept in socialization skills should care to respond to an examiner in a test situation or a teacher in the classroom.

William Labov, a sociolinguist, presented some telling findings related to this issue. He compared the test performance of children in one of two testing situations. One was a typical classroom setting; in the second a friendly examiner went to the child's home, got down on the floor with the child, and gave out Fritos while the child answered questions. Labov (1966) found significantly higher test scores in the pleasant, informal situation with immediate reinforcements than in the standard school testing. This verified the unused intelligence that Riessman discussed. Another one of Labov's demonstrations was equally convincing. I attended a couple of scholarly conferences where he played two audio tapes. The first was in a classroom where poor black children were asked questions and essentially could not answer or gave monosyllabic responses. Listening to this tape, one would conclude that the children's language skills were primitive and inadequate. The second tape was of the same-aged children playing a game common in poor black neighborhoods named "the dozens." This is a game of insults in which players take turns trying to one-up the previous insult. In this game the children were verbally adept and quite effective in the use of language.

These examples highlight the error in assuming that test scores are an exact readout of ability. A child's performance on any task reflects three factors: a variety of cognitive abilities (e.g., memory and reasoning), the exposure the child has had to specific information on the test, and the child's motivational system. Considerable work has now been done showing that middle-class children are much more motivated than poor children by the inherent satisfaction of being right and/or the approval of the test-giver or teacher. Reinforcing Labov's work, my studies indicated that both retarded and poor children of normal intellect perform better under conditions when they receive a tangible reward rather than only the satisfaction of being correct. This is indeed a cultural difference, but it is one that has real consequences. A test result is just an example of a child's behavior, and if his or her motivation inhibits test performance, it will also attenuate performance in real-life situations akin to the testing situation—including the all-important classroom.

This fact was readily buried by participants in the raging civil rights movement. Some vocal minorities, victims of poverty, "bleeding hearts," and repentant wealthy and/or white liberals demanded equality for all. A backlash began to brew that rejected the existence of deficits within the culture of poverty or racial group. It was most evident inside the CAP, discussed later in this chapter, and blossomed into such contemporary movements as "black pride." A pioneer in the movement was Riessman, whose two books are filled with evidence of the strengths of children who experienced poverty. For example, Riessman reported findings of a study in which over half of the children who had learned to read before coming to school came from lower-income homes. It appeared that their older siblings had taken the trouble to teach them. Poor or not, it is rare to find a parent who doesn't want his or her child to do better in life than the parent did. Indeed, Riessman's contemporaries Sears and Maccoby (1957) found that poor parents were more concerned that their children do well in elementary school than were middle-class parents.

Riessman was not the only scholar in the 1960s pleading that the strengths and abilities of poor children, in particular poor black children, and their communities be acknowledged. Two prominent scientists advancing this point of view were Kenneth and Mamie Clark (1950). In a shocking demonstration they had shown that the continuous denigration of poor black children led many of them to prefer white over black dolls. These findings were noted in the Brown desegregation decision in 1954. They were living proof that the deficit model and words surrounding it such as "cultural deprivation" were hurtful. They hurt the children whom we were trying to help by conveying the message that they were somehow inherently defective.

I witnessed the backlash to the slightest negative attitude toward the poor from Mamie in our deliberations on the Head Start planning committee. Toward the end of our sessions I was attempting to develop rating measures to assess the progress of children attending Head Start during its first summer. My measures upset Mamie a great deal because I was measuring improvements, implying there might be something about these children that could be improved. Being young and not particularly diplomatic, I finally asked her, "If these children are perfect in every way, why are we here in Washington designing an intervention program?"

Here then was the central quandary of the Head Start planning committee and one that Riessman also faced. In discussing the many strengths of the poor, he introduced the caveat, "I do not intend to romanticize or idealize poverty or the poor" (1976, p. 6). In this regard, it would be hard to underestimate the difficulty of the framing task that faced the planners. We had to find and champion a middle ground between the negative deficit model and the optimistic, romantic view that poor people were so strong they didn't need any help.

Head Start's planners, both blacks and whites, firmly embraced the civil rights movement. We rejected the deficit model and consciously adopted a cultural-relativistic approach that respected Head Start families' racial backgrounds and cultures. One vehicle of this approach may be seen in our emphasis on parental involvement. Head Start parents would not only participate in the daily activities of the program, but they would have real decision-making power in all planning and administrative aspects of their neighborhood centers. This was a major break from past practices in which educated professionals dictated the operations of poverty programs and often imposed their own cultural standards. Of course, our job as planners was to prepare children to succeed in a school environment that was structured around middle-class traditions and values. We had to assure they learned "school behavior" without abandoning their cultural identities. Ultimately the planners decided that Head Start would not try to make poor children emulate the middle class but instead try to build on the strengths they bring to the program.

Designing Head Start's Structure

With these theoretical issues addressed, the planners tackled the more practical task of structuring Head Start's content. We knew that our charge was to design a school readiness program, but 40-plus years ago—when it was not uncommon for children to show up in first grade without having attended kindergarten, much less preschool—there was no consensus on what exactly comprised readiness. The members represented a variety of disciplines, and each was convinced that his or her field was critical to preparing children for school. As we listened to one another's point of view, we realized that we were all correct.

Although medical professionals dominated the committee, they did not have to twist any arms to convince the others that good physical and mental health, including good nutrition, are imperative to a child's success in school.

Likewise, no one disagreed that social and emotional functioning are important to a child's ability to work within a group setting and develop a positive approach to learning. That preschool education would be the centerpiece of our school readiness program was a given.

The planners also agreed that healthy development depends on the relationships the child has with important adults. The first and foremost relationship is that between parent and child. Parents would therefore be offered a special place in Head Start, participating in both the classroom and administration and having opportunities to enhance their own learning. At the time, this philosophy was unique in that parents were commonly blamed for children's learning problems and not treated as part of the solution. Parent participation also fit in well with the "maximum feasible participation" mantra of the War on Poverty efforts. Finally, at Bronfenbrenner's urging, the local community's influence on child development was recognized. We agreed to encourage ways for Head Start and the community to strengthen one another. In essence, the committee envisioned a "whole child" approach to school readiness.

Our recommendations were presented to Shriver in February 1965—not even 2 months after the planners first met and a short 4 months before Head Start was to open its doors. The "Cooke Memorandum" outlined seven objectives of a comprehensive preschool program:

A. Improving the child's physical health and physical abilities.
B. Helping the emotional and social development of the child by encouraging self-confidence, spontaneity, curiosity, and self-discipline.
C. Improving the child's mental processes and skills with particular attention to conceptual and verbal skills.
D. Establishing patterns and expectations of success for the child which will create a climate of confidence for his future learning efforts.
E. Increasing the child's capacity to relate positively to family members and others while at the same time strengthening the family's ability to relate positively to the child and his problems.
F. Developing in the child and his family a responsible attitude toward society, and fostering constructive opportunities for society to work together with the poor in solving their problems.
G. Increasing the sense of dignity and self-worth within the child and his family. (Recommendations for a Head Start Program, 1965, pp. 1–2)

Clearly, the plan was only a conceptual model that did little more than lay out what the component services of Head Start should be and specify what aspects of the child's functioning the program was meant to impact. In the tight timeframe we had, it was impossible for us to write a practicum and detail exactly what workers should do to achieve the goals. That task would go to Dr. Julius Richmond, who would shortly be appointed Head Start's first director, and Jule Sugarman, executive secretary of the planning committee and a highly effective manager.

Our hastily prepared plan was of course subject to a great deal of criticism, much of it in the wisdom of hindsight. A complaint I raised myself over the years is that the seven objectives were not specific enough to be well understood or soundly evaluated. This was one reason why early assessments targeted increases in IQ scores as the measure of Head Start's success. The planning committee was certainly wise enough about the failure of IQ-raising efforts in the mental retardation area to consciously avoid IQ changes as a goal of Head Start. Although Shriver thought IQ improvement was possible, he certainly did not begin the program for the primary purpose of boosting intelligence. However, when early results indeed showed rises in IQ scores, there was no stopping him from bragging about this outcome. I personally spoke to him many times to attempt to deter him from selling Head Start on the basis of IQ. In retrospect, I believe Shriver was torn on the IQ issue, but at the time it was the only result that could be neatly explained to policymakers and the public.

Trials of Crafting Preschool Education

A related criticism is that the planners neglected Head Start's early education component. Some skeptics went so far as to suggest there was some sort of professional hierarchy in the planning committee in which members representing early childhood education were viewed as second-class scholars by the others. Nothing could be further from the truth. As noted, planners James Hymes and John Niemeyer were famous early childhood leaders, and their professional stature probably outranked that of many of the other members. Further, Head Start's first director was Dr. Julius Richmond. Although he was a pediatrician, he was well versed in the knowledge of human behavioral development. As described in Chapter 1, he had mounted an early childhood intervention with his colleague, Bettye Caldwell, one-time president of the premier organization for early childhood educators, NAEYC. Soon, an educational psychologist, Ed Gordon, was added to Richmond's staff.

Both Richmond and Sugarman felt they needed more hands-on expertise to deal with the preschool education component. The planners had become the steering committee by this time and were helping with the details of implementing the program. Planner Jimmy Hymes was recruited to work within the

Head Start unit at OEO and took on the leadership task of developing the preschool education piece.

Hymes was also very concerned that there was not enough expertise about children's learning at the Head Start office. He discussed this with William Rioux, another early education expert (from the Merrill-Palmer Institute, a well-known center for early childhood education), who was leading the Title I effort under the new Elementary and Secondary Education Act. Rioux, in turn, discussed the matter with Francis Keppel (head of the Office of Education). Keppel then asked Shriver that a representative from the Office of Education be attached to Head Start to advise on the educational component. Shriver agreed, and Keith Osborn was detailed to Head Start. Osborn was a leading early childhood educator, also from the Merrill-Palmer Institute. He joined the planning and steering committees and became the daily head of the preschool education operation. As visible proof that preschool education was being taken seriously, Osborn notes that he was given an office in close proximity to that of Hymes (personal communication, May 3, 1977).

Osborn recalls the specific precipitant for his invitation to join the planning committee. Oblivious to what the committee was doing, the Community Action people were proceeding with their own plan for Head Start. Osborn writes, "The bureaucrats at OEO were going 'full steam ahead' on Head Start and they were tooling up rapidly. . . . Actually they were extremely dedicated people, but they really knew nothing about the young child" (personal communication, May 3, 1977).

As an example Osborn cites an early OEO memo suggesting that Head Start centers be arranged in clusters, with one aide and 15 children each, and that a head teacher supervise five of these groups. The planners in the meantime had unanimously agreed that there must be low child-to-teacher ratios to allow for individual attention and promote close relationships. Osborn says, "Fortunately the professionals on the planning committee stopped the proposal before it got off the ground. . . . However, it was because of that proposal that I joined the planning group. . . . It was felt that I would have more 'clout' with some of the OEO people if I was also a Planning Committee member." He emphasized "that the OEO bureaucrats were not 'hostile' or 'anti-child,'" but they just did not understand child development.

Maris Vinovskis (2005), an expert in the history of education, also believes a major weakness of Head Start was its inadequate education program, which he feels was underemphasized by the planners in favor of other services provided to the children and parents. Ron Haskins, once Senior Advisor to the President on Welfare Policy for George W. Bush, likewise sees a conflict between comprehensive services and school readiness. The comprehensive services approach was what made Head Start different from all previous early intervention programs. In the whole-child approach to readiness the planners advanced, child development is viewed within the context of a number of subsystems, such as cognitive, socioemotional, and physical health. These subsystems are synergistic and in a constant state of interplay, so it is ill-advised to try to focus on one to the exclusion of its partners. For example, does Vinovskis or Haskins, or any reader of this book believe that good health is not a factor contributing to school readiness? Today, comprehensive services are widely accepted as key to the effectiveness of intervention, although obviously agreement is not unanimous.

The attention given to staffing Head Start's education unit alone shows that Vinovskis and others are incorrect that little emphasis was placed on Head Start's education component. In any preschool intervention program, education and learning have to be the acknowledged core. Admittedly, the planners did not prescribe a specific curriculum for use in Head Start centers. We could not justify doing so because there was no evidence proving the superiority of one curriculum over another, and later searches gave no definitive answers (Miller, 1997). We have learned that children have different learning styles, so different approaches are more effective with some students than others, and that the value of any curriculum is only as good as the teacher who implements it (Sale, 1997). However, the critics are correct in their view that preschool education in Head Start was not of sufficiently high quality.

Leading figures in the early education field were quite aware of the short-comings of Head Start's education component (e.g., Omwake, 1997). Indeed, though hopeful and optimistic, Osborn notes, "We were always concerned about the massiveness of the program and the lack of trained staff" (personal communication, May 3, 1977). There was fear "that we would end up with one large reading program and there would be no concern for the total child," and that "well meaning elementary school teachers would be concerned with teaching kids curriculum and lose sight of larger goals." He worried "that these teachers would not work with parents." Years later, Osborn's trepidations were resurrected in response to the George W. Bush administration's attempts to make Head Start a literacy program.

Education in Head Start was very handicapped by the lack of expertise in the nation at that time. In 1965, there were not very many teachers who had worked with children under five, and even fewer experienced in working with poor families. Hymes and Osborn knew there were not enough trained early childhood educators to staff Head Start classrooms, so they devised a massive training program that rolled out across the United States, the Virgin Islands, and Guam. Some 40,000 teachers attended these 1-week sessions. Osborn remembers that he felt this training was successful. The logistics were indeed impressive. The National Universities Extension Association recruited over 100 universities on short notice. Some of these universities very quickly took on the task of housing, feeding, and training as many as 1,200 students.

Another example of the hyperactive thrust for training comes from Osborn's recollection of a meeting that took place near Easter in 1965. Because of the many tourists in Washington, Richmond and Osborn had to share a hotel room at the Lee House. The Head Start advisory committee came to their room for their weekly meeting. After discussing the dire need to train staff, they decided to ask America's premier academic children's film maker, Joseph Stone at Vassar, to produce some training films. The fly in the ointment was that Stone was recovering from a recent heart attack. Nevertheless, Osborn called Stone, who came to Washington the very next day. Amazingly, Stone produced 22 films in 30 days, which "has to be some kind of record in filming circles" (Osborn, personal communication, May 3, 1977).

It is amazing that while all of this was being done, the entire permanent staff of Head Start consisted of Richmond, Sugarman, Osborn, and a secretary. The fact that they were able to pull the training off in such a short time is commendable if not heroic. However, we are skeptical of Osborn's assessment that the training was successful. A subject as complex as teaching poor pre-school children cannot be learned in a week. The teachers in Head Start that first summer ranged from some first-rate early childhood educators to the semiliterate parents and their neighbors that Vinovskis notes.

Program Size and Length

The interventions that preceded Head Start were either school-year or year-round programs. It was little more than pragmatics that determined Head Start would originate as a summer program. In 1965, schools were mostly empty in the summer, leaving ample classroom space available. Further, there was a supply of teachers not working in the summer who could be employed by Head Start. Of course, even in 1965 we knew that high-quality preschool education required developmentally appropriate practices carried out by trained early childhood specialists rather than third- or fourth-grade teachers. The ideal staff did not exist, so we had to take what was available. Head Start owes a debt of gratitude to the thousands of public school teachers who gave up their summer vacation that year to serve our neediest young children and their families.

The size of the program was another issue that was outside of the planners' control. The early planning that took place in OEO prior to the appointment of the formal planning committee used a target of 100,000 children for the first summer. That is the number Cooke's committee worked with, but we did not know where it came from. The month before our first meeting, Shriver had asked a nationally known child development scholar, Jerome Bruner at Harvard, for his opinion on the size of the program. Aware that qualified early childhood teachers were rare, Bruner recommended no more than 2,500 children. But Shriver was running a war, not a skirmish, so he firmly rejected that number, and it was never heard of again. The planning committee members were not comfortable with the 100,000 figure, worried that the program was beginning much too fast and much too big. Our chairman, Bob Cooke, tried to allay our concerns by telling us he remembered when the Peace Corps consisted of Sarge Shriver and one secretary. It quickly grew into an immense and successful program. Head Start had the same captain, and his track record was good.

We were also very confident in the abilities of our executive secretary, Jule Sugarman, who would have the job of actually implementing this huge effort. Sugarman remained optimistic throughout. For every managerial problem or snafu, he quickly developed a solution, giving us a semblance of hope that somehow it would all work.

The day after Shriver received the Cooke memorandum, he presented it to President Johnson. He mentioned that the planners "recommended" serving 100,000 children in the first summer. (That number definitely did not come from us.) Johnson said, "That's such a magnificent idea. Triple it," which "was music to Shriver's ears" (Stossel, 2004, p. 422). Shriver had been under verbal attack by "rapid reformists" within his agency, as well as the militant radicals attached to many local Community Action programs. Within OEO, those who wanted the world changed overnight gossiped that the planning committee sided with Bruner's suggestion and wanted Head Start to be a relatively small program. OEO staffers accused the planners of plotting to experiment with the children, enrolling only enough to fill their research needs.

The fact is the planners were never asked how big we thought the program should be. We watched incredulously as 100,000 became 300,000, then 400,000, and finally 560,000 children. There was nothing close to a group sense that we should rebel against this mammoth plan. We were not policy-makers, elected officials, or presidential appointees. We had been recruited to plan the best program we could, not fund it or implement it (although some of us did volunteer to help with the launch). The planners were asked one relevant question about the size of the program—whether we had enough knowledge and experience with preschool education and could provide the rational under-girding for the huge effort being proposed. We concluded that we did.

Vinovskis asserts that the close, personal relationships the planners had with Shriver deterred them from actively questioning the large size and short duration of the first summer's Head Start program. This was certainly not the case for me. Although I was the youngest member on the committee, I had the hubris of youth and no reluctance in challenging anyone. Maybe there was a degree of group-think in the committee's deliberations. We were all nervous about the huge enrollment scheduled for our untried program. Yet there were enough physicians among us to remind us of the medical dictum, "first, do no harm." We agreed that no Head Start child would be harmed by getting a hot meal and medical care, and that parents would not suffer by being offered social services and education in child rearing.

I was personally reassured by Julius Richmond, Head Start's first director. At the time OEO was housed in a dilapidated building that had been the site of the New Colonial Hotel, a former brothel. The lobby contained a small lounge and bar, where Richmond and I would often have a drink together and compare notes. I expressed my worries about the huge number of children who would soon be entering an untested program. Richmond was concerned too, but he said that this was a window of opportunity to help young poor children, and if we didn't climb through it, we might lose our chance. This reminded me of the 1935 Social Security program, which, when it began, was little more than a recipe for poverty in old age. Over time, the program evolved into an economic safety net for the elderly. My hope was that, like Social Security, Head Start would improve as it matured and we learned more about early intervention.

Finishing Touches

I made a few recommendations about the Head Start model that created some controversy. For one, I questioned the wisdom of having a preschool program populated only by poor children. Such segregation runs headlong into John Dewey's dictum that education is not only about learning academics but about how to live in a democracy. The civil rights movement of the time was trying to end racial segregation. I thought it was equally inappropriate to segregate children by socioeconomic status. I argued that Head Start centers should include middle-class children. Not only would heterogeneous enrollment be ethical, but social modeling theory espoused by scholars such as Bandura and others suggested that poor and middle-class children could learn important skills from one another.

Some members of the planning committee disagreed with my idea, arguing that Head Start was part of the War on Poverty so limited funds should not be spent on children who did not "need" the services the program would provide. Still, the moral issue was a potent one, so we reached a compromise. My original proposal was that one-third of the children be middle class. The other members thought that was too many and eventually agreed that 10% of Head Start slots could be filled by children above the poverty line. (The 10% rule still exists, although many centers do not have funds for all the poor children in their service areas so the heterogeneity rule is more a statement than a practice.)

I threw another bombshell toward the end of our deliberations. I was a basic behavioral scientist who at the time lived and breathed empirical research. In character, I recommended that we mount at least a small evaluation to assess the efficacy of the summer Head Start program. The results could give some insight into what was working, what we needed to do differently, and show policymakers what benefits they were purchasing with this huge expenditure. To my surprise, not a single member of the committee agreed with me. Everyone said that the services we were introducing—for example, preschool education, health care, and family support—were valid and worthwhile practices on their face and needed no further proof. They also pointed out that the small federal Head Start staff were as busy as they could be, and no one had the time to create a good evaluation. My adversaries were correct on this point. It takes money and a lot of time to develop measures and prove their worth, train testers, handle the flow of incoming data, and interpret the results. However, to a 35-year-old Ed Zigler, being told something could not be done was a challenge I could not resist.

The debate over evaluation continued through the last two or three meetings of the planning committee, and I am sure everyone was getting tired of me. I could have been easily outvoted, but, because of the mutual respect among us, a vote was never taken. By this time, Julius Richmond had arrived to be Head Start's director. He was busy with a thousand and one administration responsibilities, but he would often look in on the planning committee meetings. He overheard our argument about whether to have an evaluation and made up our minds for us. Richmond called me into the hallway and said he had decided I was correct, but with time and money in short supply, I would have to put the evaluation together myself. I certainly tried. I will save the embarrassing details for Chapter 3, admitting here only that it was probably the worst study of Head Start ever conducted. The only value in that first effort is that it put Head Start on the path of using science and evaluation as tools for innovation and improvement. I believe Richmond, in his wisdom, foresaw this when he broke the Gordian knot that encircled the planning committee and endorsed an evaluation component.

Some of my antics aside, the interactions of the planning committee members were amicable and a consensus was quickly reached on most major issues. There was, however, one outlier, Dr. Myron Wegman. Wegman reports that his first contact with the Head Start program "came with a surprise telephone call from Sargent Shriver, followed by a week of persistent attempts to persuade me to become the director" (1997, p. 109). When Wegman insisted he could not leave his job in Ann Arbor, Shriver asked him to join the national planning committee. (The same thing happened when Shriver recruited Richmond to become the Head Start director. Dr. Richmond was the newly appointed dean of the Medical School of the Upstate Medical Center at Syracuse and was not inclined to take the job. Shriver's charm and enthusiasm made it difficult to say no to him. Richmond eventually agreed to work part-time in Syracuse and part-time in Washington. Despite these two sets of enormous responsibilities, Richmond proved to be an inspired leader for Head Start.)

During the planning committee deliberations, Wegman was negative about many decisions. He writes, "Other members of the Planning Committee must surely have thought of me as a contentious person" (1997, p. 111). Wegman was concerned that Head Start would be wasteful in that it overlapped many existing services. "I was deeply bothered by the attitude of the Planning Committee that we were going it alone," seemingly "unaware or unheeding of admittedly inadequate ongoing efforts aimed ... in the same direction" (1997, p. 110). Wegman also wanted Head Start to be much smaller in scope, running selected projects in targeted regions instead of attempting nationwide coverage. This way of thinking was of course one of the major complaints about the planning committee by the "rapid reformists" in CAP, who believed we wanted Head Start to be a small experimental program. With the wisdom of hindsight, it is clear Wegman would have had a hard time as director of Head Start. He would have been in constant conflict with Shriver, who was bound and determined to have a very large and very visible Head Start program that first summer.

I do concur with one important point made by Wegman. He writes "I would want to concentrate enough services to really give everyone involved the extra attention that is needed, for a long enough time to make a difference" (1997, pp. 111–112). Forty years of subsequent research have now proven that there are two determinants of a program's efficacy: quality and intensity. The idea that any 8-week program could have a significant impact on the growth and development of economically disadvantaged children is nonsense. Sister Jacqueline made this point succinctly: "Unless we can succeed in changing the public school experience where formal education takes over, the initial investment will be squandered" (Wexler, 1997, p. 113).

So yes, the planners anticipated the "fade-out" of program benefits that longitudinal studies would eventually reveal. They understood there was no magic inoculation for children living in poverty. The purpose of Head Start was to produce some positive momentum in children's development, but then the ball had to be picked up by the schools. As for program intensity, after the first summer Head Start quickly became a more meaningful academic-year program. Decades later the debate continues about the added value of having children attend for 2 years instead of one.

Despite the flaws in Head Start's design and implementation, the sheer number of innovative ideas produced by the planners and administrators is admirable. More impressive is the fact that an unprecedented program of Head Start's complex scope and immense size went from the drawing board to full-scale implementation in a matter of months. Most unfortunately, the capacity of Head Start to provide a universally high-quality program was simply defeated by the impossible timeframe and the shortage of the required manpower and resources.

The Community Action Program: Another Vision of Head Start

Unlike Community Action, Head Start was not written into the bill creating the OEO. The program came late to the scene, and instead of being given an independent place within OEO, it was made part of Community Action. At several of the planning committee meetings, the head of CAP showed up briefly just to remind us that we were part of Community Action. I honestly had no idea what this meant.

As mentioned earlier, Shriver had asked CAP staffers to design a preschool intervention program before he convened the official planning committee. The committee's executive secretary, Jule Sugarman, was the only individual at the table who had a foot in both camps. Yet he never informed the planners of the thinking about Head Start that was taking place within the CAP. In fact, in a recent interview he told the authors he recalls no formal plan emanating from the Community Action people that was acceptable either to him or to Shriver. Although no record of the CAP plan exists, the agency's approach to poverty was very different from that taken by the planning committee, and it is clear they had a different vision for Head Start.

According to Polly Greenberg, who was detailed to OEO in its early days from the Office of Education, the formal birth of Head Start as a program took place at an October, 1964 meeting at OEO: "Shriver tossed to his senior staff his bombshell of an idea for a massive . . . program for children on the brink of entering kindergarten or first grade.... Shriver's top staffers exploded in an enthusiastic response.... Everyone was thrilled with Shriver's brilliant idea, and instantly, imaginatively elaborated on it" (1998, p. 57). She relates that the CAP plan contained a heavy emphasis on health and nutrition. Some attention apparently was given to preschool education, based on the OEO memo suggesting the cluster teaching arrangements described above and Greenberg's statement that she was asked to write the education piece (2004). She also says she wrote the parent involvement part, chiding the planning committee for crediting themselves with the "innovation" of including parents. "The Poverty Warriors ... smiled at what they saw as the experts' conceit" (2004, p. 66).

CAP's notion of involving the poor in antipoverty efforts was to give them total control of their destinies and the power to change the social structure as needed to permit their rise out of poverty. Whereas the Head Start planning committee had to develop a response to the deficit model, the CAP visionaries focused only on the strengths of the poor, denying any sense of deficits, or lingering effects of deprivation, or performance in need of a boost. To the thinkers in Community Action, the problems to be corrected were not of the poor adult or child, but rather of the entire American system that deprived economically disadvantaged citizens access to community services, good schools and jobs, and a voice in government. Thus, the emphasis in Community Action was on changing the "system" to make it fair and egalitarian.

There was also the realistic recognition that money is power. A major thrust in OEO was to get poor people into meaningful, decent-paying jobs. Many OEO programs, Head Start included, offered employment opportunities to poor participants. Of course, like many federal positions, jobs were also given as patronage for individuals favored by local Community Action leaders. Bolstering the earnings capacity of the poor was so critical to OEO's mission that Greenberg suggested it as a measure of the success of antipoverty programs. After her stint at CAP, she moved south and became part of a huge Head Start effort known as the Child Development Group of Mississippi (CDGM). Head Start became a major industry in Mississippi, much to the unhappiness of southern politicians and many residents who disliked the program's racial integration policy. In her book about the CDGM, *The Devil Has Slippery Shoes*, Greenberg (1969) argued that Head Start should be assessed by the amount of money that is poured into Mississippi rather than by Shriver and the planners' goal of children's school readiness.

There was a downside to CAP's joint initiatives of providing jobs and showcasing the strengths of the poor. Professionals (e.g., teachers, social workers, psychologists), with the possible exception of MDs, came to be viewed as part of the system that had already failed Head Start families. Marian Wright, a lawyer active in the civil rights movement, asserted that the poor could do a *better* job than the pros (Kuntz, 1998), and indeed they were some-times hired for CAP jobs that normally required professional credentials. (Of course, when Head Start became a school-year program and the licensed teachers who had taught in the summer were unavailable, parents and others with no classroom experience were needed as pinch-hitters. Even today, Head Start's roots as a job source for community residents conflict with the children's needs for highly trained teachers.) The general suspicion of professionals was sometimes warranted. Many had bought into the deficit model, so they had difficulty establishing rapport with poor parents from cultures they viewed as having few assets.

Turning the tables, the poverty warriors viewed *professionals* as having little to contribute. The hostility of the Community Action people toward the outside experts on the planning committee was abundantly clear. Greenberg insists there was no real confrontation between the two groups because each was totally irrelevant to the other. "We paid 'outside experts' no more mind than they paid *us*" (2004, p. 63). Greenberg viewed the efforts of the planning committee as a mere distraction to the in-house Community Action people who were frantically engaged in more important tasks essential to the entire antipoverty effort. Their work was to change the system on behalf of the underclass, a mission that could never be accomplished "by most of the middle class ... or by liberal politicians, professionals, and academic gurus" (1998, p. 69). Organizing the poor was the route to the goal—with strength in numbers they could pressure the system to enable them to better their own lives: "*Significant* social change—without which poverty will be reduced only in small, safe, institutional inching forward, on a one-by-one snail's pace basis—comes from masses of frustrated poor people, emboldened, organized, and guided by a well-informed, charismatic, and trusted leader (usually a former poor person)" (Greenberg, 1998, p. 69).

A Literal War *on Poverty*

In their mission to change the world, some militant Community Action agencies engaged in protest marches, sit-ins, and physical intimidation of public servants and officials. Police were often called, and sometimes the National Guard was deployed to quell the constant clashes between "the people" and the social order. These altercations shared the stage with the raging civil rights protests of the 1960s, ratcheting up percep-tions of a siege of violence.

A recognized poster person for Community Action and a radical community organizer was Saul Alinsky. He was a long-time supporter of militant combat against the powers that be, a view obvious in the title of his book written back in the 1940s, *Reveille for Radicals*. Throughout the War on Poverty he was in great demand as a speaker to inspire communities in their organization and action agendas. Another activist trooper was Richard Boone, Director of OEO's Policy and Development Division and one of Shriver's right-hand men (Greenberg, 2004). Not only did he invent the phrase "maximum feasible participation" of the poor, but he purposefully used it repeatedly until it was written into the Economic Opportunity Act and became CAP's marching song (Stossel, 2004). Even though he was a leader at OEO, he eventually found their efforts too timid and left to form an outside advocacy group, potently named the Citizens Crusade against Poverty.

It is easy to see why OEO in general and the Community Action Program in particular quickly became worrisome to the establishment. It is hardly surprising that only a few months after the birth of OEO, the House of Representatives formed a committee to investigate the agency (Greenberg, 1998). Actually, policymakers were on alert much earlier when they were still in the process of creating OEO, *before* any bad behavior occurred. When the Economic Opportunity Act was working its way through Congress, it was widely expected that Adam Yarmolinsky, special assistant to the Secretary of Defense, would be appointed as Shriver's deputy and second in command at OEO. Yarmolinsky was a liberal political activist and a brilliant tactician who had worked closely with the Kennedys and was frequently referred to as the "chief midwife" of Johnson's War on Poverty. Yet he was never even nominated to become Shriver's deputy, partly because Southern conservatives feared he was too radical and might attempt to desegregate all OEO programs (Vinovskis, 2005). To facilitate debate on the bill, the White House had to promise that Yarmolinsky would not be appointed, despite Shriver's strong support of his candidacy.

The militancy, the radical organizing in the Saul Alinsky mode, and the inflammatory rhetoric of the poverty warriors quickly led to a backlash against Community Action. It is inevitable that when you fight the system, the system fights back. For example, Mayor Yorty of Los Angeles banded together with other mayors and tried to make it impossible for Community Action agencies to set up in their cities. Chicago's mayor Richard Daley went directly to President Johnson with his complaints. "What in the hell are you people doing?" he said to Bill Moyers, a key aide to Johnson. "Does the president know he's putting M-O-N-E-Y in the hands of subversives?" (quoted in Stossel, 2004, p. 495). Shriver, of course, was well aware of the animosity of the power structure toward what many felt was the heart of OEO, namely the CAP. This is likely why he placed Head Start in the agency instead of giving the program its own administrative structure. He hoped that as a program for small, needy children, Head Start could mitigate the growing hostility toward Community Action.

Head Start was given the status of a National Emphasis Program within OEO. These were federal programs originating from Washington but administered at the local level, usually through the local Community Action agency. Shriver had high hopes that the National Emphasis Programs would counterbalance the negative views many had of CAP by delivering desirable services that localities needed. Shriver writes that without these service programs, "The Community Action Program would be looked upon exclusively as an effort to empower the poor politically and economically. We knew that endowing a particular group in a community with money and political power would generate hostility from others in that community" (1997, p. 60). Although the intention was good, many politicians were incensed by OEO's practice of sending federal money directly to local communities rather than through the conventional channel of sending it to the states, which controlled doling it out at the local level.

To be fair to history, two points must be emphasized. One is that President Johnson and Shriver were liberals, not militants. Neither had any patience with confrontational tactics and lawlessness. Second, while many Community Action agencies did support rabble-rousing, many others did not. Instead, they concentrated on providing worthwhile services in their neighborhoods that had been developed at OEO, for example, health centers, Head Start, and the Job Corps. Community Action agencies exist across the nation to this day. For the most part, they provide the poor with support services like heating oil subsidies and Meals on Wheels for the elderly. In Fiscal Year 2003 (the latest published data), Community Action agencies were the grantees for 32% of Head Start programs (U.S. Department of Health and Human Services, 2003). Unfortunately, the noisy, radical Community Action participants roused the attention of the media and local leaders everywhere and tarnished the entire group of affiliates.

Irreconcilable Differences

Looking back, it is easy to see that the two different purposes of the two groups that each independently invented Head Start were on a collision course. The goal of the planning committee was healthy child development. Their Head Start would give children the academic and socioemotional skills they needed to be ready for school and support their families in the vital task of child rearing.

The Community Action people were an integral part of OEO. They saw them-selves as selfless, idealistic poverty warriors with a messianic desire to correct all of the wrongs that society had perpetrated on the poor. To the planning committee, the Head Start program was the entire ball game. To those at Community Action, Head Start was relatively small change in the overall effort that was all about social reform.

Shriver was aware that many of his Community Action employees didn't see as particularly important the goal of delivering services like Head Start. He writes, "Some of the philosophers or theorists of community action did not believe in what they called 'services.' They believed that OEO should not give services to poor people. Rather we should *empower* poor people politically and economically [so they] will pull themselves up by their own bootstraps" (1997, p. 60). Service programs like Head Start were considered of little value since they did not lead to "transferring power."

Although Shriver didn't champion their views, like Sugarman he was sympathetic to their approach and accepted it as part of his own action plan. He felt that both service programs and power realignment were needed. This position did not reconcile the poverty warriors. Shriver relates that

> Saul Alinsky . . . started out by being a very good friend of mine for fifteen years, and then ended up attacking us and OEO relentlessly. He called our whole effort at OEO "political pornography." What he meant was that we were not really giving poor people the power to change their own conditions . . . that OEO was therefore palliative and all we were doing was spoon-feeding the poor with programs like Head Start. (1997, p. 60)

The conflict between empowerment and service provision became obvious when some local agencies did not even want to mount a "wimpy" program like Head Start, which they saw as part of the problem instead of a piece of the solution.

With the passage of time, the animosity of the Community Action poverty warriors toward the Head Start planners became quite palpable. To illustrate, Greenberg stated in print that Sugarman, her colleague in Community Action, was the "de facto director of Head Start . . . 'from before the beginning'" (1998, p. 61). She credits Julius Richmond, who was appointed to the post by Shriver, as being merely "the part-time national director" (2004, p. 67). (Richmond [2004] has rebutted this directly.) The planners came to be treated as inter-lopers who were upending the Head Start design CAP had already constructed. Carolyn Harmon describes this sentiment: "It was only through the interven-tion of unnamed planners in OEO and/or spontaneous efforts by Head Start parents that the program became a vehicle for empowering the disadvantaged to challenge oppressive social institutions . . . but in the end, conservative forces triumphed, and Head Start was redirected to changing individual parents and children rather than society" (2004, p. 86).

Harmon, a key special assistant to me during my years in Washington and probably one of the few scholars who closely read the 800-plus-page opus containing Greenberg's biography of CDGM, notes that since that book's publication, "the notion has been making the rounds that Head Start was diverted from its true purpose as a community action program by craven liberal politicians, elitist academic developmental psychologists, and an American political system that would not tolerate true reform" (2004, p. 85). This same revisionist view can be seen in two books by Ames and Ellsworth (1997; Ellsworth and Ames, 1998). The contents lament the loss of Head Start's potential as a force for social change and assert that a heavier emphasis on parents and communities would have made the program more successful in combating poverty than merely including these elements as adjuncts to serving children.

Spatig et al. (1998) drew a succinct comparison of the two different frameworks employed by the Head Start planning committee and CAP. These scholars describe the Head Start planners as operating within a "functionalist framework," providing poor children and their families with the types of support that could enable them to take advantage of opportunities provided within the current social system. "In other words, Head Start need not fundamentally challenge the societal status quo. Rather it should be about the business of helping poor children and families function more successfully within it" (p. 74). Antithetically, Spatig et al. describe the Community Action approach as operating within a "conflict theory," aimed at exposing the social system's flaws and inequities. Given this philosophy, "it is reasonable to expect [Head Start] to challenge, rather than support, the inequitable system that continues to spawn such poverty" (p. 75).

To the planners, the purpose of Head Start was optimal child development, resulting in improved school readiness. The Community Action people viewed better performance by a Head Start child not as an end in itself but as a means to a much larger end. It was an opportunity to hire parents and locals to improve their financial situation. More important, Head Start would confront and change the system so that all poor children and adults would experience a better quality of life. To the CAP firebrands, the Head Start planners were basically traitors who accepted that the hierarchical capitalistic system would characterize America far into the future so Head Start would have to work within it.

Shriver's wish that Community Action and the Head Start program would become comfortable bed fellows was somewhat naive. This did not stop Jule Sugarman, a high-level official in both Head Start and Community Action, from trying. He was very sympathetic to the Community Action mission and attempted to pursue the inherently different goals of Head Start during the first 5 years of the program's existence. His policy of allowing Head Start funds to support Community Action activities did not sit well with policymakers or many Head Start families. As will be explained in Chapter 4, I ended this practice when I became the federal official responsible for Head Start. In a paper entitled, "The Lost Legacy," Kuntz (1998) blames me for disassociating Head Start from Community Action and thwarting the people's power struggle. Realistically, the social realignment aspect of Community Action could not have lasted very long. The antics of community activists were storm clouds over Head Start's early years, but, as we will tell in the next chapter, they were not the only ones.

3

Head Start's Early Years

President Johnson's promotion of the War on Poverty as a moral, just cause initially struck a chord in this democratic nation founded on the principle that "All men are created equal" and deserve equal opportunities. There was popular support for many of the new antipoverty programs, but the emerging favorite was the one devoted to the youngest, most innocent victims of poverty. As Head Start moved from the drawing board to the set-up phase, it very quickly brought out the best in Americans. This reaction might seem unexpected given Head Start's ties to Community Action, which was just as quickly becoming a dirty word in the common lexicon.

Head Start's huge popularity was ignited by President and Lady Bird Johnson. Alleviating poverty was close to the president's emotional core, since he had lived among the poor as a boy, and his own family later fell on hard times so he had to work his way through college (Woods, 2006). The First Lady had a special place in her heart for children and adopted Head Start with the zeal of a missionary. Even before Head Start had taken shape, she agreed to meet with Sargent Shriver and a small group of social workers at the White House to discuss the concept of a preschool program for poor children. That night Mrs. Johnson wrote in her diary, "The Head Start idea has such *hope* and challenge. Maybe I could help focus public attention in a favorable way on some aspects of Lyndon's poverty program" (1997, p. 44). Her help did exactly that, and more.

The widespread devotion to Head Start was jumpstarted at a tea in the Red Room of the White House that Mrs. Johnson hosted on February 12, 1965. (This is when she innocently talked about the horror of preschool children not knowing their own names.) Many prominent women from the business and entertainment worlds had been invited, as well as some high-ranking federal officials and their wives and a number of wives of governors. There were also a few men from the private sector, primarily church leaders including several from the black community. The planning committee members were present to explain the new Head Start program to the attendees.

As a result of this tea, Head Start was first discussed in America's newspapers. Mills (1998) notes that early stories about Head Start often ran in what was called at that time the "society pages." The timing could not have been better. Sugarman observed that this placement created "the image of an acceptable, nice program in the public mind. While Community Action . . . was being bloodied every day on the front page, Head Start was receiving glowing tributes in the society and community-news pages from local establishment leaders" (1997, p. 117).

After the tea, Shriver asked Mrs. Johnson to become Head Start's honorary chairperson. First Ladies are wary of lending their names to specific efforts and select their commitments cautiously. Yet Lady Bird wholeheartedly welcomed Shriver's invitation, balking only at the traditional definition of "honorary chairperson, which meant I was not supposed to really do any work" (1997, p. 44). As Mills points out, Mrs. Johnson insisted "she wanted to be more than a figurehead. She wanted to work at it, which she did by helping corral volunteers, visiting Head Start centers, and focusing press attention on the program" (1998. p. 50).

The Johnsons' contributions to the success of Head Start cannot be overstated. In addition to the First Lady's many efforts, the two Johnson daughters became involved in the program. For example, they volunteered at an eye clinic for Head Start preschoolers, and, at her father's urging, one served as a substitute teacher at a Head Start center near their Texas home. President Johnson himself was an avid fan of the program and became a volunteer once he retired from public service. He would periodically visit the local Head Start center with his pants pockets filled with jelly beans. The children delighted in his visits and the treats and dubbed him, "Mr. Jelly Beans." They were too young to grasp the prominence and importance of their guest and how important they were to him.

The Johnsons' devotion to Head Start and to the poor was genuine. I recall the Rose Garden ceremony at the White House in May of 1965 where the president greeted a sea of reporters and cameras and announced with great pride the new Head Start program. Again, Head Start's planners were invited to participate and be available to answer questions from the media. The scholars were standing to one side of the presidential podium and, like the rest of the audience, were awaiting the arrival of the president and Mrs. Johnson. Children make great photo opportunities, so four preschoolers and their parents from the Washington area were invited to the event. The children sparkled in their immaculate cleanliness and Sunday clothes. Yet being children, they were squirmy, and their parents seemed very uncomfortable in this atmosphere. There is something intimidating about being at the White House. That feeling apparently affected the great experts on children and families from the planning committee, none of whom had the good sense to go over and talk to the young visitors to help them feel more at ease. Soon Mr. and Mrs. Johnson came into the Rose Garden and without a bit of hesitation, walked over and played with the children and spoke with their parents in a reassuring and understanding manner. I will never forget this warm welcome extended to these guests at the Johnson home, even though they were from the poor side of town.

Head Start was an instant hit with the public, the media, and policy-makers across the liberal–conservative continuum. Volunteers came out of the woodwork. The ladies who attended the Red Room tea returned to their homes across the nation and enlisted local support. Great-grandmothers and elementary school children offered their help. Heart-throb actor Gregory Peck advertised for volunteers on television. Because of his giant stature in the medical community, Julius Richmond was able to mobilize the American Academy of Pediatrics to provide physicals to Head Start children. He secured dental services through his contacts at the Public Health Service. (Although the volunteer medicine did not last long, Richmond put into place the under-pinnings of what is an unquestionable Head Start accomplishment— improving poor children's health.) Enthusiasm ballooned. The entrance of Head Start on the social scene clearly made Americans pleased with them-selves for what they were doing for such a deserving segment of the poor. The widespread involvement of local volunteers helped Head Start not just that first summer but to this day. The helpers came to "own" the program and thus became a built-in lobby group who, along with parents, opposed political actions that could threaten their beloved Head Start. In 1965, though, there were no threats. Head Start's troubles, many put into place that first summer, were still all in the future.

Launching a Nationwide Preschool

Neither the planning committee nor the OEO decision makers anticipated the immense popularity of Head Start. No one came close to predicting that 560,000 children would be enrolled that first summer. As applications poured in, the budget exploded from $10 million to $70 million. Head Start's prenatal growth amazed even Shriver:

> This illustrates one of the fantastic aspects of OEO. I increased the funding by myself! I didn't have to go to Congress; I didn't have to go to the president; I didn't have to go to the Bureau of the Budget. Congress had appropriated money, and if I wanted to spend it on Head Start, I could spend it on Head Start. . . . I felt we had a gigantic breakthrough, so I pumped in the money as fast as we could intelligently use it. It was really quite spectacular. (Shriver, 1997, p. 56)

At the outset, the Head Start unit in OEO had three professionals and one secretary. They obviously needed more expertise, so the planning committee became the steering committee for the new program. The director, Julius Richmond, and Jule Sugarman, his right-hand man, made a good team: one an expert on children and their needs and one capable of the gigantic managerial task of launching a complex program within an impossible timeframe. The usual Washington title for the job Sugarman was performing would have been deputy director. Richmond wanted the Head Start administration to look more academic than governmental, so he bestowed Sugarman with the title of associate director (parallel to the associate professorship in higher education).

The authors certainly agree with Polly Greenberg that there is no way to give Sugarman more credit than he deserves. His feats of managerial legerdemain during Head Start's start-up period are now legend. He recruited Washington's leading female activists to volunteer in the Washington office. What would a staff of four do with a growing mountain of 3,300 grant applications? It was Sugarman's idea to work with the organization in the District that managed substitute teachers. After a brief training, these substitutes worked in shifts processing all the incoming Head Start applications.

Getting fundable applications from the poorest communities in the nation was another hurdle. Sugarman was concerned that potential grantees had no idea how to write a government project request because they had never done so. At the same time, Jimmy Hymes and Keith Osborn, the two preschool education experts who had served on the planning committee and were now helping to implement Head Start, were worried that many of those who would be requesting funds for the project probably had little knowledge of child development or how to prepare young children for school. To solve both problems, Osborn suggested that Head Start bring the nation's experts on young children and preschool programming "to Washington and teach them how to write government proposals. . . . Then, they could go to the communities throughout the country and perform two functions: a) inform the community on ways to achieve good programs for young children and b) help the community to write a government grant" (personal communication, May 3, 1977). These leading professionals performed heroically. Osborn recalls that they labored for 30 to 40 days without a break to get thousands of applications completed within the 6-week deadline.

Given the several components of Head Start, the future grantees also needed help in the application process beyond that provided by the early child-hood educators. Therefore Head Start hired psychologists, social workers, nutritionists, and other professionals to consult with the potential grantees. Aware of the enormity of the task and the inexperience of the applicants, Sugarman also recruited young civil servants from throughout Washington to travel to 300 of the poorest counties in the country to help people prepare their grant requests. These huge outreach efforts were incredibly successful, with 2,700 of the 3,300 applications received—a whopping 82%—complete enough to be funded (Richmond, 2004).

Every day between February and June 1965, 12- to 15-hour days were common for the Head Start workers. Outsiders jokingly referred to the new program as "project rush–rush." Richmond remembers taking the president of the Child Welfare League to witness the frenzied assembly line set up to process the grant applications. It was the middle of the night, and the lights were blazing. The guest observed that he had not seen anything like this since World War II. The headquarters had been hurriedly staged in an old hotel scheduled for demolition. Richmond pointed out the lack of furniture in his office and quipped how quickly one gets through meetings when attendees must stand. There were insufficient file drawers for the mounds of applications, so they were stacked in bushel baskets and in the bathtubs in the old guest rooms.

Most of the action took place in the hotel's ballroom. I stood there one day and watched the assembly line where the substitute teachers determined whether each Head Start application contained the quality indicators necessary to make the proposal fundable. The fact was that these quickly trained helpers were not looking for quality indicators and probably would not recognize them if they were there. Instead they were scanning for evidence that the components of the program as designated by the planning committee (e.g., health, education, parent involvement) were included. If these elements were mentioned at all, this was sufficient to demonstrate the program's adequacy and funding was approved. Watching this process late one night, I approached Sugarman and worried aloud that we must be funding a lot of really bad programs. Not taken aback for a second, Sugarman said, "I know that, Ed." I reminded him that it did not take an expert to realize that poor quality programs would not be helpful to children. He reassured me by saying he had a plan of action. First we had to get programs funded, to get the money out there. Once the centers were running and we had more time, we'd give them a closer look, and those that did not measure up would lose their money to better centers. Being naive as a post, I felt that this sounded sensible and that his concern about quality would be dealt with eventually. Forty-two years later, quality issues continue to haunt Head Start. To be fair, the authors emphatically add that giant steps in quality improvement have been made.

Another indicator of Head Start's hurried launch can be seen in the process of determining the amount of funds programs would get to serve each child. Shriver gave Sugarman *one hour* to calculate exactly how much money communities would be given to provide staff, materials, utilities, and so forth, for an 8-week program. Sugarman decided that $180 per child would suffice, but where this amount came from is a mystery. (Sugarman, 1997, attributes it to OEO staff.) Although Sugarman was an excellent manager, he knew little about child development or preschool programming. A respected pioneer in early childhood intervention, Martin Deutsch, immediately sounded an alarm and, based on his own experiences, said this was much too little for an effective program. When applications started pouring in, Sugarman was appalled that almost all of them asked for exactly $180 per child.

I know of one that did not. A leading developmentalist, Frances Horowitz, who was then at the University of Kansas, applied for a Head Start grant and was told that her proposed budget was too high. Mirroring Deutsch's view, she wrote to Head Start officials complaining that $180 per child was too little to mount a high-quality preschool program. The letter she received back stated that they were not attempting to mount high-quality programs but Head Start programs. Both common sense and experience tell us the higher the quality of the program, the more money it costs. The planners were certainly aware that the effects of the Head Start intervention would be commensurate with its quality. The few experimental projects that preceded Head Start and were showing at least preliminary positive results certainly cost more than $22.50 per child per week, and they did not offer the full gamut of services to be included in Head Start. I guess the planners never took the time or trouble to carefully figure out what their program would cost if delivered in the intended fashion.

Of course, one must be realistic and not design programs that are very expensive because they would not be able to serve enough children to make a real impact. In my 40 years of experience, I have discovered that many decision makers are not sufficiently conversant with the relation between the quality of a program and its effects, nor do they appear concerned about the degree of the fidelity of programs actually mounted to the model they are supposed to follow. We see this today in the push to institute universal preschool. The data show that quality preschool education prepares children for school, so many states and localities are quickly mounting programs that bear little resemblance to the famous models that produced the findings but are expecting the same results.

Understandably, that first summer officials were more interested in getting a program out in the land in a big way and were not particularly worried about quality. Further, as Jerome Bruner noted when he told Shriver Head Start should begin with no more than 2,500 children, the nation did not have enough trained preschool teachers in 1965 to mount an immense, high-quality program. Even if it did, there was not (and still is not) enough money to pay them a competitive wage. Head Start was underfunded that first summer and remains underfunded today, making it difficult to achieve its broad array of goals.

Even though Head Start was America's darling in its early years, the program suffered two serious blows. One was the loss of its brilliant director, Julie Richmond. Shriver was so impressed with Richmond that he convinced him to take over the direction of the OEO network of health centers around the country, all of this as a part-time worker who also had the responsibilities of being dean of a major medical school. These impossible demands took their toll. Attempting to do three jobs simultaneously, Richmond became ill after about a year and was forced to leave Washington. Head Start was fortunate to have the continuing leadership of Jule Sugarman, who unquestionably learned a great deal from Richmond and had experience with both the Head Start planning committee and the Community Action program. He skillfully guided Head Start forward for the next few years.

The other blow was the unrealistically high expectations placed on Head Start that, although they have constantly changed form, continue to guarantee the program will disappoint. This began before Head Start even opened. When President Johnson announced the program in the White House Rose Garden, he unabashedly told the nation, "This program this year means that 30 million man-years—the combination lifespan of these youngsters—will be spent productively and rewardingly, rather than wasted in tax-supported institutions or in welfare-supported lethargy" (1997, p. 68). He called for volunteers by charging them with a lofty goal: "We have taken up the age-old challenge of poverty and we don't intend to lose generations of our children to this enemy of the human race" (pp. 68-69). The authors agree with Mills's view that the president "planted the seeds of future discontent by overpromising the results. Because of one summer program, thousands of children were not suddenly going to emerge from poverty.... Broader, more lasting strategies for combating poverty would be needed, and with them, greater national will to do so" (1998, p. 55).

Any program must be evaluated against a realistic goal that can actually be achieved in the real world. Promising people that a brief Head Start experience will enable children to overcome the ill effects of living in poverty all the years before and the many years after the Head Start interlude was not being realistic. To this day Head Start suffers from impossible expectations. For example, the George W. Bush administration criticized Head Start because after spending 9 months in the program, children are not as school-ready as middle-class children who have had all the benefits of a comparatively wonderful middle-class life. In response, one of psychology's finest child development scholars, Jeanne Brooks-Gunn (2003), replied with a paper entitled, "Do You Believe in Magic?" She pointed out that although there is considerable evidence that high-quality preschool intervention programs have positive outcomes, they do not have supernatural powers. The achievement gap at school entry can be completely closed only by providing impoverished children with every environmental benefit experienced by middle-class children every day of their lives. Head Start could never do that on $180, nor can it do so on today's $7,200 annual per-child allotment.

Action from Community Action

Community Action's mission to empower the disenfranchised poor fed into and was fed by the raging civil rights movement bent on extracting justice for past and present sins of racial discrimination. The zeal of participants in these crusades spilled into the streets. In the late 1960s and early 1970s militant acting-out behaviors became routine, not just in the inner cities but in once-peaceful suburbs. Residents who had never before locked their doors began to do so, and shopkeepers installed bars and gates as barriers to looting and vandalism. I remember when Bob Cooke, Ed Davens, and I were visiting Head Start centers that first summer of 1965 in an area of Los Angeles known as Watts. While we were there, a riot broke out with violence, burning, and looting everywhere we looked. Police rescued these wide-eyed visitors and got us safely back to our hotel. The country would suffer a few hundred such riots precipitated by poverty, inequality, unhappiness over the escalating Vietnam War, and the assassinations of Robert Kennedy and Martin Luther King, Jr.

The mob mentality made reasonable discourse impossible. To illustrate, I attended what I thought would be a routine academic conference chaired by my friend, the scholar Ed Gordon, who would become Head Start's first research director. The audience included both scholars and some pretty militant community people. While I was speaking, one of them interrupted with a tirade accusing me of using my research subjects to advance my own professional fame and fortune. I tried to explain the purpose of my work was to further understanding of the effects of poverty on children's development and, ultimately, to design better interventions. The man wouldn't hear it and continued his attack. Surprised, I simply gave up and announced that I would discontinue all of my research with poor children and return to my earlier areas of interest, namely mental retardation and psychopathology. At this point Gordon took the prerogative of the chair and advised me not to follow this course of action because future generations of poor minority children could only benefit from the work I was doing. I'm not sure that Gordon convinced the militants, but at least order was restored, and the meeting could continue. This meeting was actually mild compared to others I experienced. As I will relate in a later chapter, it was not unusual for activists to lock the doors after I arrived, imprisoning me and my staff for hours so they could make some point.

The charge that researchers wanted to do experiments with Head Start children to advance their academic careers actually began before the program did. Speaking for the poverty warriors at OEO, Greenberg (1998) writes:

> To the few ivory tower developmental psychologists involved in early
> plans for Head Start, the prospect of "experimenting" with children was
> exotic and exciting.... Psychologists had researched their middle-class
> "lab rat" children down to the last finding and were exhilarated by
> the idea of a "laboratory" (as some literally called it) of children from
> low-income families about whom to study, publish, and present. (p. 61)

True, the War on Poverty did raise academics' consciousness about the plight of the poor, and many behavioral scientists did begin to study children in Head Start and other intervention programs. The purpose as I saw it was to learn more about the developmental effects of living in poverty and eventually, to create more effective interventions. Of course, for empirical papers to serve this purpose, they must be published so they are available to other scholars who can build on them and expand the knowledge base. However, given the militancy of the times combined with the distrust of professionals, many community people balked at allowing psychologists to use their children as "guinea pigs." Street power eventually reached the point where behavioral scientists were sometimes told they could do their research but could not publish it, guaranteeing that no one would benefit from the findings. Instead of answering these activists with the truth that the ultimate beneficiaries of the research were the children, many psychologists agreed to these draconian conditions.

A case study of Community Action's motives and methods was the highly visible Child Development Group of Mississippi (CDGM). Political leaders in this state were opposed to offering Head Start because of the program's racial integration policy. Fearing that the governor would refuse to sign off on a grant proposal to start a Community Action Agency, black leaders funneled the request through Mary Holmes Junior College. The grantee then subcontracted with CDGM to operate 85 Head Start programs in 24 counties (Stossel, 2004). Most of those running CDGM were black, as were the majority of the young Head Starters. This segregation would probably have suited the white leadership just fine except that escalating civil rights violence in the area seemed to coincide with the growth of CDGM.

The story of CDGM has been chronicled by Polly Greenberg (1969), the CAP employee and activist who left Washington to join the Mississippi group. She writes, "CDGM was run by 945 extremely poor African Americans serving on small community committees that hired the 2,272 parent employees who held all of the jobs in all of the Head Start centers serving 13,000 children in most Mississippi counties. CDGM received $12 million dollars during the first summer of Head Start and many millions more in subsequent grants" (1998, p. 71).

Greenberg, of course, was an ardent supporter of empowering the poor and of community action directed toward system change. However, her great admiration and respect for the strengths of poor people had to be reconciled with her knowledge that poor children needed the help of professionals to prepare for school. Greenberg was a trained early childhood educator who had been transferred to OEO from the Office of Education. Prior to and following her poverty warrior days at OEO and CDGM, she worked at the highly respected National Association for the Education of Young Children. Thus she was troubled that inexperienced and often uneducated local residents were hired as teachers in the CDGM preschool program. Harmon writes, "Greenberg was not a romantic on the subject of the poor and expected that training and (unobtrusive) guidance by experts such as herself would be required to achieve both the adult empowerment and program quality goals she had for CDGM" (2004, p. 91).

Greenberg's views in this regard were oblique to those of the CDGM leaders, who felt that the primary goal of Head Start was to empower parents to improve their own and their children's lives. We get a sense of how this thrust affected the quality of CDGM's preschool program in Marian Wright Edelman's Senate testimony in which she asserted Head Start needed as teachers "warm responsive bodies who can help teach kids to be free and happy" (quoted in Kuntz, 1998, p. 20). Kuntz states that Edelman went even further, telling the Senators that "these nonprofessionals were better suited than college-trained women, echoing the community action notion that institutions and experts could learn something from the poor" (p. 20). Kuntz put these views against my own when I criticized OEO's operation of Head Start in 1969, summarizing my argument that "an 'indigenous' person was not going to be effective with children simply because he or she is poor and therefore is understanding and sympathetic. Like the early childhood personnel inside OEO, Zigler argued that poor mothers required training before they could contribute effectively to Head Start centers" (p. 20). However, CDGM's mission was to raise up poor adults, and it is doubtful whether the Head Start program experienced by the children of Mississippi that first summer did much to improve their school readiness.

CDGM became an immense headache for OEO decision makers, including Shriver, who was forced to spend an inordinate amount of time on this tense issue. CDGM became enmeshed in the politics of Mississippi and in all manner of civil rights confrontations. Many poor white parents refused to send their children to the CDGM Head Start centers. Unsurprisingly, the white power structure of Mississippi and the state's Senator John Stennis were forceful foes of CDGM. Stennis's opposition led to an audit by OEO of the group's expenditures. When a number of fiscal irregularities were discovered, its grant was revoked. The reasons included paying people who did not come to work ("no show" jobs), focusing on the economic needs of adults instead of the developmental needs of children, and failure to be racially integrated (Stossel, 2004). Poor citizens lashed out at Shriver and OEO. Eventually a compromise was reached and CDGM was reorganized under new leadership and permitted to continue receiving funds, provided employees did not participate in political activities during working hours.

In the end, CDGM was not successful in the Community Action goals of empowering the poor or in the Head Start goal of preparing children for school entry. Nonetheless, a positive patina surrounds many people's remembrance of CDGM. We concur with Harmon's observation, "Without a doubt, the very existence of CDGM was enormously valuable to the cause of freedom and equality for the viciously oppressed Black population of Mississippi" (2004, p. 90). Further, the struggle produced many young black leaders. Marian Wright Edelman is a shining example. This attorney founded and still heads our nation's most visible child advocacy group, the Children's Defense Fund. (As I will relate later, Edelman's adversarial style, honed in Mississippi, caused me many a sleepless night.)

Research Steps Off on the Wrong Foot

The thousands of local Head Start programs mounted that first summer were done hurriedly and in many places haphazardly. As part of Community Action,

Head Start enjoyed a great deal of local control. With bare-bones guidance about the types of services programs had to provide, grantees had only hazy ideas of what Head Start was, and essentially each program was designed as the local people thought best. To make matters worse, there was no form of anything resembling quality control. Thus any evaluation attempted that first summer would be nothing more than a study of a hodgepodge of various Head Start activities. Alas, I did not know all of this early in 1965 when I argued with the other planners about the importance of doing an evaluation right away.

I really wish I had listened to my elders and not argued so vehemently in favor of an assessment that turned out to be ahead of the science. The first major problem was that there were no established measures for most of Head Start's many goals. When Richmond relented to my demands for a study, he told me I would have to design it and construct the measures. My plan was to have local Head Start staff assess children when they entered and again when they left the program through simple observations of their behavior. I hoped that enough children would enroll that some would be placed on waiting lists and could form a comparison sample. Having a comparison group would make it possible to tell if any improvements shown by Head Start students over the course of the summer were due to the program or simply to the maturation effects of growing older and more capable.

Summer was almost upon us, and we had to have the measures ready within 10 days. With that type of timeframe, it is obviously impossible to construct measures from scratch and do all the pretesting to make sure they are psychometrically sound. I had to try, though, or my hard-fought battle would be a wasted victory. I returned to Yale and recruited some of my best graduate students to help. Even cloistered graduate students loved Head Start and were willing to work around the clock. They all contributed their services because I had no budget. The Yale Psychology Department contributed the facilities and materials.

We came up with some original ideas but also stole liberally from existing instruments. Our final product included observational measures that teachers and volunteers could use to assess children's social, emotional, and cognitive development and parents' child-rearing skills. Before measures could be used in a federal program, they had to be approved by the Office of Management and Budget (OMB). In those days we had no copiers or laser printers and still used mimeograph machines. We had the last measure on the machine ready to run off copies when Ed Gordon arrived from Washington to pick up the tests. He was taking the next plane back to DC and did not have time to wait for copies because we were running into the OMB deadline. He took the messy, ink-laden master in two fingers and flew it to Washington, where the mimeographing was completed and the battery submitted just in time. Why it was approved I will never know.

Fortunately, Julius Richmond did not put all of his eggs into the Yale basket. He asked his colleague, the prominent early childhood educator Bettye Caldwell, to construct an observational measure that could be filled out by Head Start teachers. Like the Yale group, she included a broad array of developmental domains such as cognitive and social skills. Although her test was also made up hurriedly, it was likely based on measures already developed and in use at the Children's Center she and Richmond ran in Syracuse. With better psychometric properties, the Caldwell measure proved to be useful and was employed for several years in the field of early childhood development. The Yale measures sank into the oblivion they richly deserved.

After Head Start was up and running, I found that my adversaries about doing an evaluation were not just the members of the planning committee but Head Start workers everywhere. They were so full of optimism and had such strong belief in the value of the program that they thought even the idea of looking for proof was an insult. They were working hard and were sure they were seeing improvements in the children every day. I traveled the country that first summer and everyone I met castigated the measures, complaining that completing them took precious time away from working with the children. I heard the same response a dozen times: "If you want to see if Head Start is working or not, just come to our center and open your eyes." Not only did I have a hard time convincing them to fill out my awful instruments, but there is no way they were going to try to round up the wait-list children and assess them too. Without the needed comparison group, it was impossible to tell if improvements were caused by Head Start or the passage of time. The whole data set was useless.

The tension and animosity between program staff and evaluators that I encountered in 1965 lingers to the present day, but it has gotten better. One of Head Start's victories over the years has been to bring about better understanding between those who run the programs and evaluation scientists. This movement has been helped along in recent years by a biennial research-to-practice conference held in Washington and attended by both behavioral scientists and Head Start practitioners. Evaluators are better at seeking the input of those in the trenches about what they think is important to include in an evaluation. (A glaring exception is the National Reporting System, which was imposed on all Head Start centers by the George W. Bush Administration. We will cover this incident in Chapter 12.) Program people have come to realize that it is fully legitimate for evaluators and policymakers to want to know exactly what has been accomplished with the money spent. In this age of account-ability, everyone is aware of the high stakes involved in program evaluation. Budgets in Head Start have fallen and risen in response to assessment results. When practitioners overcome their fear of evaluation, they realize the data can be extremely helpful at the center level by highlighting program strengths and weaknesses and pinpointing specific areas in need of improvement so the children and families will reap greater benefits.

The IQ Trap

My flawed attempt to discover if the Head Start summer program had any benefits did not begin to answer the question. Fortunately, scientists' curiosity was piqued, and soon several local and much better studies were under way. Unfortunately, researchers were not given any clear clues from the planning document about what to study. The wide variety of services that Head Start programs were trying to implement, each in its own way, did not make it easy to grasp what they were trying to do and therefore what effects should be assessed.

The planning committee's conceptual statement of what Head Start was designed to accomplish did not explicitly state that the ultimate goal was school readiness. Instead, the statement rambled on about better physical and mental health, enhanced cognitive skills and socioemotional development, and stronger parenting and family and community life—all contributors to school readiness but too sprawling to reveal a direct, measurable link. Lacking a ready definition of school readiness, and not able to decipher one from the planning document, researchers focused on the one listed objective they completely understood: "Improving the child's mental processes and skills." Thus the IQ measure became the standard measurement technique in assessing Head Start and other early intervention programs, but only by default.

I have nothing against intelligence tests. They are very solid measures in terms of reliability and validity and are relatively easy to administer, especially in shortened versions like the Peabody Picture Vocabulary Test. Further, the IQ score is related to school performance and therefore is a reasonable candidate to include in an assessment of programs designed to prepare children for school.

Another attraction of the intelligence test is that it began to yield positive findings. For example, Leon Eisenberg reported that Head Start children demonstrated an increase in IQ of 8 to 10 points after the summer session. In a letter to Lady Bird Johnson in June 1966, Shriver enthusiastically noted that Head Start children entered school with greater intellectual capacity (Mills, 1998). He also showcased the IQ gains at congressional hearings when asked about the War on Poverty's greatest success that could actually be measured.

Nevertheless, Shriver was ambivalent about the role of the IQ measure in evaluating Head Start. Although dazzled by the IQ findings of Susan Gray (Chapter 1), once higher IQs were found during Head Start's early days Shriver made clear that IQ improvement was not his goal for the program. He stated, "If we at OEO had not done anything more than to show how foolish IQ tests are, how little predictive value regarding competence, and how much people can do if given a chance, the right environment and supervision, then I feel we made one terrific contribution to our society" (1997, p. 59). While keeping the IQ findings in his back pocket for when he needed them, Shriver believed Head Start's purpose was to promote school readiness.

I knew and admired Leon Eisenberg as a careful scientist. I did not doubt that he found the amazing IQ gains he reported. However, I was aware that the IQ is a highly stable measure that no one had had much luck in changing. I therefore sought some other explanation for Eisenberg's findings. My colleagues and I conducted several experimental studies that indicated the IQ increases were not caused by truly expanded cognitive ability but by better test-taking capabilities. For example, children had less wariness of the examiner and test situation, more persistence and confidence, and greater familiarity with the test items and materials. I concluded that the Head Start experience had helped the children use their intelligence rather than giving them more of it.

The IQ became somewhat of a curse for Head Start as the program became more visible and more studies were done. As time progressed, unwelcome findings began to spoil the party. Indeed, Wolff and Stein (1966) reported the common increase in IQs of Head Start children but discovered the gains were ephemeral and dissipated over time (the famous "fade-out" phenomenon). One reason is that children who did not attend intervention caught up to peers who did after they began elementary school. Another is that children whose IQ test performance was boosted by intervention soon lost their initial advantage because of continued exposure to deprived living conditions, the low-quality schools they attended, and failure of the schools to build on their early gains.

Almost 50 years of research have now confirmed that the IQ gains typically found after just about every intervention program eventually fade out over time. The only program that has ever demonstrated lasting IQ improvement is the Abecedarian project (Campbell et al., 2001). The reported gain was approximately 5 points, which, although statistically significant, is not practically significant. Further, I am a bit skeptical about this finding because it was obtained by researchers assessing their own intervention model rather than by an independent and disinterested investigator. This in no way implies the Abecedarian research is inaccurate but only that it would be most credible if replicated by outsiders.

If intelligence is not a human trait amenable to quick and sizable change, using it in evaluations is a recipe for disaster. I was harshly reminded of this fact right after the first summer by a senior scholar who candidly told me I was "dumb." He said no one with an ounce of sense would use change on the most stable measure psychology has ever constructed as the ultimate criterion of a program's success. I did not make IQ increases the benchmark of Head Start's effects, but it is easy to see how this came to be. I tried to help Head Start escape the burden of demonstrating improvement in IQ scores when I became responsible for the program (see Chapter 5). Until then, the practice caused a lot of damage.

The Westinghouse Report

The most important study ever done to evaluate Head Start (prior to the Cornell Consortium and the more recent Head Start National Impact Study) was the famous, or infamous, Westinghouse study, conducted by the Westinghouse Learning Corporation (1969) and Ohio University. It was a terrible study, both methodologically flawed and misguided in its choice of outcomes used to determine the program's efficacy. It also became a political football, initiated and used by those interested in dismantling OEO. It resulted in a serious attempt to close down Head Start. The story of the Westinghouse Report lends insight into the workings of politics, the emergence of applied research in the social policy arena, and the turbulence of Head Start's growing years.

Early on, impact evaluations of Head Start were done by local researchers or by the programs themselves. In addition, many studies were being conducted or supported by Head Start to find better ways of serving low-income children and their families. In fact, there were so many research activities under way that the original research committee composed of Bronfenbrenner, Gordon, and Zigler was expanded. Renamed the Research Advisory Council, two members were added, Edward Suchman and Boyd McCandless. The council initiated many evaluations, including a major longitudinal study by the Educational Testing Service. As described by Datta, "The council believed that adequate evaluations would be longitudinal, comprehensive, involve a priori multiple comparison groups, and require a great deal of information about the families' and children's experiences before, during and after Head Start" (1976, p. 178).

By the late 1960s, both the Bureau of the Budget and Congress were pressuring OEO to demonstrate accountability for its many programs, including Head Start. In autumn of 1967, OEO established an evaluation division headed by John Evans. There is considerable conjecture as to why

Head Start was selected as one of the first programs at OEO to be evaluated. One factor may well have been the hostility existing between the Community Action people and Head Start. This feeling went beyond the CAP poverty warriors' belief that Head Start was not doing enough to challenge the power structure that oppressed the poor. Head Start was very popular and was being allocated so much money, relatively speaking, that the CAP workers felt their other vital efforts were being "starved." There was a definite sense within Community Action that Head Start (nominally a part of the CAP) was now the tail wagging the dog, and many in the agency would have liked to see Head Start get its comeuppance. As Datta notes, one view of the Westinghouse study was that "the real purpose of the evaluation . . . was to find a way to kill Head Start or to mutilate it" (1976, p. 131).

Certainly Evans and the OEO evaluation office had nothing against Head Start and saw themselves as simply doing the job assigned to them. The charge of the evaluation office essentially made the tension between the Community Action Program and Head Start irrelevant. Policymakers wanted accountability, and they had to provide it. They contracted the Westinghouse Learning Corporation and researchers at Ohio University to design and conduct an evaluation to produce the answers. Little noticed at the time and not fully appreciated even today is the fact that in the process of designing the Westinghouse study, Evans amended the planning committee's general goal for Head Start.

The planners certainly did not believe that Head Start was some sort of inoculation that could protect children from the incremental risks of growing up in poverty. They believed that poor children would be less disadvantaged upon school entry if they had had Head Start's preschool experience and the comprehensive health, nutritional, and social supports typically enjoyed by more advantaged children. However, Evans took this hope one step further and decided they should *remain* less disadvantaged ever after. The Westinghouse study was an attempt to determine whether taxpayers were getting their money's worth by seeing if Head Start children did better on standardized tests 1, 2, and 3 years after entering public school compared to similar children who had not attended Head Start.

One might ask why stop at third grade? Why not look at sixth grade, or high school? The reason is pragmatic. Head Start began in 1965, so the longest possible follow-up in the fall of 1968 was third grade for those children who had entered first grade immediately after the first summer session. This immediately introduced a confound because some states had kindergarten but many did not. Thus, some children entered first grade shortly after leaving Head Start, others went to kindergarten, and some stayed home and then entered first grade over a year later. Another confound is that some Head Start programs continued through the school year. Seventy percent of the children in the study had experienced only the summer program, while 30% had a much longer stay. Comparison children were selected at random and were matched for age and gender with Head Start participants. Other variables such as parental income, teacher, and time of testing were left uncontrolled. The hope was to control the differences between experimental and comparison children by using questionable statistical methods. The premier methodologist of the twentieth century, Donald Campbell, told me that the ex post facto design used in the Westinghouse study should never be used in an evaluation under any circumstances.

The Head Start Research Council thought the Westinghouse study was redundant in that a methodologically excellent study had already been contracted with the highly respected Educational Testing Service. This was a longitudinal study in three different communities that would assess general outcomes as well as the variation observed across Head Start sites. The council argued the inadequacy of the Westinghouse study up the chain of command to Bertrand Harding, OEO's then acting director. They pointed out the superiority of the Educational Testing Service design, but Harding's response was that OEO did not have the luxury of time required to complete a high-quality longitudinal study. As Datta states, the research council's "arguments and the Evaluation Division's replies then were much the same as the extensive criticisms and equally extensive rebuttals that appeared later" (1976, p. 132).

The Head Start programs themselves were also not given the luxury of time to iron out their start-up kinks. It was much too early to evaluate Head Start, which was really not an established program but nothing more than 2,500 communities' ideas of what Head Start should be. A famous dictum from Donald Campbell is that you should never evaluate a program until you have firm evidence that the program is "proud." Indeed, what a program can accomplish is limited by how well the program model has been implemented. The textbook approach today is that first one does a process or formative evaluation to determine if a program is providing the services dictated by its model in the intended manner. Only when fidelity to the model is established can the program be considered "proud" and an outcome evaluation initiated. The Westinghouse study was conducted when Head Start was brand new and many staff members were still trying to figure out what they were doing.

Yet Congress had indicated evaluation could not wait, so the Westinghouse study was commissioned. In addition to the direction given by the evaluation office at OEO, the study group benefited from the counsel of two eminent evaluation experts, Stanford University's William Madow and Harvard

University's Sheldon White. These two scholars made a number of sound suggestions that improved the methodological rigor of the study at least a notch. Nevertheless, the final Westinghouse product was scientifically ridiculous and was attacked by legions of methodologists, theorists, and academics. Madow himself repudiated the analysis so completely that he refused his pay and requested his name be taken off the title page of acknowledgments. The statistician then published his own scathing critique (Madow, 1969).

The results contained in the Westinghouse Report focused on academic achievement. Although social adjustment and a few nonacademic factors were assessed, the measures were not robust and the findings were dismissed. No achievement differences were found for the children who had attended the summer program compared to controls. Positive findings were found for the full-year programs, but only in the first-grade comparison. (Later reanalysis of the data revealed a few additional positive findings.) The initial advantages disappeared by third grade. Remember that the majority of the children had attended Head Start for just weeks, and the programs themselves had had just weeks to prepare. Including children from the first summer program was essentially loading the dice against Head Start.

The Westinghouse scientists' interpretation of their findings was quite blunt: "although this study indicates that full-year Head Start appears to be a more effective compensatory education program than summer Head Start, its benefits cannot be described as satisfactory" (quoted in Datta, 1976, p. 134). Although not commissioned to do so, the authors went on to make a number of recommendations suggesting different types of program that might be more effective. The generally negative conclusion was trumpeted by the *New York Times*: "The most comprehensive study ever made of the Government's widely admired Head Start programs asserts that poor children who participated in them were not appreciably better off than equally disadvantaged children who did not" (Semple, quoted in Datta, 1976, p. 138).

The report's impact on Head Start was magnified when it was quickly followed by Arthur Jensen's famous monograph in the *Harvard Educational Review*. Jensen (1969) argued that compensatory education had failed to date and must inevitably fail because heredity, not environment, was the primary determinant of intelligence. Jensen wrote:

> Why has there been such uniform failure of compensatory programs
> wherever they have been tried? What has gone wrong? In other fields,
> when bridges do not stand, when aircraft do not fly, when machines do
> not work, when treatments do not cure, despite all conscientious
> efforts on the part of many persons to make them do so, one begins

to question the basic assumptions, principles, theories, and hypotheses that guide one's efforts. Is it time to follow suit in education? (1969, p. 3)

Jensen was wrong in fact. Earlier in this book we described pre–Head Start early intervention programs that did work. However, to acknowledge them would threaten his thesis that intellectual functioning could not be influenced by intervention.

Had Jensen limited himself to the conventional review of the behavior genetics literature concerning IQ, his paper would never have received the worldwide attention it attracted. Its great visibility came from his assertion, in so many words, that the intellectual inheritance of blacks was inherently inferior to that of whites. Indeed the term "Jensenism" became synonymous with "racism." Jensen felt that IQ could only be raised by intervention in those cases when genetic potential had not been allowed full expression. In disputing Jensen, White (1970) asserted this was exactly the case for poor black children, a position confirmed through behavior genetic research on intelligence in poor children, both blacks and whites (Watt and Bradley, 2006).

The *Harvard Educational Review* was soundly criticized for publishing the Jensen article without including commentary by other scholars. Six papers refuting Jensen's position on black–white differences were published in a subsequent issue, and Jensen was given space to reply to these rebuttals. Unfortunately, the six commentaries were obviously written hurriedly and came out weak, employing more heat than scholarly analysis. On the other hand, Jensen's reply made a stronger case for his arguments than did his original paper.

Although Jensen had nothing to do with the Westinghouse study, the two occupied headlines around the same time and had an additive effect on public opinion. Datta described the one–two punch: "The Westinghouse and Jensen reports have to be looked at together. The impact from the Westinghouse was that Head Start wasn't working, and from Jensen, here's why it wasn't working, and won't ever" (1976, p. 136). White added that the Jensen paper, "appearing at about the same time as the draft of the National Impact Study [the formal name of the Westinghouse study], abolished any faint hope that the study might be nonpolitical and neutral because, in many minds, it set the seal on the negative findings of the study" (1970, p. 181).

The notion that it may not be worth the time and effort to offer early intervention to poor children would have been considered heresy during Head Start's lovefest years, but times had changed. By 1969, national priorities had shifted from social action to the Vietnam War. Money was getting tight, and disillusionment was setting in about the value of social programs like Community Action. President Nixon entered the White House in January of 1969, and he had little sympathy for Johnson's War on Poverty. As with most new presidents, Nixon felt it was time for a new approach to old problems.

Before the results of the Westinghouse study were issued on June 12, 1969, its negative conclusions were leaked to both Congress, which was then considering the OEO budget, and to the Nixon White House. Patrick Moynihan, an advisor to Nixon and a social scientist himself, took great interest in the report, particularly because it bolstered his own serious reservations about the War on Poverty and service programs like Head Start. His preference for fighting poverty was income redistribution, as will be explained in our later discussion of his Family Assistance Plan. Nixon's own response to the Westinghouse Report was relatively muted. In an address to Congress, he said he would treat Head Start as an experimental program, thus suggesting it would have another chance. The *New York Times* reported that "Mr. Nixon has said nothing disparaging about Head Start and indeed appears to have decided to have another go at making it work," treating it more like an experiment rather than the "final answer" (quoted in Datta, 1976, p. 139).

Head Start found a new important friend in Robert Finch, whom Nixon named his Secretary of Health, Education and Welfare. Finch criticized the Westinghouse Report in formal testimony before a congressional committee: "I challenge the basis for the report. It was not broad enough.... Some people in our department feel the data were sloppy. The only thing we got out of the preliminary report was that the summer programs are not as effective as full year programs, and we know that from other studies" (quoted in Datta, 1976, p. 139).

Finch was certainly on solid ground in criticizing the lack of breadth of the Westinghouse study. The researchers had overlooked many of the objectives of Head Start. They had no adequate measures for social and emotional development and totally ignored such goals as improved physical and mental health, better parenting behaviors, and positive changes in the community as a result of Head Start's presence. Nevertheless, the White House and Pat Moynihan doggedly stuck to the value of the Westinghouse study because it was crucial to policy decisions they wished to make.

This put Moynihan in a ticklish situation. A great many respected members of the scientific community had denounced the Westinghouse Report as so badly flawed it could reveal nothing about Head Start's efficacy. Prior to joining the Nixon White House, Moynihan had been a professor at Harvard. He could not detach himself from his academic roots and simply ignore the myriad scientific critiques of a study whose findings he liked very much. He therefore went to his academic contacts to find someone with credibility who could write a scholarly paper defending the Westinghouse Report against its many critics. He chose his former Harvard colleague, Sheldon (Shep) White, a widely respected child psychologist who had been an advisor to the study.

White wrote a surprisingly positive endorsement of the Westinghouse findings: "I was a consultant involved with the effort, and, while I believe there are flaws in it, I also believe that the flaws are not critical and that the study's general conclusions are sound. None of the arguments I have yet seen has changed my mind about this" (1970, p. 163). He then went far beyond defending the accuracy of the Westinghouse Report, echoing Moynihan's distaste of the Community Action Program and its system-change philosophy.

White ranged further, essentially stating that the Head Start program should never have been mounted in the first place. He wrote: "In the light of what was known then, the Head Start program must be seen as a bold gamble, which drove over theoretical and practical hesitancies and which sought to bury them under the weight of a *fait accompli*" (1970, p.164). Challenging the conclusion of the planning committee that there was sufficient empirical evidence to support launching Head Start, White asserted that only by "picking and choosing" through the literature could academics embrace a positive view about the potential of the new program. He also built on Bruner's earlier views, saying that Head Start was an ill-advised venture because "the country did not have the resources, in experienced personnel or in established facilities, for a national network of compensatory preschools" (p. 165). However, consistent with the thinking of the planning committee, White expressed faith that needed resources would grow with the program. History shows this is exactly what happened. When Head Start began, the entire field of early intervention and preschool education was energized. Many volunteers who came to Head Start decided to make careers in early childhood, and the field has burgeoned over the last 40 years.

The authors do agree with White's assertion that at the outset Head Start was not a standardized program. Noting the lack of a national curriculum, White concluded, "Head Start has been, and is, the corporate name for a nationally implemented series of preschool programs" (p. 167). He forgives Head Start for this, pointing out there was no general agreement on the one best preschool education curriculum. Further, in keeping with Head Start's practice of local control, the choice of curricula was left up to local centers. Later, it became evident this leeway was too lenient. Some programs had no lesson plans at all, and the children just wandered about all day. Once standards for Head Start were developed, a designated curriculum became mandatory. Although this got more staff thinking about lesson plans, the standard was hard to enforce until later when it was required that curricula be written. The George W. Bush Administration finally ended the tradition of local choice and told Head Start programs which curriculum they had to use—the Circle Curriculum developed by Susan Landry in Texas.

White, like other scholars, was well aware that the knowledge base concerning effective preschool curricula was quite primitive during the mid-1960s. Although much has been learned in the ensuing decades, there is still no solid evidence proving that one particular curriculum—including the Circle Curriculum—is best. Yet White argued reasonably that Head Start was simply too big and too expensive to permit OEO to delay an assessment of the program's value to taxpayers.

Perhaps he was right, but his support of the poorly done Westinghouse study startled many in the scientific community. Anticipating such a response, White's chapter included the statement, "On the social science side, one had an unpleasant rhetoric by some in or near the public press, immoderately concerned to 'protect' the program by refusing to admit that any problems could or did exist for it" (1970, p. 183). While there has been a tendency among Head Start advocates to circle their wagons, I for one have criticized Head Start for poor quality since it was getting off the ground. A *Los Angeles Times* journalist, Kay Mills, described my reputation: "Zigler is like a pit bull about Head Start. He can rip into it with the best of them because he knows what it should be doing, but he will stand and defend it when the program is threatened because he knows what it has done" (1998, 226).

In a way, Shep eventually did the same thing. While it was ironic to find two brilliant methodologists like Donald Campbell and Shep White in opposing corners over the Westinghouse study, in later years the two teamed up on Head Start's Blue Ribbon Research Panel, which was charged with developing a broad forward research strategy to evaluate the program. White not only produced impressive work on Head Start over his lifetime, but he was a leader in shaping the field of applied developmental psychology, encouraging scientists to put their research to work in bettering children's lives and teaching their students to do the same.

We had the honor of a lengthy interview with Shep before his death in 2005. He candidly told us he was under a great deal of pressure from Moynihan to produce an article favorable to the Westinghouse Report. Moynihan repeatedly called him at home to check on his progress. Shep confessed to us that back then he was ignorant to the ways of politics and not fully aware of how his chapter would be used in national policy. He was a young scientist and was excited and honored when Washington called. He was undoubtedly more socialized than I was and felt a duty to comply with the requests of national leaders. Once the administration realized they had a naive scholar they could employ to unknowingly do their dirty work, they put White's name on their short list of candidates to become the federal official responsible for Head Start. They were drawing up plans to phase out the program, and Shep admitted to us he was gullible enough to do it. He expressed his happiness that I was the one who was eventually chosen to lead Head Start. He devoted the rest of his career to advancing the cause of applied psychology and cross-training students in both science and social policy so they would not become lost in the political circuitry that entangles the policymaking process.

Head Start's Move to the Department of Health, Education and Welfare

Just as Moynihan was the catalyst for White's chapter defending the Westinghouse Report, we see him at work when Head Start was transferred from OEO to the Department of Health, Education and Welfare (HEW). Head Start had to be moved somewhere because, although the Economic Opportunity Act gave OEO the power to start new programs, within 3 years the programs had to be delegated to another agency with OEO oversight. After 5 years, there would be a permanent transfer.

Shriver authorized Jule Sugarman, by now Head Start's acting director, to explore the possibility of delegating Head Start to HEW. But where in HEW? Sugarman and everyone else close to Head Start were concerned that the program would go to the Office of Education, which had no expertise with preschool education and no clue about comprehensive services, which were outside of schools' traditional mandate. Sugarman worked directly with Wilbur Cohen, Secretary of HEW, who felt that the Children's Bureau would be a better home for Head Start. Harold Howe, the Commissioner of Education, agreed that an Office of Education placement would not be a good idea. (According to Vinovskis, 2005, Howe later changed his mind and argued forcefully that Head Start belonged in Education.) Cohen then appointed Sugarman as Associate Chief of the Children's Bureau in anticipation of Head Start's move.

From his position on the White House domestic policy staff, Moynihan disagreed with the other decision makers and wanted Head Start to be placed in the Office of Education. He did not openly dismiss opponents' fears that the education agency would emphasize academics and slight the other essential components of the Head Start model, for example, health. Nor did he address concerns that the agency's Title I program, the remedial education program for students that began at about the same time as Head Start, had a bad track record in creating opportunities for poor parents to become involved in the schools. Parent involvement was of course a pillar of Head Start.

Management issues were the basis of Moynihan's contrary position. Head Start grants were made from the federal government directly to local grantees, bypassing state and local governments. Head Start is the only federal program with this feature. Sending Head Start to the education agency meant it would become a block-grant program, that is, grants would be made to state education departments that would allocate the money locally as they saw fit. The only restraints would be some federal guidelines that history has shown states freely ignore. Individual governors would become the primary decision makers. This would have pleased the governors, a group who has always objected to the fact that Head Start money is sent to their states without their having any say about it. Moynihan's views were consistent with Nixon's "new federalism," in which power was transferred from the federal government to the states.

This important decision was being made during the period that the Johnson administration was transitioning to the Nixon administration. Johnson did not wish to hamstring the new president in any way, so he refused to move Head Start from OEO himself. The transfer was made by key leaders in Nixon's Department of Health, Education and Welfare where HEW Secretary Robert Finch and Deputy Secretary John Veneman were very sympathetic to Head Start. The heated debate about where in HEW Head Start should go was quelled by creating a brand new agency, the Office of Child Development. OCD consisted of two components, the Head Start program and the well-established and highly respected Children's Bureau. OCD was placed in the Office of the Secretary, which gave the new director direct access to the head of HEW (a very important factor in whatever successes OCD later achieved).

Another key person in creating Head Start's new base was Robert Patricelli. Patricelli was young, bright, and effective and was much in demand across power points in the new Nixon administration. Prior to Nixon's election, he had been working as minority counsel to the Senate committee on which the powerful Jacob Javits of New York served. Patricelli made a decision that probably changed the entire course of the Head Start program. He was offered a job to work for Moynihan in the White House and was also invited to work for Robert Finch at HEW. He chose the HEW job because he could continue working on issues that captured his interest during his time with Javits in the Senate. Had Patricelli chosen to work for Moynihan, he would have had to concur with Moynihan's preference for sending Head Start to the Office of Education. Instead, he took a strong supportive role for Head Start in the Secretary's office at HEW. He also had much of the responsibility for choosing the first director of OCD.

Rocking the Boat at the Children's Bureau

The marriage of the old, venerable Children's Bureau with the new Head Start program was definitely not a match made in heaven. The underlying tension sprang from the fact that the Children's Bureau had always been apolitical, whereas Head Start, based as it was in CAP, was entrenched in politics. This dichotomy weighed heavily when it came time to choose someone to lead the two agencies under the new OCD umbrella. Before we turn to that topic, it is helpful to understand the Children's Bureau's history and the respected role it had long held as the national voice for America's children.

Establishing a federal office for children was a grassroots process begun in 1903 by two early social reformers, Lillian Wald of New York's Henry Street Settlement House and Florence Kelley of the National Consumer's League (SSA, n.d.). President Taft signed into law the bill creating the Children's Bureau in 1912. The stated purpose of the new bureau was to investigate and report "upon all matters pertaining to the welfare of children and child life among all classes of our people" (SSA, n.d.). The Children's Bureau continually compiled national statistics on child and family issues and made recommendations directly to the president and to Congress.

The Chief of the Children's Bureau was appointed by the president and required confirmation by the United States Senate, making clear the great importance of this position. Requirements for the job typically included being a prominent advocate for children. National elections came and went, but the tenure of the Chief of the Children's Bureau continued. To illustrate, Julia Lathrop was named the first chief and served for 9 years, and the second chief, Grace Abbott, served for 13 years (Smuts, 2006). Lathrop worked very hard to ensure that the bureau would never be viewed as politically partisan. As time passed, the agency became involved in weighty issues such as child labor, infant and maternal mortality, juvenile delinquency, mothers' pensions, child abuse, and foster care. Perhaps the most popular publication produced by the federal government was the Children's Bureau's periodically revised booklet, *Infant Care*, which gave mothers the latest expert advice on child rearing. Smuts, who wrote a very accessible history of the Children's Bureau, judged that "Lathrop's most striking achievement may have been the relationship she created between the bureau and the nation's mothers. One wonders if there has been any other government bureaucracy so trusted and loved" (2006, p. 102).

One gets a sense of the special status of the Children's Bureau by the background of its last chief prior to Nixon. Pardo Frederick Delliquadri (Fred) was sworn in on June 21, 1968. Over his lifetime, he was dean of four major schools of social work, a director for children and youth services in three states, and U.S. representative to the Executive Board of UNICEF. He was sworn in at the White House by Justice Byron R. White. At the ceremony, President Johnson spoke about the many problems of our nation's children and the adults they would become. He said: "What we do now in our families, in our churches, schools, and homes, and through agencies such as this wonderful agency—the Children's Bureau—to strengthen, to guide, and to care for our children" will determine their well being and future (Woolley and Peters, n.d.c). He predicted that Delliquadri would be a great force in improving the lives of children.

Despite Johnson's words of praise, the Nixon administration defied over 50 years of tradition surrounding the Children's Bureau and decided to replace Delliquadri after only about a year in his position. Sugarman, an old Washington hand, remembers that the chief's position "had always been considered as exempt from politics and the [Children's Bureau] staff was very disturbed by the change" (personal communication, June 27, 2007). Sugarman was asked to serve as acting chief while the administration sought a new appointee. The members of the bureau did not care either for the Nixon administration that had precipitously fired their leader or for their new superior, Sugarman, who did not have professional credentials in social work or child advocacy. This feeling is evident by the actions of Arthur Lesser, a well-known physician who headed the Bureau's Division of Maternal and Child Health. His distaste for the situation and unhappiness in taking orders from Sugarman lead him to use his connections and move his division out of the Children's Bureau into an adult health agency in HEW. As I will relate in Chapter 4, this move proved to be damaging both to the division and to Head Start, which could have benefited from the division's resources to improve its health component. With the departure of the Maternal and Child Health program, the Children's Bureau's responsibilities were limited mainly to foster care and adoptions. It had no permanent leadership but did have many seasoned, knowledgeable, devoted, and unhappy employees.

Choosing a Director for OCD

The Department of Health, Education and Welfare had to recruit a director for the new Office of Child Development with some obvious constraints. Typically such a job would go to a political appointee as a reward for support of the administration in power. Yet the Chief of the U.S. Children's Bureau did not serve "at the pleasure of the President" but had to be confirmed by the Senate. It had to be someone who knew a great deal about child development and had professional credentials. HEW Secretary Elliot Richardson noted that President

Nixon initially imposed fewer restrictions on political appointments than did many of his successors (1976). Robert Patricelli, who interviewed the candidates, pointed out "we chose all kinds of people with nontraditional Republican backgrounds" (quoted in Zigler and Muenchow, 1992, p. 77).

The only two contenders for the OCD director's job who I knew about were Urie Bronfenbrenner and me. Jule Sugarman, who was OCD's acting director, would have liked the job, but his very liberal views and his close ties with Shriver undoubtedly made him unacceptable to the Nixon administration. Bronfenbrenner, a fellow planner who was teaching at Cornell, was a more senior scholar than I was. He was a true icon as a developmental thinker, but he and everyone around him knew he simply did not have the temperament to function in the pressure-laden milieu of Washington "wheeler dealers." I too was an academic, not a politician. In fact, I was surprised I was even being considered for the job because I was not affiliated with either party. In terms of management ability, I did not have the background to run a candy store much less a federal agency with a budget in the hundreds of millions of dollars.

Many years later I was stunned to learn from Sheldon White that he too had been a candidate for the OCD job and had been interviewed by the same powers at HEW. Again we see the long arm of Moynihan, who, on the basis of the Westinghouse Report and his own negative attitude toward the value of social services, had decided that Nixon should discontinue the Head Start program. Surmising from White's chapter in support of the Westinghouse study that he would be willing to close Head Start, Moynihan entered White's name as the White House's candidate for the OCD job.

How can a perfectly well-qualified individual nominated by an influential man at the White House not get the position? This is not as strange as it sounds. There is considerable tension between the White House and secretaries of the various departments. Cabinet-rank officers are political appointees and must display some sympathy toward the president's agenda. On the other hand, these influential decision makers have views of their own and sometimes find themselves at odds with the White House. As noted above, Finch had much more positive views about the future of Head Start than did Moynihan. This was also the case for Patricelli and other higher-ups at HEW. At this point in time the Secretary and his staff may not have even known about Moynihan's plan to end Head Start (which was probably more his idea than Nixon's). Certainly no one at HEW with whom I interviewed, including Finch, gave any indication that the job would be anything other than running the Children's Bureau and the Head Start program. They did ask my views about the merit of the Westinghouse Report, which were much closer to the position articulated by Finch than was White's very positive opinion. Thus, being "Moynihan's candidate" may have actually been a handicap for White.

Moynihan's failure to sell White as first director of the new Office of Child Development does not detract from the undeniable fact that he had great influence with President Nixon. Nixon liked Moynihan; White House assistant John Erhlichman's handwritten notes from the period contain the frequent reminder to place Pat "near the President" (quoted in Zigler and Muenchow, 1992, p. 65). Moynihan was the one who wrote Nixon's "First Five Years of Life" speech that emphasized the need for government to ensure the optimal development of children during this critical period.

This speech actually put Nixon into something of a bind vis-à-vis Head Start. The speech could certainly not be followed by closing down Head Start in response to the negative findings of the Westinghouse Report. Yet behind the scenes, Moynihan expressed disappointment in Head Start. He wrote: "Head Start wasn't working: The children were getting their teeth fixed but little else that could be quantified" (quoted in Zigler and Muenchow, 1992, p. 66). He dismissed the many methodological critiques of the Westinghouse Report as yet another indication of the liberal "unwillingness to face the finding of failure where it appeared, as recurrently it did" (quoted in Zigler and Muenchow, 1992, p. 72). In later years it is not surprising that Moynihan became an early recruit to the neoconservative movement.

Nixon's First Five Years of Life speech was well received, and he mentioned it with some frequency. In 1969, when the president announced the creation of the Office of Child Development, he renewed his pledge to a "national commitment to providing all American children an opportunity for healthful and stimulating development during the first five years of life" (quoted in Zigler and Muenchow, 1992, p. 74). This commitment, and that wonderful speech, weighed strongly on my decision to take the job as director of OCD.

There were, of course, other factors. One is that I strongly believed in the value of the Head Start model and wanted to help it become a more effective program. I was also appalled that the badly done Westinghouse study had become a threat that might deny poor children the clear benefits of participating in Head Start—for example, from health and nutrition services. The prospect of defending Head Start against this inadequate study actually made the job more appealing to me. From the time I had questioned Sugarman about the poor programs that were being funded, I had become more and more concerned about the quality of Head Start and knew that it had not yet become a program that merited an outcome evaluation. I wanted to see it become such a program.

Another reason I was willing to entertain the possibility of heading OCD is that, since my work on Head Start's planning committee, I had become intrigued with the potential of using the knowledge gained from empirical research to improve the well-being of children. I had spent my professional life in an academic milieu where scholars worked hard in their laboratories, formulated theories, and tested hypotheses. Those leaving the lab to apply their knowledge to real-world problems were considered suspect and certainly not true scholars. Indeed, a leading scholar told me that I could become a first-rank child psychologist if I would just give up this "policy nonsense." Yet several admired figures in my life space had moved into the social arena to utilize scientific knowledge to improve society's treatment of children. Two of these role models were part of the Head Start story—Julius Richmond and Urie Bronfenbrenner.

After my sojourn on the planning committee, I became increasingly aware of the limiting nature of the research enterprise. I was conducting experimental studies, writing up the results, and publishing them in professional journals. The audience was probably a few hundred readers. My job as a basic researcher was to expand the knowledge base, not produce best sellers. Compare this to my experience on the planning committee, where my research was used in formulating the whole-child approach that characterized the Head Start effort and was of immediate value to 560,000 children and their families. For all these reasons, I was willing to consider becoming the first director of the Office of Child Development, but my secret hope was that someone else would be offered the job and I would not have to make a decision.

When I was offered the position, I had to deal seriously with my ambivalence about leaving a situation where I had demonstrated competence and entering a post where I would be a novice at best. I consulted with Donald Taylor, then Chairman of the Psychology Department at Yale. Taylor was in the field of industrial psychology, a subdiscipline that had no reservations about applying psychology to improve the functioning of businesses. He advised me to take the job and said he would arrange a 1-year leave from Yale that could be extended into 2 years. At the time, I was the head of Yale's Psychology Department's program in child development, and Taylor made it clear that he wanted me to return to the Department. He pointed out that my serving in Washington would add luster to Yale's child development program.

Although I could leave my departmental commitments behind, I had another huge responsibility that I could not abandon. I was the principal investigator in a large program grant that employed 25 to 30 people spread across five different projects. I talked to a friend who was the dean of the Medical School at Albert Einstein who once took a leave to serve in

Washington. He advised me to continue my research on weekends. Following the "craziness" that was Washington, he thought this weekend work would be therapeutic. So I accepted the job. For the next 2 years I worked 5 days in Washington and Saturdays and Sundays in my laboratory in New Haven, where my family remained. I still remember how hard it was to tell my 7-year-old son I would not be home every night. There were, of course, a few crisis weekends when I could not make it home. Those crises, and the weekday ones, are covered in the next chapters.

4

A Conflict of Cultures

I thought moving to Washington would be just like any other temporary move I had made during my academic years, but it soon felt as though I had moved to another planet. I almost found a way out of it. The first thing I did as I prepared to assume my job as the director of the Office of Child Development (OCD) was to submit my resignation. The man who had chosen me for the position, HEW Secretary Robert Finch, had developed health problems and resigned before I came on board. He was replaced by Elliot Richardson, whom I had never met. I didn't think my new boss should be saddled with an employee he did not choose himself, particularly when it came to the head of a brand new agency. I thought Richardson would want to shape OCD according to his own vision and therefore would want to select his own person to take charge. I asked for a meeting and was instantly awed by how comprehensive and intelligent Richardson was. He said he was well aware of who I was and mentioned some of my credentials that had led to my selection for the position. He told me warmly and decisively that I was *exactly* the person he wanted to direct OCD. Thus began a collegial relationship and friendship that lasted for decades.

Richardson was the fastest learner I ever encountered. He was brilliant and was able to master demanding developmental concepts and complex data sets at one sitting. I heard many people say Richardson "thinks in paragraphs," and it was true. Probably because we had great respect for one another's intelligence, Richardson and I bonded very quickly. In fact, we did not disagree on a single substantive issue in the 2 years plus that I served under him. I wish I could say the same for the rest of the people I encountered in Washington.

I got my first taste of Washington politics when I was assigned an official to brief me about the interviews I would have with eight Senators prior to my confirmation hearings. I could not fathom why a briefing was needed.

I thought they would ask me honest questions and I would respond with honest answers, just the way I was used to in front of the classroom. Well, I soon learned government is not the classroom. Questions are chosen in the context of political agendas, and the answers are vetted ahead of time to concur with the administration's position. I was not a professor guiding students' pursuit of knowledge but a voice for the Nixon administration. This was very foreign to a young scholar grounded by Yale University's motto, Lux et Veritas (light and truth).

My swearing in, though sufficiently pompous and ceremonial for me, was a much more low-key event than those for previous chiefs of the Children's Bureau. Richardson, who had been Attorney General of Massachusetts, did the swearing in himself, with my family in attendance. Afterward a party was held at the new OCD offices, and the staff sang a song that had been written in my honor called, "We Love Zig." When I came to work a few days later, I learned that my new staff not only did not "love Zig," but they were against me before I even began.

People Problems

OCD was a huge bureaucracy. There were the federal Head Start office, 10 regional Head Start offices around the country, and the revered, newly transplanted Children's Bureau that was older than I was. I hoped that Sugarman, a career civil servant, would stay at OCD as my deputy. He knew a great deal about the ways of Washington, and I knew nothing. Plus I needed a manager for day-to-day operations, and management was his forte. I guess I wanted to recreate the Richmond–Sugarman alliance that had proven so effective at OEO. Yet soon after I was named director, Sugarman was informed by the powers that be there was no place for him in the new organization. He had been serving as acting director and, not wanting to fall too far down the ladder, was trying to negotiate a position as co-director with me. Rejecting his job demand was the gentleman's way around firing him. In actuality, Sugarman's views were much too liberal for him to be acceptable to the Nixon administration.

With the wisdom of hindsight, it is probably best we went our separate paths. I am simply not the nice, low-key man Richmond was. Further, Sugarman was much more sympathetic to the Community Action aspect of Head Start than I was and not nearly as concerned about the quality of the services children and families were experiencing. Sugarman had been running Head Start since 1965 and was relatively satisfied with the program. I was anything but satisfied.

This personnel problem did have a happy ending. Mitchell Ginsberg had been a member of the Head Start planning committee and, like the other members, was very impressed by Sugarman's strong abilities during our deliberations. When Ginsberg decided to leave New York City Mayor Lindsay's administration where he was serving as the administrator for human resources, he recommended Sugarman as his replacement. Mayor Lindsay recruited Sugarman to head the agency, where he began a long, accomplished career in human services. (Jule Sugarman and I have remained friends. In fact, he was extremely helpful in sharing his remembrances for this book.)

Dissension within the Ranks

Within a month I realized that I was in a real mess and castigated myself for ever thinking I could perform such a complicated task as running a huge bureaucracy. Both the Head Start and the Children's Bureau staff appeared to have ingrained animosity toward Nixon and everyone in his administration. I was a Nixon appointee, so they saw me as one of the bad guys. On the Head Start side, I had inherited a staff mostly put together by Sugarman, many of whom were veterans of OEO and adherents of the Community Action philosophy. Their purpose in life was to empower the poor. My goal was to promote child development and school readiness by delivering a quality program to poor children and their families. We just weren't speaking the same language. Some staffers who sensed trouble brewing managed transfers to other agencies, as was their right under civil service procedures. Others decided to wait me out. I am sure that was my fault. In the early weeks, I made the greatest mistake a bureaucrat can make if he wants to build a team and enact new policies. Always given to candor, I let it be known that I was only planning to be at OCD for a couple of years. In Washington there is an old refrain used by civil servants in regard to appointees: "I was here when you got here, and I'll be here when you're gone." Thus waiting me out was not a bad strategy.

Needless to say, it is impossible to get anything done with a staff that is waiting around for your departure. In those first few weeks I was sabotaged at every turn. People ignored or botched tasks I asked them to do. Some acts of revolt were quite egregious. For instance, soon after I started I was pleased to learn that a group from the White House was coming to visit OCD and welcome me aboard. Just before they arrived, by happenstance I went to the men's room where I found a picture of Nixon taped to the wall. I of course took it down, never discovering who the culprit was.

Some problems that interfered with my plans for Head Start had more to do with philosophical differences than with outright defiance. For example, at the time the Head Start Bureau was headed by Richard Orton, who had been working under Sugarman since late in 1965. My interactions with this key person were cordial enough, but it was apparent that he was a Sugarman clone. I remembered vividly my conversation with Sugarman at the birth of Head Start when we both agreed we were funding some poor-quality programs, but the plan was to replace them later with good ones.

So shortly after arriving at OCD I asked Orton to come see me. I told him of my talk with Sugarman, pointing out that it had now been 5 years since we awarded those initial grants. I asked him how many of the first programs we had closed. Orton said none. When he saw the shocked look on my face, he quickly added, "But Ed, we almost closed one once." Apparently in this particular center the teachers were hitting the children with long sticks. A team from the Head Start Bureau had been sent to investigate and found that the parents wanted their children to be disciplined by getting hit with sticks. Orton's logic was that the principles of parent involvement and local control held sway, so he decided to let the practice continue. I told Orton this is not what parent involvement meant to me, and the Head Start Bureau had no business abdicating its responsibility by allowing parents and staff alone to decide what constitutes a good program. I pointed out we should have taken advantage of this teachable moment and trained parents in better child-rearing practices. I said the Head Start Bureau's response was totally unacceptable, and I immediately put out a nationwide announcement that no child in any Head Start center would ever be subjected to corporal punishment.

I saw here the conflict between the parent-empowerment goal of the Community Action Program and the child-centered goal of Head Start's planners. It was clear to both Orton and me that we were not on the same wavelength. Not long after, Orton told me he was "burnt out" and needed to resign. Even though he held a high grade (i.e., GS 17 or 18) in the civil service, he had no prospects of further employment. He asked if I could help him find a position. He knew little about children but was an experienced bureaucrat with solid management skills. I called a friend of mine, Jeanette Watson, who had been appointed by the governor to head Texas's OCD, a counterpart of my agency in Washington. Lo and behold, Jeanette was having the same problems at the state level that I was having at the national level. She needed an experienced manager so hired Dick Orton, who has lived in Austin to this day.

The staff situation in my first days at OCD struck me as somewhere between noncompliance and mutiny. I was soon to discover that this state of affairs also existed among the OCD personnel at the regional offices. That summer Jule Sugarman and I were scheduled to speak at a meeting of the American Psychological Association in Miami. Without my knowledge, the regional office in Atlanta (a region that included Miami) sent letters to parents warning them that some disaster in Head Start was imminent. To the best of my knowledge at that time, there was no dark cloud on the Head Start horizon. This was a standard academic convention, and to everyone's surprise the large auditorium was invaded by a couple dozen shouting protestors carrying signs. The session's chair, my graduate student mentor Harold Stevenson, was able to get the protestors to wait outside the door until the meeting was finished.

Attending the session was a dear friend from my graduate student days, George Moushegian. Like me, George had grown up as a tough kid in a large city where one learns to scuffle at an early age. He did not want me to meet with the protestors alone and insisted on accompanying me. They demanded a formal meeting right away. However, with the convention going on, every meeting room in the hotel was in use. The only place I could think of to meet was in my rather small hotel room. With my friend George riding shotgun, we all crowded in and sat on the bed and floor. It turned out the group was simply trying to protect their program, and I was able to allay their fears. I was annoyed at the regional office for sending that letter that was sure to stir up animosity. It was well-known at OCD that I would be speaking at the conference, and the regional office at least should have sent someone to Miami to help me diffuse the situation.

My ability to survive those first few months at OCD was largely due to two people. As soon as I arrived in Washington, I recruited Carolyn Harmon. Carolyn had once been my assistant at Yale, and later I had supervised her dissertation on the topic of children's political socialization. She was extremely bright, very articulate, and much better at managing people than I was. My style has always been to demand the best that a person can produce, which I am sure earned me the reputation of being impossible to please. This is characterological, and there was not much I could do about it.

Of course, I could not manage a huge place like OCD with Carolyn Harmon alone. At Yale I had mentored a medical student, Donald Cohen, who impressed me greatly with his abilities. He was now working in the U.S. Public Health Service. I used my influence at the higher levels at HEW to recruit him to OCD as my second special assistant. Donald was a very astute, young child psychiatrist with good people skills. Not only was he able to head many important efforts requiring an expert on mental health, but he also became the in-house psychiatrist, speaking with individual employees to help smooth the waters and keep things functioning. (I brought Donald back to Yale when I returned, and he later became *my* boss as the director of Yale's Child

Study Center.) However, Donald did not understand the bureaucracy any more than Carolyn Harmon or I did.

I badly needed a high-level experienced administrator who understood the minutia of bureaucratic functioning, who knew how to "move paper" and actually get things done once a decision had been made to do them. My superiors at HEW were very supportive, so I asked for their help in finding a first-rate civil servant who could take on the day-to-day management of OCD. I envisioned a situation similar to the Richmond-Sugarman duo at OEO, where Richmond provided the knowledge about children and Sugarman did the implementation and administration. Although the people at HEW were sympathetic to my plight, they offered no help whatsoever.

I was becoming desperate, so I turned to a good friend who was a professor of management, first at Yale and then at Harvard, Chris Argyris. He was an international authority on management, and just getting him to consult with me for a couple of days impressed my superiors at HEW. Argyris suggested an organizational study of OCD. Lawrence Lewin and Associates, a consulting firm in Washington, was hired to do the job. Lewin's analysis revealed just how difficult building this new agency would be. Lewin told me, "You're exactly what this organization needs, but you are not all that it needs." I agreed and assigned Lewin the task of finding me a deputy who understood the federal bureaucracy. Then along came along my salvation in the person of Saul Rosoff. Saul had himself mentored many outstanding bureaucrats who invariably praised him to the sky.

Saul was an experienced professional and had once pulled off the immense task of moving a large section of the Public Health Service from Washington to Baltimore. He was an absolute master at bringing out the best in staff. He could not only convert a project staff into a team, but he was willing to talk as long and provide as many donuts as necessary to help them complete a project. I became the front man with the ideas, but it was Saul who turned them into programs. Saul mentored me in public administration, and I mentored him in child psychology. He learned enough to run OCD after I returned to Yale.

I had a little competition with Saul about who could get into the office first. My work day was typically from eight in the morning until six at night, with a couple more hours spent reading and preparing at home. I had worked my way through college by unloading freight cars serving the Kansas City produce market. I had to be at work at four in the morning, and ever since then I've had an aversion to getting up early. However, it bothered me that Saul was always in the office before me. I started coming in at seven, but invariably he was already there. I tried six-thirty, and then six o'clock, but he was always there when I arrived. I gave up and went back to coming in at eight o'clock.

My next managerial task was to recruit some key staff members whose views were close enough to mine that they would be willing to pursue my agenda rather than their own. Early in my new job I was often asked whether so-and-so was loyal to me. I had no idea why this was important. As a college professor, the last thing I desired of a student is loyalty. On the contrary, I always admired students who took issue with everything I said and demanded evidence supporting accepted positions because this is how learning takes place and how the field of knowledge moves forward. I came to learn that in a bureaucracy, loyalty is absolutely paramount. Otherwise people will quietly do what they want to do, not what you want them to do.

A key person in an agency head's life is the executive secretary, who keeps the director on schedule. Unfortunately, the executive secretary assigned to me proved to be disloyal, or else she was just incompetent. As luck would have it, I had gotten to know James Farmer, a civil rights leader who was Assistant Secretary of HEW. In my meetings in Farmer's office, I was very impressed with an executive secretary I met there, Dee Wilson. I was learning the bureaucratic game and was not above pirating exceptional people from other agencies. So I stole her. Dee became my executive secretary and essentially ran my life throughout my stay at OCD.

One further coup took place as a result of a meeting I had with Sid Marland, head of HEW's Office of Education. Sid and I had disagreed on some issue or another, and we met in an attempt to resolve our differences. Sid was accompanied by one of his lieutenants, Harley Frankel. Harley debated me more effectively than his boss. I heartily admire good debating skills (in high school I was on the debate team and won the city oratorical championship), so I later asked Harley to join me in running the Head Start program. He asked me why I was not angry because of the way he had confronted me at the Marland meeting. I told him that debate and disagreement did not upset me because in my scientific world, defending oneself against critics with opposing views is quite common. I said I admired the strength of his rebuttal of my position, and I wanted him to join OCD so he could fight just as hard and effectively on my behalf as he had for Marland. He did join me and proved to be as good as I thought he would be. He eventually rose to be Chief of the Head Start Bureau, was on Carter's White House staff, worked as an effective advocate at the Children's Defense Fund, and helped maintain Head Start in the face of the Reagan administration's proposed changes to the program.

I did not have to bring in all new blood to get OCD functioning smoothly. I was able to make friends with at least some of the staff who were there when I arrived. One was Clennie Murphy, who was the Head Start Bureau's key liaison to the 10 regional offices. Clennie had a master's degree in child development, so he had a lot more to contribute than his management skills. He was comfortable enough with me to ask if I would critique his master's thesis. I eagerly did so, happy to finally do something at which I was good. Clennie was invaluable in helping the Washington office essentially make peace with the regional directors.

I found that the regional offices were difficult to synchronize with the national office. Part of the reason was confusing authority lines. A bigger part is that some of the regional directors were holdovers from the Sugarman years and worked closely with the Community Action people who often ran local Head Start centers. Several disliked President Nixon, his philosophies, and his political actions. Further, about half of these 10 regional Head Start chiefs were members of minority groups, and there was still a lot of racial tension in the early 1970s. With Clennie as referee, I began meeting regularly with the directors to get their input on policies I was thinking of implementing. In my home I have a memento of those meetings—a drawing by a cartoonist in the Children's Bureau, who illustrated many of the agency's publications. There I am, standing in front of a group of 10 figures with a shiny red apple on my head, William Tell-style. The 10 people facing me all have bows and are shooting arrows, hopefully at the apple. Evenually we came to trust one another, and these meetings became extremely productive and helped me to finalize my plans.

Clennie was so good at negotiating difficult situations that later, when he had risen to become head of the Head Start Bureau during the Reagan years, he was referred to as "Mr. Kissinger." I became very fond of Clennie and realized I had seen the "Mr. Kissinger" side of him in the early 1970s when he had helped me convert the regional directors from foes to allies. This was a critical change because the quality of Head Start programs across America is probably influenced as much by the regional offices as by the powers in Washington.

I found other allies in the Head Start Bureau among the professionals who worked there. Unlike the Community Action types in Head Start, they seemed pleased to have a fellow professional as their supervisor. Each component of Head Start had a specialist at the national level to track and upgrade the relevant services, for example, a parent involvement specialist, a pediatrician for the health component, and an early childhood educator for the education component. Gertrude Hunter, a pediatrician, was responsible for health services, and I found her to be an excellent partner in improving service quality. The early childhood educator was Jenni Klein, who had been mentored by Jimmy Hymes— a Head Start planner and master authority on early education. A woman well into her seventies, Sue Sadow, was Head Start's nutritionist (a section of the health component). She taught me why it was so important for each service area to have someone knowledgeable who cared about it. She was in my office constantly, and if she had her way, Head Start would exist solely to improve the nutritional habits of poor children and their families.

This nutritionist's zeal made me realize why Head Start's mental health component was (and remains) a disappointment. There was no one in the Head Start Bureau whose primary concern was children's mental health. (Although we did have a pediatrician, this profession is concerned primarily with physical health, and most members are not specially trained in mental health.) Donald Cohen and I attempted to remedy this omission by hiring Paul Wohlford, a community-oriented psychologist, as director of psychological services. Alas, his position was kept only as long as I was in Washington and was delegated to a consultant after I left. It is therefore not surprising that the literature is filled with critiques describing the poor job Head Start has done in serving mental health needs. The problem will not be corrected until someone in the federal office "owns" the component and gives it her or his all.

Discontent at the Children's Bureau

By 1971, Harley Frankel had become the very competent director of the Head Start Bureau, and Saul Rosoff had seen to it that the entire Bureau had incorporated good management practices. However, I could not turn my attention over to the primary task of improving Head Start until all of OCD was a smoothly functioning organization. The Head Start Bureau had progressed nicely, but the Children's Bureau presented me with a different set of problems. For the most part the staff there were professional people who were free of any Community Action orientation, but they were annoyed with the Nixon administration for breaking tradition and dismissing their chief after just a year's service. Burned once, they really didn't want to have anything to do with me. Further, working in the venerable Children's Bureau seemed to go to the heads of some employees, who saw themselves as having a hallowed status and not having to "play by the rules." Others were just set in their ways. Delliquadri had not lasted long enough to have much impact on this very old agency, and the Bureau was badly in need of a knowledgeable leader. I saw this as my job.

A serious defection had occurred at the Children's Bureau prior to my becoming chief. As mentioned in Chapter 3, Arthur Lesser was a physician who headed the Bureau's Division of Maternal and Child Health. He apparently rebelled at Sugarman's direction as acting chief and wanted his division moved. He could have lobbied for placement elsewhere in OCD, but the agency was new and its ways of operating were still unknown. Lesser therefore negotiated a move of his division to a health services section of HEW. There he quickly learned an unfortunate fact of big bureaucracy: when children's services are combined with adult services, the children do not get their fair share of attention and resources. This happened with community mental health agencies and other health services, and it was happening to Lesser's Division of Maternal and Child Health.

Not too long after my arrival in Washington, Lesser came to see me and asked if I would make his case with the head of the agency where his division was now located. As Chief of the Children's Bureau based in the HEW Secretary's office, this was an appropriate course of action and I pursued it. After this occurred a few times, Lesser and I began serious discussions about moving his division back to the Children's Bureau, where it had been for decades. We both thought this was a good idea. Unfortunately, with the many time-consuming crises I was confronted with during my short stay in Washington, we never did accomplish the transfer. This was a loss to Head Start, which needed the division's expertise, and to the division itself in terms of accomplishments and clout.

Although it was unfortunate to lose the tradition of the Division of Maternal and Child Health, other traditions at the Children's Bureau needed to be lost. One involved the policies of the research director, whom I had known for several years. He was not doing his job the way I thought it should be done. The research division had considerable funds to mount and evaluate child-oriented initiatives around the country. However, the research director made all the funding decisions himself. It seemed to me he was acting as if this money was his own and was essentially handing it out to his friends. I had served on research committees at the National Institutes of Health where grant proposals were carefully reviewed by outside scholars to choose those most deserving of support. I demanded that we put in place a similar peer review system at the research division. After all, the Children's Bureau, like the National Institutes of Health, was a part of HEW and should adopt its best practices.

My conflicts with this research director did not end there. Research supported by the Children's Bureau often involved troubled youth, many of whom were black. There was a job opening in the research division, and I thought it made sense to ask the director to search for a qualified black scholar to fill the position. Week after week I inquired about his progress and always got the same answer, namely that he could find no qualified applicants. I had had enough and decided to find a slate of candidates myself. I called some friends in academia, and in about an hour, I had a list of six very promising, young black candidates, each of whom had rave reviews from his or her mentor. I gave the list to the research director and asked him to select the best person to work for him. Even as late as 1970, the active recruitment of a black scholar was unusual. Nevertheless, given the nature of the population we were serving, I could not tolerate an all-white staff who often had to decide how best to help black children.

After a time, the director informed me that not a single one of the candidates struck him as being up to the job. This report signaled the end of my patience. I cooled down a bit and then asked him to come to my office. I told him I viewed his behavior as rank insubordination and that there was no longer any place for him in the Children's Bureau. I gave him two alternatives: he could voluntarily leave, or I would place a letter in his civil service file presenting evidence of his racism. Being a long-time veteran of the Children's Bureau, and knowing that I would only be at OCD for 2 years, he took advantage of a federal program that allowed high-level bureaucrats to take a 2-year leave to attend a university and hone their skills. (The program also allowed scholars to spend 2 years working in the federal government to learn how to better interface the academic world to the needs of the government.) The research director enrolled in this program and of course returned to the Children's Bureau when I left OCD.

I became something of a hero to leaders at HEW in that I was able to ease two super-grade civil servants out of their positions at OCD. (The Orton departure had been friendly, but this one was not.) I learned that the red tape involved in firing a "super-grade" was so great and the process so long that most agency heads in my position just found a desk somewhere for the noncompliant employee and let the federal government pay him or her until retirement.

The research director's leave-taking did not end all my trouble getting the Children's Bureau in hand. One high-level worker invariably reeked of alcohol whenever I met with her. I privately asked several of her colleagues whether she had a drinking problem. I explained that there were federal programs available for employees with substance abuse issues, and I wanted to help this knowledgeable woman get treatment. Each and every one of the people I asked insisted the woman had no drinking problem. All I could do was turn to my ace in the hole, Saul Rosoff, and ask him what to do. Saul advised that I had too many important things on my plate to take this amount of time dealing with one alcoholic employee. He wisely recommended a change in administrative structure and created the position of associate chief of the Children's Bureau. We hired a warm, intelligent physician for the position, Fred Green. His job was to oversee the Bureau's daily operations, including handling personnel problems. This freed me to focus on my mandated responsibilities to the Children's Bureau, advocating for all of America's children.

It should be noted that by 1970, the Children's Bureau had become somewhat moribund. Certainly the great love affair between the American people and the Bureau had cooled noticeably. Although it still turned out useful pamphlets such as the one on infant care, these materials were given to members of Congress who sent them to their constituents. Thus many Americans believed these materials came from Congress and did not give the Children's Bureau due credit.

Further, although the Bureau maintained close ties to the Child Welfare League of America, its activities were hampered by its failure to develop an effective lobby for children and families. This vacuum became obvious to me when I attended a meeting with the head of the agency on aging. He bragged that he could make three phone calls to organizations representing senior citizens and get 3 million letters to Congress within a week. This made me green with envy. I called together some senior staffers and recounted what I had just heard about making three phone calls. I asked them if there were organizations we could contact to get public support for our initiatives. They assured me there were and came back with a list of literally hundreds of organizations—the Boy Scouts, the Girl Scouts, PTAs, 4-H clubs, and the list went on for many pages. I pointed out that in terms of effective political action, having hundreds of organizations to rally was equivalent to having none. Issues come up suddenly in Congress and must be dealt with at that point in time or your efforts are useless. It would be impossible to rouse a gaggle of groups on the spur of the moment.

My vision of myself as America's advocate for children soon ran headfirst into the power of politics. I traveled across the country giving my standard Chief of the Children's Bureau speech, enumerating the bad news about how children and families were faring, for example, the higher infant mortality rates in America than in many other industrialized nations. After one such speech I returned to Washington the next morning and received word that a counselor to the president wanted to meet me at the White House as soon as possible. He recited some word-for-word quotes from my speech the previous night and asked if I had really said these things. I said I was presenting known facts derived from empirical evidence collected by the Children's Bureau. The president's counselor asserted that children could not possibly be faring so badly "since Nixon is in the White House." I realized then and there how hard it would be for the Children's Bureau to try to fix problems that were not even permitted to exist. Truthfully, though, I did not find this head-in-the-sand attitude commonplace in the Nixon administration.

Of course, the budget of the Children's Bureau was infinitesimal compared to that of the Head Start program. On the heels of the Westinghouse Report, the crisis confronting Head Start made it impossible for me to give the Children's Bureau the time it deserved. This saddened me because I was a great admirer of the Bureau and took my role as chief very seriously. Nonetheless, with stable management finally in place in both the Head Start and Children's Bureau, I could turn my attention to saving Head Start.

Making Peace with Parents

Head Start parents were the people who knew the program best and never wavered in their support. They were always on high alert for perceived threats to their treasured Head Start, fearing political skullduggery would take it away. I discovered this before I even got to Washington. When word of my nomination became public in 1970, for some reason Head Start parents sensed that their program was in danger. This is when I realized that people who did not know me personally believed I was an extension of President Nixon. In point of fact, I was neither pro-Nixon nor anti-Nixon. Granted, a key factor in my decision to take the OCD job was Nixon's inspiring speech on the importance of the first 5 years of life and the nation's need to foster children's development during this critical developmental period. (The first time I met with Nixon, I complimented him on that wonderful speech. The president sloughed off the compliment by telling me Moynihan wrote it and I should give him the credit.) Since I was a presidential appointee, I suppose it was natural for people to associate me with Nixon. It would take several months for me to develop a public identity of my own.

I did not know any of this while I was still at Yale awaiting the formal job offer. My first confrontation with Head Start parents was at a luncheon address I gave before the New England arm of the National Association for the Education of Young Children (NAEYC) at the Park Plaza Hotel in New Haven. Walking across the New Haven green from my office to this meeting of predominately white, middle-class nursery school teachers, I had no idea I would be met by an angry picket line. At the hotel I was greeted by about 30 sign-carrying Head Start mothers, mostly black women, who had rented a bus to come from Rhode Island to voice their grievances. They were demanding entrance to the luncheon address but could not pay the $6 fee. This was a highly confrontational period, and the conference organizers dealt with the situation poorly. They were offended by what they saw as the Head Start group's unruly behavior and their refusal to pay for lunch. I would have gladly paid for their meals out of my own pocket, but I think the group of some 400 NAEYC members was actually frightened by these 30 mothers. The women were only carrying signs and posed no real threat to anyone, but the organizers locked them out and called the police.

I realized Head Start parents were my new constituency and wanted my first public exchange with them to be pleasant. After my address, I implored the hotel management to provide a space where I could meet with the mothers. The management agreed on the condition there be a police officer stationed at the door. (Some of the signs they carried were hostile toward President Nixon, a sentiment certainly not uncommon in poor communities.) Despite the distraction of a glaring policeman watching us, our meeting went smoothly. The mothers had only one concern: Was I going to defend, protect, and save Head Start? One mother asked me pointedly, "Are you going to cut the budget?" I explained that I had just been nominated, had not been confirmed by the Senate, and did not yet have any say on Head Start's budget. Another mother said, "We just want you to know what a good program it is." Another woman quickly added "and to let you know we can't stand any more cuts."

Before this encounter, my only real connection to Head Start had been as a planner, researcher, and visitor. I learned at this first meeting that Head Start was not just a standard government program provided to the poor but a partnership between the federal government and parents. When we adjourned about three o'clock, I realized these women probably had not had anything to eat since breakfast. The fact that they were willing to travel 100 miles and go hungry all day in order to make the case for "their program" certainly earned them my respect.

After I officially became the director of OCD, I met regularly with Head Start parent groups across the country. I thought of them as my new family and wanted to learn from them and help where I could. Unfortunately, many of these sessions were too confrontational and emotional to be of value. The meetings were as predictable as if they had been scripted. The parent groups would invariably bring a tape recorder and inform me everything I said would be taped. This bothered me because I had been reared in a milieu where a person's word was his bond. The group would then announce they were there to make "nonnegotiable demands." I always wondered why they spent the money to come. If their demands were not negotiable, why not just send me a written list? Their real purpose was probably a display of power over the person in charge. My role was to provide the coffee and cookies. Despite the power plays, I actually think I got more heat from the Nixon White House than I did from Head Start parents.

Mob Mentality

One constant problem during these years of civil unrest was that just about every group of demonstrators I encountered called themselves Head Start "parents." There was no way of knowing how many were actually parents and how many were community activists bent on showing power and "raising Cain." One of the relatively few times the distinction was clear was during a visit I made to the Chicago regional office. The director there asked if I would speak to a community group presently meeting in a building within a city park. As was becoming commonplace for the times, a huge riot was in progress in the park. Fearing for my safety, the regional people thought the best plan was to have the police take me to the meeting, guard me while I was there, and then take me back to my hotel. I learned a lesson that troublesome night I will never forget. The last place anyone would want to be during a riot is riding in a police car. The car was bombarded with large rocks hitting the roof, hood, and sides but thankfully missing the passengers. If I had to do it again, I would have had someone from the regional office sneak me through the park to the meeting. In the end, my rather standard talk was well-received, and the community people were thankful that I was willing to brave such violence to meet with them.

Not all of my encounters with community groups—sometimes under the guise of Head Start "parents"—were so positive. Thanks to Clennie Murphy, I was getting along better with the regional directors and was comfortable that I would never again experience the sabotaging behavior that had occurred in Miami (when irate parents confronted me after getting misinformation from the regional office). My sense that all was well was dashed during a visit to the regional office in San Francisco. Several members of my staff and I, including Clennie and Jenni Klein (the very competent national preschool education director), were there to visit the Head Start center in Marin County. There is little question that the regional directors, many of them holdovers from the Sugarman years, were sympathetic to the Community Action aspect of Head Start. Furthermore, social activists at the local level were naturally hostile to me since I had essentially cut off the funds that supported their activities. (I will explain this decision later in the chapter.) Thus my staff and I walked innocently into the lion's den.

After our visit to the Marin Head Start center, the regional director asked if I would meet with a "few" Head Start parents. I always made a point of meeting with parents, so despite my tight schedule I agreed. The director escorted us to a huge World War II Quonset hut situated a few yards from the Head Start center. We walked in and were met by some 800 obviously angry people. How many were parents and how many were community activists I will never know. It was obvious this meeting had been arranged and was well-orchestrated. Throughout the hall microphones had been set up so members of the audience could be heard. There was a stage in front with the exact number of chairs for the visitors from Washington. The regional director had lured us there, giving us absolutely no indication of what was happening.

We were no sooner seated than all the doors to the Quonset hut were shut, and we were told by a man who appeared to be the leader that we could not leave until our captors decided we could. With such a big crowd in this tin hut, it was very hot and physically uncomfortable. The mob was clearly agitated, and we feared that at any moment this huge group of angry people would storm the stage. Jenni Klein, who had fled Hitler in 1939, became extremely frightened and told me, "This is just like Nazi Germany." She began hyperventilating and said she was going to pass out and that I had to do something. I walked up to the microphone and said I would stay as long as they wished and would answer all of their questions to the best of my ability. I added that one of my staff members was ill and needed to leave immediately. They allowed her to leave, and then the questioning began.

Most people who spoke at the microphones asked no questions but made long statements that brutally vilified me and everyone in the Nixon administration, with special vitriol directed at the president. At first I was unsure what the group was so unhappy about. I surmised they were protesting a proposed $5 million budget cut for the following year. (This proposal originated in the House of Representatives, which was still being influenced by the Westinghouse Report and by some liberal members who wanted to punish me and Head Start after I cut off the use of program funds for Community Action efforts.) Actually, the Nixon administration had requested a $14 million increase for the fiscal year, not a cut. I never needed this defense, however, because most of the questions and comments had nothing to do with Head Start.

In the midst of this explosive situation, I had one of the warmest experiences I ever had that underscored the importance of Head Start to poor families in America. During the 3 hours or so that we were restrained in the building, an elderly black woman came up to the microphone. Unlike the speakers before her, she used halting words that were far from reassured or oratorical. I got the impression this was the first time she had gotten up the courage to speak directly to an authority figure in front of a crowd. She said that her daughter had been killed in an automobile accident so she was raising her two grandchildren. One had attended Head Start but the other had not, and she could see how much better the Head Start child was doing. She said she was on Social Security and that if I would not cut the Head Start budget, then the government could keep her Social Security checks. She thanked me for whatever I could do on behalf of her decimated family and sat down. I have never been more touched in my life. I knew her comments were not the type of scientific evidence needed to prove the effectiveness of Head Start. However, I am certain that responses like this from those who had the Head Start experience have a lot to do with the program's longevity. This was the one positive incident during a long, hot, tense afternoon.

I stood on the stage in the stifling heat of that locked hut and took a verbal beating for what seemed like forever. The meeting came to a head when a middle-aged black woman asked me how much money Nixon was spending that year on the Vietnam War. I honestly replied that I didn't know since my responsibility was Head Start and I had nothing to do with the war. She exploded and shouted into the microphone, "You don't know nothing. You ain't nothing but a boy. Why don't they send a man to talk to us?" At that point the academic Ed Zigler vanished, and the government Ed Zigler vanished. Who stepped forward was that young man who had been raised in the very tough north end of Kansas City. I told the woman and the assembly, "I don't like it when black men are called 'boys,' and I won't be called a boy either." I challenged anyone who doubted my manhood to step outside with me. Suddenly the doors were flung open and the meeting magically came to an end. As we were leaving, several members of what had just been a hostile crowd approached me and told me what a great guy I was. This event is simply reflective of the times we were living in during the 1960s and 1970s in America. It was a time of riots, confrontations, and demonstrations.

I will describe one more capture that finally brought me into contact with Donald Rumsfeld, then director of OEO. In November of 1970, the Secretary of HEW, my boss Elliot Richardson, decided to hold a retreat with his key staff members at Camp David. The purpose was to brainstorm a number of issues confronting the agency, although Head Start was not high on the agenda. As the meeting was about to begin, Richardson took me aside and said he had gotten word that some 500 parents of Head Start children from as far away as Mississippi were occupying the HEW auditorium back in Washington. They were demanding to talk to the Secretary about possible cuts in the Head Start budget. This seemed like an excuse for a riot because the administration's budget request for Head Start was higher, not lower. (The increase was not sufficient to cover inflation, so we were preparing for a possible reduction in services, but the mob was not privy to this information.) Meanwhile, the Senate was asking for a $73 million increase, so there really was no looming threat to instigate a protest at this stage of the budgetary process. Richardson asked me to go back to Washington to deal with the demonstrators.

When I walked up to the HEW auditorium stage, I could see that the crowd was angry. I was not there for 5 minutes before they started chanting, "Zigler must go! Zigler must go!" Ed Zigler, the professor, again wondered what a respectable academic was doing in such a dangerous place. (Actually, at the time college campuses were also filled with demonstrations, but there I was invited to the party and wasn't its target.) I tried to talk about the many constructive activities going on in Head Start, but the crowd was totally uninterested in anything positive I had to say. I was given the by now standard ultimatum that I could not leave until the leaders said so. After about 6 hours of my being stuck there, Richardson was forced to return and address the crowd. He promised to urge a conference committee to give Head Start enough money to go forward without any cuts. Although this promise did not exceed what the administration had already requested, he made it sound like a major concession. Secretary Richardson was then allowed to leave and go to a special office provided for him in the building.

The big problem was not in satisfying the demands of the demonstrators but how to get them out of the HEW auditorium. Evidently while I was still stuck there, Rumsfeld had been called from OEO to join Richardson in his emergency office. I asked the group leader if I could leave to consult with Richardson, but he initially refused. I gave him my personal word that I would return, but he said he had heard that from other high-level detainees who never came back. I promised that my word of honor was very meaningful to me and that I would try to convince Richardson to move things along in the direction the group would like. The leader relented, and I joined Richardson and Rumsfeld. Our only discussion was about how to get the crowd out of the auditorium. Our bind was that calling the police and having them physically evicted would hurt the image of both HEW and Head Start, so we didn't want to take that route. Among the three of us, we could not come up with a viable solution. As promised, I returned to the auditorium to once again become captive. The hour was growing late, and there was no further public discussion or hint of just what it would take to get them to leave. It seemed to me that the occupation itself was the ultimate goal of the takeover.

The dilemma was finally solved by James Farmer, Assistant Secretary of HEW. Farmer had been a forceful and effective civil rights advocate as head of the Congress of Racial Equality and had coined the term "freedom rides" for the bold attempts of black and white commuters to challenge racially segregated transportation in the South. He confidently walked up to the stage, knowing that his civil rights fame would give him credibility with the predominantly black crowd. He told them it was way past dinnertime, and he knew they had been there all day without eating. He said he had arranged for dinner to be served to them at a nearby school cafeteria, and he would be pleased to join them. That did it. Everybody left the auditorium and went with Farmer to dinner.

I breathed a sigh of relief and escaped out the back door to freedom. Outside I bumped into Daniel Schorr, who was covering the demonstration for CBS news. His wife Lee and I had been friends for years as a result of our mutual friendship with Julius Richmond. Schorr said to me, "Not much like academia, is it, Dr. Zigler?" (Zigler and Muenchow, 1992, p. 98). That is exactly what I was thinking.

Over the years I have been amazed at the evolution in the ability of parents to deal with the system. They have learned how the complex world of government works and where the appropriate pressure points can be found. Long gone are confrontations, sit-ins, and meetings with unconditional demands. Along with Head Start staff, parents have built a money-poor but experience-rich lobby, the National Head Start Association (NHSA). This group not only effectively lobbies for Head Start on the Hill but advises national leaders and trains parents and staff to be knowledgeable and effective forces in shaping policies that affect the program. NHSA does not have the power of other lobbyists who have the resources to contribute to politicians' campaign funds. Nevertheless, this group of underpaid employees and parents managed to become a force to be reckoned with in Washington and have done much to protect and improve Head Start. The executive branch as well as Congress often reach out to the NHSA for early council on any Head Start action that they propose to make, knowing from experience they would much rather have them as an ally than an opponent.

Divorcing Head Start from Community Action

Some of the confrontations just described, and hundreds if not thousands of others that took place across the nation, may have been financed at least in part by Head Start money. Recall that with the departure of Julius Richmond, Head Start was essentially in the hands of Jule Sugarman from 1965 until I took over in 1970. Sugarman embraced the Community Action philosophy and chose to apply Head Start funds to both the child and family piece and the social action side. I inherited this situation and, after being trapped in too many rooms by too many revolutionaries, soon realized that the two roots of Head Start were in opposition. Head Start had to become either the social change program envisioned by the Community Action people, who continued to run many of our nation's Head Start centers, or a program dedicated to enhancing the development of poor children and their families, as envisioned by the Head Start planning committee. To me, the choice was easy. I simply announced that no

Head Start funds were to be spent on Community Action initiatives. Head Start was to be a child development program.

Philosophically, I was not opposed to efforts to make our society more sensitive to the problems and needs of the poor. However, I did not believe that chaos, riots, or kidnappings were the way to achieve social change. Political science teaches that social systems work to maintain themselves and respond to attack with counterattack. I believed that once the attacks and revolutionary fervor died down and people learned to play within the accepted rules dictated by the system, change would be more achievable. Working outside the system with sit-ins and confrontations was proving to be counterproductive, alienating key policymakers who could actually make desired changes.

Whatever my own views were, I was under great pressure from all sides to get Head Start out of Community Action escapades. My superiors, from President Nixon through Secretary Richardson, had next to no sympathy for the social activism component of Head Start. This had been evident before I was hired. During the confirmation process I made courtesy visits to eight Senators, including Russell Long, Chairman of the powerful Senate Finance Committee. Senator Long lectured me that he did not want any more Head Start funds going to Community Action activities.

My final decision to end the relationship was forced not by the powers in Washington but by the power of Head Start parents. Their program time was being taken up with instruction in social action and "confidence-building" exercises so they could discover their hidden strengths and fight harder for the cause. For example, in some places parents were asked to attend a form of psychological group therapy called T-groups, which were a fad at the time. These groups promoted self-analysis and reflection, but the evidence of their efficacy was never particularly convincing to me, and I had trained as a clinical psychologist.

Congressmen from many districts began receiving letters from parents who complained they did not understand what social activism training or all the mysterious self-help procedures had to do with Head Start. Congressmen saw little connection either and were soon calling me to meet with them at their offices on the Hill to explain the purpose of such expenditures. They essentially saw Head Start like I did, as a program to get poor children ready for school and to incorporate parent activities that would help parents help their children.

Another factor in my decision was money. Tens of millions of Head Start dollars were being spent on social action efforts and pseudopsychological treatments that many parents did not want. I wanted quality improvements that would strengthen Head Start services and enhance child outcomes, and these would obviously come with a cost. While my decision that Head Start would no longer finance Community Action was welcomed by policymakers and parents, it infuriated the nationwide network of social activists whose livelihoods depended on Head Start money.

This network formed a representative group and demanded to meet with me. Sitting around a conference table in my office (where I could not easily be held hostage), I quickly spotted their leader. Each member who spoke would look to him for some sort of reaction. At first he said very little. I explained to them that the purpose of Head Start was to promote school readiness and healthy child development, and there was not enough money in my budget to do this *and* to change society. I remained very firm and made clear that I would not rescind my decision. At this point the leader of the group became very frustrated and could maintain his silence no longer. He stood up and in a raised voice said, "Dr. Zigler, you don't understand. We are interested in systemic change. We are willing to give up a whole generation of our children in order to get it" (Zigler and Muenchow, 1992, p. 111). I stood up and countered that while he might be willing to give up a generation of children, I was not. Their children had a right to be all they could be, and that was what Head Start was going to work to achieve. If they did not like my decision, their only recourse was to go to my superiors in HEW or to their elected officials. With my fiat, Head Start could become a program focused on children and their families. I breathed a sigh of relief that the ambiguity of the first 5 years had finally come to an end.

The pain of defeat has still not healed among some hard-core community activists. (Some radical feminists also continue to disparage me in the literature. They disapproved of my actions because they viewed the community action within Head Start as a promising vehicle for poor mothers to demonstrate their strength and assert their power.) A small group of scholars presenting chapters in Ellsworth and Ames's (1998) *Critical Perspectives on Project Head Start* are of the opinion that, in ending social activism in Head Start, I severed the portion of the program that had the greatest potential for ending poverty in America. They believe that if Head Start had put all of its effort into community change, communities would have changed, and the poor would have come closer to achieving social and economic parity. However, in one chapter Kathryn Kuntz concedes that had I not taken this action, Head Start probably would not have survived. Kuntz writes, "Zigler used [children] to protect Head Start as a noncontroversial early childhood education program. . . . Millions of children in thousands of communities continue to benefit from Zigler's political maneuvering in the early 1970s" (1998, p. 33). She recognizes that an alternative to my action would have been to try "to maintain the balance between a focus on community and one on children. While this is generally what occurred inside OEO between 1965 and 1969, it is unlikely that the uneasy alliance could have held indefinitely" (p. 33). Finally, she admitted "It is difficult, then, to assert that a community-action-style Head Start would have succeeded in changing local institutions as effectively as the preschool-style Head Start succeeded in serving children in the last two decades" (p. 33).

In the end, my decision to divorce Head Start from Community Action saved the program on the political front, and it saved me from being overwhelmed by the craziness of politics, activism, and public life. Free of Community Action, I could focus on something I understood—child development.

Out of My Element

Until I arrived in Washington, I had never experienced any sense of inferiority and never had a doubt that I could accomplish anything to which I set my mind. Indeed, my weakness was probably thinking too highly of myself and carrying a dangerous amount of hubris. After all, I had risen from the poverty of a Depression-era slum to become a tenured, full professor at Yale University at a young age. I had already received some national academic honors, and my research was being funded with large amounts of public and private support. Transplanted from my cozy, ivy-covered tower (a literal description of Yale's architecture), I suffered culture shock. My response to it was far from praise-worthy. I was lost. I felt like a nobody. I became despondent, convinced I was doomed to fail and would reap a great deal of shame in the process. I even began developing psychosomatic symptoms such as a continuously dry mouth, which is a symptom of anxiety. Worse still, I took refuge in continuously running away.

My new position demanded more work than any one person could possibly do, and I should have worked day and night to at least try to keep up. As luck would have it, because of my rank I was inundated with invitations to speak all over the country. I accepted way too many of these engagements and was therefore out of town a great deal. I have always been an effective speaker, and giving addresses gave me a feeling of success, whereas performing in Washington left me with a sense of imminent failure. All of this behavior was maladaptive, and I am indebted to this day to a wonderful colleague at HEW, Connie Newman, who had a hand in my being offered the job and who certainly wanted me to succeed. My nationwide speeches resulted in positive press about me and the new office, but Connie wisely saw that I needed to be on the ground in Washington, needed to be available to decision makers, and needed to get on with the work of building OCD and strengthening Head Start.

Connie did not confront me directly with her concern about my excessive travel. Perhaps she saw that direct criticism from a superior at HEW might have caused me to throw in the towel and advise them to find someone better at the task. Instead she brought the issue up with my special assistant, Carolyn Harmon, whose office adjoined mine. Newman suggested that Harmon "mention" my frequent absences and the concerns they were precipitating. Although my new position did require considerable travel and speech giving, from the Newman incident forward I tried to keep this aspect of my job to a minimum. I realized that my basic problem was not understanding the bureaucratic maze that is Washington and how one goes about getting things done in this complex arena, and that I would never learn if I was never there.

Even after I stopped escaping, I continued to suffer a real identity crisis. Was I an academic or was I a high-level decision maker? Even my physical setting never felt like home. Instead it seemed unreal, especially compared with the modest surroundings of a college professor's lab. OCD took up a whole building, not to mention the 10 regional outposts. My office was huge and contained a conference table, not one but two couches, and the giant HEW flag. I even had a private restroom. One perk that grated the basic academic in me was the use of a chauffeured limousine to get around the city. I was a young college professor who either walked or drove my humble family sedan to move about the sprawling Yale campus. I viewed limousines as ostentatious and a prime example of Veblen's "conspicuous consumption." I tried the limousine a couple of times but felt foolish, so I informed my executive secretary that from now on I would take taxicabs. My decision was prompted not only by my academic reluctance but by the fact that I was running Head Start, a program for the poor.

Cabs worked fine for a couple of weeks until one day when I had an interview at a local television station situated a good distance away on Wisconsin Avenue. That is pretty far from the Capitol and its office buildings where I had an important meeting later in the afternoon. After the interview I tried to catch a cab and discovered it is next to impossible to find one in Washington at that time of day. There I stood on the street, feeling helpless, hailing every taxi I saw only to have them all drive by me. At the meeting I was supposed to attend, people from various HEW agencies were to make a decision about whether to fund a $15–20 million initiative. My study of the proposal led me to conclude it was weak and not worth the money. The project ended up being funded, and I will never know if the outcome would have been different if I had been there. The next morning I told my executive secretary that hereafter I would use the limousine for my trips in the district. We hear a great deal about waste in government, and I am sure that there is more than a little.

However, in Washington I learned that what may appear wasteful can be absolutely necessary if leaders are to work effectively.

Strange Customs

Another episode of culture shock was my discovery that in Washington I had many superiors to whom I had to answer. Being a professor in a university is like being an independent entrepreneur. You alone decide how to teach your classes and which students to mentor. At a research university like Yale, you are expected to obtain research funds from public or private agencies by writing an application describing the work you want to do. Once you receive support, the only requirement is that you conduct the research you proposed in the stated timeframe. In my laboratory at Yale, the final decisions about each stage of the process were mine alone. A college professor does have to answer to the department chair, but once he or she is tenured, the chair and the professor are essentially equals.

My autonomy and decision-making authority were somewhat curtailed in my new job. Since OCD was in the Secretary's Office, throughout my tenure in government I considered HEW Secretary Elliot Richardson as my primary superior. Although I needed his approval before taking any major steps at OCD, Elliot and I respected each other and shared the same values. I do not recall our having a single disagreement on a decision. I was also responsible to the undersecretary and the various deputies in the Secretary's office, but I really had little to do with them. Even when I disagreed with Richardson's deputy, John Veneman, my decision usually stood. The HEW hierarchy was the easiest for me to deal with. After all, they had hired me, and my failure would reflect as much on them as on me.

However, I also worked for OEO. Recall that Head Start had been delegated, not transferred, to HEW. Thus Head Start's money was still given to OEO, and even though it was then transferred to HEW, the Office of Management and Budget (OMB) saw OEO as having responsibility over the program. Rumsfeld, the new director of OEO, and his second-in-command, Richard Cheney, had little love for Head Start. Technically I had to get approval from OEO for just about every action I took. I attempted this early in the game, but most of the reactions to my proposals were negative. Their responses carried no weight, however, because HEW was really in charge. After a while I learned to proceed with the work Richardson had approved and not bother sharing what I was doing with OEO.

The most formidable bureaucratic boss in Washington is the OMB, which oversees every agency and is very involved in determining every budget that will be submitted to Congress. Despite the fact I had good relations across HEW and with my more immediate superiors, I still had to answer to OMB. When I had my first meeting with budget officials, which incidentally was held not at HEW but at OEO, they put up a chart and ordered me to cut Head Start by one-third the first year, another third in the second year, and the rest in the third year. I would never have taken the position of director of OCD if I had known my job was to end Head Start. In a state of shock, I requested an urgent meeting with Secretary Richardson. I told him what had transpired at OEO and declared that if this was the agenda I was to follow, I would resign that day. Richardson calmly told me to give it no further thought and to get back to work. He promised to go to the White House and straighten things out. He evidently did because I never heard of the 3-year phase-out plan again.

In addition to HEW, OEO, and OMB, I soon realized that every member of Congress and all of their staffers felt that they should be able to influence my activities. When I got calls from these staff members, I learned I could not possibly act on all their concerns, so I got into the habit of listening politely. The calls from members of Congress I took more seriously and often had to drop what I was doing to be cooperative. One would think that the executive branch would have the most authority over me, and it did sometimes seem that every 25-year-old staff member at the White House felt he or she could order me about. In actuality, I found I could deal with their demands rather easily. During my stint in Washington I generally had little to do with the Nixon White House. I met with the president a few times and periodically was called to the White House to take part in a press conference or other routine event. I did work closely with the president's chief advisor, Pat Moynihan, and his lieutenants on Nixon's welfare reform plan. This engagement will be discussed more fully in Chapter 6.

Dealing with so many superiors was certainly foreign to me, but so was the Washingtonian manner of dealing with others. I mentioned earlier how I stupidly announced to my workers that I would only be staying for a couple years, which gave them an excuse to ignore my demands, and how I had to begin gauging employee loyalty, something that would never enter a college professor's mind.

Cooperation among equals was another area interpreted very differently in Washington than in academia. Secretary Finch's early discussions with me as well as his press release describing my new post indicated OCD was to coordinate children's programs throughout HEW. The White House too wanted me to be the administration's point person in dealing with children's issues throughout government. To an academic, coordination is a positive term, such as when researchers in different laboratories or disciplines work on different aspects of the same issue. I soon found that coordination across agencies in Washington is next to impossible. An agency head must protect his or her turf. I remember a meeting with Secretary Richardson when I noted there were literally hundreds of programs for children spread out across at least a dozen agencies within HEW. I explained that my intention to coordinate across these agencies was met with a favorable response even by OMB, which typically hates everything. However, I was encountering little enthusiasm for coordination as I discussed the possibility with the agency heads. Richardson burst into laughter. "Coordination may sound like a great idea to you, but to a bureaucrat it means you want to take over his program and put it in OCD" (Zigler and Muenchow, 1992, p. 93).

Even though I had been warned that the task would be difficult, I pushed forward. After all, President Nixon had made a point of emphasizing the significance of the first 5 years of life. Wouldn't it be nice to know exactly what HEW was doing in terms of programs for children in this age group? I invited the heads of the relevant agencies to OCD to discuss our efforts targeting this age so we could identify overlaps and gaps and develop a more rational overall set of policies and programs.

The first meeting was an absolute disaster, with much discontent. The problem was that I had stupidly designated myself as chairman, so the participants immediately saw the meeting as the first step in a takeover of their programs by OCD (just as Richardson had warned). In my scientific world every group has a chairman, who is an equal among equals. This academic practice did not work in Washington. I turned to my professional contacts to recruit an outside chairman, Brewster Smith, who was a leading social psychologist and a past president of the American Psychological Association. I then joined the other agency heads as a member of the group instead of as a threatening leader. We developed a topographical overview of all the children's programs in HEW and identified those that should work together and also found some unmet needs of children from birth to age 5 that we wanted to address. Incredibly, OMB was happy with this effort and praised me for pulling it off. (As an agency, OMB is notoriously long on criticism and short on praise.) Emboldened by my success, Edith Grotberg, a staff member who worked with me on the project, decided to attempt the same type of effort with adolescents, which did indeed become our second success story.

From Professor to Pedestrian

In the 1970s academics were held in pretty low repute by Washington decision makers. Even today, we are viewed as spending our lives in ivy-covered towers out of touch with the real world, whereas decision makers see themselves as pragmatic and hard-headed men and women of action. One has to admit that there is a certain degree of truth to these characterizations. The world of academia is paced, whereas the world of Washington is fast. Scholars think, study, and lead very reflective lives. In Washington there is simply no time for thorough study of problems or solutions.

When I moved into my office I found a rubber stamp that printed the letters OBE, meaning overtaken by events. There is no being overtaken by events in academia, where we can schedule our work a year or more out and then stay the course. I asked what I was supposed to do with this stamp and was shown an in-basket filled with memoranda to which I had to respond. After reading some of these papers and perhaps making a check mark about my preferred course of action, I realized many were no longer relevant because action had already been taken at a higher level or because certain events had precluded making a decision at the time. These were stamped "OBE." I used this stamp a lot in Washington, but needless to say, I left it there when I returned to Yale.

The conflict between policymakers' needs for immediate answers and academics' tendency to focus on the unknown is evident in an anecdote that has long made the rounds in Washington. Supposedly a congressman remarked that what America needs is a one-armed psychologist. He was frustrated from hearing psychologists' testimony in which they invariably say, "On this hand . . . but on the other hand," essentially avoiding taking a stance. True, in scientific papers there often is a reluctance to draw a firm conclusion. Findings are discussed with a range of implications, and the scholar is honor bound to point out weaknesses in the study that cast doubt on its validity or application. The most common conclusion is "More research is needed." Such an approach is alien to a decision maker, who by definition is charged with making decisions. Policymakers do not expect infallibility. They want an expert opinion about the best course of action based on the best information we presently have, even if that information is incomplete.

Another contrast is that scholars are trained in the pursuit of knowledge and obliged to keep science pure and uncontaminated by preconceived notions or personal opinion. The legislative process, however, is driven by politics and ideology. Often a congressperson has already made up his or her mind about an issue and invites experts whose testimony will support a planned policy. A couple of real-life illustrations will make this clear. During the Carter years the Senate Operations Committee held hearings on the president's proposal to move Head Start from HEW to the newly formed Department of Education. My own Senator, Abe Ribicoff, had often sought my counsel on Head Start issues in the past. I met with him in his apartment at Watergate and explained to him why I thought the move was a bad idea. He told me how much he valued my advice but that he could do nothing in this instance, since all he was doing was "carrying the President's water."

I remember another incident in which I testified before Mondale's Senate committee hearings on the Comprehensive Child Development Act of 1971, which would have provided our nation with a formal, good quality child care system. (This bill will be discussed at length in Chapter 6.) The Republican Senator from New York, James Buckley, was opposed to the bill and found a PhD-level psychoanalytic social worker to testify against it. As an expert on the effects of social deprivation on children's behavior, I was appalled by his testimony. The witness mentioned the famous "hospitalism" study done by Rene Spitz. This well-known study examined the effects on very young infants of being reared in custodial institutions, where they received food and shelter but had little stimulating interaction with caregivers. Some developed a profound syndrome (hospitalism) in which they withered away and often died. The drama of this testimony belied the fact that infants only spend the length of the workday in child care settings, few if any of which resemble custodial institutions. Although conservatives like Buckley were unsuccessful in that the bill passed both houses of Congress, they went on to play a key role in Nixon's decision to veto this landmark act. My point is that whereas science is never totally neutral, policy is always ideologically driven, making it acceptable to pick among the evidence only that which supports a chosen position.

Another side of this problem is the mistaken notion that members of Congress know a great deal about every subject, ranging from war policy to special education to coal mining. This is of course unrealistic. I was very surprised to find that most policymakers knew very little about child development. Considering that many of them have backgrounds in law or business, I really shouldn't have expected them to be experts in a field that takes years of study to master. I must add that in all my decades of working with policymakers, I have generally found them to be eager to learn.

I discovered one of the reasons lawmakers have a generally skeptical attitude toward academics when I testified at one of my first congressional hearings. An elderly congressman approached me as I sat at the witness stand and said, "You don't sound like a professor—you're peppy, and I could understand everything you said." I thanked him and said I had not always been a professor but was once a truck driver, which was true. The exchange taught me that what often defeats academics in Washington is their love of their own jargon, which often means little to most listeners. Try explaining "ego strength" to a congressman sometime. The problem with scholars of course is that they are used to communicating with their peers rather than with the public. Yet freeing myself of professional jargon did not necessarily make me more likable. I had to learn to make the distinction between a congressperson's reaction to me as an academic in Washington versus a representative of President Nixon, with neither persona generating much esteem.

I learned at another congressional hearing that my Nixon persona was indeed the less popular of my two identities. Before the formal hearing began, a committee member engaged me in a friendly conversation and praised the work I was doing at OCD. Once the hearing began, however, this same congressman became very belligerent in his questioning and downright nasty to me. I could not help but wonder what was going on and if this was really the same person I had had a cordial conversation with moments before. After the hearings the congressman told me, "Dr. Zigler, I'm sure you know that all that I was doing was making a record. Please know that I think the world of you." I did not have the slightest idea what "making a record" meant. I later learned that every word, both the questions and answers, at a hearing is recorded verbatim in the *Congressional Record*, which is quickly available as a publication. What this friendly–nasty congressman was doing was getting on the public record how severe he was in his dealings with the Nixon administration and its agents. Thus, our exchange could be used as publicity in his next campaign, which he was running on an anti-Nixon ticket. I had never witnessed anything of this sort in academia, where there is no rationalization for being two-faced. Thus, I found myself being socialized in a world where I had to operate but did not understand.

Although I did my best to sound like a Washington bureaucrat, I guess my years in academia left me with a tendency to sound professorial. At congressional hearings I had to read the official testimony written by OMB, so I necessarily sounded like the administration. Afterward you are asked questions and you have to be careful your spontaneous answers hue the policy line. I was unaware that representatives from OMB monitored my answers to make sure I did not "leave the reservation." I learned of this practice inadvertently from Secretary Richardson. He told me reports of my testimony had been sent to him by the OMB monitors to inform him about my performance, good or bad. He admitted he was not supposed to tell me of their judgment but that he was so amused by it he simply had to share the review of my testimony from the previous day. The report essentially said, "Zigler gave his usual tutorial. It was extremely well received by the committee." Richardson knew me well, so why he was so amused by this evaluation I will never know. Perhaps he had his own prejudices against academics, although I repeat that he and I got along very well. I remember one meeting I had with Richardson to update him on OCD's progress toward various subgoals we had set as steps toward achieving our final goal. My report showed we were progressing quickly and were on track. Richardson started to compliment me by saying, "Who would have thought a college professor. . . ." He heard what he was saying and sheepishly stopped midsentence.

I found that being an academic had certain positive consequences at least in terms of my doing my job. Functioning agencies in Washington are filled with generalists (e.g., lawyers, political scientists, economists) who can perform a multitude of tasks. Other than a few old timers in the Children's Bureau and the education and health specialists in Head Start, I encountered few people who had specific knowledge about children. To most Washingtonians, Piaget is a watch, not the great scholar in cognitive development that child psychologists know him to be. Although I was lost and confused in the world of politics, the one solid asset I could contribute to the policymaking enterprise was understanding of the nature of children's growth and development. This knowledge served as my north star. When conflicting interests were trying to influence my decisions, I asked myself the simple question of whether a potential action was conducive to improving the lives of children.

Eventually members of Congress came to respect my judgment and began to turn to OCD to answer pertinent scientific questions. One such topic was the overuse of Ritalin, the medication used to treat attention deficit disorder and hyperactivity (often referred to as ADD and ADHD). The issue had particular valence for the Congressional Black Caucus since there was some evidence that black boys were prescribed the drug to a greater degree than white boys. Of course the sensational media reports were often overblown, but they incited many letters to congressmen imploring them to do something.

Congress asked me to mount an effort to illuminate this issue for them. The overuse of Ritalin seemed like a legitimate concern for OCD, so I convened a distinguished group of national experts representing a swath of disciplines. This commission was headed by a colleague at Yale, Daniel Freedman, a psychiatrist and one of our nation's leading psychopharmacologists. The group unveiled their final report at a very crowded press conference with many policymakers in attendance. At the time the issue was a heated one, and I remember the atmosphere in the packed room was emotion laden. Here I again saw the difficulty scholars have operating in the Washington milieu. Freedman presented the findings clearly but his attitude seemed to be, "I am a great scholar [which was true], and therefore you should not question anything I tell you." This of course is not the style of either the Capitol media or Congress. As the questions to Freedman became more prickly, he rebelled and made clear his resistance to waste his time with such ignoramuses.

Thankfully the vice chairman stepped forward, pushed the angry Freedman aside, and began answering the tough but reasonable questions being put forth by the audience. Since OCD's reputation was at stake, I too was concerned about the tempestuous nature of what should have been a straightforward report and joined the vice chairman. In the end, the Ritalin commission was a success and OCD received a great deal of positive press.

Dr. Freeman was certainly not alone among the ranks of college professors who found Washington to be an impossible environment. Yet some professors have worked successfully in the political machine in the executive, legislative, and judicial branches of power. When I returned to Yale, Richardson gave me the Secretary's award for my accomplishments in government. Many years later he gave me a greater accolade by saying he considered me one of the two best bureaucrats with whom he had worked over his entire career. Of course, all I could remember was my dry mouth and sense of failure when I got to Washington.

What I resented about my Washington days was that it took me so long to learn this new culture. It slowed me down and led to my accomplishing less than I could have. My graduate training and experience in academia simply did not prepare me for the world I would encounter on Capitol Hill. I guess I was in the same camp as my colleague Sheldon White, who confessed he thought that somehow good elves would do all the work and that all he would have to do was to sit there and think wise thoughts. Our ignorance convinced us to rally some like-minded colleagues to create programs to cross-train students in child development and social policy. There are now over 40 such centers in universities across the nation, training psychologists and members of other scholarly disciplines about the policymaking process and policymakers about the needs of children and families. How I wish such training had been available to me when I blindly stepped onto Capitol Hill.

Posterity will have to decide whether my actions in Washington were successful or not. I know I take pride that over 40 years later almost 1 million children and their families profit each year from the Head Start program. This outcome seemed impossible so many years ago when I arrived in what to me was an alien culture, where my staff hated me, I had no idea what I was doing, and my first marching orders were to close the Head Start program—the program I had left my comfortable university life to run. I had to forget about being intimidated and devote all of my energy to saving Head Start.

5

Reinventing Head Start

The summer of 1970 was not a promising time to assume leadership of Head Start. The federal budget surplus that had been spent so freely during Head Start's early years was gone, depleted by the war in Vietnam. Structural changes were taking place at the White House that threatened to lessen the influence of Head Start's strongest allies. Moynihan had been promoted to Counselor to the President in November, 1969, and in early March the Urban Affairs Council Moynihan had run was replaced by the Domestic Council. John Ehrlichman was named the head of the new council and the president's Chief Domestic Assistant.

According to Ehrlichman, the administration was considering massive changes to and even the elimination of several key antipoverty programs, including the popular Job Corps. On the subject of Head Start, Ehrlichman's view was that "it may be too late to abolish it" (Zigler and Muenchow, 1992, p. 75). He noted that House Education and Labor Committee Chairman Carl Perkins was too powerful a supporter of the program for the Nixon administration to act hastily. But the president was clear in the spring of 1969 that no increases should be considered so long as Head Start retained its present form. I definitely was not planning to maintain Head Start in the form that characterized it in 1969.

Although President Nixon was never hostile to Head Start, the controversial invasion of Cambodia placed all the administration's more constructive domestic proposals in jeopardy with a testy Congress. This took a toll on Head Start's budget, with appropriations slipping from $349 million in FY67 to $325 million in FY70. Some program funds were diverted from direct services to research and development. The House of Representatives was proposing a further reduction in the program's budget. Even though the

Nixon administration was planning to request a small increase for Head Start to $339 million for FY71, this was actually $30 million less than it had requested the previous year.

Without question, Head Start's future was precarious because of the program's association with the War on Poverty. One of the president's closest advisors had strong influence at the White House and little use for Head Start. Moynihan was undoubtedly the mastermind behind the Head Start 3-year phase-out plan shown to me shortly after I arrived at OCD. After all, he had championed another nominee to be the first director of OCD, Sheldon White of Harvard, who would have carried out the order. After successfully prodding White to write a scholarly paper defending the poorly done Westinghouse study, Moynihan made sure President Nixon continued to note the study's negative findings in his references to Head Start. For example, in a message to Congress on educational reform, Nixon included Head Start in a general dismissal of compensatory education: "The best available evidence indicates that most of the compensatory education programs have not measurably helped poor children catch up" (Zigler and Muenchow, 1992, p. 78). He again alluded to the Westinghouse Report, stating: "In our Headstart program where so much hope is invested, we find that youngsters enrolled only for the summer achieve almost no gains, and the gains of those in the program for a full year are soon matched by their non-Headstart classmates from similarly poor backgrounds" (p. 78). This speech must have been written by Moynihan, who was a scholar but certainly not an expert in compensatory education. Although our relationship remained cordial, Moynihan was a formidable enemy targeting Head Start from a lofty position at the White House.

Where to Begin?

A month before I was scheduled to become the first director of OCD, I attended a far-ranging press conference where, in retrospect, I barely touched on some of the many enormous issues I would soon have to confront. I began by criticizing the Westinghouse Report, a problem that would shortly take up an unfair amount of my time. I warned that although the Westinghouse study did not use the IQ as a measure, the only measures it had that were worth using at all gauged intellectual functioning, which in most people's minds is represented by the IQ. I explained the poor predictive value of a young child's IQ to successful adjustment in school and later life. I stated that I was "more concerned with the type of character we build in kids than with elevating IQs" and pleaded that we "don't crucify children on the cross of IQ" (Shelton,

1970). Fearful of the overpromises being made, I warned that we must be realistic about the possibilities of early intervention programs and pointed out the folly of believing we could inoculate a child against the ravages of poverty by a short stint in Head Start. Consistent with an earlier speech by President Nixon, I stated that the first 5 years in a child's life are a critical period but that the years 5 through 10 and 10 through 15 are also critical developmental stages. I said I wanted to convince policymakers and the public that development takes place from conception to old age, so we should not give preferential treatment to one single year and ignore all the others.

When the press asked what my agenda at OCD would be, I could only voice the charges given to me during the recruitment process by leaders at HEW and the congressionally mandated charge of the Children's Bureau. I said I would run social action programs for children like Head Start at the highest quality possible, unaware of what a massive job this would become. I also mentioned my interest in integrating children from different social classes in Head Start and my intention to replace the summer programs with full-year sessions. I voiced my hope that OCD would be given responsibility for federal child care programs that were in the planning stages. At the time, President Nixon's welfare reform proposal, the Family Assistance Plan, was being drafted. To get single mothers off welfare, there had to be access to child care. There was considerable debate about whether the child care component should be housed in OCD or in the Department of Labor, and I appealed for its placement in OCD. In the tradition of the Children's Bureau, I also promised to be an outspoken advocate for children, adding "I don't think we have had the kind of advocacy for children that they deserve to get.... We can do better by our children than we have been doing" (Shelton, 1970).

As I geared up for my new job, my plans became more detailed and probably more grandiose. Another press conference held shortly after my swearing in was reported in the New York Times under the headline, "Provocative Child Agency Head" (Herbers, 1970). Because I certainly did not sound like a Nixonian conservative, the reporters asked me several times about my political affiliation. I said that I was basically a scholar and all I had to bring to the table was knowledge about child development. I told them I was essentially apolitical, concluding "my politics are children." I again vigorously defended Head Start against the Westinghouse Report, lecturing that its cognitive emphasis was an inappropriate way to evaluate the impact of the program, which was designed to promote an array of child, family, and community achievements. I promised I would do my best to change the goal of raising IQ scores to encouraging children's everyday social competence. I predicted that America will eventually see the start of formal schooling for all children at the age of 3. My confidence was showing when I said, "The commitments of President Nixon and Secretary Richardson to improving the quality of life for children will guarantee the success of the new agency."

The new OCD was described by others as "established by President Nixon as a point of coordination for federal programs for preschool children and all other . . . youth." This indeed gave me a very large, blank slate. The *New York Times* took note, stating "Dr. Zigler is starting out with the zest and self-assurance of one who has a broad mandate," and "provocative statements flowed from him faster than reporters could take them down" (Herbers, 1970). The truth, however, is that I actually had no specific mandate from anyone. I was armed with nothing more than some sketchy thoughts about what was expected of me. It was both exciting and frightening to realize that I would have to develop my own agenda. At least I knew my starting point: improvement and innovation in Head Start. The program was in danger, and I had to do something to keep it alive.

I learned this would be easier said than done at a hearing held by Rep. Carl Perkins, Chairman of the Education and Labor Committee, which was responsible for Head Start's oversight. The hearing began rather well. Perkins asked about how many volunteers were coming to Head Start centers and the numbers were quite large, which pleased him. He then inquired about my views of the Westinghouse Report. I gave my standard critique, which he applauded. The hearing was essentially over at that point and I should have thanked the chairman and left. However, I wanted to be honest so I added that there was one aspect of the report with which I agreed, namely that the short length of the summer program made it pretty useless in preparing poor children for school. I noted that Westinghouse reported some promising benefits for the minority of their sample who had attended full-year programs. I logically concluded that the evidence suggested it would be better to serve fewer children in a full-year program than more children in a summer program.

I was totally unprepared for the explosive response I received. Perkins became very angry and red in the face, and he literally shouted at me that if I closed even one summer Head Start program he would subpoena me. I left the hearing totally befuddled as to what I had done to incite such an attack. I spent the next week asking my superiors at HEW and everyone else I knew in Washington to explain what I had said that so angered Perkins. No one would tell me. Finally I spoke to John Brademas, who was a member of the committee and was present at the hearings. At first he just said some deferential things about "the Chairman." I just could not get a straight answer. John, a Rhodes Scholar with a Harvard PhD in political science, finally took pity on me and engaged me in a Socratic exercise. He asked me, "Who worked in the summer programs?" I replied, "school teachers." He then asked, "Who mans the phones for Perkins at election time to get out the vote?" I said "school teachers?" and John nodded sagely. In solving the mystery I got an important lesson in government. The very nature of the system is such that getting reelected takes precedence over just about everything else, particularly in the House where members face reelection every 2 years. As one congressman in a different context informed me, "I can be of no help to you if I am not here next term."

I now found myself in a quandary. Richardson's predecessor Finch had voiced his dissatisfaction with the summer program, and my own reading of the evidence convinced me it was imperative to redirect the summer program money to full-year programs as soon as possible. However, the chairman of Head Start's oversight committee was ordering me to waste money on the ineffective model rather than use it for a more promising one. I thought long and hard about what Head Start could realistically accomplish with an 8-week summer program that might be of measurable use to children living in poverty. I decided that in such a short period we could at least provide health screenings and follow-up services many of these children needed. OCD thus funded 29 health demonstration projects called Health Start to serve children enrolled in summer Head Start as well as their younger siblings. However, Health Start had the shortcomings of the summer Head Start programs, namely it did not last long enough and there was not enough time for follow-up treatment. Health Start was declared a failure and was soon ended. Unfortunately, the political support for summer Head Start programs made it impossible to close all of them for too many years after their lack of efficacy had been documented.

While I was getting OCD and my vision for the new, improved Head Start off the ground, the negative conclusions of the Westinghouse study remained an albatross around my neck. I had to hurriedly find a way to counter the by now famous report. I scanned the existing evidence on Head Start and found a quite positive study by Kirschner Associates (1970). The study clearly reflected the Community Action mentality in which the benefits of the program were assessed by improvements in poor communities rather than by better performance of poor children. The findings showed that communities that had mounted a Head Start program evidenced many more improvements in general health and educational facilities than comparable poor communities that had no Head Start center. However, this finding has never been replicated, which is the best evidence of the validity of a finding.

I also employed other, less scientific evidence indicating the value of Head Start. For example, Richmond had pointed out (Hicks, 1970) that 34% of Head Start preschoolers had not seen a doctor in the 2 years before their enrollment, and one in four had never been to a dentist. With the obvious and close relationship between a child's general health status and ability to learn, it has always surprised me that Head Start's great health benefits have essentially been ignored by lawmakers as well as by scientists. The fact that Head Start employed and trained so many poor parents also won little approbation, as did the social support services to parents that undoubtedly improved the child's home environment. To my sorrow, I learned that nobody cared. The only change precipitated by Head Start that interested decision makers was cognitive improvement. I knew I had to make two crucial moves: (1) convince people that Head Start is about greater school readiness and social competence, not about higher IQ scores; and (2) gather some sound scientific evidence on whether or not Head Start has a meaningful impact on participants. I will talk more about the first thrust later in this chapter. The second effort will be detailed in Chapter 7.

All of this might be viewed as wishful thinking on my part, because in 1970 Head Start was not a very good program. I admitted as much in a meeting when Secretary Richardson asked me which program in HEW held the most promise for children. I later learned several of the participants there fully expected me to say Head Start. I could not possibly have said Head Start because at that time it did not have very good quality and there was little evidence that it merited the funding it received. Instead I told Richardson that I thought efforts in maternal and child health held the greatest unambiguous promise for improving children's lives. He asked if I could recommend a specific effort in this area that would do the most good. I targeted the dangers of lead in the environment and suggested that widespread lead abatement would greatly benefit children's health and well-being. Richardson was interested in anything that used volunteers, and between us we thought of a plan to have volunteers go into the inner cities and strip lead paint from children's homes. Richardson ran the possibility by his dollar-conscious assistant secretary for planning and evaluation. The cost was calculated to be in the billions of dollars, and that was the end of that idea.

I did not have to sell the merits of children's well-being to Elliot Richardson. His family background, which contained professionals who worked with children, and his own value system made him instinctively committed to bettering children's lives. His concern for and desire to help children became obvious to me at a large meeting of his key staff. By way of background, the sheer number of programs and agencies in HEW made Richardson's job extremely demanding. All of us who worked for him admired his intellect and leadership and had no doubts that he was up to doing the job. Nevertheless, his inner staff was constantly trying to reorganize HEW so that fewer individuals would report directly to the secretary. I went to a meeting one morning and on the blackboard was a new organizational chart for HEW. The diagram showed

I would no longer interact directly with Richardson, nor would my counterpart at the agency for the elderly. I was given no warning of this reorganization so I was more than a little shocked. I knew that the successes I had so far could never have taken place without the Secretary's close support. He was the one who out-argued others at the White House to keep Head Start in place after I received the 3-year phase-out plan. Our close personal relationship made him a constant ally in the efforts I was pursuing.

Richardson asked the attendees to study the chart and share their reactions. I studied it for about 30 seconds and raised my hand. I said something like, "Mr. Secretary, a society is judged by its treatment of two dependent groups— children and the elderly. I think it is important that the heads of the agencies representing children and the elderly have direct contact with you so you can give these two groups the special attention they need and that I am sure you feel they deserve." Richardson did not hesitate and, to the annoyance of his personal staff sitting next to him, he walked over to the blackboard and drew a straight line between both OCD and the agency for the elderly directly to the Office of the Secretary.

This meeting had great portent for the history of Head Start because I was able to recreate the program with the Secretary's advice and blessing. After I left Washington, the HEW managerial types had their way, and the head of OCD and its successor agency, the Administration on Children, Youth and Families, no longer had direct contact with the Secretary. My successors reported to an assistant secretary, who in turn answered to the Secretary. I continue to feel this has been a great loss to America's children. There is no strong lobby or political constituency that is effective in demanding solutions to the many problems that confront our children. The Children's Bureau, with its great tradition of advocacy for children, has its glory days behind it. Reorganization in 2006 created the Office of Head Start, which replaced the Head Start Bureau, that appears to be directly under an assistant secretary. With the increasing politicalization of government, though, I wonder whether an honest and effective advocate for children can exist with such close proximity to the powers within the executive branch. Indeed, shortly after I left, the decision was made to move the position of Chief of the Head Start Bureau from the civil service to a political appointee, suggesting that expertise on children's issues would take a back seat to political connections.

Confronting Issues Bigger than Head Start

The Westinghouse study and its negative conclusions were a huge threat to Head Start when I took over at OCD, but it was a threat I felt competent to address. After all, I was a scholar and research scientist, and critiquing empirical studies was something I did every day. Yet coming from a liberal, northern university, I was not at all prepared to deal with the racial and socio-economic tensions that were invading Head Start from the larger society. As an undergraduate, I aspired to be a statesman. When I joined government, I realized how difficult that career path would have been.

One societal problem that presented itself in Head Start really took me by surprise. HEW had a civil rights officer whose job was to assure that no program in the department trampled on the civil rights of any American. The first time I met him he accosted me with what he perceived to be a crisis: minority group members were overrepresented and Caucasians underrepresented among Head Start participants. He saw this imbalance as threatening the civil rights of Caucasian families who were not in the program in the numbers that they should have been. (Although blacks and Hispanics are more likely to live in poverty than Caucasians, the absolute number of Caucasians living in poverty is higher than the number who are minorities.) I explained to the official that I believed this state of affairs was the result of two factors. First, in 1970 there was little enthusiasm for integration by white southerners, so eligible white families did not want to enroll their children in Head Start. Second, many blacks held leadership roles in local Head Start centers, giving white families the perception that Head Start was meant for minorities. The fact that the Congressional Black Caucus made Head Start a favored program also gave Caucasians the view they did not belong there.

I could not take issue with the enforcement official. The numbers were the numbers. I essentially threw myself on his mercy and asked for time to address the situation. I pointed out that my first priority was to improve the quality of services because in 1970 it was an open question whether Head Start was a worthwhile program for either minority or white children. He decided to give me some breathing room, for which I will always be grateful. Unfortunately, to this day Head Start does not enroll Caucasian children in numbers consistent with the ethnic makeup of families living in poverty.

Without prodding from a civil rights officer, I tried to address the issue of socioeconomic segregation in Head Start. By law, the program was limited to serving children and families living below the poverty level. I always thought this was wrong. Philosopher and educator John Dewey argued that an important aspect of schooling is to prepare students to be effective citizens in a democracy. Democracy is about equality, which is not consistent with tracking children by race or wealth. This is why I convinced Head Start's planners to permit programs to open 10% of their slots to children from middle-class families (see Chapter 2). I felt intuitively that the optimum mix would be about 50–50 poor–not poor, but I could not muster agreement for even a 70–30 mix. I knew that a 90–10 ratio was not sufficient integration, but at least the 10% rule sent a signal that the planners were aware that a socioeconomically integrated setting was a better developmental setting for children than segregated schooling.

In several interviews I did shortly after arriving in Washington, I announced that I was going to try to integrate Head Start so that it did not segregate poor children from the rest of the world. I was not the only person in Washington who felt this way. Two members of Congress who were taking the lead on improving the lives of poor children were Walter Mondale in the Senate and John Brademas in the House. Both had introduced bills that would bring together child care, Head Start, and other federal children's programs into a unified child care system (discussed in Chapter 6). A key provision would allow nonpoor families to enroll their children for a fee based on their income. In essence, poor children would still receive Head Start services while all children of working parents would have access to the same high-quality child care services. The wisdom of this proposal was supported by the findings of Jim Coleman that poor children may do better developmentally when they are grouped with middle-class peers.

Interestingly, in the first summer of Head Start some program administrators decided on their own to integrate poor and middle-class children in Head Start classrooms. Later, the federal and regional offices ruled against this practice. One program that had to stop integration was run by early education expert Marilyn Segal in Hollywood, Florida. Her rationale was that "you can only break down stereotypes if you work and play together." She recalls "when we had the socioeconomic mix, all of the parents, including the upper-income parents, would visit the program and get close to the children" (Zigler and Muenchow, 1992, p. 127).

I had an ulterior motive for wanting to socioeconomically integrate Head Start. Poor parents do not have the political influence in Washington that wealthier parents wield. When polls of voters are conducted, education invariably appears as one of the top concerns. Middle-class parents crowd school board meetings, join PTOs, circulate petitions, and get out the vote when issues affecting their children's education arise. I doubt whether public schools would garner any attention if they were for poor children alone. In European countries, preschool programs are generally universal, available to all children. Therefore all segments of society have an investment in the program and protect it against detractors. Thus I believed that Head Start needed the political clout that could come from including the large middle-class constituency.

I telegraphed what I was going to do in a *Washington Post* interview. I said that middle- and lower-class children would both grow from integration, that it was wrong to send poor children to one set of centers and more affluent children to another, and that I would open Head Start to nonpoor children. Middle-class parents who wanted to enroll their children would pay tuition calibrated to the family's income. I was very confident while I awaited the reaction of both the Head Start and non-Head Start communities. I believed I could sell the idea to Secretary Richardson, who just about always agreed with me, and even to the White House, framing my proposal as consistent with Nixon's view that Head Start was not a finished product. I also thought that with Mondale and Brademas taking the lead, I could sell the plan to Congress.

My confidence turned out to be false. I was shocked to discover the strongest opposition to my integration proposal came from the Head Start community. Their reaction was essentially that Head Start was a program for poor people, and I was trying to take it away from them. They feared that middle-class parents would take over and poor parents would lose their voice. Soon an editorial in the *New York Times* accused me of being a reverse Robin Hood, taking from the poor to give to the rich. I wrote a letter of rebuttal, but the fact is I found no support for what I wanted to do anywhere in Washington. Although I had learned as a tough kid growing up in a slum never to back away from a fight, I decided to back away from this one. I simply had too much on my plate trying to run OCD, Head Start, and the Children's Bureau.

Decades later, I remain conflicted about whether I should have fought harder for socioeconomic integration. Consistent with my views in the 1970s, today we have considerable evidence that poor children profit from attending class with middle-class peers (Rusk, 2006). I smiled when I read a front-page article in the *New York Times* describing how the Raleigh, North Carolina school district found a great improvement in poor children's performance once they were integrated with middle-class children (Finder, 2005). Economists who argue in favor of financing preschool programs for poor children alone have seized upon findings that they benefit more from preschool than wealthier children. However, they ignore evidence that although the improvement is not as great, middle-class children's later school performance is also raised by preschool education. When we speak of the achievement gap in this country, we are typically referring to the gap between middle-class and poor children. Yet there is also a sizeable gap between middle-class and rich children. If we want all of our children to do well academically, school readiness programs should be open to everyone.

Although Head Start remains primarily an economically segregated program, some headway has been made. The 2007 reauthorization permits grantees to open up to 35% of their slots to families earning 100%–130% above the poverty line. Head Start is still mandated to serve the neediest families, so whether room is available to permit this expansion remains to be seen. Another push toward integration came about from welfare reform in 1996 that created a need among poor and near-poor families for full-day child care so parents could enter the workforce. Today approximately half of Head Start sites offer full-day, full-year services. By braiding Head Start dollars with federal and state dollars provided for child care, many Head Start centers are now serving children from over-income families. Fuller integration has taken place in a large national school reform movement called the Schools of the 21st Century, which consists of some 1,300 schools in 20 states. Of these school programs, 40% also include Head Start and manage to achieve the full integration of poor and more affluent children.

There is one area where my efforts to integrate Head Start by including underserved children were successful. Shortly after I arrived at OCD, Senator Walter Mondale asked me why Head Start did not serve children with disabilities. I had no satisfactory answer, so I asked Ray Collins to begin trying to mainstream handicapped children into Head Start classes. We found there was a general reluctance among local center employees to include children with handicaps. Their sense was that it was difficult enough to serve poor children and that it would be even harder to meet the greater needs of those with disabilities.

Head Start workers did not have much choice after 1972, however, when Congress mandated that at least 10% of the program's national enrollment consist of children with disabilities. The innovation we had begun toying with was about to become a requirement long before we were ready to go live nationwide. Our pilot became a nucleus of 14 resource access projects, funded jointly by Head Start and the Office of Education's Bureau of Education for the Handicapped. We provided training and technical assistance to Head Start teachers working with handicapped children and worked closely with professional associations to develop a series of training manuals. In just a few years, 13% of Head Start's population consisted of children with disabilities.

It must be remembered that, at this time, public schools had no legal obligation to serve children with handicaps. This changed in 1975 with Public Law 94-142 and its successor, the Individuals with Disabilities Education Act. This legislation did not require mainstreaming, as was the case in Head Start, but appropriate education in the least restrictive environment. Head Start did not have the option to place special needs children in classrooms by themselves. Collins recalls, "ducking the issue was not an option, so we simply stole the best of the state of the art, and it worked" (Zigler and Muenchow, 1992, p. 164).

Head Start's success serving disabled children eventually inspired the 1986 amendment to the Education of the Handicapped Act, Public Law 99-457. The law requires states to provide free appropriate education to children with handicaps between the ages of 3 and 5 and provides grants to those states that choose to serve younger children. (All states now do so.) The mandated services are clearly aligned with Head Start practices, requiring the full range of comprehensive services for handicapped children, individualized programming to meet their specific needs, and strong parental involvement.

Two groups among the poor who needed *separate* services were Native American children and the children of migrant workers. Integration in regular Head Start centers was not pursued because of the unique needs of these populations and their often isolated physical locations. Head Start developed a special division for these two groups combined, and the basic program was amended to better serve them. For example, children of migrant workers were enrolled before they reached preschool age and extended-day services were offered because their parents spent long hours in the fields. And, although Head Start has always incorporated cultural relevance, the significance of Native American customs and heritage to tribal members necessitated different practices and curricula. Over time the single division was divided into separate units for each of these two populations. The 2007 Head Start reauthorization contained special expansion provisions for the Indian and Migrant-Seasonal branches.

Introducing Quality Controls

When I visited the first Head Start classrooms in the summer of 1965, I saw exactly what one would expect of a program serving 560,000 children that had been planned just a few weeks earlier. Those visits convinced me that if Head Start was to achieve at least some of the optimistic goals that had been set for it, the quality of services had to be raised. When I took over the program 5 years later, there still were no uniform standards and no monitoring to determine what exactly the centers were providing. Each did its own thing, making Head Start more a collection of centers than a defined program.

I decided to gather some data on just how well Head Start centers were delivering the services outlined in the planning document. I charged Clennie Murphy and the regional offices to take the first official look at how each component of Head Start was being delivered at the local level. This preliminary analysis revealed that not a single component was being delivered in a satisfactory fashion. This proved to me that the Westinghouse study had been much too premature. The Head Start program was not nearly good enough in quality to merit an outcome evaluation. We also found that individual centers had different profiles in their accomplishments, each demonstrating its own strengths and weaknesses. Truthfully, as a behavioral scientist I would have great difficulty defending Head Start as it existed in 1970. OCD had to get cracking in standardizing the service model and improving quality.

Developing Performance Standards

Harley Frankel, who was responsible for Head Start from 1971 to 1975, described the program's status in 1970:

> For the most part Head Start was not in great shape in the early
> 1970s.... It had a good reputation but for the most part kids weren't
> getting good services. It was a great concept and in my view very
> important, but it didn't have meat on its bones.... Some people had
> picked up on it really well, but others hadn't. They were all very decent
> people, committed to kids, [but] many needed a more solid idea of what
> they should be doing. (Mills, 1998, p. 221)

Clearly, we needed some type of performance standards to give clarity to what exactly was required of a Head Start center to be a Head Start center.

I launched this project with Frankel and the very talented Ray Collins. Frankel recalls, "We did it not by sitting in Washington saying that this is what makes sense, but we went around the country and got a consensus on what it would take to make it a great program" (Mills, 1998, p. 221). We closely examined the practices of 150 of the largest individual Head Start programs in the nation. We then studied the 50 best of these programs to be sure we would recommend practices already in place and therefore achievable. Our framework was built on the vision of the planning committee. The program model dictated by the performance standards consisted of a quality, traditional classroom-based program in which educational activities are enriched by health services and parental involvement and supplemented by services supportive of family life. With the new standards, local centers had clear guidelines to follow for each component of the model. Of course, given Head Start's philosophy of local control, centers were allowed some leeway to accommodate conditions and preferences unique to their neighborhoods.

The best standards in the world are useless if they are not enforced. We put into place a quality control system that included an annual self-assessment by each Head Start program. External reviews of every program were to be conducted every 3 years by the regional offices. Because the regional offices were key in the management of Head Start, we had to upgrade their knowledge of what constituted a good Head Start program. For example, the education component never received the attention it deserved as the heart of an early childhood intervention program. Remnants of the Community Action philosophy stressed the importance of hiring parents and other untrained residents of the poor communities as teachers instead of qualified early childhood educators. Thus it is not surprising that in the early years, many Head Start sites did not even have a curriculum. The standards dictated that centers employ a curriculum, although they did not mandate a specific one. Early in OCD's existence, we conducted a comprehensive comparison of the value of a half dozen or so different curricula. We found that while no one curriculum was clearly superior, in all cases having a curriculum resulted in better outcomes for children than not having one. Even more important than the choice of curriculum was the ability of the staff to use it properly. We therefore needed an effective training and technical assistance infrastructure to support local sites in implementing the new standards. Jenni Klein, Head Start's early education director, made sure each regional office included a staff person knowledgeable about early childhood education.

The training and technical assistance system was of course not limited to the education component. All of the program components needed upgrading. We sought to reinforce the regional offices with the staff capability to implement the standards in all service areas. In addition to this in-house training, we made money available to Head Start personnel to afford the education necessary to upgrade their skills. This was in total opposition to the Community Action ideology of respecting the strengths poor people already had. By professionalizing nonprofessionals, we hoped to equip them with new skills so they could carry out the performance standards. We were realistic and did not expect all of this to be done overnight. Although the standards were ready by late 1972 or early 1973, Head Start centers did not legally have to comply with them until 1975. I did not remain in Washington that long, but the effort was continued by my successor and deputy, Saul Rosoff and Harley Frankel.

It is fair to say that the performance standards ended the program that had existed since 1965 and created a new Head Start model that exists to this day. Mills observes that Head Start in its previous form was alive but very much at risk by 1970. "Once the performance standards had been developed, Zigler went to his boss at HEW, Secretary Elliot Richardson, and laid out what had been done." She quotes Frankel's recollection that "Richardson really trusted Ed, and that was crucial.... Nixon's people wanted to make government work, but they wanted to make government work differently" (Mills,

1998, p. 222). The performance standards did make Head Start work differently. This gave the Nixon Administration a stake in a program created under a predecessor.

The standards were not perfect, but at least they made Head Start a relatively uniform program instead of thousands of different programs operating under the Head Start umbrella. The job of quality improvement is a continuous one, and my hope was that the performance standards would evolve as new knowledge came to light, best practices were upgraded, and the needs of the target population changed over time. Alas, revisions were slow to arrive. It is sad to point out that the Program Performance Standards written in the early 1970s remained in force until they were finally updated in 1998 during the Clinton administration. The amendments addressed oversights in the original standards such as mandating that curricula be *written* instead of just being required. They also included for the first time programs serving children from birth to 3 years.

Management Issues

Why had Head Start fallen into such a sorry state between its birth in 1965 and 1970? Two insiders very close to Head Start in the early days, Carolyn Harmon and Ed Hanley (1997), argue that the culprit was an inadequate management system. Head Start employed a "recipient-participant model," whereas most federal programs employed the "classical accountability model" of management. The classical model emphasizes uniform program design and delivery systems, a structure that lends itself to standard techniques of evaluating success. In the recipient-participant model, the only accountability to the federal government is the satisfaction of grantees and the recipients of the services. As long as local Head Start administrators and participants were satisfied, the program had demonstrated accountability. Harmon and Hanley explain that this model was a barrier to efforts to standardize practices across Head Start centers. They also point out the inevitability of introducing a concrete form of program accountability to justify continued federal support from the Office of Management and Budget and even the friendliest Congress. They state, "from the beginning [the recipient-participant model] had its detractors within the career civil service, a minority of the Congress, most state, county, and municipal governments, and much of the nonrecipient public, who held the classical view" (p. 385). They also note that the official view of the new Nixon administration shifted toward the classical model. This meant that changes in Head Start administration had to be made quickly if the program was to survive.

Having performance standards and some mechanisms to be sure they were being followed were only first steps in implementing a new model of accountability. With roots in Community Action, Head Start could not easily give up its federal-to-local management design. Unquestionably there is much stronger financial oversight in the accountability model, where funds go from the federal government to the states. Each state then gives the money to local sites and is responsible for monitoring them. The states are monitored by the feds. Head Start funds instead go directly from the federal government to local grantees. Oversight of the grantees is the responsibility of the 10 regional offices. However, as originally conceptualized these regional offices were not viewed as watchdogs but as partners with the local sites, helping them to solve problems and function smoothly.

They were not the only federal officials who appeared to be too lenient with their flock. A short time into my stewardship of Head Start, a financial problem was brought to my attention from the regional office level that made me furious. A local Head Start director (who happened to be a black minister) had been given funds to purchase lumber to renovate his Head Start center. Instead he appropriated the lumber and built a house for himself. I had to decide what the Head Start Bureau's reaction to this malfeasance would be. In the normal world, when thievery takes place the police are called, and the criminal justice system runs its course. I was very angry and wanted to pursue the most severe course of action possible. I myself could not take any action but had to discuss the issue with HEW's chief attorney, who was the one who would conduct whatever response HEW wished to pursue.

I charged into the lead attorney's office and exclaimed that I wanted the man arrested, punished, and made an example for others in the Head Start community. I was rather agitated, but my colleague was anything but. He begged me to calm down, explaining that the situation was actually routine and unimportant. He then gave me a tutorial on the history of graft in government. He pointed out that when immigrant groups of any ethnicity finally achieved some political power, they invariably engaged in patronage and graft. They saw this as nothing more than their legitimate right after having suffered hardships and discrimination. He pointed out that for the first time African Americans had some control over government funds and were behaving in the same manner as other ethnic groups at that moment in their histories.

What was left unsaid, but certainly implied, was that making a big hubbub over a little lumber would put Head Start in a bad light on the Hill, and we certainly did not want this image of Head Start to make the news. After his rather lengthy discourse, this head of the HEW legal office asked me,

"What do you really want to do to this man?" It was clear to me that the right answer to this little test was "nothing." However, this was more than citizen Ed Zigler could tolerate, so I asked if maybe we could just get the lumber back. He guided that I was much too busy with major issues to worry myself about such a small degree of malfeasance. To this day I do not know exactly what course of action HEW pursued, but I do know the incident was never publicized or even leaked to Congress. I am sure hundreds of such events have occurred in Head Start over the years, just as they have in every other federal program.

These scandals sometimes make the local papers and someone brings them to the attention of the top layers of Head Start's management. A crime involving millions of dollars occurred in Denver, which is the home of one of the 10 regional offices. The assistant secretary of HEW responsible for Head Start at that time, Olivia Golden, went to Denver herself to resolve the blatant criminality there. However, nothing much was heard of the incident in Congress. It was just one of many Head Start programs that lost their grants during the Clinton years. The Clinton Administration was aggressive in policing Head Start centers, revoking more grants than the number rescinded in all of Head Start's prior history. Although it was implied that these programs did not measure up to the performance standards and were terminated because of poor quality, the fact is that many of these closures were due to missing or misappropriated funds. When serious malfeasance is discovered, the standard procedure is to give the grantee the choice between returning the stolen money or giving up the grant without further appeal. Unsurprisingly, the common choice is to let the grant be transferred to a new grantee.

During the George W. Bush years, a case of blatant thievery at the Head Start program in Kansas City, MO, was the subject of detailed reporting by the *Kansas City Star* and was actually brought to the attention of members of Congress by the Republican senator from neighboring Kansas. The program was run by a nationally recognized director with a reputation for mounting first-rate Head Start centers. I had a déjà vu moment when I heard Rep. George Miller's response to the news. He asked the simple question, "Why didn't someone just call the police?"

Why did the Kansas City scandal come to light in Washington, while so many earlier ones did not? I think the answer lies in the George W. Bush Administration's attitude toward Head Start. There is a general view in the Head Start community, which the authors share, that this President Bush disliked Head Start and did everything in his power to end the program in its current form. (George W. Bush's actions against Head Start will be discussed in

Chapter 12.) Thus, rather than conceal transgressions, the Bush people were pleased to have Head Start's shortcomings trumpeted in Washington.

This approach backfired when a member of the administration itself was implicated in questionable financial activities in Head Start. At the time, the Chief of the Head Start Bureau was Windy Hill. She was at the forefront of efforts to publicize "cases of financial mismanagement, in what providers describe as a campaign to undermine public support for them" (Schemo, 2004). Prior to assuming her job in Washington, Hill was director of a large Head Start program in Texas. An internal audit prompted by the National Head Start Association revealed that she had mismanaged the program and improperly spent tens of thousands of dollars in vacation pay and bonuses for herself and others. After a formal federal investigation, Hill was allowed to quietly resign from her federal post and no criminal charges were filed.

Although financial malfeasance in Head Start over the years has been higher than it should be, it certainly is the exception and not the rule. Head Start is a multibillion dollar program with over 1,600 grantees and nearly 19,000 centers, so it would be naive to think the government can account for every single dollar. Further, we do not know how much mishandling of funds is due to poor management rather than criminality. For the most part, Head Start directors come from disciplines like early education, social work, or other human services. They are not necessarily well-versed in accounting and administrative practices. Being a Head Start director today is very much like running a small business with a sizable payroll. One solution some programs have tried is to hire a for-profit company to take over formal management of the grant so the director can concentrate on program services. Better administration can result in cutting costs to the degree that these savings cover the price of the contract.

Head Start management was not nearly this sophisticated when I took over in 1970. The tens of millions of dollars freely and hurriedly dispensed to the first Head Start grantees drew a strange mixture of takers. The story told emphasizes that Head Start attracted wonderfully idealistic and dedicated individuals from communities across the nation. The untold story is that it also attracted street hustlers and opportunists who viewed Head Start money as a source for personal gain. Truthfully, most of the early grantees had absolutely no experience running a program of any size and no idea they were accountable to taxpayers for the money they received. As for the hustlers, I had to accept that it is next to impossible to have a huge federal program totally devoid of graft and theft. Publicly demanding punishment and restitution could only have stirred a general aversion to giving the program any more taxpayer dollars.

Turning Head Start into a National Laboratory

At OCD the changes I was making to Head Start were referred to as the improvement and innovation agenda. The need to improve Head Start was obvious, but why innovation? The impetus for my decision to experiment came from many sources. When Head Start began, it had the excitement and fervor that comes with a brand new endeavor. After it had been operating for a few years, complacency set in. For example, I never considered Head Start the one perfect model to serve poor children and their families, nor did I think that OCD had superior wisdom to determine what to do differently. I thought that those in the trenches would have some good ideas about strengthening services, filling service gaps, or new approaches to doing what we were trying to do. Thus an invitation was sent to all Head Start centers to apply to add their own innovative program to the basic Head Start protocol. All they had to do was send the national office a description and the theoretical rationale that convinced them the effort was worth trying. The national office would then review the plans and fund those that appeared promising. At OCD we referred to these potential projects as Project X. Alas, with all the new demands being made on them for program improvement, it is unsurprising that the local personnel did not rush to put more work on themselves by undertaking new projects.

There were many other reasons for the innovation effort. One was an article that had a great impression on me by Donald Campbell (1969) titled, "Reforms as Experiments." Campbell's idea was to try out programs without falling in love with them, evaluate them, and discard what did not work and refine and expand what did. Using Campbell's "experimenting society" as our methodological map, every new program we mounted had a built-in evaluation plan to determine its efficacy. An even more important impetus came from President Nixon. I was quickly learning how to play the political game, and I seized upon Nixon's remarks that he wanted Head Start to be an experimental program rather than an operational one. It was important for the Nixon administration to see Head Start as something new and not the Head Start they had inherited from the opposing political party. Further, my immediate boss, Elliot Richardson, was himself a creative thinker. He believed in experimentation and was willing to attempt innovations that might end up as worthwhile efforts and reflect well on his department. Richardson controlled a budget that was larger than the expenditures of many countries, so he could always find funds here or there to support ideas he liked.

In addition to having a supportive boss, I was incredibly lucky to have a first-rate manager. Ray Collins had an uncanny ability to take a rough idea and in a short time turn it into a workable program. My greatest strength is in generating ideas, but my greatest weakness is in knowing how to move them from my head to a real program on the ground. Collins was a genius at this. We established a Head Start research and development unit at OCD, and I placed him in charge of the program development division with a budget of $12 million and a staff of about 25. My vision was for the unit to spawn a collection of undertakings that would earmark Head Start as a national laboratory attempting a variety of solutions to the difficulties confronting children in poverty.

Building Out

Health Start, which was my failed attempt to ring value from the summer programs, was not the first experimental effort made under the Head Start banner. Two earlier efforts had been mounted well before OCD came into being. The first was Head Start's Parent and Child Centers (PCCs), which offered comprehensive health and education services to low-income families with children under the age of 3 years. The program began in 1968 as a result of recommendations made in 1966 by two committees, HEW's Task Force on Early Childhood Development and the White House Task Force on Early Childhood. These groups concluded that by the time a poor child reaches age 3, it could be too late to overcome the intellectual and emotional damage already inflicted by being reared in poverty. Whereas the basic Head Start preschool program could be considered remedial, the PCC concept was seen as preventative. Another rationale was that access to medical and developmental services early in life could lead to the identification and treatment of handicapping conditions before they become irreversible.

When Head Start was moved from OEO to HEW, the PCCs were moved too. However, three of these centers were kept at OEO where they were renamed Parent and Child Development Centers and became part of an intensive research and evaluation program. The center in Houston (headed by Dale Johnson) in particular received a great deal of visibility as a result of groundbreaking research demonstrating the significance of developmental processes in infants and the important role of parents in child development. I thought these PCD centers were quite synergistic with the innovation effort OCD was mounting, so I worked behind the scenes to get them back. My efforts bore fruit after I left Washington, and these three centers were eventually reunited with the Parent and Child Centers at OCD.

The second pre-OCD innovative effort was Project Follow Through, which was conceptualized at OEO but was conducted by the Office of Education in

HEW. Shortly after the birth of Head Start there was a growing realization that a quick intervention in the days before formal schooling begins is not enough to thwart the developmental harm caused by poverty. The inoculation view began to give way to a more realistic appraisal of how much is necessary to put and keep a child on an upward growth trajectory. Similar to the case of Head Start, a planning committee was established to develop an extended program of Head Start-like services. The committee was chaired by Gordon Klopf, the Dean of Bank Street College, and contained some members of the original Head Start planning committee, including Bronfenbrenner and me. Our plan was simple and direct. Extend the comprehensive services of Head Start into the early years of elementary school. The idea was to solidify the gains made in Head Start and build a solid foundation for later learning.

Although there was complete unanimity on the potential of this approach, Follow Through as implemented had no resemblance to our carefully drawn plan (Doernberger and Zigler, 1993). By this time the Vietnam War was draining federal coffers, so there was simply not enough money to support the program we had envisioned. Instead of continuing health, educational, parent participation, and support services, Follow Through became little more than a comparison of 13 different curricula in the early years of school. Other than refining the curriculum models involved, the program had little value. No consensus was ever reached on which curriculum is best. For some reason Congress continued funding this program long after there was any hope that it would provide the nation with much useful information. One consolation is that today we have sound evidence that preschool followed by a dovetailed program in the early grades results in a better outcome than preschool alone (Reynolds, 2003), which of course was the original intent of Follow Through.

We did not give up on the concept of extended services. When it became obvious that Follow Through would not amount to much, I conceptualized Project Developmental Continuity (PDC). I did not stay in Washington long enough to launch the program. It was initiated in 1974 by my deputy director Saul Rosoff, who took over as acting director when I returned to Yale. Similar to the Follow Through plan that was never realized, the purpose of PDC was to offer continuous educational and other Head Start services to children throughout the first 3 years of primary school. The most important objective was to develop a sequential and continuous program for children with the move from Head Start to the primary grades. A simultaneous objective was to ease the transition from preschool to formal schooling. Such major life transitions can be difficult for families, particularly poor Head Start families. For example, many Head Start parents find that public schools are not nearly as welcoming to parent involvement as Head Start. In the PDC effort, the school was considered the basic unit of change.

Probably OCD's most ambitious effort was the Child and Family Resource Program (CFRP), which combined the concepts of targeting very young children, preschoolers, and children transitioning to elementary school. This program offered comprehensive services to children and families from the prenatal period through 8 years of age. Eleven demonstration sites were funded in 1973, and they continued to exist for many years. I conceptualized this program not only because of my belief in developmental continuity but because of my concern about the rigidity of the basic Head Start program, which demanded that families fit themselves to the Head Start model regardless of their individual needs. There is great variability among families living below the poverty line, but Head Start operated as a "one size fits all" program. As described by Valentine, "the primary goal of the CFRP [was] to provide and integrate the delivery of comprehensive services to families and children, on an individualized basis, throughout early childhood" (1997, p. 354). Of special importance is the fact that families enrolled in CFRPs rather than children. A family needs assessment was made for each family and each child, and the staff coordinated the necessary services to meet their identified needs. The current family support movement in America can be traced back to CFRP.

Other Ideas

Full descriptions of OCD's early innovative efforts are offered by Valentine (1997) and Henrich (2004). Here I will dwell on several that together illustrate the multiple directions I was pursuing in my quest to renew Head Start. One new program called Home Start proved successful and remains part of Head Start offerings today. Both Bronfenbrenner and I were strong believers in the central role of parents in a child's development. The influence of parents goes beyond the critical nature of their relationship and interactions with the child. In the early years of life, the parent determines the child's daily environment and the majority of his or her experiences. Thus in Home Start the guiding principle is that parents are the first major educators of their children, and they are encouraged to create various enriching experiences. Like Head Start, Home Start offered health and social services to the children and families enrolled. The key to the operation of the program was the home visitor, usually a community resident who had training in the principles of child development and the program goals.

Research showed Home Start to be as effective in promoting developmental processes as the Head Start center-based program. The one difference was that children in center-based programs received more preventative health care. Although the Home Start demonstration ended in 1975, six training centers were established to disseminate the model to Head Start centers that wanted to incorporate a home-based option. Currently about 48,000 children participate in home-based services. In the field of early childhood intervention, Home Start proved to be a historic event in that it was one of the first programs to employ home visiting as a mechanism to enhance child development.

Another innovative effort, Education for Parenthood, was probably the most controversial program initiated by OCD. The purpose struck me as innocuous enough, namely to teach the fundamentals of child development to teenagers before they became parents. We developed a curriculum for high school students to learn about the nature of children's growth and developmental stages not only to help them be more informed parents when that day arrived, but to lessen the likelihood of child abuse. Many behaviors children engage in precipitate abuse because adults do not understand the reasons behind them. For example, an infant who repeatedly drops a rattle on the floor is not misbehaving but is engaging in a knowledge-building activity Piaget called object constancy—awareness that an object continues to exist when it is out of sight. Abuse also arises from expecting too much from a child at a given stage of growth, like wanting a child in the "terrible twos" to be quiet and cooperative or trying to toilet train a 6-month-old. We also thought the program might help prevent teen pregnancy, which was an immense problem at that time. The course was offered to both boys and girls, and part of the training was actually working with young children in nurseries, child care centers, and Head Start.

The curriculum was developed by the Education Development Corporation in Massachusetts, who also did an evaluation and found many positive outcomes. Nevertheless, while the program spread to 3,000 schools and cost very little, it became a target of criticism. Some saw it as yet another infringement by the government into private family life. Another critic charged that, to save money, I intended to substitute Education for Parenthood with Head Start, which was absurd. Although this program did not outlive my years in Washington, it got the ball rolling. Today parent education courses are offered in many high schools.

The costs of my improvement and innovation efforts did leave me with almost no discretionary funds. I could not hope for an increase because federal funds were tight. In fact, some decision makers were seeking to replace Head Start with something far less costly. Sid Marland, commissioner of the Office of Education in HEW, called together a meeting of the department's power structure. Many participants were enamored with the TV program Sesame

Street and dwelled on the fact that it was so inexpensive: "We can get 'Sesame Street' to reach poor kids by spending sixty-five cents per child. . . . Why should we spend over a thousand dollars per child on Head Start?" (Zigler and Muenchow, 1992, p. 165). They wanted me to help fund Sesame Street out of the Head Start budget. I told them that as much as I liked the program, I had no money to spare. The group was not about to take "no" for an answer. John Veneman (the undersecretary) could have ordered me to spend my funds on Sesame Street, but I guess he knew I would appeal his decision to Elliot Richardson. As the pressure on me mounted, I said I would give Head Start money to Sesame Street if they could answer one question: "How long would a poor child have to watch Sesame Street to get his or her teeth fixed?" With this question they dropped the issue. History now shows that both Head Start and Sesame Street have prospered and remain forces helping children learn and grow.

The Child Development Associate

The Child Development Associate (CDA) credential was one OCD innovation that has had great impact and a long life. CDAs acquire competence in understanding and meeting children's developmental needs through training and practical experience. The idea for the program grew out of the pragmatic problem that Head Start needed highly qualified teachers but there was not enough money to hire them. Head Start's roots in Community Action, which dictated hiring poor parents and community members, addicted congressional budget writers to cheap labor. Although Head Start did employ many college-trained teachers, the majority of the staff were poor and had children to support, so the traditional college training was not a realistic option. At the same time, I was becoming more and more interested in the child care crisis. As Nixon's Family Assistance Plan was being drafted, it was apparent there would be a great need for qualified caregivers to work at child care centers as mothers left welfare for employment. Thus the nation needed a large cadre of trained entry-level assistant teachers in Head Start as well as trained caregivers in child care settings who were knowledgeable but at the same time affordable. There had to be a way for personnel to improve their skills in working with children outside of the costly higher education system.

I began thinking seriously about a competency-based child care credential after a conversation with Bettye Johnson, a friend who was an extremely well-qualified early childhood educator. Bettye was the wife of the governor of American Samoa and decided to run Head Start-like programs on the island. She had a single assistant who was a native Samoan and had some training in teaching young children. They advertised on television for people who wanted to take a couple of weeks of training in child development. The trainees then returned to their villages and set up the programs. Johnson and her assistant carefully observed the new teachers in the classroom and then decided which ones would be hired. I asked Bettye how she could tell from this short observation who was qualified and who was not. We were sitting side by side on a couch, and she nudged me in the side with her elbow and said, "Oh Ed, you know."

She made me realize that some people really do have a way with children and that these are the people we needed to work in Head Start and child care centers. The problem was how to capture this talent in some verifiable way. I initially ran my thoughts by Jenni Klein, Head Start's national education director. Her reaction was positive. She thought that having more competent teachers was essential to our goal of improving Head Start quality. Her view was that no matter how many performance standards were established, change could not come around by edict. If Head Start staff were going to implement the standards, they would have to understand and believe in them. She felt the only way that would happen was through training. She also agreed with my view that we mount a new form of training. At the time the only education available was a college degree. Klein's hope was that CDA trainees would learn under a master teacher in early childhood settings.

Establishing the CDA required the work of many people. First we had to convince the reluctant early childhood education establishment that competency-based training was valuable. These people had fought for years to create bachelor degree programs in early childhood education and thus saw the CDA as undercutting what they had tried for so long to achieve. Fortunately, not all of these professionals felt that way. I remember a conversation with Marilyn Smith, Executive Director of the National Association for the Education of Young Children (NAEYC), who served as chair of CDA's board after we got the program going. She questioned whether a BA in early childhood education adequately prepared a student to be a first-rate preschool teacher. Smith thought that getting a BA should be followed by earning a CDA to assure that the individual had the competencies essential to good performance as an early childhood educator. I did not pursue this because I knew early childhood professionals would never accept such an idea, although I did agree with it.

In January 1971, OCD sponsored a meeting to address the need for qualified personnel in Head Start and other early childhood programs. The meeting was chaired by my friend Barbara Biber, a leader in the early childhood education field. We decided on the competencies needed to work with young children, the type of training to build these skills, and ways to measure them.

Marilyn Smith led the feasibility study on how to administer the CDA credential. I still remember vividly how dedicated these individuals were to making the CDA a reality.

The program was first administered and the credential awarded by a consortium of 10 leading national organizations that formed field evaluation teams to assess each candidate's competency. With the passage of time, colleges became more involved in the process, particularly community colleges. Part of the reason is that Head Start staff who were studying for the CDA felt they should receive college credit for their efforts. Today awarding CDAs is the task of the Council for Professional Recognition, which has close ties to the Office of Head Start and NAEYC. More than 200,000 CDAs have been awarded, and applications now number over 15,000 each year as the demand for trained child care staff increases (Council, 2008). The CDA has certainly come of age, as can be seen in the fact that 49 states now recognize the credential in their state child care licensing requirements. The CDA also received the endorsement of Congress. The Head Start Expansion and Improvement Act of 1990 mandated that by 1994 every Head Start classroom of 20 children must have one teacher with at least a CDA or an associate's degree in early childhood education. Actually neither Jenni nor I thought of the CDA as the ultimate goal for training but rather as a first step on a career ladder. We certainly never thought that the CDA would qualify someone to be a lead teacher in a Head Start classroom—an assistant teacher perhaps. Unfortunately, there were so many Head Start teachers with no formal qualifications that the CDA represented a superior level of training. Although Congress has frequently mandated that increasing percentages of Head Start teachers have bachelor's degrees, the money to pay BAs a competitive wage has not materialized so they are often wooed to public school positions. But progress has been made, and over 70% of Head Start teachers have at least an associate's degree in early childhood education (Office of Head Start, 2007).

Policy Changes

Parent Participation

Head Start's planners established that parent involvement was a key objective. However, the concept had no clear meaning. To some it meant allowing parents complete control over Head Start, whereas to others it meant hiring parents as staff. The meaning of parent participation in Head Start as we know it was developed by Bessie Draper, who joined the national Head Start staff in 1966. When Draper realized that parent involvement had not been defined in federal rule or policy, she asked Jule Sugarman, her boss, for direction. He replied, "If we knew what parent involvement should be, we wouldn't need you" (Zigler and Muenchow, 1992, p. 104). In her quest for a workable definition, Draper examined the Economic Opportunity Act of 1964, where she found only the vague phrase, "maximum feasible participation of the poor." She interpreted this to mean parents should be full partners in the design and delivery of services. I liked Draper's interpretation since it meant that parents were neither in charge nor were they underlings. Rather, they were part of the team.

When Draper began her job, parent involvement was not a separate component of Head Start but was a division of social services. The parent component thus suffered the same fate as the mental health component in that there was no strong leader in charge of that piece. She found the attitude of her supervisors in the social services department toward poor parents as patronizing, not unlike the education establishment's treatment of parents in those days. She also found a sense that since parent involvement stretched throughout the whole program, no dedicated staff for the theme was necessary. Draper correctly felt that if parent involvement was everybody's job, it would be nobody's job. Thus she placed parent specialists at every level of the Head Start program, from the national office to the 10 regional offices to individual centers.

In charting what she knew to be new territory, Draper's first step in defining parent participation was to assemble a group of consultants from a broad array of disciplines including sociologists, educators, and psychologists. She carefully selected these experts so they represented all the ethnic backgrounds of the families Head Start was serving. This committee did yeoman's work and provided thorough recommendations that Draper then used to devise a parent involvement component. In 1967 she wrote into the Head Start policy manual four basic factors of parent involvement: (1) participation in the decision-making process about the nature and operation of the program; (2) participation in the classroom as paid employees, volunteers, and observers; (3) receiving home visits from Head Start staff; and (4) opportunities to attend parent educational activities. Draper was well aware of the need for professional staff if Head Start was to become a quality program. Thus, in this first manual she mandated that parents be given preference for employment as *non*professionals in Head Start.

Draper wove in roles for parents at various levels of the Head Start hierarchy. There was to be a parent advisory committee at the center level, a policy advisory council at the grantee level, and a policy advisory committee at the national level. Half of the members were to be parents of Head Start children, with the others representing professionals and community organizations concerned with children. The policy manual gave parents on the advisory group the right to participate in program governance but not the power to approve staff selection. Under Draper's direction, the parent involvement policy evolved toward an approach that helped parents gain the organizational skills necessary to be full partners with the staff in running the program and in choosing the kind of educational programs they wanted. (For a more complete description of Draper's groundbreaking work, see Zigler and Muenchow, 1992.)

The confusing overlap between Head Start and the Community Action Program caused Draper grief, just as it did for me. For example, she discovered that not all Head Start "parents" on the advisory committees really had children in the program but were social activists using Head Start as a launching pad. After I forbade the use of Head Start funds for community action purposes, I decided that federal policy should give parents clear authority to determine the nature of local programs. I asked Draper to develop a policy to enforce the decision-making role of parents. A key change in the new parent involvement policy was that half the seats on the policy councils be reserved for parents of Head Start children, rather than local residents in general. Kuntz writes, "This rule ensured that the councils were not filled with activists who, in Zigler's view, cared more about systemic change than the opportunities provided to . . . young children. Perhaps more than any other change, this one signaled that Head Start would focus on specific children rather than broader communities" (1998, p. 29).

Employing Draper's plan, we issued the controversial 70.2 policy mandate that for the first time spelled out the responsibilities of the policy councils at the center, delegate, and grantee agency levels. Of great importance is that the name of the policy-setting groups was officially changed from policy advisory council to policy council. The council was specifically given the power to approve hiring decisions as well as the program budget. To avoid putting parents in over their heads, we funded training in how to function on the policy councils.

As soon as we issued the new parent involvement policy, my phone began ringing off the hook. Many Head Start grantees, particularly those in public school settings, threatened to abandon the program if I insisted on giving parents so much authority. I pointed out the loss this would mean for their communities but stated the policy would stand. We did de-fund Head Start programs in Kansas City and Omaha because they refused to comply with the new policy. We threatened to de-fund some others which then somehow found a way to comply. I felt this new policy reflected the planners' intention that Head Start has as much to do with the development of parents as it does with children. With Bronfenbrenner and many others, I believed that parents are the most important determinate of the child's growth trajectory. If children are to succeed, they must not think that because they are poor they are incompetent. A positive self-image is encouraged when the child has parents who themselves feel effective.

Given the controversy over my parent policy, and always being the empiricist willing to change my views if hard evidence contradicts them, I commissioned what we called the MIDCO study. The findings showed a direct relation between children's progress in Head Start and the degree to which parents participated in the program. This was just a correlation, so what is cause and what is effect is hard to surmise. I can envision a circular effect in which parents improve the quality of their own behavior, which inspires children to improve their behavior, and with that improvement the parent is inspired to become more involved with the child's program.

It has been interesting to watch the evolution of the education establishment's view of parent involvement since OCD issued 70.2, when educators were so opposed to giving parents any authority. Not even a generation later, one goal of the Educate America Act was more parental involvement in schools. In response to mounting evidence of the value of parent involvement, New York City placed a parent coordinator in each and every city school. Henrich and Blackman-Jones (2006) reviewed the research and concluded that for poor and probably more affluent families, parent involvement in the schools leads to better educational outcomes. Parents simply are too important in children's lives for educators not to get them involved in the educational process.

Redefining Head Start's Goal

Most of the early evaluations of Head Start, including the Westinghouse study, used either IQ change or improvements in IQ-related measures to assess the program's benefits. Yet no one from the planning committee forward had ever designated IQ gains as the purpose of Head Start. The problem is the planning document simply had too many goals and no concise statement of the overall point. Thus the IQ goal was essentially forced on Head Start by the early childhood research community. Those friendly to Head Start saw no reason not to use findings of IQ increases because they were numerous, striking, and desirable. When the Westinghouse study showed these instant cognitive gains were transient, people were again left wondering about what is the point of Head Start.

It was becoming obvious to me that Head Start needed a clear goal statement to replace the long list of objectives provided by the planners. I knew in my heart that we were hoping to prepare children for school physically, academ- ically, socially, and emotionally. In other words, we were trying to boost their social competence, or everyday functioning in all areas relevant to successful schooling. In the federal government, an agency head can make a decision and it automatically becomes an agency policy. I therefore simply announced that the goal of Head Start was to improve children's social competence. Lo and behold this immediately became the official goal incorporated in all Head Start materials. Although the meaning of the term was fairly clear in my mind, it needed a good definition and ways to measure it.

Thus began the expenditure of several million dollars to delineate social competence, money that was essentially wasted. Contracts were given to the Educational Testing Service and then to Mediax to provide the government with a prescribed set of measures that could be used to quantify a child's social competence (Raver and Zigler, 1991). I attended the national conference of noted scholars at the first ETS effort. Here I learned that too many academics have no idea what the government needs to carry on its work. If you cannot tell a congressperson in 5 minutes what you are measuring, don't bother. Over this 2- or 3-day meeting, the participants came up with so many measures of social compe- tence that a child would be grown and married before we could complete all the testing required. Mediax made a second attempt that narrowed the possibilities somewhat but still delivered no answer. The Reagan administration eventually cancelled most of the project, which was by then devoted to creating assessment tools. The only part left standing was the one developing measures of cognitive improvement, which is exactly where we started.

Meanwhile, the Head Start community was happy working with social competence as the program goal because it made sense despite the lack of measurement. With the wisdom of hindsight, I should have just put into words my sense of what social competence is when I declared it to be Head Start's goal. Then I could have designated a short number of assessment instruments. I did not do this until I returned to Yale. My colleague Penelope Trickett and I wrote a paper in which we defined social competence as having two compo- nents: (1) the child's ability to meet age-appropriate social expectations, and (2) the child's self-actualization (Zigler and Trickett, 1978). We narrowed the elements of social competence to four features, all of which were amenable to measurement. These are the child's health, cognitive ability, achievements, and social and emotional functioning. Interestingly, when George H. W. Bush and the nation's 50 governors adopted national educational goals, the first was school readiness. A technical workgroup for Goal 1 provided a five-factor definition of school readiness similar to our four-factor definition of social competence. In 1998 Congress legislated the official goal of Head Start as school readiness. Although social competence is a much broader concept than school readiness, at the age of 5 the two concepts are really the same (Zigler et al., 2007).

All of my grand plans to refresh Head Start, structure the program better, experiment a little, clean up bad habits, and most importantly, build quality, could never be accomplished during my short stay at OCD. My capable successors, Saul Rosoff and Harley Frankel, took over the mission and were still implementing some of my ideas years after I left Washington. Truthfully, the improvements in Head Start I initiated and the innovations I conceptualized would have fizzled out without these capable civil servants.

The one piece of the new Head Start I wish I could have moved along faster was research and evaluation. It is one thing to show people that a program is deserving by lavishing it with intensive attention as we were doing. It is quite another to prove the program's worth with sound empirical data. The Westinghouse study tainted Head Start in many people's minds, and the best way to counteract the damage was with better research. Good studies take time to design and conduct, but I needed evidence right now to show if Head Start had any benefits. So in addition to all the ways I was changing the program, I was also trying to build a scientific base to establish Head Start's credibility. This thrust is the topic of Chapter 7.

6

The Failed Union of Head Start and Child Care

Some independent events that were to become interrelated during the late 1960s and early 1970s came within a breath of expanding and joining Head Start to a national child care system. This system would have been a giant leap toward meeting the child care needs not only of poor children but of all children of working parents in America. Many Head Start advocates were not particularly enthusiastic about the program becoming a relatively small part of a much larger combined effort, and they were unhappy with the idea of allowing wealthier parents to join and potentially wrest control from the poor families Head Start had been created to serve. I was fighting to keep Head Start alive after the Westinghouse study and the haunting memories of the Nixon administration's plan to phase out the program. My own view was that Head Start would have a better chance of survival if it were part of a larger system that had a broader and politically stronger constituency. Further, my research and scholarship on child care made me aware of how important good care is to every child's development, school readiness, and family life. Saving Head Start and providing access to high-quality child care at the same time seemed like an ideal plan of action to me.

The time was right. During the 1960s the United States was undergoing a rapid change in the demographics of family life. The stereotype of the typical family in the 1950s, with the father as the breadwinner and the mother taking care of the children and home, was evaporating. American women were increasingly joining the out-of-home workforce, and young children were increasingly being cared for in out-of-home settings. Although many attribute this change to the impact of the women's movement, this demographic shift was more likely driven by economics rather than ideology. The jobs that permitted a father to earn enough to support a family comfortably were steadily decreasing in number. Thus both spouses often found it necessary to work to generate enough income to sustain what has over the years become the American way of life. Child care was becoming an essential service to the two-earner family.

Adding to the growing need for child care was a second demographic shift, namely a huge increase in the number of single-parent, female-headed families. Prior to major welfare reform in 1996, single mothers were given money through Aid to Families with Dependent Children (AFDC) to help support themselves and their children. This was in keeping with the American ethos that revered motherhood and the child-rearing role. However, this rationale for welfare became pretty untenable once middle-class mothers began to leave their home jobs for paid employment. Once that happened, the days of AFDC were numbered. In fact, the Nixon administration was working on a welfare reform plan that would require recipients to secure jobs. The plan could only work by expanding access to child care services.

While I was still at Yale, I had joined the board of the Day Care and Child Development Council of America, led by a Baltimore socialite, Theresa Lansburgh. The board members included business executives, politicians of both parties, early childhood educators, and researchers. For a period, Mrs. Richard Nixon served as the honorary chair. Because of its prestigious membership, this organization became the leading advocacy group for child care on behalf of working parents.

My work on the council brought me into contact with other scholars who had been studying child care much more intensely than I. Our discussions led to my observation, impressed upon me further after my going to Washington, that there was a total disconnect between how child care was viewed by decision makers as opposed to people knowledgeable about human development. Many decision makers to this day view child care primarily as a service that parents need in order to go to work. Once I began pursuing my own studies on child care, I began to advance the position that rather than being a service for parents, child care must be viewed as an environment where many children spend a significant part of their growing years. As such, what happens in child care has considerable influence on the course of child development, just as the educational environment influences the child's learning trajectory. Thus I felt that policymakers should be just as concerned and supportive of good quality child care as they are of good schools.

Under ideal circumstances there would be no difference between a good educational setting and a good child care setting other than the length of the day and year. Think of a child in a school classroom. Even though the primary purpose there is to learn, the child is simultaneously receiving child care. This explains why many mothers join the workforce once their children are of school age. However, while education is invariably accompanied by child care, child care is not invariably accompanied by education. The average quality of the child care available to most American families is somewhere between poor and mediocre, a problem we will return to later in this chapter. But now we had a wonderful chance to do something about it.

Attempts to Develop a Federal Role in Child Care

In America, child care has historically been treated as a private family matter. With the exception of child care centers supported by the Lanham Act during World War II, the federal government paid little attention to the plight of parents who needed care for their children while they worked (Zigler and Lang, 1991). Even today, many working mothers feel that they made the choice to work and to place their children in substitute care, and thus believe child care is a personal responsibility rather than having anything to do with the common good, as in the case of public education. The exception to the government's laissez faire stance toward child care has been in the area of welfare reform. In the 1960s, for example, a number of welfare reform programs such as the Work Incentive Program, or WIN, were tried with the goal of weaning mothers off public assistance by requiring them to secure work or training. The federal government funded child care services for these poor mothers but gave no thought to the child care needs of nonpoor working families.

In 1969 a special Head Start Advisory Committee was formed, chaired by Charles Schultze, a former director of the Bureau of the Budget. The group reported that "the objectives of day care and Head Start are in many ways similar, though not identical" (quoted in Zigler and Muenchow, 1992, p. 125). Schultze thought that much of the knowledge gained in the Head Start program could be applied to child care, an effort that would be easier if the two programs were jointly administered. Nixon's HEW Secretary, Robert Finch, agreed. He announced that the Office of Child Development would be the focal point within HEW for child care and preschool programs. Indeed, a brochure about the new OCD stated the agency would have a major responsibility for child care.

Of course, HEW practices were not always consistent with the rhetoric. The OCD had operating responsibilities for Head Start, whereas responsibility for child care programs was spread across half a dozen agencies in HEW. New legislation was required to unite these two important streams of services to children and families. Congress took the lead, and such legislation was moving along rapidly.

Senator Walter Mondale and Rep. John Brademas both introduced bills in 1969 that would join Head Start to a new national system of child care open to all children who needed it, regardless of family income. The increase in women working outside the home was not unique to America but was occurring throughout the industrial world. In response, other nations were putting into place child care systems to accommodate this new form of family life. These new bills were an effort to fill the vacuum in America's policies to benefit working families and also the national economy.

In the late 1960s and early 1970s, Mondale in the Senate and Brademas in the House were something of an advocacy tag team for America's children. Everything from the National Institute of Education to the first national child abuse law was herded through Congress by these two legislators. They were often viewed as sharing a single ideology, but close examination of their bills and actions made clear to me there were considerable ideological differences between the two. Mondale leaned more left on the liberal continuum than did Brademas, who was more a pragmatist than an ideologue.

"Fritz" Mondale had a deep and real concern for our nation's children and a true desire to better their lives, but he was trying to achieve other ends as well. His 1969 bill, the Head Start Child Development Act, proposed a massive expansion of Head Start from $325 million to $5 billion over a 5-year period. The bill would have extended the program to nonpoor families, who would pay for the service on a sliding scale based on their income level. The proposed funding was enough to ensure quality child care services. This emphasis was child oriented and in keeping with my own hopes. However, elements of the bill seemed to be directed at shoring up the Community Action Program, which was close to Mondale's heart. Preference for applications to run child care centers would be given to CAP agencies. Head Start would stay in OEO, and there would be a renewed emphasis on hiring low-income residents to work in the centers. These provisions were clearly prompted by fears that the Nixon administration's plan to move Head Start to HEW was the first step in abolishing the CAP. I opposed giving preference to CAP instead of awarding grants based on the quality of the application. In essence, Mondale was trying to rejuvenate Head Start's Community Action roots, using the program to organize communities to fight poverty. With the new Nixon administration's desire to dismantle OEO, returning Head Start there was a long shot at best. Mondale certainly did not want Rumsfeld and Cheney (both then at OEO) to have the final say on Head Start.

The 1969 bill introduced by Brademas was more consistent with my own views. The key objectives of his Comprehensive Preschool Education and Child Day Care Act were to bring together children's programs including Head Start. Instead of scattering responsibility for child care across seven federal agencies, he wanted all early childhood programs to be located in the Office of Child Development. By making OCD the lead agency for these programs, Brademas hoped to undercut the tendency to subordinate children's needs for good care to other goals, such as getting their parents off welfare or using child care as a source of jobs for low-income people.

A key witness at the hearings on his bill was Milt Akers, head of the National Association for the Education of Young Children. When asked what the principal lessons learned from Head Start were, he said, "For a while we wanted to give jobs to everybody—that was the important thing. But now parents are beginning to see their kids are being sold short without competence" (quoted in Zigler and Muenchow, 1992, p. 126). Akers's testimony was pretty much on target. Over the years one of the strongest voices for improving the quality of Head Start programs has been the National Head Start Association, whose membership is comprised of Head Start staff and the parents of participating children.

Brademas was a Rhodes Scholar and possessed an impressive intellect. A primary reason he wanted to coordinate child care programs with Head Start was his concern that existing federal policy was promoting socioeconomic segregation. It placed poor young children in one set of programs such as Head Start, while children of more affluent parents received care and education elsewhere. Brademas believed that this policy undermined civil rights policies the government was trying to enforce. He also thought that quality care was important to children's well-being and learning, so his bill required the construction of clear quality standards.

The key battle that would seal the fate of the final bill, the Comprehensive Child Development Act, 2 years later could already be seen in 1969. The primary difference between the Mondale and Brademas bills concerned whether federal funds should flow directly to communities through CAPs or be channeled through the states. Whereas Mondale was attempting to strengthen the CAP, Brademas was trying to design a new system encompassing all publicly funded early childhood programs. Brademas was willing to turn over to the states the power to distribute federal child care funds. In his 1969 bill, state commissions composed of representatives from local agencies, CAPs, and public and private child welfare groups would prioritize grant applications for approval by the HEW secretary. After 2 years, the states themselves would have the power of approval and distribution of the federal funds. Brademas was careful to retain some protection for existing Head Start programs. First, CAP agencies would have representatives on state commissions. Second, his legislation mandated that the commissions give priority to funding Head Start programs in existence prior to 1969. Still, many Head Start and CAP advocates thought that any state involvement would undermine the leadership role of poor and minority parents in the program.

Building Momentum

Between 1965 and 1970, the number of working women with children under age 14 soared 45% from 3.5 million to 5 million. It is not surprising that a June 1969 Gallup poll showed two out of three Americans were in favor of federal support for child care (Zigler and Muenchow, 1992). What was needed to move the child care bills along was to frame the problem and build a more organized base of support. In 1970 two national conferences were held that spotlighted the child care needs of American families and energized momentum toward legislative solutions.

Not long after I took the helm at OCD I convened a conference at the Airlie House in Virginia. There were 1,000 participants including experts on child care, local providers, community people, and a sprinkling of decision makers from localities across the nation. The focus of the conference was on family day care, where a woman cares for five to six children in her home. Child care is much too complex to be tackled as a single issue. To capture the variety of child care services in our nation, one needs a three by three typography (three types of care by three ages of children). In addition to family day care, there is also center care and kith and kin care (individually provided by a babysitter, relative, or neighbor). Although there is considerable overlap in the ages of children served by each type, centers in general cater to preschoolers and school-age children, whereas infants and toddlers are often cared for by kith and kin. Family day care is the most likely to serve children of all ages.

Parents of infants and toddlers particularly like family day care because it is more homelike than the larger centers and can be more reliable than a relative or friend. I had a special concern about the quality of family day care, which I once described in testimony I gave before a Senate subcommittee as a "cosmic crap shoot." You could knock on one door and encounter a wonderful caregiver for your child and a warm, caring person who really wants to help you, much as if you had found a new sister. On the other hand, you could knock on another door, drop off your child, and the child could be dead that night. The *New York Times* used my phrase as the title for an editorial and supported my views by pointing out the number of children who had burned to death in family day care homes in New York City.

The goal of the Airlie House conference was to improve the quality of care children received in family day care settings by producing guides for providers that spelled out the essentials of good care for infant, preschool, and school-age children. A subsidiary purpose was to give the child care issue the visibility it deserved. (There had been no national child care conference since the one held by the Women's Bureau in 1960.) We accomplished this through the great press coverage our meeting received. The conference helped set the stage for child care policy in Congress and the evolution of the child care component in Nixon's welfare reform plan from an afterthought to a designated program that had its own important role in welfare reform. We will have more to say on this plan shortly.

The momentum was developed further at the national White House Conference on Children that met in Washington in December of 1970. This conference used to be held in Washington every 10 years, placing children front and center in the nation's consciousness for 3 days or so. The president typically gave the keynote address. Some 4,000 experts and knowledgeable laypersons came to Washington, representing each of the states. The general purpose was to identify problems affecting children, which participants would present to their legislators face-to-face while they were in town.

I needed the help of the participants on another matter that pertained to all children but would never surface at the state level. OCD had not been legislated by Congress but was created by an executive order. Thus my agency was vulnerable that another executive order could easily disband it, sending Head Start to the Office of Education (a great fear of Head Start people) and sending the Children's Bureau to be a joint organization of the Women's Bureau. The conference was run by Steven Hess, with whom I worked closely. I lobbied Congress to provide Hess with the funds he needed to conduct this event, yet it took considerable arm-twisting on my part to get him to include a single sentence mentioning OCD in President Nixon's keynote address.

My goal was to have OCD legislated. I turned to my many friends who were attendees at the conference and asked for their support. I hoped they would make this a recommendation of their conference and carry the case to their legislative representatives. I made my pitch, but the participants said they wanted to do better than that for OCD. They said they would work to get a cabinet-level agency for children and would recommend me as its first secretary. Here I was proposing a doable task that would likely have received no opposition from the Nixon administration, and the advocates' response was a totally unrealistic plan that did not have the slightest chance of being achieved. At the time of the White House conference, OCD had only had a permanent director for less than a year. Their pleas to elevate this office to cabinet rank would have fallen on deaf ears in both Congress and the executive branch. Although I tried to dissuade them and recruit their efforts to my more modest goal, they chose to proceed and satisfy themselves with the emotional catharsis that came from talking about a cabinet-rank Department of Children.

Nevertheless, the 1970 White House conference was important in moving child care legislation along. At previous conferences, the participants drew up huge lists of needs and concerns they wanted the federal government to address. Faced with these laundry lists, policymakers had no idea where to begin. For the first time, at the 1970 conference the attendees voted on their top concern. They chose the need for good quality, affordable child care as the biggest issue facing our nation's children and their families. Many people from Congress attended the conference, and many of the attendees went to the Hill to make the child care problem visible to their representatives.

I was at the conference and met with a variety of people both to express my concerns and to hear firsthand the concerns bubbling up from the nation as a whole. I met with a friend, Mary Keyserling, who was the executive director of the National Council of Jewish Women (NCJW). They had just completed a huge national evaluation of the quality of child care in America that included both centers and family day care homes. They found that many children were receiving terrible child care: "growth in services available has failed to keep pace with rapidly rising need. Large numbers of children are neglected; still larger numbers now receive care which, at best, can be called only custodial and which, at its worst, is deplorable. Only a relatively small proportion are benefiting from truly developmental quality care" (Keyserling, 1972, p. ii).

The study was conducted as a public service by NCJW, whose members volunteered their time. They visited child care settings nationwide and reported what they saw. Had such a study been done by the federal government, it would have cost several hundred thousand dollars at the least. Keyserling told me that the data had been collected and analyzed, but NCJW did not have the $4,000 needed to publish and disseminate the findings. Seeing this as a bargain for the Children's Bureau, which should be conducting this type of study, I gave the group the funds to finish their project.

The report, titled *Windows on Day Care* (Keyserling, 1972), had a huge impact. Decision makers and parents were appalled at the findings and the negative implications for our children and society as a whole. Policymakers in both parties were finally coming around to believing it was time to do something about the atrocious state of child care in our nation. (Alas, NCJW conducted a parallel study in 1999 and discovered that child care was of no better quality than it had been 30 years earlier.)

The Comprehensive Child Development Act

The time was right for child care legislation. The Airlie House conference and the White House Conference on Children had spotlighted the child care crisis affecting our nation's children and families. Early releases of the NCJW findings showed the urgent need to improve the quality and availability of child care services. Most importantly, the Nixon administration was proposing major welfare reform devised by Daniel Patrick Moynihan. Under their Family Assistance Plan (FAP), welfare families would work for a guaranteed minimum wage, which would necessitate an expanded role for the federal government in child care. The original conception of child care in the proposal was only as an add-on to free mothers to go to work. Indeed, in the 100-page bill that passed the House in April of 1970, only three pages addressed child care. The language was vacuous, mentioning only that choices of child care settings should be provided and grants should be given to agencies "that demonstrate a capacity to work effectively with the local manpower agency" (Zigler and Muenchow, 1992, p. 129).

Secretary Finch was already on record as saying that OCD would be the focal point of child care in HEW, where FAP would be administered. I was determined that the child care provided in FAP would be of good enough quality to give children a good start in life. Poor child care can lead to poor school readiness, which can cycle into poor school achievement and eventual welfare dependency—exactly what FAP was trying to change for their parents. Elliot Richardson, who replaced Finch, was enthusiastic about my view that FAP be a two-generation program and that the child care portion deserved attention in its own right. He carried this idea to Moynihan and Nixon at the White House, and they agreed.

Quality Standards

Just as I had insisted that performance standards were needed to assure quality in Head Start, I argued that we must have enforceable standards in the child care component in FAP. I was surprised to discover that standards already existed. In 1967 Congress had mandated that all federal agencies that were providing child care comply with a single set of standards to ensure children's safety (Segal, 1989). Jule Sugarman was given the task of drafting what was called the 1968 Federal Interagency Day Care Requirements (FIDCR). I studied this document and found it wanting. Sugarman was a civil servant whose knowledge of child development was pretty much limited to what he had learned through his close association with the Head Start program. Sugarman was a very liberal thinker and had depended primarily on input from Head Start advocates to define quality child care. Unsurprisingly, he and his staff constructed a set of ambitious standards that were popular with children's advocates because they championed comprehensive Head Start-like services in child care. According to Segal (1989), the problem was the "high-cost requirements could result in fewer children being served and less parents working." (Remember that at the time OCD did not exist and various agencies in HEW had responsibility for managing child care programs that were launched to support other purposes like welfare reduction.) "Therefore, they drafted a set of ambiguous, unenforceable, and unenforced goals that had little practical effect on the operation of child care programs." Indeed, Sugarman cut a deal with relevant agencies and decreed the standards would never be enforced (Zigler, Marsland, and Lord, 2009).

The Office of Management and Budget (OMB) and the Department of Labor were already having trouble with my desire for good quality child care. The Department of Labor would be responsible for the employment features of FAP and wanted to run the child care component as well. Labor's mission was to place welfare mothers in the workforce, and child care was nothing more than a means to that end. Their view of child care was custodial, where children would be watched, fed, and kept safe until parents picked them up after work. My view was that child care should be educational and promote physical, cognitive, and socioemotional development.

Both Elliot Richardson and I agreed that no federal money should ever be spent on purchasing child care that is not conducive to overall child development. This goes beyond the health and safety concerns of the Labor Department. However, standards must be realistic and cannot require every single service one would like children to have because this would make the cost prohibitive. Thus "standards" or "requirements" are not the absolute best we can do for the children. Rather, they should be the threshold, defining the minimum acceptable quality. I explained to decision makers that there were three types of child care: custodial, developmental, and comprehensive. Comprehensive care was advanced in the 1968 FIDCR, whereas custodial care was being championed by the Labor Department in their effort to obtain responsibility for child care under FAP. I placed OCD in the middle of this spectrum, arguing that standards must assure developmental care that promotes healthy growth and learning.

As I began working on fleshing out the child care provision of FAP, I quickly revised the 1968 FIDCR. It was obvious that a single set of standards would not work for children of different ages. Child care is typically classified into three age groups: infant and toddler care (birth to 3), preschool care (3s and 4s), and school age (5 to about 13). I consulted with some of the child care experts who had been at the Airlie House conference and had worked on the lists of what constituted quality care at each of the three age levels. I was amazed at how little disagreement there was on such technical features as child–staff ratios and group sizes. This made my task surprisingly simple.

The 1970 FIDCR were to be enforced in HEW, and I had several meetings with Elliot Richardson before he would sign off on the standards and make them part of his own criteria for quality child care. Richardson knew we must confine regulations to what is truly important to children's development and not over-regulate. Thus before giving the 1970 FIDCR his imprimatur, he demanded some changes. I am still embarrassed to think of the minutia I had inserted. I guess I was being too responsive to the experts by including such details as the number of inches off the floor the children's drinking fountain had to be. Elliot convinced me to focus on the forest and not the trees.

After winning Richardson's acceptance of the slightly revised 1970 FIDCR, I had to prove they would not be too expensive to implement. The early figures on FAP were that we would care for 450,000 children in the first year with a budget of $750 million. Richardson, the White House, and OMB wanted assurance that the type of child care I wanted to provide fit into this budget. I discovered that no one bothers to cost out requirements they impose upon a program (hence the exasperating term, "unfunded mandate").

Child care is very labor intensive, with approximately 75% of the cost going to personnel. Care becomes progressively less expensive as children age since an individual caregiver can care for more older than younger children, and older ones spend less time there on school days. The most expensive care is for infants and toddlers. The FIDCR required an adult:child ratio of 1:3 for this age group. The debate continues whether that number should be 1:4, but I chose 1:3 because in the 1970s there was still argument about whether infants under 1 year old should be in child care at all. Thus I thought I should be particularly conservative in regard to care for infants and toddlers.

Our calculations indicated that the budget money was sufficient to serve the number of children expected in the first year of FAP. With these figures in hand, Richardson went to the White House and won for OCD the authority to manage the child care component at FAP. I was pleased to discover that my two-generational approach to FAP received wide acceptance in the Nixon administration. The president himself was positive, stating "The day care that would be part of this plan would be [of] a quality that will help in the development of the child . . . and would break the poverty cycle for the new generation" (quoted in Zigler and Muenchow, 1992, p. 129). My battle for quality child care seemed to be won.

Drafting the Child Care Bill

Mondale and Brademas were again preparing child care bills for the Senate and the House, respectively. Because of the child care component in FAP, these two pieces of legislation were joined at the hip—the child care bill could provide the delivery system for the child care required by FAP. The more we could do to make the child care bill synergistic with FAP, the greater the likelihood it would be supported by the Nixon administration and Republican lawmakers. Thus Elliot Richardson and I constantly attempted to navigate the 1971 bill so it would mesh with FAP's child care piece.

At the same time, Brademas and Mondale worked closely on the development of their versions of the Comprehensive Child Development Act (CCDA), introduced in the spring of 1971. The two bills matched on many points. Taken together they constituted the most far-reaching child care legislation Congress has ever proposed. As in the 1969 bills, Head Start would be grandfathered into a new child care system. Child care centers throughout the nation would be open to all children regardless of family income, while the Head Start programming would be for those children living in poverty. Since both poor and more affluent children would attend the same centers, we would achieve the socioeconomic mix that was important to Brademas and to me. Looking back, universal access to child care services was by far the most dramatic aspect of these bills. This was a marked break with the past, where the family sphere was considered inviolate and government only intervened when the family had failed, as in the cases of child abuse or families so poor they needed AFDC. Mondale and Brademas's great ideological breakthrough was treating child care in the same way children's advocates did, namely as a social good much like public schooling and Head Start—programs needed to improve the life course of children and thus the future of society.

Both the Senate and House bills emphasized the importance of the quality of child care. They called for federal standards for child development programs, including Head Start. Funds were earmarked for pre-service and in-service training for all child care staff, matching the new training provisions that OCD was incorporating into the Head Start program. The federal government would help finance the renovation or purchase of child care facilities, which would improve the physical environment experienced by Head Start children.

Mondale and Brademas also patterned Head Start's comprehensive services into their proposed child care practices. Like Head Start children, those in child care would have access to physical and mental health services. And just as Head Start was beginning to do, child care providers would strive to identify and include children with special needs. OCD would be legislated as the principal agency for administration of the bill and for coordination of programs related to child development.

The views of Mondale and Brademas were shared by many legislators of both parties. In the 1970s there was still a strong liberal wing of the Republican Party. In the Senate, Jacob Javits of New York and Richard Schweiker of Pennsylvania joined with Mondale and other Democrats as initial co-sponsors of the bill. In the House, four Republicans were among the nine original sponsors of the legislation. Eventually 120 members signed on as co-sponsors, over one-third of whom were Republicans (Zigler and Muenchow, 1992). Orval Hansen, a Republican from the conservative state of Idaho, spoke on behalf of the CCDA: "This legislation before us today is truly landmark legislation in terms of its potential effect on the future of the country. The good it can do can have a more far-reaching impact than any of the major education bills enacted during the past 20 years" (quoted in Zigler and Muenchow, 1992, p. 136). This is a very potent statement coming from such traditional quarters.

Building Support

After working closely with Mondale and Brademas to draft the child care bill and get features into it that I thought were important, I was determined to do everything I could to get the CCDA signed into law. What more could I have dreamt of than having Head Start stabilized and expanded, with high quality guaranteed? Joining Head Start with a nationwide child care system would give the program a broader constituency of parents who cared about it and would demand that their representatives support it.

Passage of the 1971 Comprehensive Child Development Act would have the added benefit of allowing me and OCD to escape from a touchy situation I was facing. Even prior to proposing welfare reform, Nixon and his administration were highly motivated to get poor women off the public dole and into the paid labor force. Although other federal agencies were already running child care programs, the administration was pressuring me to provide child care for the many poor mothers whose children were attending Head Start. I would have been happy to do so if I had the money needed to turn the conventional half-day, 9-month Head Start session into an all-day, full-year program. However, the Head Start budget was extremely tight. It was all I could do to squeeze out the money needed for the improvements and innovations I was undertaking. I argued that Head Start was an intervention program to improve school readiness, not a child care program to free parents to work. Further, there was no strong developmental case that could be made for subjecting 3- and 4-year-old children to an extended-day program. This was long before educators began discussing the value of full-day kindergarten classes. Experts were divided on whether too long a day would lead to fatigue and disengagement in very young children. There is no question that if Head Start were invented today, it would be a full-day, full-year program providing both early intervention and child care services.

In my mission to grow support for the CCDA, I enlisted the help of my fellow scientists. I hoped to get the Society for Research in Child Development (SRCD) to publicly endorse this legislation on the grounds that it would benefit the healthy growth and development of our nation's children. My goal was facilitated by a serendipitous event that took place at the national SRCD conference in Minneapolis in 1971. SRCD was the premier organization of research scientists devoted to expanding the knowledge base through rigorous empirical study. Applied psychology was treated as "lesser" science. But the times were changing (see Zigler, 1998).

From the planning of Head Start forward, more and more behavioral scientists who studied children were becoming interested in social action programs like Head Start. One reason is that many child psychologists became involved in Head Start as volunteers and consultants. Another is that a leading developmental thinker, Urie Bronfenbrenner, was championing his bio-ecological paradigm for understanding human development. His model viewed children's development as a function of both proximal and distal factors in the child's total ecology. Proximal of course was the great influence of family, but Bronfenbrenner argued that the child is also influenced by the social and economic status of the community and country as well as by decisions made by state and federal governments. In fact, a new subdiscipline was emerging that encompassed child development *and* social policy, made up of scholars who worked at the intersection of our knowledge base of human development and social policy construction.

A pioneering leader of this movement was my graduate school mentor, Harold Stevenson, who in 1971 was the outgoing president of SRCD. Stevenson made the brave decision to replace the standard president's address with a symposium of three Washington decision makers and three experts in human development. He thought this would facilitate a dialogue where the Washington people would tell scholars how they could be of help in improving policymaking for children, while the scholars would give the decision makers recommendations, emanating from the knowledge base, about children's developmental needs. Fritz Mondale, the Senator from Minnesota where the meeting was held, led the three-person Washington contingent. The others were Representative Orval Hansen, who gave the Washington group a bipartisan flavor, and I, the only one who was a member of SRCD.

The conference was held in a downtown hotel, and it was there that I learned of the right-wing opposition to the CCDA, which at that point was working its way through Congress. A group of demonstrators was picketing the hotel with signs that denounced the legislation and mentioned both Mondale and me by name. It was no secret that I was working closely with Mondale and Brademas in drafting the bill. I was not a loose cannon in the Nixon administration but worked directly with Elliot Richardson. Although he and I were in total agreement and enthusiastic about the bill, we still had not received the nod of approval from the Nixon White House. However, we saw ourselves as being loyal to Nixon in that we were helping to develop the child care component of his Family Assistance Plan, which would eventually fall to Richardson's agency to manage. Mondale had evidently been picketed prior to the SRCD conference and was less perturbed by it than I was. Yet I too would soon become blasé about the picketing because after Minneapolis, I was picketed at any public appearance I made anywhere in the nation. Consistent with my academic background, the first couple of times I encountered these dissenters I tried to speak with them and discuss the pros and cons of our two positions. I found out this was like talking to a tree stump. They felt their opposition to the child care bill was dictated by God who knew how He wished children to be raised.

The picketers in Minneapolis did not deter me from my goal at the SRCD conference. I mobilized my good friend Urie Bronfenbrenner to make a motion at the business meeting that SRCD should officially endorse the 1971 Comprehensive Child Development Act. The motion passed handily in spite of SRCD conservatives who argued it was not the place of behavioral scientists to get involved in policy issues. In the end, this endorsement probably made little difference one way or the other, but it did make public that our nation's greatest experts in child development approved the bill.

Political Wrangling

In both the House and the Senate there was bipartisan support for the 1971 child care bill and support for the Family Assistance Plan in the House but not the Senate. Although there was a general air of optimism about the CCDA, a major pragmatic hurdle soon developed that would eventuate in the bill losing

Republican support in Congress and jeopardizing the Nixon administration's endorsement. The conflicted issues were the pathway by which the federal money would get to local centers and the size of the population areas that would be eligible to receive federal grants. With the exception of Head Start, most large federal programs are block-granted to the state governments, which then partial out the funds to local communities. The Nixon administration would have preferred 50 state grants for the child care money, but it was willing to follow existing law and continue to permit Head Start funds to go directly to Head Start grantees at the local level. Thus local centers would be funded by the state for the child care component and directly by the federal government for the Head Start services.

As they had in their 1969 bills, Mondale and Brademas disagreed on the role states should play. Mondale preferred the Head Start model, meaning federal child care funds would flow directly to local agencies. Brademas favored delivering the funds through state commissions, believing that some state supervision was needed to manage the money. "Administrative workability was very important in my mind," said Brademas. "The idea that the federal government would have to be in direct touch with thousands of community agencies all over the nation would have been an administrative nightmare" (quoted in Zigler and Muenchow, 1992, p. 137).

Brademas was a political realist and was fully aware that Republican support for his bill depended on granting some role to the states. He therefore included a provision giving prime sponsorship of child development programs to states and to cities with populations of over 500,000. Local communities would submit applications to the prime sponsor, which would forward those it approved to the federal government. The civil rights issue was still salient in 1971, so Brademas built in some protections to assure racial integration in child care centers just as there was in Head Start. To avoid discrimination and prevent favoritism for grants going to white applicants (particularly in the segregated South), the bill gave the HEW secretary the right to override the prime sponsor's recommendation and directly fund a local program.

As the debate continued in the House, the bill was revised to allow cities with populations as small as 100,000 to serve as prime sponsors. The committee thought this number would meet with White House approval because this was the number the Nixon administration had proposed for its manpower development programs. Since I was to be the federal official responsible for administering the child care program, this was a critical number for me. It would determine how many grants OCD would have to review, implement, and monitor. I was fairly comfortable with the 100,000 figure, which would play out as 50 state grants plus roughly a similar number of city grants. One hundred grants spread across my 10 regional offices struck me as a doable workload, although the new combined system of Head Start and child care meant we would have to monitor a much larger number of Head Start grants. Even though the 100,000 figure would put us up to the limit of OCD's administrative capacity, I thought we could do it.

Mondale argued against states being prime sponsors: "I think it is time we learned that money sent out from the Federal Government by way of the States, through the State bureaucracy, to the localities gets to be pretty thin by the time it reaches the end of the pipeline.... It is terribly important that we make money available directly to the community groups and local governments" (quoted in Zigler and Muenchow, 1992, p. 138). This position was unquestionably spearheaded by the very powerful Marian Wright Edelman. She became a primary advisor to Mondale, who often appeared to be legislating whatever Edelman recommended. She never seemed to make it into Brademas's orbit.

I interacted with Edelman a great deal during these years and came to admire her for both her outstanding intellectual power and her determination. She had come of age during the civil rights movement, when she was a key figure in the Child Development Group of Mississippi (Chapter 3). Edelman saw firsthand how the state government of Mississippi fought Head Start tooth and nail because of its integration policy. She later moved to D.C. where she founded the Washington Research Project, the predecessor of the famous Children's Defense Fund she has headed for decades. One of her first initiatives in Washington was the study of the implementation of the Elementary and Secondary Education Act of 1965. She found that while a lot of federal money was going to state education agencies, very little of it was reaching poor children. Thus she saw efforts to transfer the new combined Head Start and child care to state agencies as a threat to Head Start's existence. To protect Head Start, she brought together an ad hoc coalition that included several labor unions, the National Organization for Women, the National Welfare Rights Organization, and the Day Care and Child Development Council of America. (I had withdrawn from the board of the latter when I joined the Nixon administration in 1970.) This coalition did indeed work hard in support of the CCDA. To Edelman, though, child care was not a primary concern. She stated, "My goal was to protect Head Start, but to couch it in terms of child care," claiming victory when "there was a separate section near the end of the bill that protected Head Start, which was my primary agenda" (quoted in Zigler and Muenchow, 1992, p. 134).

Edelman was adamant on the issue of federal-to-local administration. In Senate testimony she stated, "The heart of this bill is the delivery system. Those of us who have worked with the poor, the uneducated, the hungry, the disenfranchised, have had long and bitter experience in how legislative intent is thwarted in the process of implementation; the way money is spent often is more significant than the fact that it is spent" (quoted in Zigler and Muenchow, 1992, p. 138). She further warned that those concerned with equal opportunity and civil rights would oppose any state control of the child care funds.

At the time I had considerable empathy for Edelman and her views. However, the prime issue in this bill for me was not the delivery system but the deplorable state of child care in the country and the promise the bill had for creating a quality child care system responsive to the needs of America's working families. The House subcommittee headed by Brademas did approve the 100,000 population requirement. However, it became clear that the matter was far from resolved when the bill came before the Education and Labor Committee, chaired by Carl Perkins. Speaking on behalf of the many small communities in rural America, Perkins wanted to eliminate or reduce the 100,000 threshold. He was an extremely powerful figure in the House and was senior to Brademas. I still admire Brademas's courage in taking on Perkins and holding to 100,000. Brademas was aware that, like Mondale and Edelman, Perkins was demanding an administrative monstrosity that without question would weaken Republican support for the bill.

Endorsement by the Nixon Administration

President Nixon's interest in the CCDA was predicated mainly on his interest in reducing welfare. While Brademas and the majority in the House were in favor of FAP, Mondale had deep reservations about the legislation. Like Edelman and the National Welfare Rights Organization, he viewed FAP's demands that poor women work as an attack on minorities and motherhood. Liberals preferred the AFDC approach that supported poor mothers so they could stay at home and raise their children. Mondale and Edelman could not see that the practice of supporting poor women to stay home was doomed once so many middle-class mothers joined the out-of-home workforce. Interestingly, when President Clinton signed welfare reform into law in 1996, Marian Wright Edelman's husband Peter resigned his post in the Clinton administration in protest. However, by this time there was considerable agreement that AFDC was not working in solving the problems of poverty. Today there is a general consensus that, although far from perfect, the current rules that impose time limits on welfare payments are more effective than AFDC, which many saw as perpetuating poverty from generation to generation. The authors' primary reservation about the welfare reform of 1996 was that not nearly enough attention was given to the quality of care children would experience when their mothers joined the workforce. In 1970, quality in child care was front and center.

Although Richardson and I were working directly with Congress to shape the CCDA in a way that would undergird the child care component of FAP, the Nixon administration as a whole was divided on the bill and continued to vacillate. There was considerable opposition at OMB, which objected to the $13 billion, 4-year price tag and wanted to define the child care component of FAP by itself (thus leaving open the custodial vs. developmental quality issue). Brademas was on Nixon's enemy list, which didn't help matters any. Because of divided views, Secretary Richardson had to cancel his scheduled testimony on the bill three times. In June of 1971, Richardson finally won out over those in the administration who opposed the bill. With White House approval, he sent a letter to Senator Mondale stating his general support for comprehensive child development legislation that would consolidate and coordinate federal child care and child development programs and provide a delivery system for both services. Richardson also reiterated his support for my revised FIDCR and noted these standards would govern child care under the 1971 version of FAP. This letter was the breakthrough we had been awaiting.

Stephen Kurzman, the HEW assistant secretary for legislation, and I were then sent to deliver testimony on the bill before the responsible Senate sub-committees. We stated that the administration endorsed the principle of a delivery system for child care and child development services for all income levels. On the delivery system issue, we repeated that the administration preferred to deal with states and cities with populations exceeding 500,000. We pointed out how hard it was to ensure quality in the Head Start program with over 1,000 grantees and warned that many times that number "would require a much, much larger Federal bureaucracy . . . to manage and monitor effectively the quality of the services provided" (quoted in Zigler and Muenchow, 1992, p. 142). Richardson's letter and my testimony with Kurzman seemed to provide a green light for child development legislation. This was probably the high point of the 1971 child care initiative.

Losing Ground

Many child care activists, led by Marian Wright Edelman, were not satisfied and appeared willing to lose the bill unless every local community could get a grant. I had little sympathy for their view after Richardson and I had worked so hard to get the administration on board. Various advocates for the bill were concerned enough about the situation to feel the need for an off-the-record meeting where positions could be stated and hopefully disagreements could be resolved. Terry

Lansburgh hosted the meeting at her home in Baltimore. The event was cordial and the tone remained optimistic. Knowing the importance of the size of the grantee to the Nixon administration, I informed the group that I feared a veto if they did not compromise on the demand that every small community in America be eligible for a grant. Characteristically, Edelman stood firm and continued to champion the Head Start federal-to-local model. Edelman is one of the most magnetic human beings I have ever met, and it was clear to me that she was effectively directing the advocates' thinking.

Edelman and I were friends and had always gotten along on issues having to do with poor and minority children. In desperation, I took her aside to talk. I implored her to compromise on the size of the grantee issue. I told her we should both track the system once it was in place, and if we saw any injustice as a result of the delivery system, I would join her in asking Congress to make changes. I begged her not to let this once in a lifetime opportunity for children and families slip away because of administrative details that could always be corrected in future legislation. Her reply consisted of little more than pointing out my naiveté. She informed me that I "just didn't understand politics" and that Nixon could never veto a child care bill with an election year coming up. I agreed that I was just a child development expert out of my element, but said there was nothing wrong with my hearing and I was beginning to hear "veto" from within the administration.

Edelman found a powerful ally in the liberal democrat, Carl Perkins. Remember that Brademas had succeeded in sustaining the 100,000 population requirements for prime sponsors in the committee over the objections of Chairman Perkins. Perkins got his revenge when the bill reached the House floor. He proposed an amendment slashing the population requirement to 10,000. Brademas remained philosophic about this, realizing that Perkins represented a district in Kentucky where 10,000 was a big number. Perkins pointed out that his own Pike County, the largest state county east of the Mississippi, had a population of only 60,000 and would not qualify as a prime sponsor under Brademas's mandate. Brademas patiently explained that the population limit did not mean that smaller areas would not receive child care services. They would still be able to submit grant applications, but the federal government would deal directly only with larger units. Republicans attempted to support Brademas, warning that further reduction in the population require-ments would jeopardize their backing. But Perkins prevailed in the floor vote, reducing the population requirement to 10,000.

Perkins further punished Brademas by pursuing a very unusual com-mittee policy. Because there were still differences in the House and Senate versions of the child care legislation, the bills had to go to a joint conference committee. Perkins decided that Brademas would not be one of the House conferees. There was no precedent for the author of a major piece of legislation to be excluded from a conference committee. The absence of Brademas made the final bill even less palatable, reducing the population requirement for a prime sponsor to 5,000. As a final blow to the administration, the conference report mandated that programs follow the 1968 FIDCR rather than the revised FIDCR we had developed at OCD to give quality control real teeth. Thus the final bill would give America an unmanageable system with unenforceable quality standards. Still, it was better than nothing. Richardson and I swallowed hard and decided to continue to support the bill even in its weakened condition. We were correct in feeling this opportunity would not come again soon.

The End

The 5,000 prime sponsor number infuriated the Republicans, and they dropped off the bill, just as they had threatened they would. A particularly ardent supporter of good quality children's programs was Al Quie of Minnesota, who had been an original co-sponsor of the bill with Brademas. In an address to the House floor he ruefully stated, "I wish I could come before you and urge you to support the conference report but I cannot. . . . [This] report is an administrative monstrosity. It is impossible for it to work properly" (Cohen, 2001, p. 41). Jack Duncan, staff director of the House Education and Labor Committee that sponsored the bill, worked alongside Brademas to maintain bipartisan support. Duncan believed that the president would never risk a veto if congressional Republicans continued to favor the bill.

Elliot Richardson knew the bill was headed for trouble with the White House and met with the president and John Ehrlichman, Nixon's chief advisor. They informed Richardson that right-wing opponents of child care were pressuring the president to veto the bill. Richardson eloquently argued that if the administration decided to oppose any federal role in child care, that position would be inconsistent with their involvement in the process of shaping the legislation. Richardson, who had given positive testimony on the bill with the president's blessing, said an about-face would put him "in an exceedingly embarrassing position" (Zigler and Muenchow, 1992, p. 145). He also reminded the president of his own public statements on the importance of quality child care for welfare mothers. The meeting ended with Ehrlichman telling Richardson to keep the president in touch, without making any final decision one way or the other. Richardson lobbied hard and wrote a memo stating, "It is my belief that a Presidential veto would be a major error. The credibility of the President's commitment to the first five years of life is certainly at stake, as is the integrity of our relationship with those Members of Congress who have done so much to bring about the result we have repeatedly claimed we wanted" (Zigler et al., 2009).

Right-Wing Attack

Just as the bill was having problems on the left with both Edelman and Mondale insisting on an unmanageable child care system, the opposition from the right was reaching a fever pitch. The White House was being flooded with mail (much of it form letters) opposing the child development legislation on the grounds that it would destroy the American family. It was my sad lot that all these letters were brought to my agency so my staff could reply to each and every one. There were literally dozens of boxes of this mail, which I stored in my private restroom. I went through a couple of the cartons and could not find a single letter supporting the legislation. I had to wonder what happened to all those people in the polls who said they wanted their government to take a leading role in child care. I was even more disappointed to find no indication of support from the women's movement, which had much to gain from national child care legislation. Although part of Edelman's coalition, the National Organization for Women did not make the 1971 child care legislation much of a priority.

The right-wing activists were making their position known not only to the White House but were inundating Congress with letters opposing the bill. They found an eager accomplice in Senator James Buckley, who was not a member of either major party but of the Conservative Party of New York State. Buckley claimed this proposal for federal child care would "threaten the very foundation of limited government and personal liberty" (in Zigler et al., 2009, p. 35). In the House, Democrat John Rarick of Louisiana characterized the bill as "replacing U.S. parents with the Federal Government and the home with a national institution" and asserted "this power grab over our youth is reminiscent of the Nazi youth movement; in fact, it goes far beyond Hitler's wildest dreams or the most outlandish of the Communist plans" (in Zigler et al., 2009, p. 35). In response to all of this, congressional conservatives began to mobilize for a veto. They even circulated a "Dear Colleague" letter to gauge whether enough members would vote in favor of sustaining a veto. This served not only their interest of seeing whether they could guarantee the veto would not be overridden, but it planted the idea in recipients' minds that is was okay to vote against this popular bill.

The euphoria I felt after Richardson's breakthrough in getting President Nixon's support gave way to disappointment as I witnessed all this right-wing activity. I had deluded myself into thinking that Congress could not possibly believe these charges that the bill was some sort of Nazi or communist plot. It was a child care system for crying out loud, a system that would have easier access and higher quality than the places children of working parents were already attending. With this logic on our side, Richardson I continued to think that the primary stumbling block was the size of the population area represented by the prime sponsors. We needed a system that could be managed and monitored properly to assure the quality of services that everyone had agreed was important. The guiding light to me during this time was John Brademas and his clarity of thought. I felt we had a good chance of avoiding the veto being engineered by the far right if we could just get agreement on Brademas's position of grants serving areas of no less than 100,000 in population.

The Veto

While the right wing was finding a voice in Congress and inundating the administration with anti-CCDA mail, a conspiracy of sorts was taking place within the White House. Advocates from the far right found a kindred spirit in Pat Buchanan, who was then an advisor and speechwriter to President Nixon. Among his various duties, Buchanan controlled the daily news summary presented to the president. He leveraged his relationship with the conservative newspaper, *Human Events,* and columnist James Kilpatrick to shape Nixon's opinion. Buchanan would arrange to have someone write a conservative column on the child care act and then put it into the president's daily news briefing. Kilpatrick proved to be a willing conspirator and personally wrote a 1971 editorial entitled, "Child Development Act—to Sovietize Our Youth." Another front-page article demanding a presidential veto claimed, "This sounds dangerously like the kind of eugenics and thought control the civilized world learned to revile when practiced in Nazi Germany and in the Soviet Union" (in Zigler et al., 2009, p. 34).

I remained hopeful when the bill passed both Houses of Congress, the Senate handily and the House by a small margin. The Comprehensive Child Development Act of 1971 was sent to the president for his signature. The president met with Ehrlichman and George Shultz, who was director of OMB, and decided to veto the bill. His speechwriter, Pat Buchanan, was assigned to work on the veto message. Buchanan was told to "put in what the right wing wants to hear" (Zigler and Muenchow, 1992, p. 146). Buchanan inserted some of the same language that had been used by Kilpatrick and even quoted from some of the letters and op-ed articles proliferating from the opponents. In his veto the president scolded: "for the Federal Government to plunge headlong financially into supporting child development would commit the vast moral authority of the National Government to the side of communal approaches to child rearing over against the family-centered approach" (Woolley and Peters, n.d.f). The wording was vitriolic and had a deadening effect on future efforts to build the type of government-sponsored national child care service available to parents in other industrialized nations.

I was in San Francisco when Nixon decided on the veto. One of the first people to be informed of the president's decision was Richardson, who quickly called me to break the bad news: "Ed, I know how long you've been working on this and how much the bill means to you, and I wanted you to hear it from me and not on TV or in the news." I tried to eek out a very small victory in what was surely the greatest defeat of my professional life by asking Richardson if I could write the veto message. I would have pointed out the inadequacies in the bill while affirming the great need for a system of quality, affordable child care available to all working parents and reiterating Nixon's belief in the importance of the first 5 years of life. Thus I would have left the door ajar for a better bill. Richardson said he would check with the White House and call me back, which he did in less than an hour. The answer was "No." I was not surprised. Although I was apolitical, it was well-known in Washington that I was not a Nixon loyalist.

Few believe the veto was due primarily to the right-wing attack, although it clearly played a role. Child care historian Kimberly Morgan concluded "the passions of both the left and the right jointly defeated an attempt to form a national, unified day-care policy," which is likely closer to the truth (in Zigler et al., 2009, p. 38). There were other reasons as well. Moynihan had left the White House, and interest in his Family Assistance Plan followed him out the door. Although the administration continued to push for FAP, its passage seemed less likely. Without FAP, the administration would have no use for an expensive, new child care program. Richardson believed that the cost and unworkability of the child care legislation led to the death of the CCDA. Indeed, Nixon's veto mentioned the "new army of bureaucrats" that would be created with the participation of thousands of prime sponsors. Richardson noted that had Nixon really thought the federal government should not be involved in child care, he would not have continued to support it as a provision of welfare reform. Since Nixon had decided to nix the bill anyway, perhaps he just used the occasion to placate the conservative part of his base.

Ed Zigler Goes Home

After Nixon's veto I knew I could no longer honestly serve in the administration. I went to Elliot Richardson, my friend and superior, and told him I had no choice but to resign. Richardson, who also felt somewhat bruised by the child care veto, responded by saying, "I wouldn't blame you if you went back to Yale and your hour-long lunches—but look, we're still going to get FAP through and you are the only person in Washington who is concerned with the quality of child care in that bill" (in Zigler et al., 2009, p. 39). He invoked our close relationship, saying it was important to him that I stay and continue to work with him on matters of mutual concern.

I was adamant that my most important asset, both as a scholar and as a federal official, was my credibility, and the president's veto put me in a totally untenable position. Everyone knew I was in favor of a national child care system, so there was no way I could suddenly support my boss's veto. Elliot said he really wanted me to stay and would go to the White House and see if he could work out some sort of accommodation. Later in the day he called me to his office and happily reported that he had reached an agreement with the White House that would allow me to remain in Washington. The deal was really not one that I liked, namely that I did not have to support the veto, but I could not attack it. I asked the Secretary what I was supposed to do when reporters asked me point blank, "How do you feel about the president's veto of the child care bill?" He gave me a one-word answer: "waffle." This is a familiar term to those in politics: it means speak in such a way that you do not commit yourself one way or the other. Although politicians are adept at this practice, it was quite distant from my standard direct and candid style. However, I was genuinely concerned about the child care experiences that hundreds of thousands of poor children would have as a result of FAP. By staying at OCD I was in a position to shape the child care component in FAP the way I wanted. The second factor in my decision to stay was my great admiration and affection for Elliot Richardson. He deserved some reward for all the efforts he had made so that I could continue working under him.

I did stay and did my best to be a first-class waffler. In addition to FAP, I still had much work to do on the improvement and innovation strategy I had mounted for Head Start. Soon, however, it became clear that Nixon's welfare plan would not be enacted into law. This time I did leave Washington and returned to my academic home at Yale.

As relieved as I was to go home, I arrived with a heavy heart that weighs on me to this day. We had come so close. Our nation's working parents almost had access to a wonderful system where their children would receive great care and have experiences conducive to learning and social–emotional growth. They would not be confronted with the serious problems of finding reliable child care and figuring out how to pay for it that face so many families today. America's young children would not be plunged into child care settings of mediocre or awful quality, or have to fend for themselves outside of school hours. But we lost. It is rather sad to see that the nation has regressed rather than move forward from the 1971 child care efforts. Welfare reform finally did come to America in 1996, but the child care component of the legislation does little to guarantee that children of mothers leaving welfare will receive quality care that can help them achieve a welfare-free future themselves.

I am still haunted by the absurd arguments the right wing used—and still uses—to thwart a regulated child care system. Their arguments were totally out of touch with the reality of child care in America. The fact was that child care existed for decades before the 1971 bill was proposed. It was not considered un-American or destructive of the family. Indeed, the high-quality child care centers that were mounted during World War II under the Lanham Act made it possible for women to work in defense plants, and the entire enterprise was considered the height of patriotism. Further, just like Head Start, the proposed child care program was voluntary and no family was forced to use it. The existing nonprofit and for-profit child care providers could stay in business, and parents could choose the settings they preferred. The charge that the child care act would allow government to wrest control of child rearing from families was totally unfounded.

The right-wing's opposition to child care was and remains a smokescreen for their opposition to the phenomenon that makes child care a necessity, namely mothers leaving the home to join the workforce. Their strategy is to oppose any legislation that will make it easier for women to join the labor market, be it child care or paid infant care leave. They do not want to acknowledge the fact that as the years have gone by, more and more mothers of even very young children have joined the out-of-home workforce, primarily because of economic necessity. Even as the need has increased, the right wing was able to fight off several pieces of child care legislation. A federal child care bill was not passed until 1990—the Child Care and Development Block Grant, signed into law by President George H. W. Bush. Conservatives fought just as vehemently against this bill and proposals leading up to it as they had in 1970, including charges that federal involvement in child care would "sovietize" the American family and be "anti-religious" (Schlafly, 1988a, 1988b).

There is an old saying that "demographics drive social policy." By this time, so many women had joined the workforce that the arguments of the right had little salience. Interestingly, a leading supporter of the effort in 1990 was Marian Wright Edelman, who 20 years after the 1971 bill was quite willing for federal child care funds to be block-granted to the states. Alas, current federal child care dollars are spent in the existing hodgepodge, nonsystem of care, with no guarantees that children receive good quality care.

Elliot Richardson's days in the Nixon administration were also numbered. He left HEW in early 1973 when he was appointed U.S. Secretary of Defense. After just a few months, he became U.S. Attorney General. When Nixon ordered him to fire the special prosecutor investigating the Watergate scandal (which ultimately led to Nixon's resignation), Richardson refused and immediately resigned. Unlike me, however, he remained in public service and held various cabinet and ambassadorial posts. While I have served as a consultant to every administration after Nixon, I have done so as an academic, outside the world of politics. I have continued my battle for quality child care for all of America's children, but I have not been very successful. I can only trust in my students to continue the good fight.

7

Coaxing Science to the Rescue

During my stay in Washington, I knew I was out of my element. I was a college professor and research scientist, struggling to grasp the inner workings of policymaking and the realities of politics. Thus I could forgive myself when things did not quite go my way or took longer than they should have. The one area where I refused to accept defeat, however, had to do with the misunderstanding and mishandling of research. After all, this was my strength, my area of expertise that had led to professional recognition, generous grants to conduct my work, and indeed the job I held in Washington.

Let me briefly explain how the world of empirical research works. Using the scientific method, an investigator develops a hypothesis, usually based on a scientific theory, and then devises ways to test it. In designing the study, he or she typically examines the literature and brainstorms with colleagues to create methodology that will test the idea fairly. Once the data collection is complete and the results statistically analyzed, the project is written up and submitted to a scholarly journal. There the editor determines if the study has scientific merit and, if so, assigns it to several reviewers, typically experts in the subject area, for critiques. They may recommend further statistical analyses, gathering more data, and so forth, and ultimately whether or not the study is a meaningful contribution to the literature and should be given space in the journal. Such peer review is a way of ensuring scientific integrity. Once the paper is published, it is not unusual for other scientists to agree or disagree with the findings or route taken to obtain them. They write letters to the editor, present their opinions at conferences, and may undertake their own studies to try to replicate, expand, or disprove the original work. This is how the knowledge base is built and how scientific understanding progresses.

Not so in Washington, I learned to my dismay. Studies are contracted to research companies, many of which are quite professional and follow the procedures described above. The findings, however, are rarely peer-reviewed before they are submitted to the contracting agency. Once they are released, they are often treated as Truth by both policymakers and reporters, the majority of whom do not really understand the scientific method. After that, it is exceedingly difficult to correct mistakes in the research or conclusions or to change public perceptions. This is exactly what happened with the findings of the Westinghouse study, which seemingly indicated that Head Start had no long-term effects (Westinghouse Learning Corporation, 1969). Although the many scholarly criticisms of the study and my relentless complaints about it to both the Nixon administration and Congress eventually led to a decrease in the credence given to the findings, conventional thought had embraced the view that the benefits of Head Start soon fade away.

The Educational Testing Service Study

My defenses against the damaging effects of the Westinghouse study began with exactly what one would expect of a research scientist—designing a better study. I had tried to stop the Westinghouse effort when I was on the Head Start Research Council before I got to Washington. We met with Bertrand Harding, the head of OEO, to expose flaws in the study's design and focus when it was still in the planning stage (see Chapter 3). Congress was demanding account-ability, however, so the study was commissioned flaws and all.

Both Urie Bronfenbrenner, who was also a member of the Research Council, and I were appalled at the methodological inadequacies of the Westinghouse proposal. Urie put our feelings bluntly:

> The proposed design was an overly mechanical and mindless plan for
> massive computer analysis of data regarding changes in intellectual
> development of Head Start children, obtained for noncomparable
> groups of children under noncomparable program conditions. The
> most predictable result of the proposed analysis . . . would be the
> finding of no differences, whether or not differences in fact existed.
> (1997, p. 87)

We were both empirical scientists and knew that the best way to measure any lasting benefits of Head Start was to follow the same children over time rather than compare children 2 years out of Head Start with a different sample 3 years out as the Westinghouse design would do. With a third member, Ed Gordon, we designed a straightforward, 3-year longitudinal study. Unlike the faulty Westinghouse methodology, we wanted experimental and comparison groups formed at the outset of the study, an approach still standard in evaluation research. Another reason for launching the study was to demonstrate to the powers that be that Head Start welcomed an assessment of its effectiveness and did not oppose the Westinghouse effort on grounds other than its poor design.

Almost simultaneously with the start of Westinghouse project, Head Start officials approached the highly respected Educational Testing Service (ETS) to conduct the longitudinal study. Our choice of ETS was based on their expertise. Scholars working on the ETS study included Scarvia Anderson, Walter Emmerich, Sam Messick, and Virginia Shipman. By this time Lois-ellin Datta had replaced Ed Gordon as Head Start's key research person. Datta recalls, "I remember the meetings [on] the ETS longitudinal study which had so much going for it in design, in the diversity and care of measurement" (personal communication, October 27, 2006). She had sat in on the meeting with OEO when "You and the Committee laid it all out and argued with utmost eloquence that the [Westinghouse] study was fatally flawed and the results would not add knowledge but hard-to-overcome ignorance about Head Start. You all were over-ruled, a sad day in the history of Head Start."

Working with the ETS people, we designed a deeply textured evaluation. The study was to be conducted at multiple Head Start sites in three cities around the country. To start, ETS collected unique data on child development before the child's Head Start experience, data on parent and community context, and considerable data on the programs themselves. The day-to-day conduct of the study was placed in the capable hands of Virginia Shipman, a well-known pioneer in the field of early intervention. Datta remembers how well-funded the ETS study was. We saw this money as being well-spent inasmuch as this was to be Head Start's answer to the Westinghouse report that we knew was coming down the track.

Because of the longitudinal nature of the ETS study, we understood we would have to wait 3 years for the results. The findings should have been available by 1972, when I was still in Washington desperately trying to hold off the negative impact of the Westinghouse Report. But I did not get them, and neither did anyone else for nearly 2 decades. Even though we emphasized to the ETS people that we had to know the outcome of the study as soon as possible, they simply would not produce. Datta recalls "the Steering Committee was 'called in' to reason with ETS" (personal communication, October 27, 2006). I too remember these terribly frustrating meetings in New Jersey. Datta concludes from these discussions, "where overt resistance diminished, foot dragging set in." The problem, again in Datta's words, was that within ETS there were "heated debates on whether this was a research study or an evaluation study and a great reluctance to do the analyses that would look at development as a function of participation in Head Start." She further notes, "there were internal personnel problems too ... and new ETS contracts and enthusiasms came along." Eventually the principal researcher working on the study, Virginia Shipman, asked me to help her get another job. With the lead investigator gone and disagreement over the types of analysis to conduct, the data languished in ETS files. I can only conclude that ETS failed Head Start and the larger cause of early childhood intervention.

A set of inadvertent circumstances resulted in the ETS findings finally being compiled and made public, but not until 1988 for one key paper and 1990 for the second. The heroine in getting the study published was Jeanne Brooks-Gunn, a senior research scientist at ETS where she was making the transition from basic research to more applied work. (She has since become one of our nation's most respected workers navigating the inter-section of the knowledge base and social policy construction.) She was joined by two postdoctoral fellows, Valerie Lee and Elizabeth Schnur. Their work was facilitated by Ernie Anastasio, vice president for research at ETS. He and others still remembered the Head Start project and wanted something done with all the data that had been meticulously collected by Virginia Shipman. He suggested Brooks-Gunn undertake this task and gave her release time and some funding to complete the project. It is not easy to enter cold files and try to make sense of 3 years' worth of old data. Brooks-Gunn remembers, "The data were a bit daunting (25 huge code-books). We treated the challenge as an archeological dig" (personal com-munication, January 6, 2008). Analyzing this data necessitated some sophisticated statistical controls. These young scholars were fortunate to have a senior statistician at ETS, Don Rock, as a consultant.

The first paper was reported under the title, "Does Head Start Work?" (Lee, Brooks-Gunn, and Schnur, 1988). The Westinghouse Report had created a bias by positing that unless the benefits accruing by the end of the Head Start year were maintained well into the school years, the program could not be deemed effective. This expectation was certainly not in keeping with the goal of Head Start at its inception, which was to prepare children for the challenges of elementary school. In this first paper Lee et al. chose to assess whether Head Start accomplished what the planners had intended, that is, whether Head Start children performed better than appropriate comparison groups at the end of the preschool year. Using the rich design of the ETS study, the scholars compared the performance of 967 children across three groups: (1) those who had attended Head Start, (2) poor children who had attended other preschool programs, and (3) poor children who had no preschool in the years 1969–1970. The results were clear and indicated Head Start children demonstrated greater gains than children in the other two groups. These benefits were found in both intellectual and social–emotional domains.

These findings were similar to those reported by many other investigators. Yet Lee and her colleagues drilled deeper into their data and provided some interesting—and still useful—insights. Their study demonstrated that Head Start children were more disadvantaged than either of the two comparison groups, which were comprised of children who also lived in impoverished neighborhoods. They argued that a failure to adjust for the lower initial starting point of Head Start children was a major reason for the Westinghouse study's finding that graduates were not much better off than those who did not attend Head Start. By looking at the end point and not the greater progress the children had to make to get there, "the beneficial effects of Head Start were seriously underestimated in the Westinghouse Report" (Lee et al., 1988, p. 211). Study after study has now revealed that Head Start children are at higher risk than comparison groups of disadvantaged children, so their actual progress is understated. From the program's inception, centers have been instructed to recruit the neediest children in their neighborhoods, and they appear to have lived up to this commitment.

Lee et al. also found that the greatest benefits of Head Start attendance accrued to children with particularly poor cognitive and demographic characteristics and that black children benefited more from Head Start than white children. The authors offered two interpretations, one substantive and one artifactual. The substantive argument was that black children had experienced poorer demographics and lower cognitive stimulation than white children, which would leave them more room to improve. The second interpretation was that there were too few white children in the study to provide the statistical power to fairly assess their comparative gains. In a later study in which whites were also underrepresented in the Head Start sample, they were found to benefit *more* than blacks, although Head Start attendance was related to lowered later crime rates for the black participants (Garces, Thomas, and Currie, 2002). The authors agree with the recommendation of Lee et al. that race be examined in all Head Start studies, particularly because today a large number of children in Head Start are Hispanic whites.

Lee et al. made a point of noting that "despite substantial gains, Head Start children were still behind their peers in terms of absolute cognitive levels after a year in the program" (1988, p. 210). I have pointed out many times over the years that we were much too optimistic when Head Start began and did not fully appreciate just how difficult it is to improve the performance of children mired in poverty. Yet the impossible dream that poor children will rise to the level of more affluent children after a year or two in Head Start will not die. For example, many years after the observations of Lee et al. the George W. Bush administration criticized the program on the grounds that after a year of preschool, Head Start graduates do not attain the same level of school readiness as middle-class agemates. It is fully appropriate that one of the authors of "Does Head Start Work?" wrote a response to this view entitled, "Do You Believe in Magic?" (Brooks-Gunn, 2003).

Overoptimism about the powers of early childhood education is not confined to Head Start but has spread to preschool programming in general. Advocates emphasize what we can achieve and use sophisticated cost–benefit analyses to predict vast financial payoffs if society would just embrace preschool education. What they fail to realize is the fact that even model programs do not produce the level of performance in poor children as middle-class children achieve in the years before elementary school. Thus just as at the beginning of Head Start, today's workers strike me as wildly optimistic in thinking a typical 1-year preschool experience can change lives. Do they really want to suggest that the 13 years spent in grades K through 12 carry less weight than a single year of preschool? Rothstein (2004) pointed out the same folly, noting other factors such as health, housing, neighborhood safety, and job security that in total have more cumulative impact on a child's growth trajectory than a year or two of preschool. The Lee et al. paper demonstrated once again that while children made substantial gains during their Head Start year, these benefits are limited.

The issue about whether children continue to perform better after preschool was dealt with in the second ETS report, "Are Head Start Effects Sustained?" by Lee, Brooks-Gunn, Schnur, and Liaw (1990). This study was limited to 646 black children in two cities. Data were collected at the end of Head Start, kindergarten, and first grade. Again, both intellectual and social outcomes were examined, since both are important in school performance. The primary finding was that the Head Start graduates maintained their advantage over the two comparison groups at both the end of kindergarten and the end of first grade. The differences were not as large as those found at the end of the Head Start year, a finding the authors surmised could result from differences in the quality of subsequent schooling or the home environment. They also argued that a program must have sufficient intensity to overcome the harm caused by poverty and a 1-year program is insufficient to this task. At the time it was still somewhat rare for behavioral scientists to write about the policy implications of their work, but Lee et al. included such a discussion. They said their results supported the continuation and perhaps expanded funding for intervention programs like Head Start for disadvantaged children.

Lee and her colleagues correctly warned that the ETS findings might have limited usefulness because the data had been collected nearly 2 decades earlier. The nature of Head Start changed dramatically during the early 1970s when I implemented uniform standards and quality controls. Thus the children evaluated in the ETS study attended a different program than the one in place by the time the findings were published. Nevertheless, my life and Head Start's would have been much easier if I had had the results of the ETS study available when I was in Washington, desperately trying to fight off the negative findings of the Westinghouse Report and defending Head Start to the skeptical Nixon administration.

More Tries and Another Disappointment

I of course never anticipated that the ETS findings would be delayed so long. Still, because the study was longitudinal, I knew I would not have the results anytime soon to counteract the Westinghouse Report—or even if the results would be positive enough to serve as a good defense. The future of Head Start was shaky, and while I awaited the data I had to do something to save the program from extinction.

As noted earlier (Chapter 3), the Westinghouse findings were bolstered by Arthur Jensen's (1969) monograph, which was published at about the same time. Jensen argued that compensatory education could not work because intelligence is largely determined by genes, rendering the environmental changes inherent in intervention powerless. The essential dynamite in the Jensen paper was his assertion that blacks have an inferior gene pool for intelligence compared to whites, so nothing could be done to improve their cognitive development or performance. This was a vote of no confidence in Head Start, which served many black preschoolers whom Jensen apparently decided were destined to fail with or without intervention.

Soon after I assumed my duties in Washington, the White House approached HEW Secretary Richardson about his views on the Jensen report. He in turn asked me about the possible implications for Head Start. I wrote my usual two-pager, concluding that the Jensen report was essentially irrelevant to Head Start since it concentrated on black–white difference in intelligence. Head Start was about improving the daily performance of poor children regardless of race, and this improvement was not to be defined by raising IQs. Both the White House and Secretary Richardson were comfortable with my position, and it became their own.

I knew Jensen well and always thought he was an intelligent, careful scholar. Still, I personally considered his views erroneous and knew the only way to discount them was with a better analysis. Thus I listened carefully when Henry Riecken, head of the Social Science Research Council, told me the group was planning a comprehensive review of the evidence on race and intelligence. The work would be conducted by Gardner Lindzey, perhaps the leading behavioral geneticist at the time. The problem was that the council only had money to support about half the cost. Riecken asked if OCD would fund the other half. I could have easily done so with the money I had for such purposes in the Children's Bureau.

As an academic, I value deeply the marketplace of ideas. However, I was not an academic in Washington. I was a decision maker whose top lieutenant in the Children's Bureau and many people running the Head Start program were black, to say nothing of the tens of thousands of black children and families participating. Although I could have chosen to fund the project and that would have been the end of it, the Jensen issue was far too explosive for me to act in such a highhanded fashion.

I decided to have a meeting with my high-level black colleagues at OCD. I explained why I was thinking about funding this effort and that I did not want to make a final decision until I had their input. There was still a great deal of racial tension in the early 1970s, and I quickly learned we could not have a straightforward discussion in which we each presented our views. The group said they would have to caucus among themselves and get back to me, thus excluding me from the deliberations. After their caucus, they informed me they were totally opposed to the project. I understood their concern—OCD contributing support to the Lindzey project could be interpreted to mean that the federal government was giving some credence to the assertion of the racial inferiority of blacks. Not stopping there, the group was explicit in their threats to resign if I funded this work.

I spent a very sleepless night worrying about what would happen if key staff members actually quit. I could see their point but felt that OCD was either in the truth-seeking business or it was not. Seeking truth was consistent with the long and illustrious history of the Children's Bureau I had always admired and was proud to head. The next day I called the staff together and told them I had decided to fund the project. I said I would be saddened if anyone quit at this critical juncture in the development of OCD, adding that such an action would not hurt me or Jensen personally, but that it would certainly hurt black children and Head Start. The academic in me made this decision (plus maybe a little of the poker player who felt his colleagues were bluffing). No government official in my place would have put his whole agency at risk by funding a small piece of scholarship. Fortunately for me and for Head Start, no one quit.

I also funded two other scholarly reviews I did not think would offend my staff. Although the Westinghouse findings were drawing the most attention, I knew there were many studies at the time that indicated some positive effects for Head Start. Early in my tenure at OCD I commissioned two reviews of the potential for long-term benefits from Head Start and other early intervention programs. What I wanted was an honest review of all the evidence to date to determine if the gains children make from intervention are sustained. The first review was conducted by Sally Ryan, a Cornell scholar who had studied under Bronfenbrenner and had his good critical acumen. She also worked for me at OCD, so I thought she would have kind words to say about Head Start. (Even though I was a scientist committed to scientific truth, I was desperate and admittedly was trying to stack the deck a bit.) She did have kind words, concluding that early intervention programs had a lasting positive effect on reading achievement and social adjustment, and that the potential of intervention programs such as Head Start to improve children's future everyday competence was clearly present. However, Ryan was a very young scholar and her paper never received much attention.

I also asked Urie Bronfenbrenner to conduct a similar review. Even prior to serving on the planning committee, Urie was a force in supporting preschool intervention in Washington. He had met personally with Lady Bird Johnson to further this issue and testified before Congress to convince policymakers of the value of early intervention. Further, he was a member of the Head Start Research Council that had tried to squelch the Westinghouse project and had contributed a lot to designing the ETS longitudinal study, which was to be a much more sophisticated and sound evaluation. I did not ask Urie to review the evidence on early intervention because I thought he was certain to deliver a positive report, although the fact that he was as negative about the methodology of the Westinghouse study as I was didn't hurt. I chose him because he was a leader in the field, knew more about early intervention than just about anyone, and was a respected scientist. He was also a well-known synthesizer of data, often finding a signal where others saw only noise.

I was stunned when I read Urie's review. He essentially agreed with the conclusions of the Westinghouse study that the early gains accruing as a result of the Head Start experience faded out over the next few years. His words carried immense weight. Whereas the Westinghouse authors were not particularly famous, Bronfenbrenner was an icon not only in the field of early intervention but in the general field of developmental psychology. His bio-ecological model of human development went on to become developmental psychology's leading paradigm. Urie knew the precarious position Head Start was in following the release of the Westinghouse Report, and he had to have known the situation would become worse when one of Head Start's founders attacked the program he helped design. For all these reasons, Urie's public position that there was no evidence of long-term effects for early intervention was more damaging than the Westinghouse Report itself.

Bronfenbrenner reviewed seven programs that had follow-up data and divided them into two types: (1) group programs, reminiscent of Head Start, and (2) home-visiting programs, in which a home visitor works with parents to improve their child-rearing skills. His conclusion about Head Start-type programs was unequivocal in declaring that the positive effects found at the end of the intervention "tend to 'wash out' after intervention is terminated. The longer the follow-up, the more obvious the latter trend becomes" (1974, p. 286). For some reason he ignored several programs that were reporting long-term effects, including the one we were evaluating at Yale that followed children from Head Start into New Haven's Follow-Through program in the public schools. He did point out a number of methodological flaws across the seven studies he reviewed, an important one being their strong reliance on cognitive benefits to the exclusion of other developmental domains. Another weakness was that to qualify for the review, a program only had to have 2 years of follow-up data, hardly enough to measure long-term effects. He did not mention the Westinghouse Report because it was not an experimental study.

Urie knew his report would ruffle my feathers, and this is probably why he included some praise for the experimental Home Start program I had mounted to provide Head Start services directly to families in their homes. This program was in keeping with Urie's bio-ecological model in which the role of parents is so central that you cannot help the child without helping the family. Thus his own focus was on improving the relationship between parents and children. However, although Home Start is certainly consonant with the bio-ecological model, the Head Start model is even more congruent because it works not only with parents but with the community surrounding the family, which Urie also saw as an important influence on children's development.

After giving short shrift to group programs like Head Start, Bronfenbrenner championed home-visiting programs (without mentioning Home Start), arguing that they did have long-term benefits because they helped parents become agents of change. So empowered, parents could continue to promote positive traits in the child long after the program's end, unlike time-limited group programs that simply stop. As proof, in these seven studies he found evidence that the younger siblings of children of home-visited parents also benefited. This sibling effect has been found in more recent programs but has generally been underexplored in Head Start research.

Although I could not take serious issue with Urie's thoughtful review, I simply disagreed with his conclusions. For example, Head Start parents also receive home visits and have much more frequent involvement in the daily Head Start program than the parents in any of the home-visiting programs Bronfenbrenner reviewed. Simply because parent participation in Head Start had not been appropriately studied was not a good enough reason for him to dismiss the program in favor of "pure" home-visiting models. I had too much respect for Bronfenbrenner to try to rebut him, nor did I bother to point out the different conclusion reached by his student Sally Ryan after she reviewed the same database. In fairness to both of them, in 1970 there was not much evidence on the long-term effects of early intervention programs, and what there was was not always scientifically sound. I could only assume that Urie gave the evidence a knowledgeable reading and reached what he thought was a fair conclusion. What hurt was that Bronfenbrenner was a brilliant thinker and wise in the ways of policy formation. He knew full well that the opinion he publicly shared at my personal request would add to my difficulty in keeping Head Start alive during this critical period.

When I commissioned the two reviews, all I was seeking was an immediate answer to the basic question of whether a good quality preschool program could achieve lasting effects. The Westinghouse report said "no," and the famous and respected Urie Bronfenbrenner who helped create Head Start essentially agreed. If fade-out was real, Head Start appeared doomed. Logically, it seemed reasonable to expect that if the program did a good job preparing children and their families for school, they would have a better chance of succeeding. What I needed was some solid empirical evidence that at least some of the benefits accruing during the Head Start year carried over into better performance during the school years. With ETS not coming through, I was defenseless—a scientist without science. I was still that tough kid from the streets of Kansas City, however, and I could not give up the fight. It was not until I left Washington that I was instrumental in finally winning it.

The Consortium for Longitudinal Studies

When I left Washington in 1972, the Head Start program was in much better shape than the one I inherited when I arrived. Instead of following their whims, all centers were gearing up to provide specific component services. Quality controls were being put into place to assure that they did, and training and technical assistance was available to help them with problem areas. Public perceptions of Head Start, however, remained jaded. The negative and highly publicized findings of the Westinghouse Report, corroborated by the famous Urie Bronfenbrenner, had deflated hopes that Head Start could be an effective weapon against poverty. Reflecting the lack of confidence, the program's budget and enrollment fell in some years and barely budged in others. To make matters worse, more studies appeared that seemed to confirm the alleged fade-out of gains made in preschool as children went further into the elementary grades.

In 1975 I was asked to give the keynote address at the huge annual conference of the National Association for the Education of Young Children (NAEYC). I used this speech to issue a challenge to the popular belief in fade-out. I reminded the audience there was one frequently replicated finding that had been nailed down, namely that by the end of the Head Start experience children performed better than comparison children who did not attend. If this advantage faded after students spent time in elementary school, this could just as easily be interpreted as an indictment of schools rather than an indictment of Head Start. By this time I had some data from my New Haven study and was aware of the data of some others indicating Head Start does have lasting effects, particularly if it is followed by further programming in the early grades. This smattering of longitudinal evidence was not enough to disconfirm the existence of fade-out, but it was certainly promising. I told the crowd, "I would like to issue a serious warning against the popular 'fade-out' notion.... This has been repeated so often that many now treat this conclusion as beyond question. I choose to question it" (Zigler, 1997, pp. 371–372). I then directed my remarks to decision makers in Washington as well as to fellow scientists:

> All that I am doing is asking decision makers not to set social policy on the basis of the conclusion that there are no long-term effects of Head Start attendance.... Bad science makes for bad social policy. I ask my colleagues in the research community to forego the temptation of delivering definitive pronouncements concerning the fade-out issue and await instead the collection and analyses of more data. (p. 372)

I referred the audience to an unpublished paper written by a recognized scholar in the field of early intervention, Frank (Francis) Palmer, who also concluded it was premature to accept fade-out as inevitable. Frank was at the conference, and later we had the opportunity to talk about the issue. Between the two of us we could think of many projects like his and mine that had collected longitudinal outcome data. We then discussed the matter with a friend and highly visible scholar, Irving Lazar, who also had doubts about the fade-out hypothesis.

Lazar was the scientist who had headed the creative and important Kirschner study—the only study I had available to me when I arrived in Washington that showed Head Start had benefits outside of the narrow cognitive domain (Kirschner Associates, 1970). Lazar examined the impact of Head Start on communities and discovered changes that were beneficial to children. Lois-ellin Datta points out how the design was consistent with the thinking of Head Start's planners, who "never saw children as isolated entities to be worked on by programs, but as part of families, whose well-being could notably affect child development." She noted that the planners saw "families as part of communities" and emphasized the "interaction between communities, families, and children" (personal communication, January 6, 2008). This thought is most evident in the writings of Urie Bronfenbrenner, who, it seemed, had given up on Head Start.

Lazar found that in places where Head Start existed, communities recruited and found resources for pediatricians, increased health outreach efforts, and kept health clinics open late so working parents could bring their children. Equally dramatic changes were found in their education systems. Schools were more likely to be welcoming to Head Start parents, worked to smooth transitions from preschool to kindergarten and first grade, and sought teaching staffs with experience working with children of low-income families. In some of these places, community colleges reached out to Head Start parents, encouraging their further education and access to better employment.

Lazar's report arrived in Washington at about the same time as the Westinghouse Report. Although I repeatedly noted it, I could not get the decision makers to pay much attention. True to this day, they were caught in the trap of believing that if a program does not have demonstrated, durable cognitive benefits, it doesn't have any benefits. Trying to show them Head Start impacted the phenomena that mediate durable benefits down the road was an exercise in futility. Although Lazar's report never achieved the prominence it deserved, its theoretical approach has been rediscovered. We now know more about what mediates children's successful performance, like their families and communities. Improvement in these mediators has obvious value. For example, a substantial body of evidence has demonstrated neighborhood effects on children's development, as may be seen in the works of Larry Aber, Jeanne Brooks-Gunn, Greg Duncan, and Robert Sampson.

Lazar and Palmer used the annual meeting of the field's premier scientific organization, the Society for Research in Child Development, to hatch an idea. They met with the investigators of many early intervention projects to assess their willingness to participate in a cross-project analysis. The idea was to pool their data to look for common long-term effects produced by intervention. Everyone seemed enthusiastic. To go ahead with the project the group needed financial support, and this is where I was able to help. Otherwise, I tried to keep my distance so no one would think my close ties to Head Start would somehow slant the outcome. I still had considerable influence at OCD, which had been renamed the Administration on Children, Youth and Families (ACYF). I continued to work closely with my wonderful deputy, Saul Rosoff, who had become acting director. My great colleague Elliot Richardson did not remain at HEW for very long after my own departure. He was replaced by Caspar Weinberger, who probably heard great things about me from Richardson and asked me to be his consultant. I emphasized to everyone I knew at ACYF how important it was to collect further data on the fade-out issue.

The head of the research shop at my old agency was Edith Grotberg. She and her knowledgeable colleague Bernard Brown immediately saw the value in this effort. Soon John Meier was appointed second director of ACYF. Like me, he had a scholarly background in mental retardation. Unlike me, he had much more large-scale administrative experience. He too arrived to find Head Start in an uncertain position, including rumors that there was to be an "imminent phase-out" of the program (personal communication, January 17, 2008). He met with Irving Lazar and approved the Consortium grant. With Meier's blessing, Grotberg and Brown became friendly critics and active collaborators in this effort.

Edith Grotberg is an extremely important figure in the history of Head Start's research efforts. Prior to coming to Washington, she had headed the network of Head Start Research and Evaluation Centers. The centers were founded on the premise that "there is interplay between knowledge and practice, so that research and evaluation should be a continuous improvement strand in Head Start" (Datta, personal communication, January 6, 2008). The Head Start Bureau provided long-term funding to the 14 (later 12) centers, which were headed by some of the best workers at that time in child development and early intervention research, who attracted some of the best graduate students.

Under Grotberg's direction, these centers were given two tasks. Half of the funds could be used for any sort of research related to Head Start. The other half was dedicated to coordinated national evaluations. Datta reports, "The evaluations, intended to be annual and cumulative, were designed co-operatively by

Center Directors, under the general leadership of the Head Start director of evaluation." She notes that the research side was quite productive, but "For the evaluation, timeliness was the Achilles' heel." The centers simply could not meet the timelines Washington required, so hopes for a series of evaluations were never fulfilled. To the extent that they put into the field a large cadre of researchers, the centers nevertheless were a success. Grotberg's experience with coordinating and combining the work of a number of research sites undoubtedly made her easily receptive to Lazar's idea for a research consortium.

Lazar was committed to producing an analysis of the long-term effects of early intervention that was beyond reproach. The extremely complicated and demanding effort he was planning would be expensive to complete properly. In addition to the funding from ACYF, the project received some support from the Education Commission of the States. Lazar also took the lead in approaching private foundations to ask for their help. He was not very successful. Lazar later discovered that the foundations were employing Urie Bronfenbrenner as a reviewer, and his advice was that the project did not merit support. In fairness to Urie and the foundations, by this time enough studies had reported the fade-out phenomenon that people thought we already knew early intervention had no long-term effects. Although Bronfenbrenner himself had found lasting benefits for home-visiting programs, he evidently came to feel these were not particularly impressive.

Head Start and early intervention in general had received a terrible blow from Bronfenbrenner in a presidential address he delivered before a major division of the American Psychological Association in 1974. In discussing early intervention projects, Bronfenbrenner stated, "Although there were some modest achievements, by and large the results were disappointing. The effects were at best short-lived and small in magnitude.... In short, my optimism about the plasticity of the developing organism and its responsiveness to environmental change turned out to be ill-founded" (quoted in Palmer and Andersen, 1997, p. 435). This extremely strong statement by an icon in the field of child development and a planner of Head Start explains why foundations would turn to Bronfenbrenner to assess the possibilities inherent in the Consortium study.

Not all private donors rejected the proposal. Lazar recalls that one year when the dates of the federal fiscal year were changed, the study faced a funding gap between the end of the old grant and the start of the continuation grant.

A new foundation, the Hewlett Foundation, had just opened its doors, and a letter to them about the predicament was promptly answered with a check. At about the same time, Dr. Jules Richmond, the original Director of Head Start, became Surgeon General. He assured that between the Children's Bureau and Head Start that the Consortium would receive what was needed for at least five years (Lazar, personal communication, May 26, 2008).

It did.

The Study

The Consortium for Longitudinal Studies was officially formed in 1975 by Irving Lazar at Cornell University. It was the cooperative effort of the principal investigators of 14 longitudinal research and demonstration projects that had been conducted in the 1960s, starting both before and after the birth of Head Start. Most of the famous projects of the time joined, including the Gray project in Nashville, the Deutsch project in New York, the High/Scope Perry Preschool project in Michigan, the Gordon project in Florida, and Phyllis Levenstein's home-visiting program. The scientists agreed to pool the data they had collected individually and to collaborate on a common data collection and analytic effort. All data were sent to Cornell to form a Consortium databank. A top-notch statistician and methodologist, Richard Darlington, joined the project in 1977 and with Lazar was responsible for the final analyses and write-ups.

To be included in the Consortium, the sample size of a project had to be sufficiently large to permit later follow-up. (There is always some attrition in longitudinal studies.) In addition, the investigators had to have a scientifically acceptable research design, that is, an experimental or sound quasi-experimental design. Each project must have been well-documented so the nature of the intervention was clear. Type, duration, and intensity of the intervention, as well as the ages of children varied across the 14 studies.

Although each of the studies was designed to determine whether a particular treatment was effective, as a group they could provide an answer as to whether early intervention programs in general can be effective. The variety of programs included allowed for conclusions that no single study could. For example, together they represented three types of intervention: (1) those that worked directly with the child, (2) those working primarily with the parents, and (3) those that worked with both generations. The Consortium examined the responses of 600 parents across the interventions and unsurprisingly discovered that only a tiny percentage did not believe the program benefited their children. In regard to the comparative advantage of type of program, the conclusion was drawn that across outcome variables there was no reason to conclude that one type of program was better than another.

The outcome measures that had previously been examined differed across the interventions, so the Consortium decided to concentrate on measures that could be found in several of the individual projects. These included assessments of IQ scores, reading and math achievement, grade retention, and special education class placement. The importance of the last two measures is that there is significant financial cost to schools and personal cost to students to be placed in special education or to repeat a grade. Darlington notes that the special education variable was added out of necessity. It turned out that many of the children were in special classes and did not take standard achievement tests; since they were not a random sample, "there was no good way to use the [achievement] test data" (personal communication, May 27, 2008).

The 1976 follow-up sample was composed of 2,008 children ages 8 to 18 from 11 projects. The majority were black. The measures noted above were collected in a common format by each investigator. To guard against artifactual results due to differences between and among the projects, subjects were never pooled into a single large sample. Instead, all tests compared treatment children to control children from the same project site, and then the results were statistically pooled.

The results indicated that intervention strikingly increased children's IQ scores by the end of preschool. These increases were found for at least 2 years after the program, with evidence of smaller increases for 3 or 4 years after, and then vanishing (the usual fade-out finding). Intervention participants also had significantly fewer school failure experiences than did the control groups. Across the seven projects that had this data, the median rate of failure to meet school requirements was 45% in the control group, but only 24% in the project group. Analyzing the two indicators of school competence separately, intervention had a greater effect on special education assignment than it did on grade retention. The Consortium also discovered some positive effects of intervention programs on standardized achievement tests in reading and arithmetic. Since these results were not as strong and consistent as the other findings and the patterns across projects were so complex, the achievement scores were more or less ignored, particularly since they were already reflected in the school competence variable. Lazar and Darlington made an unusual and wise decision to repeat their analyses after deleting the project with the strongest findings on each measure. Even with this extremely conservative procedure, the results remained highly significant. A second follow-up conducted in 1980–1981 confirmed the earlier findings, as did the results of partial follow-ups during adolescence and young adulthood (Lazar, personal communication, May 26, 2008).

The Consortium also examined whether certain groups of children benefited more from intervention than others. Unlike ETS and some earlier studies, the benefits seemed to hold across all children in the programs. The positive effects on school competence were not related to the child's pre-program IQ score, gender, mother's education level, family structure, family size, or ethnic group. The authors concluded, "These school performance results indicate that the earlier pessimism about the long-term effectiveness of early education programs was premature" (Darlington, 1981, p. 42).

Renewing Hope in Early Intervention

The Consortium study placed early intervention and particularly preschool education into a new light. Unlike ETS, the Consortium scholars fully appreciated the importance of getting their report to their funders as soon as possible and of undergoing peer review by the community of scholars. The study was so revolutionary in its impact that Lazar and Darlington published different versions of their report in major journals appealing to diverse audiences. An early, short version appeared in the illustrious journal, *Science* (Darlington, Royce, Snipper, Murray, and Lazar, 1980). A more comprehensive report was written for the prestigious monograph series of the Society for Research in Child Development (Lazar et al., 1982). The complete study was contained in the book, *As the Twig is Bent: Lasting Effects of Preschool Programs* (Consortium, 1983).

Lazar had experience with Washington and knew that publication in scholarly journals was important to science but was not the way to achieve political action.

> As soon as the findings were ready for dissemination a separate effort was mounted to get them in the mass media. Interviews with science writers led to long and strong articles in The *London* (England) *Times,* The *New York Times,* The *Los Angeles Times,* The *Washington Post,* and The *Chicago Tribune.* Arrangements were made for Consortium members to be interviewed by their local newspapers and a feature article in *U.S. News and World Report.* (personal communication, May 26, 2008)

The group produced a set of graphics they used in presentations to state education commissioners and governors and to all the individual members of the congressional committees responsible for Head Start. Lazar recalls, "At a Senate Hearing, where an official in the Administration was advocating that

Head Start be transferred to the Office of Education, and its budget distributed to the States, a Senator rose up, waving a copy of a Consortium Report, and said, in a loud voice, 'It's not broken; we don't need to fix it.'"

Unlike the Westinghouse Report, which had never undergone the peer review required for scientific publication and elicited a multitude of rebuttals, the Consortium's work had been done so meticulously that not a single substantive challenge was ever offered to the study. The multiple-site aspect of the project plus the very conservative analyses employed by Lazar and Darlington made a convincing case that quality early intervention holds value. The findings were quickly incorporated into mainstream thinking and became the new conventional wisdom. Indeed, more recent studies have confirmed the Consortium findings and have discovered positive effects that extend into adulthood. The Cornell group only looked an average of 8 years after intervention. Of particular significance is that the Consortium searched beyond cognitive benefits and pinpointed other highly valuable outcomes, beginning a new approach in the way we judge the effectiveness of intervention.

Irving Lazar is an extremely astute scholar who is both a good behavioral scientist and sensitive to the social policy issues that are impacted by our science. He was fully aware of just how damning Bronfenbrenner's negative stance on long-term effects was to early intervention and to Head Start in particular. In a kind twist of fate, Lazar's office at Cornell was right below Bronfenbrenner's office. Lazar was a friend of Urie and kept him abreast of developments as the project moved forward, sometimes running upstairs with the findings as they came off the computer. Like most good behavioral scientists, Bronfenbrenner was an empiricist, trying to form his views not by his own preferences or beliefs but by solid evidence from well-conducted studies. Early work initially had convinced him to support pre-school intervention, and later his ponderance of the research led him to reject the concept. The Cornell findings were strong enough to convince him to change his position and again believe in the possibilities of early intervention.

In 1980 President Jimmy Carter asked me to head a panel of experts to examine the Head Start program on its fifteenth anniversary and make recommendations for the future. I had no reluctance inviting Bronfenbrenner to be a member of the committee. Urie had rejoined the Head Start family. In fact, he took great joy in visiting and advising his local Head Start center in Ithaca, New York. Although we were alienated for a short period, my life has been incredibly enriched by the friendship and close working relationship I had with this icon of my field from 1965 until his death in 2005.

Caveats

The Cornell Consortium renewed beliefs in the value of early intervention and, by association, Head Start. As mentioned above, policymakers' support of Head Start had become lukewarm in the face of repeated assertions that the benefits of early intervention were transient. The new head of ACYF, John Meier, got the impression from Congress that the elimination of Head Start was a real possibility. He had an early look at the Consortium findings and ran with them to Congress. This is ammunition I wish I had had when I needed it. Meier ascribes to the Cornell findings not only the continuation of Head Start, but its expansion as well (personal communication, January 17, 2008).

Although the end result was favorable, the proper conclusion for decision makers to take away from the Cornell report was that Head Start had a great likelihood for success if it had sufficient quality. The study certainly did not demonstrate that Head Start itself had lasting effects. One of the projects (Louisville) in the Consortium was not even a study of preschool versus a comparison, but rather a study of the relative merits of various preschool curricula. Only two of the studies in the group had anything to do with Head Start, but neither was a standard Head Start program. One was the Beller project in Philadelphia, and the other was my project in New Haven. We both found long-term effects of Head Start providing it was followed by an enrichment program in the schools. There were too few children in my sample who had not attended Head Start for me to examine the contribution of Head Start alone.

There are many other reasons why the Consortium findings should not have been generalized to the national Head Start program. For example, it was not until 1975 that Head Start fully enforced a set of nationwide performance standards. By contrast, most of the programs in the Consortium were established by outstanding scholars who built their interventions on a convincing theoretical base, carefully trained their workers, and constantly watched that the program being delivered in the field was the program they had designed. Further, some of the programs in the Consortium lasted longer and were more intense than the typical Head Start experience. Thus Head Start probably got more credit than it deserved as a result of the Consortium report.

On the other hand, Head Start has never received the credit it does deserve in areas overlooked by Westinghouse, the Consortium, and most other studies. There is no doubt that the dental and medical care and the nutritional components of Head Start benefit the child's growth trajectory. By the same token, we have repeated reports that as a result of Head Start involvement parents improve their own lives in a manner that can only be helpful to their children's ultimate progress in life (Pizzo and Tufankjian, 2004). Also ignored are findings that parents who are involved in a quality preschool program become better socializers of their younger children.

Nevertheless, there is little question that the Cornell Consortium findings turned the tide for Head Start in Washington. Meier recalls, "These supportive results happily served to not only stem any rumored phase-out of Head Start but indeed contributed mightily to a budget increase for Head Start's continued operation" as it regained status as a "bipartisan supported and positively acclaimed program" (personal communication, January 17, 2008). In finally slaying the Westinghouse dragon, the Cornell Consortium had fulfilled the goal I had for it.

Politics as Usual Under President Ford

The Cornell Consortium began as important changes were taking place in Washington. The besieged President Nixon resigned and was replaced by Gerald Ford. President Ford quickly attempted to improve the demoralized executive branch and restore confidence in the federal government by filling several open administrative positions. OCD had not had a permanent director since I left in 1972. President Ford appointed John Meier to head the agency. Because the job also included being Chief of the U.S. Children's Bureau, Meier's appointment had to be confirmed by the Senate, a step usually unnecessary for presidential appointees.

An academician and scholar, Meier was highly qualified to lead our nation's efforts on behalf of young children and their families. Like so many involved in launching Head Start, he was an expert in the area of mental retardation. He and Glen Nimnicht had run an early intervention project similar to several others in the pre-Head Start days that had the goal of preventing later mental retardation. They both worked at Colorado State College (now the University of Northern Colorado at Greeley), which was one of the sites where teachers were trained for the first summer of Head Start. Meier was appointed to Johnson's Head Start Professional Advisory Committee and served on a team of reviewers who visited the new year-round Head Start programs that were started after the first summer. He also had some contact with Project Follow Through, run by the Office of Education in collaboration with OEO, and served as a professional advisor to establish the Parent–Child Centers. Before he came to Washington, he had been director of the John F. Kennedy Child Development Center for service, training, and research on developmental disabilities at the University of Colorado School of Medicine.

For a while he split his time and served as Vice President of Education for the Hasbro Toy Corporation. In anticipation of the passage of the 1971 Child Development Act, Hasbro was planning a national network of child care centers. This ended with President Nixon's veto of the act.

His early efforts as director of OCD included a better alignment of the 10 regional offices with the Washington office. He also moved the National Center on Child Abuse and Neglect from Washington to Colorado University. Working with Grotberg, Brown, and Esther Kresch in his research shop, he approved a number of worthy projects—most notably the Consortium and the famous Abecedarian program.

Things had changed in Washington between the Zigler and Meier directorships. One change was in name only. According to Meier, Head Start advocates were championing the importance of the family and wanted to add features beyond the comprehensive services that already existed. Meier believes this was a catalyst for changing the name of the agency from the Office of Child Development to the Administration on Children, Youth and Families. Other changes were structural and not as innocuous. I answered directly to the Secretary of HEW. After I left, an assistant secretary was inserted between the Secretary and the director of OCD. This bureaucratic change greatly diminished the agency's reach, so Meier never had the authority to make policy decisions that I had. Further, while my decisions did need the approval of the Secretary, Richardson and I saw eye to eye, and he never challenged any of my policy proposals. Although Meier liked to think of his position as bipartisan, the fact is if you are a presidential appointee you work for the president. Because Richardson and I shared similar views, sometimes I did take positions that were in opposition to those of the Nixon White House (e.g., the Child Development Act of 1971). Meier enjoyed no such luxury.

Meier had the talents and background to be an excellent leader of ACYF. He was smart, dedicated to improving the lives of at-risk children, and experienced with the Head Start program and other agency initiatives. Alas, he was just as inexperienced about the nature of government as I had been. This can be seen in his statement that he came to Washington "to fill a conspicuously vacant non-political professional leadership position" (personal communication, January 17, 2008). If you are appointed by the president, you are a political appointee who serves at the pleasure of the president. When the president leaves office, the next administration can decide to fill your position with one of their own.

Meier took his government job because to him it was a wonderful opportunity to help our nation's children and families. To move to the beltway, he had to resign from the JFK center directorship, which meant giving up a visible and important position. He put a deposit on a home in the Washington area. When the Carter and Mondale ticket was elected, Meier thought he would continue to work for the new administration. He recalls that he "perhaps naively expected to be kept beyond his professional (not political) assignment, based on agency performance and a previously effective relationship with the newly-elected Vice President Mondale." This hope, and the deposit on the house, were lost when Meier was "given a precipitous notice to clear offices just before the inauguration in the same week" (personal communication, January 17, 2008). His dedication to the nation's children, however, did not end with his job. After leaving government, Meier remained active in the Head Start program and worked with leaders in Washington "to sustain and improve Head Start's growth and development" until he retired in 2005.

The redeeming trait that Meier and I shared was a scientist's respect for research. I had the courage to challenge researchers at the NAEYC conference that I would stop saying Head Start had lasting benefits if they would stop saying it did not, beseeching a truce until more study was conducted. Meier had the wisdom to support the Cornell Consortium. Although the irreproachable research from the Consortium saved Head Start, the road ahead was far from smooth.

8

President Jimmy Carter, Head Start's Misunderstood Friend

Head Start policy stayed in a holding pattern during the brief presidency of Gerald Ford. The program was limping along with little more than budget increases that barely covered inflation. The Head Start community was hopeful that their needs would be addressed by the new Carter administration. Carter had a history of supporting early childhood education. He particularly liked Head Start, beginning from the time he served on the school board of Plains, Georgia. Like most of the deep South, Georgia was having great difficulty desegregating its schools. Carter admired the full integration of black and white children in Head Start classrooms. (Of course, many southern white families refused to send their children to the integrated Head Start centers and supported the all-white academies that sprung up to circumvent the court-ordered school desegregation.) As governor of Georgia, Carter fought hard to establish public kindergarten open to all children (Vinovskis, 2002). His vice president, Walter Mondale, was a champion of child-friendly policies when he was a Senator. With this new team in power, Head Start's future seemed bright.

I did not meet President Carter until he was already in the White House. However, I had worked very closely with Senator Mondale on a variety of children's issues, including the Comprehensive Child Development Act of 1971 and the first national child abuse law. I somehow got involved in their presidential campaign even though it was against a principle that has guided me ever since my days in the Nixon administration. I have made it a point never to formally endorse a political candidate of either party, but I have also made clear that I would work with any policymaker who would like my help in improving the quality of life for children and their families. On a campaign stop in New Haven, Mondale asked me to walk across the Yale campus with him. I obliged, rationalizing to myself that welcoming an old friend to campus did not constitute a formal endorsement. I compromised my principle further when my colleague, Susan Muenchow, and I helped write one of Carter's campaign speeches on family support. Again I rationalized that I was just sharing my knowledge about child development and that I would have done so for any elected official or contender.

Soon after the election, I was suddenly awakened to the fact that my expectations of Mondale were misguided. I guess I had hoped for a return to the good old days when he vigorously advocated for children's issues in the Senate and valued my counsel about what policies could help to meet their needs. I was taken aback when I met the newly elected vice president at a party, and the first question he asked me was what I thought about the Panama Canal. After admitting I knew absolutely nothing about the Panama Canal, it dawned on me that the vice president is essentially the president's assistant. If the president is interested in the Panama Canal, as Carter was at the time, then so is the vice president. The fact that Carter and not Mondale had given the campaign speeches on family support should have been a clue that domestic policy would be spearheaded by Carter, with the help of his domestic counselor Stuart Eizenstat, rather than by child advocate friend Mondale.

There were other signs that Carter and his administration might not be the answer to the prayers of the Head Start community. Carter had been governor of Georgia, and governors have always had something of a love–hate relationship with Head Start. They love the program and its accomplishments. (Several governors have even contributed state funds to support the program.) On the other hand, they have always been resentful that they have no control over this federal money that comes into their states. Remember, Head Start is the only program managed by the federal government where money goes directly to local grantees, bypassing state authorities.

Congress passed legislation in 1974 giving the Office of Management and Budget (OMB) the authority to create sub-state planning districts to coordinate the various federal human service funds the states received. Governor Carter sent OMB a letter asking to use the new authority to take control of Head Start in Georgia. Harley Frankel, then deputy director of the Office of Child Development (OCD), believed that Carter had good intentions, but he and Saul Rosoff, OCD's acting director, felt that a loss of federal control over Head Start would be the beginning of the end of the program (Zigler and Muenchow, 1992). Working from inside government, Frankel and Rosoff manipulated the system to ward off Governor Carter's grab for Head Start.

They also approached the nation's most visible advocate for Head Start, Marian Wright Edelman, and asked her to seek help from then Senator Mondale with whom Edelman had worked so closely on the 1971 Comprehensive Child Development Act (Chapter 6). Mondale in turn contacted Senator Muskie, the chief sponsor of the bill giving OMB the authority to create sub-state districts. Muskie told OMB that if they overstepped their bounds on the Head Start issue, they might jeopardize the authority they had been given.

Caspar Weinberger, Secretary of HEW, also did not share the Nixon administration and OMB's delight with Governor Carter's request (Vinovskis, 2002). A basic tenant of the Nixon administration was the New Federalism, directed at strengthening the authority of states and reducing federal control. Weinberger had become a stalwart advocate of Head Start, questioning the Westinghouse study while at HEW, and before that, supporting some of my initiatives when he was deputy director of OMB. In response to Carter's request, Weinberger stated, "In the case of Head Start, I wanted to be assured that the money would go where it was intended. I didn't want the schools to spend money for Head Start on vocational education or some other activity" (quoted in Zigler and Muenchow, 1992, p. 177). Weinberger's opposition to releasing control of Head Start to the state of Georgia was particularly courageous and commendable inasmuch as defending the federal-to-local funding mechanism for Head Start grants was contrary to the New Federalism policy. With all of this high-level pressure, Governor Carter's request for Head Start was not approved.

The Push to Establish a Federal Department of Education (and the Counter-push to Keep Head Start out of It)

Federal education policies and programs were housed in the Department of Health, Education and Welfare. Many education people felt that their interests (and share of the budget) were given short shrift, buried by larger public health and social service responsibilities (Vinovskis, 2002). (Prior to the 2001 No Child Left Behind Act, the federal government's role in education was relatively small.) During the 1976 campaign, candidates Carter and Mondale both endorsed a separate cabinet-level department of education. Carter's campaign pledge was to consolidate the public school, job training, early childhood, and many other education-related functions into a single office within earshot of the president. As a result, the National Education Association (NEA) teachers union gave Carter their endorsement, the first they had ever given to a presidential ticket. (Vinovskis, 2002, reports that rival union American

Federation of Teachers also endorsed Carter but opposed the idea of a separate education department.) Shortly after the election NEA began pressuring Carter to make good on his promise, complaining that the association was losing dues because of its support of his candidacy. The NEA wanted a definite date when the new department of education would be announced.

In spite of his pledge to NEA, President Carter did not immediately propose the new department. Instead, he established the "Reorganization Project" in OMB, which requested time to study the issue. After some months the reorganization team recommended the creation of a broad-based Department of Education and Human Development that included virtually all of HEW except for a few programs. Head Start was on the included list. OMB emphasized that it only recommended Head Start's transfer if other human development programs were moved as well. If the new agency turned out to be a narrowly based Department of Education, the team would oppose the transfer of Head Start. They felt that if the program were run by schools, its focus would winnow to preschool education at the expense of two-generation, comprehensive services. In fact, OMB wanted a broad-based Department of Education and Human Development or no Department of Education at all. Adding to the list of unrealistic expectations placed in Head Start over the years, there was hope that this placement of the relatively small Head Start program could change the nation's entire public school system, making schools more open to parent involvement and more sensitive to the close connection between education and health and social and emotional well-being.

President Carter finally announced his general support for a broad Department of Education after the Reorganization Project released its report. Signs of conflict within the administration began to flicker when his own chief domestic counselor, Stuart Eizenstat, opposed the inclusion of social services such as Head Start in the new department. The president himself appeared to vacillate. When he sent his decision to include human development programs to OMB director James McIntyre, Carter wrote in the margin of the memo, "Be general—no specifics" regarding the particular programs to be transferred (Zigler and Muenchow, 1992, p. 181). The Head Start community kept trying without success to determine the president's position on Head Start's placement. Hearings on the bill to create a department of education were scheduled for mid-April, and by late March the president still had not decided which programs would be moved.

Despite the pressure, Carter took his time endorsing the bill that Senator Abraham Ribicoff introduced in March, 1977 to create a broad-based Department of Education. Why did Ribicoff want to dismantle HEW by removing education and a host of other programs? I personally feel that his own experiences when he was Secretary of HEW motivated this bill. I knew Abe well, and he once confided in me that HEW was impossible to manage. He felt that his only real accomplishment as Secretary was the installation of an elevator that ran nonstop to his office on the top floor. Ribicoff evidently felt that since he was unsuccessful as the manager of HEW that HEW was simply unmanageable. Thus he had been sponsoring legislation to create a separate department of education since 1965. However, with the 1977 bill he had more than half the members of the Senate as co-sponsors.

Carter Surprises

Two days before the administration was scheduled to testify before Ribicoff's committee, President Carter had still not announced which programs would move from HEW to the Department of Education, other than the Office of Education. McIntyre and Eizenstat were begging him to make a decision. Just a few hours before they had to appear before Congress, the president's memo arrived: Carter wanted Head Start placed in the new department. This was a big surprise to the senior members of his administration, most of whom had been assuming Head Start would be spared. In fact, OMB had already acted on this assumption and quickly had to change all the testimony, graphs, and charts it had prepared to conform to the president's newly announced position.

My opinion is that my old friend Mondale influenced President Carter's decision. Carter's staff consisted of relative newcomers to the Washington scene, whereas Mondale's staff was an experienced group of people well-versed in Washington politics. These political veterans were extremely sensitive to the wishes of the NEA. In fact, in a memo to Carter urging quick action on the education department, Mondale reminded the president that the NEA and other education groups liked the idea and that "We specifically supported that position" and received NEA's endorsement in return. "An extensive administration review of other options will be seen as a major retreat from our campaign pledge" (Vinovskis, 2002, pp. 40–41).

Another theory has been advanced to explain Carter's decision, this one just as politically motivated. The president may have needed Senator Ribicoff's support for a major arms sale of F-15s to the Saudis and Egyptians. Ribicoff was the only Jewish Senator who supported Carter on this sale. However, Zigler and Muenchow argued, "it is equally likely that the President simply bought OMB's vision of a broad-based education department" and felt "the broader the department, the more difficult it would be for special-interest groups to control it" (1992, p. 183).

Both because there was little agreement within the Carter administration on moving Head Start, and the fact that Carter made his decision so late, the hurriedly prepared testimony before the Ribicoff committee was weak and unconvincing. For example, the testimony given by Deputy Assistant Secretary for Human Development Services James Parham praised Head Start as "a modern success story" and said Carter pledged "adequate safeguards" to keep the program intact after the transfer (Vinovskis, 2002, p. 74). Senator John Heinz tried repeatedly to get Parham to build the administration's case or at least to tell the committee his personal opinion on the proposed move. Parham waffled to the point that Heinz admonished, "Mr. Parham, I hope you won't think it amiss if I characterize what you have just said as about the most lukewarm, half-hearted statement in support of the administration's proposal I have ever heard from someone who is part of that administration" (Vinovskis, 2002, p. 76). Vinovskis concludes that the unenthusiastic support members of the administration gave to Carter's position on a broad education department that included Head Start actually served to bolster the opposition's case.

The Opposition Rises

About this time Frankel left his position at the Head Start Bureau and moved to the Children's Defense Fund (CDF) where he and Marian Wright Edelman became potent foes of the proposal to move Head Start. Because of the large number of black children in Head Start and Edelman's own experience with the Child Development Group of Mississippi (Chapter 3), in her own thinking Head Start was a civil rights issue. She mobilized a coalition of civil rights leaders including Coretta Scott King, Vernon Jordan, Joseph Lowery, and Jesse Jackson. They sent a telegram to the President's Reorganization Project that strongly urged the administration to reject the transfer of Head Start to the Department of Education. They warned that they had already had to defend "Head Start's independence against segregationists in the South and the machinations of its bureaucratic foes in Washington" (Vinovskis, 2002, p. 56). They did not want to have to defend the program against teacher unions and school administrators, whom they believed would inevitably dominate Head Start's minority leaders in the proposed new department.

Edelman called HEW Secretary Joseph Califano and Vice President Mondale to convey CDF's objections. Califano, whose agency would be weakened by the removal of education programs, made clear that he opposed the whole idea of a department of education. In fact, he had already "assembled a small, secret task force to quickly reorganize his department and give education a more coherent role within HEW—thereby hopefully averting the need for a separate department of education," a "seemingly preemptive strike" that angered some White House advisors (Vinovskis, 2002, p. 41). Califano also recommended that Head Start not be moved and had earlier hedged his position by renaming OCD the Administration on Children, Youth and Families to emphasize Head Start's "comprehensive configuration . . . consequently keeping it in its more compatible 'home' department" (Meier, personal communication, July 17, 2007). Mondale made no such promise, a stance Edelman attributed to the administration's debt to the NEA.

I too began fighting Head Start's move. Ribicoff, the chief sponsor of the Senate bill, was my own Senator from Connecticut. Besides the fact that he represented me, I knew Abe fairly well and had dinner with him on occasion. I asked for a private meeting where I presented my arguments against the transfer. Ribicoff assured me that he admired my views but then mistakenly informed me that he could do nothing to be of help since all he was doing was "carrying the president's water." This was rather misleading in light of the fact that he had been introducing legislation to establish a department of education for years, long before Carter became president. I appeared at the hearings on the bill and said it would be a "disaster" to move Head Start to the new department. Edelman had the luck of speaking directly after Parham and used his lack of directness to support our case that Head Start would be ruined if it were transferred (Vinovskis, 2002).

Meanwhile, the Children's Defense Fund and the National Head Start Association were generating 10,000 letters a day to Congress. These were not standard form letters but individual letters from Head Start's staff, parents, and many friends. (Remember Head Start had millions of volunteers from the middle class, and they invariably fell in love with what they saw.) The Carter administration quickly realized they had something of a hot potato on their hands in attempting to move Head Start. On the same day OMB chief McIntyre testified before Congress in support of the move, he wrote a memo to President Carter urging him to call Marian Wright Edelman and Coretta Scott King to try to diffuse their opposition. Knowing how unpleasant this task would be, Carter wrote on the top of the memo, "Fritz, do this." Of course, Mondale was no more eager than Carter to place the calls. The following week Mondale went to Asia, leaving the task to his assistant, Bill Smith. Smith called Edelman and reported that "Marian will fight the transfer with every resource at her command" (Zigler and Muenchow, 1992, pp. 183–184). Hoping not to totally fail, Smith asked Eizenstat to call Coretta Scott King. He put the task off for a week and then only made the call after another request from the president. King's response was more tactful but essentially echoed Edelman's position.

Harley Frankel, then at CDF, was wise to the ways of politics and an effective lobbyist himself. One of his heroic efforts to head off Head Start's transfer was to ask former president and Head Start founder Lyndon Johnson for his help. Frankel also obtained the support of Texas Democratic Congressman Jack Brooks for removing Head Start from the Department of Education bill. Brooks went to the White House and offered to carry the bill for the administration in the House Governmental Operations Committee if Head Start was not included.

Despite all this effort, few thought the Head Start community could win this fight when the NEA, powerful members of Congress, and the president himself wanted Head Start in the new department. We were well aware that this was a do or die struggle for Head Start's existence as the wonderful program we knew. Advocates had size but not might to compete with the likes of NEA and strong leaders of critical Senate committees. The National Head Start Association (NHSA) at the time had a total budget of $8,000 a year and a little aid from CDF, not enough for a paid lobbyist. Nancy Spears, a Head Start director in Alabama and chair of NHSA's public affairs and education committee, took time off from her paid job to address the crisis. Her own board paid a quarter of her salary so that she could work on legislative issues for Head Start. She and Aaron Henry, who was from another state in the deep South, Mississippi, visited legislators and their staffs to convey how harmful the move would be to black Head Start children and families. "And in every single office, they would also encounter the lobbyist for the NEA" (Zigler and Muenchow, 1992, p. 185).

The people who finally saved the day were not skilled lobbyists or politically connected advocates but none other than Head Start parents. Their relentless letters and calls began to erode what had been broad congressional support for moving Head Start to the new Department of Education. The grand finale came when two busloads of parents, one from Connecticut and one from Illinois, set out on an all-night trip to Washington to take their case directly to their Senators, Ribicoff and Charles Percy. In probably the single most dramatic incident in all of Head Start's history, these parents were able to change the two Senators' minds. Soon after their visit, the committee voted unanimously to delete Head Start from the Department of Education bill. The committee recommended that Head Start maintain its current position in ACYF and not be moved to any organizational structure where it would be administered by state education or welfare agencies.

Shortly thereafter in the House, Congressman Brooks introduced the Department of Education bill, minus Head Start. At the time, ACYF was headed by Blandina "Bambi" Ramirez. She had been stuck with the touchy job of protecting Head Start against a move to the new education department while working for a president who had recommended it. She described the victory as "a miracle that the least empowered parents took on a President of the United States they liked and won" (Zigler and Muenchow, 1992, p. 186).

In the end, Carter kept his promise to establish a separate Department of Education, but it was not the broad agency including human development services that he and his administration had originally proposed. The department is a creature of the education establishment in the same way the Department of Labor is a creature of organized labor. Although education officials must carry out legislation passed by Congress, there has been criticism that the agency distributes federal funds to our public education system with what appears to be insufficient accountability. Unlike Head Start that is actually run out of the Department of Health and Human Services (the old HEW with Education removed) and the 10 regional offices, the Department of Education does not run programs of this size. Instead, the federal money is block-granted to the states, which then determine how to allocate the funds to local school districts. What often happens with the block grants is that state officials feel free to ignore the few regulations that accompany them and essentially run the funded programs as they see fit. For example, a program much larger and more costly than Head Start is Title I of the Elementary and Secondary Education Act, which has been managed for years by the states. Legislation has long required considerable parent involvement, but the mandate has been largely unheeded. By the same token, despite new funding formulas meant to target more Title I money to high-poverty school districts, their share of the pie has changed little since 1997 (Institute of Education Sciences, 2007).

Proposals to transfer Head Start to the Department of Education, that is, to block-grant it to the states, are periodically resurrected, most recently by George W. Bush (Chapter 12). The states' track record for preserving the integrity of block-granted programs shows this is still a bad idea. Likewise, arguments that Head Start's comprehensive services and parent involvement would be lost if the program were run by the education department are still valid. As Spears bluntly stated in testimony against Carter's proposed transfer, "Head Start is not an educational program" and does not belong in the Department of Education (Vinovskis, 2002, p. 81). Although preschool education is a core component, Head Start has much broader goals that target the whole child as well as the child's family—goals outside of the traditional bailiwick of public schools.

Friends in the White House

President Carter actually liked Head Start very much, and it is doubtful he thought moving it to the Department of Education would harm it in any way. In fact, he chose some very strong proponents of Head Start for his staff, more than any other president. Holding the prominent position of Chief Domestic Policy Advisor was Stuart Eizenstat, who became more and more interested in children's issues while in the Carter White House. (His wife, Frances Carol Eizenstat, once worked at the Children's Defense Fund and was a well-known child advocate.) This interest was buttressed further after Eizenstat brought Harley Frankel on board. I had hired Frankel into OCD as a result of a meeting I had with Sid Marland, then head of the Office of Education. Harley was his assistant and debated me very intelligently (Chapter 4). I decided I would rather have this MBA from Harvard on my side rather than the other side. Evidently the Carter White House, as a result of the battle with CDF where Frankel had moved, decided they too would rather have him as an ally than a foe. He was recruited to the White House team, where, according to Pizzo, he "was the major strategist for all the positive things that happened to Head Start" during the Carter years (personal communication, February 29, 2008).

The pro-Head Start team was strengthened further in 1980 when Eizenstat and Frankel brought Peggy Pizzo into the White House. Pizzo's addition was of great importance because she was well-trained in the discipline of human development. For the first time the White House had a real child development expert to inform the president as he moved forward on Head Start issues. Pizzo had completed master's studies at the famous Tufts University Eliot-Pearson Department of Child Study. Although her schooling taught her about children's developmental needs and how to interpret and use research, she makes clear that "it was not research that lead me to support Head Start initially. It was direct personal experience in the program" (personal communication, February 29, 2008). During Head Start's early years Pizzo had worked in Head Start centers in New York City's East Harlem and in the inner-city of Rochester, New York. She states, "I had seen with my own eyes what a good program it was, when well-run, and how much it helped children and families."

Stu Eizenstat was the de facto leader of this group of Head Start's friends that created an instant bond between the White House and the DHHS, where Head Start was housed. Both Harley Frankel and Peggy Pizzo had served stints at the Administration on Children, Youth and Families. Pizzo was the special assistant to the commissioner at ACYF, where she had been involved in some White House decision making, while Frankel once headed ACYF's Head Start Bureau. This small group of former insiders was expanded to key figures at HHS. Leading the contingent was the Secretary of Health and Human Services, Patricia Harris. She had replaced another Head Start friend, Joseph Califano, who evidently had rocky relations with the Carter White House beyond reorganizing his agency to ward off the creation of the Department of Education.

Although Carter was surrounding himself with Head Start supporters, the program's advocates did not always see it that way. One battle erupted when Bambi Ramirez was chosen to replace John Meier as head of ACYF, where she would be responsible for administering the program. Bambi was a young Hispanic scholar who had close ties to Vice President Mondale. The Head Start community contained a large number of black individuals, and many felt ACYF should be headed by a black rather than by a Hispanic. For many years the position of Head Start Bureau Chief usually went to a black person, and the blacks in Head Start resented the idea that a black chief would have a Hispanic as his or her boss.

This conflict came to a head at a national Head Start conference held in Texas. I was to speak at the conference and had arrived a couple of days early. Instead of spending time in my hotel suite working on my speech, I received delegation after delegation of Head Start people who wanted me to speak against the Ramirez appointment. I frankly thought it was a tempest in a teapot since the Carter administration had already made its decision, and it was a done deal. I tried to smooth matters over by writing a new introduction to my speech in which I pointed out that a split between blacks and Hispanics could only hurt Head Start. I stated that when the Head Start community was united we were not a particularly strong force in Washington. Division in our ranks would only weaken our influence further. I said I intended to support Bambi Ramirez in her work on behalf of our program. This seemed to quell the revolt.

The Head Start contingent at the White House also included Laura Miller, Special Assistant to Pat Harris, and later Jack Calhoun, who in 1980 replaced Ramirez as head of ACYF. Jack was an expert in children's services, and he too was once the federal official responsible for Head Start. It is interesting that with all of the pro-Head Start influence there, the Carter years are not recalled as particularly helpful to Head Start.

This informal Head Start group had three serious goals. First, they wanted to inculcate a more positive congressional and public perception of the program's effectiveness. The second goal was to get additional funding for Head Start over both the FY 1981 and FY 1982 budget cycles. Most importantly, their third goal was to stem the decrease in the quality of the Head Start program. A major cause of this erosion in quality was the very high inflation rate that characterized the Carter years. Congress was simply not providing the funds necessary to keep program costs even with the rate of inflation. When everything costs more and funding does not cover the increases, services have to be reduced, spread too thin, or downgraded. The quality and funding issues are inseparable in that real quality has a cost.

Budget Battles

The growing weakness in the quality of Head Start programs did not go unnoticed at the OMB, which has the institutional responsibility to examine the functioning of federal programs and to determine the amount of money the administration would be willing to spend on each. The pro-Head Start group was concerned that OMB would use Head Start's quality problems as a reason to oppose an increase in the budget. There was also fear that, in Pizzo's words, OMB would "insist on a fundamental restructuring of the program, using a budget examiner's perspective, not a child development perspective, as to the elements deemed essential to quality in the program" (personal communication, February 29, 2008).

OMB is essentially an arm of the White House, so Frankel and Pizzo were able to meet face-to-face with key OMB officials in an attempt to get a favorable budget decision. They were troubled to discover that OMB officials were divided as to the value of a budget increase to both expand the program and to repair the quality problems. According to Pizzo, "one influential OMB career official seemed particularly enthusiastic about using this opportunity to do precisely the restructuring of the program that experts in child development feared." She reports that Head Start again had a white knight. OMB's Program Associate Director for Human Resources, Gil Omenn, was a physician who had provided on-site health consultant services to Head Start in its early days. Pizzo reports, "He needed no extensive position papers to personally persuade him that the program was worth expanding; and he was supportive of setting aside some funds in the budget request to remove the threats to quality."

In September of 1980, "Secretary Harris sent forward a request for a $308 million increase in Head Start funds, to be divided three ways: program expansion; protection of quality in Head Start; and a cost-of-living increase" (Pizzo, personal communication, February 29, 2008). Pizzo's next task was to prepare a background memo on Harris's request for Eizenstat. She analyzed this request against several sources of other data about Head Start, including a House appropriations committee investigation of the program and appropriations hearings and decisions from 1971 to 1981.

Pizzo also used the results of early intervention research, including the Cornell Consortium study, to show the centrality of quality to positive child outcomes. In her memo she asserted, "There is clear evidence program quality is threatened" in Head Start "due to a previous Executive Branch pattern of not requesting budget increases for inflation-inspired increased costs" (personal communication, February 29, 2008). The memorandum appealed for the money necessary to offset inflation and to get the Head Start quality improvement story back on track.

The budget issue for Head Start was taken directly to the president by both Eizenstat and OMB Director McIntyre. Armed with Pizzo's memo, Eizenstat projected strong support for the increase in funding. He recalled, "OMB's job is always to say no. I pushed OMB and ultimately the President for increases for the program" (Zigler and Muenchow, 1992, p. 187). According to Pizzo, McIntyre provided reluctant support, but support nonetheless.

Eizenstat, Frankel, and Pizzo worked hard to get President Carter to announce a $300 million increase for Head Start prior to the upcoming national election. They wanted a large request so that even if Carter lost the election it would be difficult for the next administration not to provide some increase in funding for Head Start. OMB Director McIntyre did not like pre-election requests, but he agreed to write a memo recommending that the president ask for $125 million for Head Start to address quality concerns and the need for expansion. Carter, like previous incumbents, did not want to tie the hands of the incoming president. Thus OMB won, and the president proceeded to request the smaller $125 million increase. Nonetheless, Pizzo felt that the pro-Head Start group had won an important victory in that the budget request "did not call for any restructuring of Head Start along the lines that had been advocated by career budget examiners within OMB."

Pizzo was married to a prominent physician, and in December of 1980 they gave a party at their home in honor of Stu and Fran Eizenstat, both respected child advocates. Frankel arrived at the party waving a *New York Times* editorial that praised Head Start. The FY 1982 budget had been delayed in getting to the printers, so right in the middle of the party Frankel and Eizenstat adjourned to a corner of the living room and decided to make an effort to get the president to add $60 million to the Head Start program. Pizzo and Frankel were charged with drafting a memo containing the new request shortly before New Year's Eve. Eizenstat then personally made sure the memo was sent to President Carter at Camp David, where the president was spending New Year's. Unfortunately for Head Start, "the President did not adopt this—perhaps because the printing deadline had been reached before he read it" (Pizzo, personal communication, February 29, 2008).

The authors have gone into this great detail over the budget battle to offer a glimpse into how Head Start has managed to stay alive and navigate difficult political climates for well over 40 years. Without a doubt, the program's longevity is due to the dedication of many people. Among those who deserve a place in Head Start's hall of fame are the Carter White House team of Eizenstat, Frankel, and Pizzo. Undergirding their dedication was a genuine concern for poor children and how to improve their chances in life. Instead of being self-congratulatory, Pizzo still voices regret to me that her group was not able to obtain the funding so necessary for improving Head Start services. She laments that Head Start policy is too much driven by the percentage of eligible children being served rather than concern with what type of program the children and their families are receiving. As Pizzo states, adding additional children to the program is "always a favorite of members of Congress." To child development scholars such as Pizzo and the authors, the primary issue is the quality of the services the program delivers. The authors have long argued that it is a better use of money to serve fewer children well than more children not very well.

Making the Most of Research Findings

Harley Frankel was as convinced as I was that Head Start would rise or fall on the evidence regarding its effectiveness. Pizzo notes, "research was a major underpinning of Harley' strategy, especially research syntheses that were maturing in 1976–1978 (some of which had been planned, with significant foresight, during the time that Ed Zigler was chief of the Office of Child Development)" (personal communication, February 29, 2008). By this time the White House and everyone in it were aware of the results of the Cornell Consortium that showed high-quality preschool programs had long-lasting effects. On its heels another supportive study appeared. In the mid-1970s George Washington University issued a report summarizing 150 research studies on Head Start and concluded that the program "did help children make improvements in their cognitive development and health while aiding their families" (Mills, 1998, p. 225). Frankel, who was then still a lobbyist for the Children's Defense Fund, papered Congress with this report so that it too became well-known in Washington.

While the Cornell Consortium findings finally freed Head Start from the stigma cast by the Westinghouse Report, one of the Consortium projects had perhaps more historical importance. This was the Perry Preschool program in Ypsilanti, Michigan (often called High/Scope, after its designers, the High/Scope Educational Research Foundation). As Hacsi concludes, "In late 1980 a study was released that would gain more coverage in media and political debates over Head Start in the next fifteen years than any other—and it was not even an evaluation of Head Start itself" (2002, p. 36). The High/Scope researchers found that the graduates of their program at age 15 were doing much better on a variety of measures compared to their controls. The Carnegie Corporation had funded this study and approached the results as a scientific contribution but not as a really big deal. In fact, they were of the opinion that coming such a short period after the Consortium report, these findings were not particularly surprising or newsworthy.

Pizzo thought differently. She immediately realized that these further positive findings would have the same beneficial effects in support of Head Start as did the original Cornell Consortium report. From her position in the Carter White House, Pizzo convinced the Carnegie people to hold a media event. As Hacsi notes, the press conference created a firestorm. *Newsweek's* coverage at the time was typical: their story emphasized the beneficial effects of the Perry Preschool program on reading, language, and math achievement and pointed out that the program children were only half as likely to need costly special education. What was new since the Consortium report was that these children were less likely to engage in juvenile delinquency.

The finding that would most capture the nation's attention was a 248% return on the investment in preschool, resulting from benefits like fewer years spent in special education or repeating a grade, and projected higher lifetime earnings because of higher academic achievement (Schweinhart and Weikart, 1980). The investigators continued to follow the preschool graduates and reported that by age 19 the program saved $3 for every dollar invested, $7 by age 27, and over $16 by age 40. The major portion of this cost savings has been due to the lowered cost to society because of less delinquency and criminality. The High/Scope 15-year-old report did not use mesmerizing dollar figures and never would have received the media attention it did if it had not been for Peggy Pizzo's effort.

Unfortunately, in many of these news reports the Head Start program was juxtaposed with High/Scope, and many readers came away with the impression that the two programs were one and the same or at least very similar. High/Scope was often referred to as a "Head Start-like" program, and some reports even mistakenly attributed the findings to Head Start. Hacsi and many others pointed out how inappropriate it was to equate the two programs. Although the children in the Perry Preschool were poor, they were likely not nearly as poor as Head Start children, who had to be below the poverty line to be eligible. On the other hand, the children in the Perry Preschool study probably had lower initial intelligence scores. The founder of this program, David Weikart, was Director of Special Services for the public school system of Ypsilanti. Like the designers of many of the earlier intervention programs, Weikart was interested in reducing the prevalence of mental retardation. Thus low intelligence was a criterion for entry into the High/Scope project. The IQ scores of the children selected to participate were between 70 and 85.

The components of the Head Start and Perry Preschool interventions were also dissimilar. These differences were highlighted in a paper by the two authors entitled, "Is the Perry Preschool Better than Head Start? Yes and No" (Zigler and Styfco, 1994). Head Start obviously serves many more children in many more places than the 58 preschool students and 65 controls the Perry project served at a single site. Head Start is the better program in regard to the comprehensive services provided to children and families. For example, there were no dental, health, or psychological services to High/Scope children. While the High/Scope program worked directly with both children and their families, parents did not have any role in the actual conduct of the program like they do in Head Start. On the other hand, High/Scope's educational component was far superior to that of Head Start. The intervention was based on a theoretically sound set of formulations and implemented in an exacting manner in one site where the investigators could watch that it was being delivered according to plan. All the teachers were certified in both early childhood and special education. They were responsible for fewer children and were paid much more than Head Start teachers, who have considerably less education and coaching.

Zigler and Styfco concluded that if all components of Head Start were high quality, then the program could produce benefits to children and families greater than those of the Perry Preschool because of its whole-child, two-generation approach. Although in recent years the quality of Head Start has improved, it still does not compare with the quality of the High/Scope project. For this reason alone, it is not realistic to expect the two programs to achieve comparable results.

The Perry Preschool program ended in 1967, but the High/Scope Foundation has continued to collect longitudinal data on the participants under the direction of the very capable Larry Schweinhart. In a personal communication to me, Schweinhart stated, "It is ironic that Head Start has welcomed political cover from Perry without working to minimize its effective differences with Perry" (March 11, 2008). Perhaps it is true that Head Start advocates consciously or unconsciously welcomed the confusion with High/Scope and "borrowed" its positive results. But under a watchful scientific community, and having a fair share of vocal opponents, Head Start could never succeed by attaching itself to the Perry Preschool's coattails.

There is no question that Head Start advocates have tried for years to improve the quality of services "to minimize its effective differences with Perry." In this chapter alone we saw how hard the ad hoc Head Start group worked to improve quality during the Carter administration. Both authors have spent most of their professional lives attempting to raise the quality of Head Start, particularly its preschool education component. There is some evidence that quality improvement initiatives started during the Clinton administration have paid off in terms of child outcomes (Powell, 1998).

Rightly or wrongly, the longitudinal findings of the Perry Preschool program were a big help to the pro-Head Start group in the Carter White House. They did manage to win budget increases for both FY 1981 and FY 1982. The growing fame of the Perry graduates also improved Head Start's image with Congress. This may be one of the reasons that Congress protected Head Start during the troubling Reagan years.

Head Start Turns 15

One way the domestic policy staff tried to win over President Carter was to stage a big fifteenth anniversary party for Head Start. Eizenstat was the M.C., and Lady Bird Johnson was the guest of honor. Eizenstat and Frankel wrote an address for the president to deliver to the large audience invited to the White House to celebrate the occasion.

Also present was a young man who was shown in a film that had been taken when he was one of the first Head Starters 15 years earlier. In the film he appeared totally flaccid and incapable of the simplest activity. It turned out he was suffering from a curable malady that was corrected as a result of medical treatment he received through Head Start. While the effect seemed as though Head Start had performed miracles, the point was that during its first decade about one-third of participating children were found to have health problems. As with the young man at the anniversary party, about 75% of these ill children received the medical care they needed.

With both the Head Start graduate and Lady Bird Johnson there, the event was pretty emotional. The president's speech built to its high point, which was supposed to be the announcement of a budget increase for Head Start. But here the president began ad-libbing and spoke of his own early memories of Head Start when he was on the school board in Plains, Georgia. To the domestic staff's relief, after he described his deep affection for the program he returned to his prepared remarks and read the section recommending the budget increase. Carter then announced another idea of Frankel's, the appointment of a presidential blue-ribbon committee to develop recommendations to strengthen the Head Start program.

The day after the party, I was asked to chair the 15-year anniversary committee. As Peggy Pizzo recalls, I was recommended for the position not only because I was a founder of Head Start and had once been the federal official responsible for the program, but because I "was known to favor a scrutiny of all aspects of Head Start" (personal communication, February 29, 2008). She states that Frankel's conception of this presidential commission would be to "summarize all findings about Head Start, both positive and negative." Even though I was known to be a supporter of the program, I guess I was also known as a constant but constructive critic.

I selected committee members carefully because I wanted to make sure the group's recommendations would have as much credibility as possible. I invited Bambi Ramirez, the former director of ACYF, as well as unrelenting advocate Marian Wright Edelman. I also enlisted people closely involved with Head Start in its early days including Julius Richmond, Saul Rosoff, Jule Sugarman, and planner Jacqueline Wexler. One distinguished member was Urie Bronfenbrenner, the planner who had returned to the Head Start fold after the Cornell Consortium results convinced him the program was worth doing. I wanted our final report to reflect Head Start's respect for parents and practitioners, so I also invited Rosalie Carter-Dixon, who was president of the National Head Start Association, as well as a representative of the National Head Start Parents Association. (The two groups have since combined.) Hacsi observes, "It would have been almost impossible to assemble a group more knowledgeable about Head Start, or more committed to its becoming as good a program as possible" (2002, p. 35).

At that time on my staff at Yale was Susan Muenchow, a gifted writer who had once worked for the *Christian Science Monitor*. Susan worked closely with me and the committee and under my direction took the lead in drafting the fifteenth anniversary report to the president (U.S. Department of Health and Human Services, 1980). The report noted the erosion in quality aggravated by inflation and emphasized the imperative to improve services if Head Start was to have the positive effects expected of it. We made clear that quality costs money and went on record stating that a budget increase was not just desirable but essential. We admitted the unevenness in health services provided by centers around the country. We particularly focused on the low salaries and lack of benefits for workers in the Head Start program. We felt this low compensation made it extremely difficult to attract and retain excellent teachers, a key to program quality.

The committee was saddened to discover that 82 programs in 1980 were still summer-only programs. We pointed out, as I had in my testimony a decade earlier to Congressman Carl Perkins (Chapter 5), that these summer programs could have little if any effect and the money spent on them could be put to better use in Head Start. We pointed out that many of the benefits of Head Start were underappreciated, such as positive impacts on health and on parents and family life. We noted the Kirschner report that showed the beneficial changes inspired by Head Start in the communities it served. The committee supported the policy councils that had been put into place in the early 1970s, showing how they negated the deficit approach so prevalent at the time of Head Start's birth. Like the Head Start planners and early staff (several of whom were on the committee), we recommended that we always take a positive approach toward the poor families participating in Head Start, emphasizing what they can do rather than what they cannot do.

The committee members tried to be realistic and warned against overoptimism about what Head Start could accomplish in the short time it had with children and families mired in poverty. We anticipated the later birth of the Early Head Start program by recommending that Head Start begin at an earlier age and last longer than a brief academic year. We also pointed out that many poor working mothers needed a full day of child care but Head Start was primarily a half-day, 9-month program. We lamented that after 15 years, Head Start was serving only 20% of eligible children. Further, we recommended an adjustment in the eligibility criterion because many children and families living just above the poverty line were as much in need of the Head Start experience as those below it. We recommended that Head Start continue its commitment to recruiting very high-risk families.

Our primary recommendation was that Head Start should bring every single center up to the quality level dictated by the performance standards. We added that this should be followed by a carefully monitored expansion of the program. This was consistent with my personal view that it would be better for Head Start to deliver high-quality services to fewer children than poor-quality services to more children.

These recommendations were fully in keeping with President Carter's direct charge to the committee, which was essentially to strategize how to make Head Start better. Although the Carter administration embraced our recommendations, they were soon to leave office, and the incoming Reagan administration paid absolutely no attention to the report. Thus it is not surprising that the panel similarly charged on Head Start's twenty-fifth anniversary reported many of the same problems and offered many of the same solutions (Silver Ribbon Panel, 1990).

The fact that the Carter administration accepted the committee's recommendations and fully intended to implement them conveys the meaning of our chapter title that President Carter was Head Start's "misunderstood friend." Carter never received the credit he deserved for his Head Start actions. The program's budget nearly doubled during his 4 years in office, and his White House staff included many knowledgeable program advocates. Yet the Head

Start community primarily remembers Carter as the president who tried to destroy Head Start by moving it to the Department of Education. Ironically, the incoming Reagan administration is remembered more fondly for placing Head Start in a "safety net" of programs to be spared the chopping block. In reality, Head Start was asked to do more without a commensurate increase in funding during the Reagan years, and many of the quality supports that had been put into place were weakened.

9

Ronald Reagan "Saves" Head Start

Ronald Reagan was an affable man. He was witty, funny, and his experience as an actor made him at ease on the national stage and adept at engaging his audience. He adhered to very conservative Republican philosophies. His campaign platform promised to reduce the size of the federal government; return power to smaller units like states, localities, and families; and greatly reduce federal taxes so citizens could decide for themselves how they wanted to spend the fruits of their labors. His message struck a chord. He received the electoral votes of 44 states in the 1980 election, which was one of the worst defeats of an incumbent president in history. (In 1984, Reagan won 49 states, trouncing his opponent Walter Mondale, who won only his home state of Minnesota and the District of Columbia.)

Once elected, President Reagan wasted no time acting on his campaign promises. In his first inaugural address, he declared, "government is not the solution to our problem; government *is* the problem.... It is my intention to curb the size and influence of the Federal establishment.... All of us need to be reminded that the Federal Government did not create the States; the States created the Federal Government" (Woolley and Peters, n.d.g). To disperse federal power, he promoted block grants and revenue sharing with local governments to give them "flexibility to solve their own problems in ways most appropriate for each locale" (Woolley and Peters, n.d.d). He also began work on huge tax cuts to encourage investment and stimulate the economy. To compensate for the reduction in tax revenues, government spending would have to be seriously curtailed. An obvious target for elimination was a host of social welfare programs, which Reagan felt were both expensive and indicative of big government meddling and bureaucracy. Encouraged by this fraternal voice, conservative writers (e.g., Murray, 1984) argued that not only were social programs costly, but that they actually hurt the individuals they were meant to help by fostering dependency.

Reagan's conservative views, his disdain for social programs, and his voiced desire for a smaller federal government signaled that Head Start was in for a difficult period. The greatest fear advocates had was that the new administration would block-grant the program to the states, essentially ending the Head Start we knew and had worked so hard to improve and grow. Remember too that Reagan, like Carter, was a former governor. Since the inception of Head Start the governors have been troubled by the fact that large amounts of federal money for the program come into their states, and they have no control over where and how this money is spent. This gave Reagan even more reason to want to block-grant Head Start. Thus at the outset of the Reagan administration, the goal of Head Start advocates was simply to maintain Head Start as a federal program run out of Washington.

Saving Head Start

Achieving even this modest goal appeared a long shot but, as they had so many times in the past, Head Start's supporters sprang into action. Unsurprisingly, probably the first to act was Harley Frankel who, needless to say, had been forced out of his government job upon Carter's defeat. The most important fulcrum of power in the federal government is the Office of Management and Budget (OMB). The day following President Reagan's inauguration, Frankel made a call to a telephone extension he knew at OMB. It was so soon in the life of the new administration that office staff were not yet in place. As luck would have it, a deputy to the new director personally answered the phone. Describing himself as a former member of the Nixon administration (which he was when he worked for me), Frankel said, "I know you'll be cutting a lot of programs. . . . But to avoid bad press, you'll need to save a few, and let me tell you about Head Start: everybody likes it, and it doesn't cost very much" (quoted in Zigler and Muenchow, 1992, pp. 192-193).

The new Secretary of Education under Reagan was Ted Bell, with whom I had worked closely in HEW when he was head of the Office of Education during the Nixon administration. I contacted Ted, made my pitch, and he responded that he was in favor of maintaining the Head Start program because he felt that it did prepare poor children for school entry. Another powerful advocate for Head Start in the Reagan administration was Caspar Weinberger, who had become Secretary of Defense. "Cap the Knife" had a long history of supporting Head Start after he became enamored with the program when he was Secretary of HEW following Elliot Richardson, another strong Head Start ally.

Within a month into the life of the Reagan administration, a cabinet meeting took place to decide the fate of various social programs. The decision was made to maintain a "social safety net" of sorts that would protect a limited number of programs serving the "truly needy" from budget cuts. These included Social Security, Medicare, free school lunches, and some veterans' benefits—not all of which targeted "truly needy" populations (Rosenbaum, 1981). Programs outside the net such as food stamps, Medicaid, and Aid to Families with Dependent Children (AFDC) would experience deep budget cuts. The chief architect of the plan was OMB director David Stockman, who recommended that Head Start be placed in the safety net. Ted Bell and Weinberger also spoke in favor of the program. Although there might have been other factors that led to Head Start's inclusion on the exclusive list of seven social programs that would be spared the budget ax, the support of these three key leaders undoubtedly carried considerable weight.

While Bell's and Weinberger's advocacy for Head Start was permanent, that of David Stockman was not. In the fall of 1981, Stockman floated the idea that Head Start be block-granted to the states. Congressional leaders favorable to Head Start were alerted, and Senator Alan Cranston of California leaked Stockman's proposal to the press right before the Christmas holiday. Writing in the *Washington Post*, Dorothy Gilliam stated, "Just in time for Christmas, it seems we have a real-life, modern-day Scrooge" (in Zigler and Muenchow, 1992, p. 195). Nonetheless, Stockman proceeded to recommend that Head Start be folded into the Community Services Block Grant. As a result of the savings on the federal operation of the program, the 1982 Head Start budget could be cut by $130 million. Once these plans were made public, the outcry was so great the administration backed down. The lesson brought home to the Head Start community was that despite their early victories, they had to maintain their guard.

Head Start was in deep trouble even before the Reagan administration took office. The 15-year anniversary report commissioned by President Carter (Chapter 8) made clear that inflation and resulting cutbacks in staff, hours, and services had decreased the quality of the program. Class size had increased from 15 to 20 children, and the per-pupil expenditure had actually decreased slightly from 1967 to 1980 in real dollars. The heart of the program, namely preschool education, had been degraded by the extremely low salaries paid to teachers. Poor compensation led to unacceptable levels of staff turnover and forced center directors to hire whomever they could get regardless of qualifications. The key in Head Start's quality control system was the support and oversight provided by the 10 regional offices. Their staff had declined by approximately 25% since my days in 1970.

The 15-year report recommended improvement on all of these fronts, but since it had been commissioned by President Carter, it was ignored by the Reagan people. They went in an entirely different direction, arguing that through some sort of super-management at the federal level, they could maintain and even expand enrollment without any new money. To make such nonsense palatable they asserted that it could be done simply by operating more efficiently. Of course in 1981, the most efficient form of operation and certainly the cheapest to the federal government was to give Head Start to the states.

Threats from Within

After I left government, the federal official responsible for Head Start was not the head of the Office of Child Development (OCD) or its successor agency the Administration on Children, Youth and Families (ACYF), but rather the Assistant Secretary for Human Development Services, who in turn reported to the Secretary. Stan Thomas, the first Assistant Secretary in this position, was a liberal Republican in the Nixon administration who clearly had Head Start's best interest at heart. Stan's counterpart in the Reagan administration was Dorcas Hardy. (She is better remembered as Reagan's Commissioner of the Social Security Administration who advocated individually funded private accounts to supplement Social Security.) Hardy, who called herself "100 percent a Reaganite" (DeCoster, 2008), seemed to be trying to one-up Stockman. She decided that if the Reagan administration was not allowed to send Head Start to the states, she could at least slash away at the program. Thus she attempted to accomplish administratively what her colleagues could not accomplish legislatively.

She asked ACYF to prepare a Head Start strategy paper that would respect the changing role of the federal government and give the states more responsibility for the program. What she really wanted was a plan to serve more children with the same amount of money. The task of writing this Head Start manifesto fell to John Busa, then serving as ACYF's Acting Deputy Commissioner. John had worked closely with me during my days in Washington and was a member of my core policy group. Like all of my key people, he was very committed to Head Start. In approaching Hardy's assignment he said, "I tried to follow a fine line between doing what Dorcas wanted and keeping bad things from happening to Head Start. It's sort of the old story of do you spank your own child, or let someone else do it" (quoted in Zigler and

Muenchow, 1992, p. 195). He decided to do it himself, which gave him the opportunity to be gentler than the administration might have liked.

Busa's report was entitled, "Head Start: Directions for the Next Three Years" (ACYF, 1981). He underscored Head Start's benefits, which not only placed the Reagan administration on record as endorsing the program's effectiveness but would make it difficult for them to turn around and dismantle it. Echoing the Carter report, Busa noted the negative impact the low pay, the increase in class size, and inflation were having on the services supposed to be provided. He tried to please the Reagan people by pointing out the cost efficiency of so much volunteerism involved in Head Start. He also included the administration's wish to forgo the Carter administration's $125 million increase in Head Start's budget in favor of a more "affordable" increase of approximately $13 million. In an effort at bureaucratic damage control, the report put on record the assumption that a portion of the $125 million would be made available the following year as a "deferred increase."

Of course, Busa could go just so far in opposing Dorcas Hardy's wishes. Although formal welfare reform was still some years away, many were arguing that poor mothers should be joining the workforce rather than depending on AFDC. Many of these families were in Head Start, which did not typically provide the full-day and full-year child care services these mothers would need to go to work. Back when I ran Head Start there was pressure to expand it into a child care program, which I would have been glad to do if I had been given the money. Now, however, Dorcas Hardy was proclaiming the federal government was "out of the day care business" (quoted in Morgan, 1981, p. 33). In his paper Busa agreeably recommended the Head Start program should not be longer than 6 hours a day and 8 months a year.

Hardy had spoken of "studying Head Start expenditures next year to see if 'we can do a better job and serve more children' by means such as eliminating health and social services components, limiting the children's ages, the hours of the program, the number of administrative cores funded, and the support system" (Morgan, 1981, p. 34). Thus Busa suggested that Head Start's staff: child ratio be relaxed. To save additional money, he recommended that the Parent and Child Centers for infants and toddlers be converted to regular Head Start programs.

John had worked with me in establishing the Child Development Associate program meant to provide affordable, trained workers to both Head Start and child care. Nevertheless, his report recommended withdrawing the federal support that provided scholarships to poor women (often Head Start parents) to train for the CDA credential. Transportation costs would be reduced by "route restructuring," which really meant route elimination. Key research, demonstration, and evaluation activities would be greatly reduced or phased out altogether. Anyone reading this report would reach the conclusion that the Reagan administration was doing all it could to destroy the quality of Head Start, making it pretty much an empty shell while maintaining the Head Start name and flag with its famous logo.

Busa made a clever tactical move by framing his report as a "discussion draft." This allowed him to circulate it broadly, thus alerting the Head Start community and Congress to the administration's plans. Head Start's supporters rallied once again. Protest letters began pouring into ACYF and congressional offices. In February of 1982 the House Subcommittee on Human Resources, which had jurisdiction over Head Start, held an oversight hearing. As a result of this hearing the administration recanted some of its own Head Start manifesto. The new ACYF commissioner Clarence Hodges promised to maintain the few existing full-year Head Start programs, continue federal support for the CDA program, and abandon plans to convert Parent and Child Centers to traditional preschool programs.

To Head Start advocates, Busa's bureaucratic damage control was seen as a positive. However, to the Reagan administration it was viewed as no less than bureaucratic sabotage of their wishes. This incident highlights a major problem of every incoming administration, namely how to control a huge bureaucracy that encompasses a huge number of civil servants who may or may not follow the new boss's orders. The civil service appears to operate as a conservative force maintaining the status quo and slowing down the more radical efforts of any incoming administration. Thus there is a perpetual tension between political figures who view their legitimacy as a result of their having been elected, as opposed to recalcitrant civil servants who have never been elected to anything and are extremely hard to remove. In Busa's case, his efforts to protect Head Start from within resulted in his transfer to another agency.

Quality Supports Dismantled

Following Busa's report and the hearings, the Reagan administration nevertheless continued its attempts to undercut Head Start. For one, they decentralized the key training and technical assistance program. This $27 million effort had been used for on-site reviews of grantee operations, expert consultation to the programs, and training for Head Start staff. The money was also used to assist local programs in serving disabled children as well as linking staff to local colleges and universities so they had access to expertise in early childhood education. The Reagan administration essentially dismantled this network and turned over the money to local grantees with no assurance that these important activities would continue with the same level of intensity. With the money in their hands, more than a few directors used it to fund much-needed improvements in the dismal salaries and almost nonexistent benefits received by their employees. I remember recoiling at the sight of so many Head Start programs becoming little more than tokenistic efforts during the Reagan years.

To make the downward spiral worse, ACYF decided that the regional offices would no longer be required to conduct on-site monitoring of one-third of Head Start programs annually. This move defied the 15-year anniversary report that recommended *increasing* the number of community representatives to conduct on-site reviews of Head Start centers. As a result of reduced staff and travel budgets, the regional offices did little more than desk monitoring of program records for the next decade. Everything we knew then and have learned since indicates that the quality of a program determines its outcomes. My most important work during my stay in Washington was the quality controls we built into Head Start—primarily the performance standards, the training and technical assistance component, and the regional monitoring. All of this was degraded during the Reagan years.

Although Head Start had been placed in Reagan's exclusive safety net of programs that would not be shrunk, that did not stop the administration from taking further steps to reduce the program's cost. The last place they had to look was the national office. Each of Head Start's major components had an individual in the national office committed to overseeing that part of the program. There was a pediatrician in charge of the health component, an early childhood educator responsible for preschool education, a specialist in charge of parent involvement and home visiting, and so on. There was also a research director to coordinate the research and evaluation activities so important in assessing the program's effectiveness and identifying areas in need of improvement.

The highly trained professionals responsible for Head Start's components were not excluded from Reagan's "RIF" (reductions in force) campaign—the bureaucratic name for downsizing. An extremely important loss was that of Jenni Klein, who was a nationally recognized expert in both early childhood and special education. Jenni had worked with me during my stay in Washington, helping to create the Child Development Associate program among many other accomplishments. As a civil servant she could not be fired outright, so she was offered a lower-level, part-time position. She quit. Edith Grotberg, a former American University professor who was Head Start's Director of Research, was also forced to leave. Indeed, the research and evaluation unit was closed. Grotberg had been instrumental in moving the Cornell Consortium study that helped save Head Start, and her reward was being fired. Her colleagues wanted to hold a retirement dinner in her honor, but the Reagan officials refused to permit it. The National Academy of Sciences got wind of this and hosted the party at their building, an act that testifies to Grotberg's reputation in the scientific community.

Head Start's health component was also decimated. In 1982 the administration dismantled the program's national medical support network. In 1987 it closed the health services branch, moving its functions to the Division of Maternal, Child and Infant Health. Head Start's medical director was transferred as well, leaving no one at the Bureau responsible for this core program component.

Our best estimate is that about half of the Head Start staff at the national level and about two-thirds at the regional offices were eventually eliminated under Reagan. In addition, top-level positions at ACYF were left vacant, with temporary leaders serving in an acting capacity. All of these shake-ups from leadership on down essentially dismantled the effective functioning unit that was Head Start.

Holding Back the Tide

The damage of the Reagan years would have been much worse if it had not been for some key experienced staff members who, against all odds, were able to hold the program together during this tumultuous time. Some of these people had been with Head Start since the War on Poverty and were strongly committed to its survival.

Henlay Foster was the national Head Start director from 1980 to 1982. He saw his most important task as maintaining the Head Start program as he had inherited it. His greatest challenge was protecting the Head Start Program Performance Standards, which created a uniform program nationwide and defined quality. The Reagan people early on wanted to revise and relax these standards. Foster's job was to implement the administration's policies, but he did not want to see Head Start deteriorate. He stated, "I cooperated as a civil servant, but I expressed my opposition to what they were doing. Not only was the climate not conducive for changing the standards, but any reduction in the scope of the Performance Standards ran contrary, in my view, to the law and legislative intent" (quoted in Zigler and Muenchow, 1992, p. 200). While the effort to revise the standards proceeded, there were many complaints from the field that received the attention of HHS Secretary Richard Schweiker, who refused to approve the changes. Once again a Secretary thwarted the intentions of the White House.

Foster's attitude did not go unnoticed by the Reagan people, who decided to switch the Head Start director's job from a civil servant position to a political appointment. A political appointee serves at the pleasure of the president and typically is more responsive to the president's wishes than a civil servant, who except for rare instances has a lifetime job. This move lessened the authority of the head of ACYF and injected a new level of political influence into Head Start's administration.

Clennie Murphy, an Inside Hero

The many complaints registered against weakening the performance standards convinced the Reagan administration that Head Start's supporters were a force to reckon with when proposing policy changes. In choosing a new director for the program, they wisely decided to select an insider who would be acceptable to the Head Start community. Enter one of the true heroes in the Head Start story, Clennie Murphy. Murphy had worked in the Head Start Bureau since 1969 and for many years had served as the regional liaison for the national office. In this role he visited the regions quite often and interacted with Head Start directors, staff, and parents. Equally at home with fellow blacks and white bureaucrats, he became widely known and liked in the field. Clennie had worked closely with me during my time in Washington, and I will always be grateful to him for his support. He was one of the very few carryovers from the OEO years who did not look askance at me as a new interloper from the Nixon administration. He was honest and certainly outspoken. On one of our first trips together he confessed that he had heard of Urie Bronfenbrenner but he had never heard of me. Although this could have been construed as an insult, there was no way I could take umbrage at Clennie. There was no malice in him, and he was impossible to dislike.

Murphy agreed to serve in a civil service post as acting Head Start chief from 1983 to 1987. (In 1987, Bessie Ussey moved from the Reagan White House to become Head Start director for 16 months, and Clennie stayed on as her deputy.) As acting chief, it was Clennie's unenviable job to control the uproar that was being expressed nationwide by the Head Start community. In recalling those years Murphy states, "My real struggle was to represent the administration. There was not one federal official I've known who wanted to hurt Head Start; even Dorcas was supportive. But I asked her to tell me if she was going to do something, so that I did not first learn about it in the newspaper" (in Zigler and Muenchow, 1992, p. 201). So warned, whenever Reagan policies conflicted with the wishes of the Head Start community, Murphy was in a position to negotiate the differences before any damage was done. The respect he had earned from the field made it possible for him to tell Head Start supporters when to take on a fight. When he advised them to let a particular issue go, they listened. Murphy's skill in negotiating and smoothing problems over lead to his nickname, "Mr. Kissinger." Amazingly, while two administrations viewed him as cooperatively doing their bidding, the Head Start community continued to view him as one of their own.

Murphy's job was not easy. A major problem he faced was the dilution of Head Start quality exacerbated by increased enrollment. There has been a tendency in Congress to grade Head Start by the percentage of eligible children served instead of the more important yardstick of the quality of the services the children were experiencing. While Congress was raising Head Start's budget by a relatively small amount, the Reagan administration was increasing the number of children in the program by 30% at the cost of the quality control system. Hacsi writes, "by 1989 Head Start's per-child spending had dropped by more than $400, adjusted for inflation. Head Start's program quality, which had been the chief concern of the fifteenth-anniversary report, was clearly damaged" (2002, p. 40). Murphy did what he could. For example, although the Reagan administration proposed no budget increases for Head Start throughout the 1980s, they never opposed the increases appropriated by Congress. Murphy unquestionably influenced this response.

Not too long ago I saw Clennie at a national Head Start meeting and was not surprised to see how much he is still loved by the Head Start community. He certainly earned this high regard by spending the better part of a lifetime building and maintaining our nation's Head Start program. In fact, when President George H. W. Bush succeeded Reagan, Wade Horn, Bush's head of ACYF, made the wise choice of recommending Murphy for the now political post of Chief of the Head Start Bureau. Thus Murphy, with his devotion to Head Start, traversed both the Reagan and Bush administrations. A decades-long civil servant, he was conflicted about becoming a political appointee knowing full well his job could end after the next presidential election. Nonetheless, Clennie told me he accepted the switch from a secure civil servant's job to a political appointment because he had decided to retire by the end of the next administration anyway.

Advocates Win Some Ground

Two advocacy groups deserve mention for protecting Head Start from some of the threats imposed by the Reagan administration. The National Head Start Association (NHSA) grew from a loosely connected network of state chapters of parents and staff into an increasingly knowledgeable and sophisticated organization. Jim Robinson, who had been director of the Head Start Bureau from 1972 to 1980, worked diligently to build up the association. Robinson displayed his inner-Washington know-how when he suggested the group establish a national office: "I said it was important for an association with several thousand members to have an office in Washington to be their eyes and ears, and to understand how legislation is put together" (quoted in Zigler and Muenchow, 1992, p. 202). Learning the ropes of social policy formation and being next door to policymakers helped NHSA lobby for their cause. Their budget was limited, and they had only two people on staff, so their early practice was to draw up a list of NHSA members from each state who could testify on behalf of Head Start issues or meet directly with their elected officials. These individuals proved to be tremendously effective, as demonstrated by their ability to gain the support of some of the most conservative members of Congress.

To illustrate, Nancy Spears, who was one of NHSA's first volunteer lobbyists in the drive to keep Head Start out of the Department of Education (Chapter 8), went to see Republican Senator Jeremiah Denton from her home state of Alabama. Denton had a reputation as a right-wing "moral majority" leader. Spears found it unexpectedly easy to secure Denton's support for Head Start: "Denton was a family man all the way, and he saw Head Start as a family program" (in Zigler and Muenchow, 1992, p. 202). The conservative Republican Orrin Hatch from Utah also became a visible supporter of Head Start. He particularly liked Head Start's ability to attract local volunteers and its support of parents in their roles as children's first teachers.

Another heroine of Head Start's struggles during the Reagan administration was Helen Blank, who had served as the Children's Defense Fund's chief lobbyist for Head Start since 1981. Head Start is periodically reauthorized by Congress, but the 1984 reauthorization had stalled, and Congress was ready to adjourn before the bill was finalized. CDF placed an ad in the *Washington Post* with a picture of young children and the caption, "400,000 children are looking for one good senator" (Zigler and Muenchow, 1992, p. 203). Senator Hatch decided to be that senator. With the help of Republican Senator Robert Stafford (for whom the Stafford federal student loan program is named), the bill was brought to the Senate floor just before the scheduled adjournment. The bill included a badly needed $80 million increase for Head Start.

Another victory was scored in the fight over how long children and families could receive Head Start services. To fund an increase in the number of children participating, the Reagan administration tried to limit Head Start programs to half-day sessions. Further, while NHSA was arguing that some children need a second year of Head Start services, the administration wanted to restrict attendance to 1 year. This was despite the recommendation of the fifteenth anniversary committee that many poor parents only begin to feel comfortable and fully participate in the program after the first year and thus need more time. The Reagan administration was in a difficult position since federal law explicitly states that local programs have the right to provide more than 1 year of service to eligible children from age 3 to the age of compulsory school attendance. To get their way, they had to covertly encourage the regional offices to limit services to 1 year and concentrate on expanding enrollment, while publicly insisting they were following federal law permitting 2 years of participation.

Nancy Spears did not believe them, so she sent out a survey to Head Start grantees. Two-thirds of them said they had received pressure from their regional offices to enroll children for 1 year only. Spears brought her survey to the attention of Congress in the person of Dale Kildee, chair of the House Committee on Education and Labor. As a result, NHSA was able to stop the effort to deny children who needed it more time in Head Start. There are some Head Start centers with 2-year programs, and at least one study demonstrated they were more efficacious in producing school readiness than single-year programs (Wheeler, 2002). This finding is validated by the work of Arthur Reynolds (1995), who demonstrated that school readiness increased when children attended the Chicago Child–Parent Centers for 2 years instead of one.

I was awestruck witnessing the metamorphosis of the Head Start community from the antagonistic and confrontational approach they took in the early 1970s to the much more effective professional approach they took in the 1980s. Their new attitude was reflected in their response in 1988 when Congress agreed to a $50 million set-aside for Head Start salary improvements. This was a long-sought goal of NHSA and everyone who cared about improving the quality of Head Start. Nancy Spears took the lead in getting supporters to send thousands of personal thank-you letters to individual congressmen. She wanted to show them they would not hear from the Head Start community only when it wanted something. The success of NHSA and a few other advocates was showcased when President Reagan himself paid tribute to the program. In a message to participants at a 1986 national Head Start conference the president wrote, "Head Start has demonstrated its worth and effectiveness over the past two decades" (in Zigler and Muenchow, 1992, p. 203).

More Scientific Support

The willingness of Congress to support Head Start, sometimes in opposition to the administration's desires, was facilitated by positive research contributions during the Reagan years. The Cornell Consortium issued its final report in 1983, and the media again took notice of their discovery of long-term effects in the numerous early interventions they assessed.

A more relevant report was the Philadelphia study of thousands of children who had attended Head Start itself (Copple, Cline, and Smith, 1987). (Only two of the studies included in the Consortium were Head Start programs.) Like many other interventions, the Philadelphia study showed no lasting effect of Head Start on achievement test scores. However, the Head Start children were more likely than their peers to be in the right grade for their age and were more apt to attend school regularly. As it is today, the nation was concerned about the drop-out problem, and thus the impact of the Philadelphia study was quite marked.

Being on the defensive during the Reagan years, ACYF contracted with CSR, Inc. to synthesize the large body of completed Head Start research to inform programming and policy, to identify areas in need of improvement, and to be available to the research community. Ruth McKey of CSR and her colleagues (1985) examined a subset of 210 longitudinal studies limited strictly to children who had attended Head Start. Like the Consortium findings with model programs, McKey et al. also found that Head Start graduates showed initial cognitive gains that soon dissipated, but they did better than their peers on indicators such as being kept back or placed in special education. Some of the positive findings reported were based on a very few number of studies that had examined the particular factor, meaning that if more studies had looked at the same factor the result might have disappeared or in fact been stronger. There is no way to tell in the absence of data. Yet this is not the only reason the synthesis project had little impact.

Unfortunately, the McKey et al. study was simply not very good from a scientific standpoint. It had serious methodological flaws including the inclusion of poor studies and lack of attention to group selection biases. These flaws negated the worth of the analyses conducted. The standard critiques of the study from the scientific community were expected (e.g., Gamble and Zigler, 1989), just as when empiricists responded to the Westinghouse Report. What was unexpected was what can only be described as a vitriolic criticism of the study and its methodology by Bernard Brown (1985), a senior research figure at ACYF. This was rather strange and indicated to me that the head of ACYF at the time was asleep at the switch. It is unheard of that the head of an agency would allow a formal report commissioned by that agency to be released when the report's authors and one of its own senior researchers had such bitter differences of opinion. Such a situation can only impair the report's credibility and the agency's reputation and research program.

The Perry Preschoolers Grow Up

The synthesis project, and the strife it revealed within ACYF, might have attracted more attention if all eyes were not focused on the latest results of the High/Scope Perry Preschool, one of the programs in the Cornell Consortium. In 1984, the investigators released the findings of their ongoing longitudinal evaluation of the Perry preschoolers who were now 19 years old (Berrueta-Clement, Schweinhart, Barnett, Epstein, and Weikart, 1984). The data were even more impressive than those released during the Carter administration when the participants were 15 years old (Chapter 8). Program graduates earned higher GPAs than children in the control group, although the difference was small—slightly above a C average versus a C-minus in the controls (Hacsi, 2002). Thus we see once again that poor children who participate in high-quality programs show some improvement but do not necessarily become honor roll students. The investigators also found that their participants spent less time in special education and were more likely to graduate from high school, go on to college, or take postgraduate vocational training. Although the young adults had been out of high school only a short time, the preschool group was more likely to be employed steadily and had been unemployed for less time. Thus they earned more money and cost the nation less in welfare benefits.

A striking finding of this study was reduced delinquency and criminality. The preschool graduates had been less frequently arrested or charged with serious crimes. A cost–benefit analysis resulted in the most publicized finding in the entire early intervention literature, namely that for every $1 spent on the preschool program, $3 in benefits accrued to the participants or to society. (The latest report at age 40 puts the return at over $16.) The vast majority of these savings were due to lower expenses borne by crime victims who did not become victims because of the reduced crime rates. Although totally inappropriate, again there was a great deal of confusion between the Perry Preschool and Head Start—so much so that a conservative think tank called Head Start a "scam" for borrowing Perry's fame (Hood, 2004).

As we discussed in Chapter 8, Head Start is a far different program than the Perry Preschool program was. The High/Scope project was of much higher quality in terms of veracity to the model, teacher qualifications, and length and intensity of services. The per-pupil cost of the Perry Preschool was approximately twice that of Head Start. Certainly High/Scope's outcome measures assessed a wider array of results and the evaluation continued much longer than any efficacy study of Head Start or any other early intervention mounted to date. However, a caveat is in order. Most studies have ignored important factors that in all probability would favor the Head Start model. For example, many benefits unquestionably accrue to the health of Head Start children, the functioning of Head Start families, and the trickle-down effects to younger siblings. The authors have argued that if service quality is uniformly high, Head Start should produce benefits greater than those of the Perry Preschool because of its comprehensive nature (Zigler and Styfco, 1994).

Hacsi (2002) has noted at some length how the media turned the 1984 High/Scope findings into a direct endorsement of Head Start, failing to note that the 19-year-olds who appeared to be doing so well had attended the Perry Preschool, not Head Start. While agreeing that the High/Scope report had a "major impact on federal policies," Hacsi appropriately states, "Whether that influence made sense, however, was another question" (p. 43). Nonetheless, the combined effect of this and the other empirical reports released during the Reagan years was to convince policymakers and taxpayers that early intervention for at-risk children was worth doing.

Decommissioning the Measurement of Social Competence

A bedrock principle held by Head Start's planners was that school readiness is influenced by all aspects of the child's functioning (cognitive, physical, social, and emotional) as well as by parental and community support of child development. The problem with this whole-child approach is that it is vague in regard to what goal or goals should be used to assess Head Start's efficacy. As discussed in detail in Chapter 5, in the absence of such a clear goal evaluators turned to the easily used IQ test to assess the impact of Head Start. Once repeated studies demonstrated that participation resulted in immediate but not lasting IQ gains, Head Start either needed another goal or had to be deemed a failure. I made an attack on this approach when I was at OCD and officially proclaimed that a child's everyday social competence was the program's goal. What was missing was a simple way to measure this outcome, something evaluators could employ to assess Head Start and other early intervention programs.

I got busy on this task while I was still in Washington. To briefly recap, OCD contracted with the Educational Testing Service (ETS) to define and develop a viable measure of my social competence construct. They instead produced a huge laundry list of every conceivable domain that entered into social competence. The list derived from what respected scholars thought was essential to the definition, but there was no way their myriad ideas could be reduced to a useable set of measures. Those who followed me at OCD and ACYF continued this important task of trying to generate a practical set of measures that could be used by researchers to evaluate Head Start.

Following the failure of ETS, and another unproductive attempt by the Rand Corporation, the definitional task fell to Mediax Associates (1980). They began with the premise that social competence refers to the child's everyday effectiveness in dealing with the environment and responsibilities in school and life. They proposed a four-factor model including health and physical well-being, cognitive development, social–emotional features, and "applied strategies." This last domain encompasses the child's ability to devise and use effective courses of action in problem-solving situations and includes such traits as motivation, curiosity, initiative, persistence, and task orientation. (See Raver and Zigler, 1991, for a complete discussion of the efforts to define and measure social competence during the Reagan years.) Note that cognitive development was a piece but not the whole of the proposed definition. The Westinghouse Report had produced an aversion on the part of scholars to rely solely on cognition and its most used measure, the IQ. Nonetheless, we were aware that cognitive ability is particularly appealing to decision makers as well as taxpayers because of the widespread belief that any increase in IQ is beneficial.

The definitional issue resolved, the next step was to develop specific measures of the socioemotional, physical, cognitive, and applied strategies components of social competence that could be used to evaluate Head Start's effectiveness. Mediax contracted with experts in each of these four domains to create measurement instruments. This work was underway when the Reagan administration decided to end three of the contracts and only continue the one developing the cognitive assessment.

Thus, the evaluation measures and the curriculum advocated by the Reagan Head Start central administration were narrowly cognitive in orientation and brought Head Start back full circle to the IQ fixation that left the program with the impossible goal of raising intelligence, a goal that preordained it to fail. The Reagan administration just refused to learn from the past. It is probably fortunate that they produced no cognitive measure that was acceptable either to the Head Start community or to scholars in the field of evaluation. Nevertheless, we were to witness the Reagan approach pushed even further by the George W. Bush administration 20 years later (see Chapter 12).

Death of the White House Conference on Children

Children's advocates suffered another loss during the Reagan years that, although related to Head Start, was not specific to the program. I relate it here because, as both a scholar in the field of human development and a former Chief of the United States Children's Bureau, my concern was and is with the optimal development not only of poor children but of all children.

Since early in the twentieth century, children and families have been supported by a national meeting that took place every 10 years in Washington, a meeting that was closely allied with the purposes of the Children's Bureau. This was the White House Conference on Children. The keynote speaker was invariably the president, which attests to the status of the event. Other speakers were highly visible professionals (e.g., the pediatrician every parent looked to for advice, Berry Brazelton) and celebrities (e.g., Mr. Rogers was at the 1970 conference).

The national meeting was preceded by a conference in every state where public and private citizens would scrutinize problems confronting resident families and children. Then these experts, advocates, and knowledgeable laymen would gather in Washington for a 3-day conference where they could share their grievances and think about what policies would be helpful. These meetings were heavily covered by the media, so children and families were front-page news for 3 days every 10 years. Members of Congress were kept abreast of the issues raised by attending the forum themselves or sending staffers, and by receiving delegates from their home districts who would come to voice their concerns in person while they were in Washington. Thus the conference was an extremely important podium for improving the lives of children.

The last White House Conference on Children had been held in 1970 when I was President Nixon's key official responsible for programs and policies affecting children. With the election close at hand and the outcome in doubt, the Carter administration did not hold the conference on its due date in 1980. This event was cherished by children's organizations and advocates across America, and they fully expected the Reagan administration to schedule the overdue conference as soon as they got settled in their new offices.

It is easy to see why any administration would not exactly look forward to the White Conference on Children. The attendees invariably came up with many actions they wanted policymakers to take, regardless of the administration's own children's agenda. Further, it was traditional that in his keynote address the president committed himself to some action for children and families that would be met with enthusiastic approval and applause from the delegates. President Reagan had little love for social programs and had campaigned on the platform of a smaller role for the federal government. It is understandable why he had no desire to face a hall full of advocates who wanted more help and programs for children and families and in essence a larger, more involved federal government.

Reagan's solution to the impending dilemma was simply to terminate the conference. In keeping with his philosophies, Reagan recommended that rather than a national event each state should hold its own conference on children. The first and last of these state conferences were held in 1981 or 1982. I was asked to keynote the Connecticut Conference on Children, which took place in a huge, historic hall at Yale University. When I opened the invitation, I immediately realized that the conference would be nothing more than a pale copy of what had taken place over so many years in our nation's capital. To be taken seriously in Connecticut, the event should have been keynoted by the governor and held in the state's capital, Hartford.

The bulk of my address was a reiteration of the Children's Bureau and Census Bureau data showing the many unmet needs of Connecticut and American children that could get in the way of their becoming all that they could be. I also used this podium to bemoan the loss of the White House Conference on Children, spelling out what I believed to be its significance for promoting the well-being of all America's children. Noting our location far from the center of state government, I predicted that states would not continue to stage these events in the absence of the White House conference. Unfortunately, this prediction proved to be accurate.

During the Reagan years I was elected president of the American Orthopsychiatric Association, a national, multidisciplinary group of professionals concerned with mental health and social justice. As president, I decided that Ortho should lead an effort to get the national White House Conference on Children reinstated. I knew we would make little headway with the Reagan administration. I thought we would have a better chance if we approached those Democratic and Republican members of Congress who were continuing to work very hard in the interests of children and families.

I knew many of these officials personally but thought legislative action would be more likely if I could convince them this was not my personal hobbyhorse. Of course, most policymakers do not care to be pressured to take particular actions any more than an administration does. Nevertheless, children and their welfare were not a partisan issue, and it was clearly in our nation's interest for every child to achieve as much as possible. A concerted action by experts in the field and organizations known for their effective efforts on behalf of children was likely to at least get a hearing from our elected representatives. Ortho did get together a coalition of groups, including the Child Welfare League of America, and we were developing an agenda.

My memories of Washington made it perfectly clear that for the coalition to move forward, we needed the support of Marian Wright Edelman. Under her leadership the Children's Defense Fund had demonstrated skillful use of the leverage of power and had been quite successful in the political arena. I wrote to Marian requesting her assistance and participation. I was surprised and disappointed when I received no response. I later learned that Marian had reservations about the value of the White House conference. Perhaps her great fame and visibility made her believe the only entity our nation's children needed to protect their interests was the Children's Defense Fund. Unquestionably, CDF has had tremendous influence, and one can only admire its many achievements. However, CDF was essentially Marian Wright Edelman, who was intolerant of any difference of opinion from within or outside her organization. Another possibility is that from her early days in the Child Development Group of Mississippi, Edelman has been particularly concerned about poor African American children and not necessarily children in general. With the cold shoulder from Edelman, I decided to discontinue my efforts to get the White House conference reinstated.

Our nation's infrastructure that supports the well-being of children and families has withered away since President Reagan ended the White House Conference on Children. The Children's Bureau has continued to weaken and no longer has its own chief. Its advocacy role for children, once so vital and effective, is now gone. The House Subcommittee on Children is gone. What children and families have left is a good number of Democrats and Republicans in the House and Senate who continue to work tirelessly for children. I immediately think here of Senators Dodd and Hatch and the late Senator Kennedy. In the House we have Miller, DeLauro, and Woolsey. In 2007 Nancy Pelosi, the Speaker of the House, gave the entire field a concrete reason for optimism. She chaired the Children's Summit in Washington, where a good number of our nation's experts spoke about the determinants of child development. Many congresspersons came to listen to the speakers throughout the day. The purpose of the summit was to give policymakers the opportunity to gain information so they could draft an effective children's agenda. It is always a good sign when decision makers want to avail themselves of sound knowledge concerning children and their healthy growth and development.

Surveying the Damage

How then to sum up the Reagan presidency's impact on Head Start? Head Start suffered but survived. The mantra of the Reagan administration seemed to be to serve as many children as possible, but to do so as cheaply as possible. Perhaps Reagan felt pressured because Head Start's waiting list was growing longer, and many poor children and their families had to be turned away. Hacsi (2002) reports that in 1978, 25% of eligible children were enrolled in Head Start. By 1987, this number fell to below 19%; and in April 1988 *Education Week* reported that only 16% of children eligible for Head Start were participating. Further, this drop was taking place at a time when the number of children in poverty was rising to an "appalling" 25% in 1983, up from 17% in the 1970s.

To serve more children without a commensurate increase in Head Start's budget, we saw that the Reagan administration cut quality controls and gutted the professional staff in the national office. To make matters worse, while Head Start was seemingly protected in Reagan's safety net, cuts in other programs that Head Start relied on had a deleterious effect on service quality. For example, federal food and Medicaid grants were reduced, forcing Head Start directors to consume more of their budgets for food and health care, leaving less for other services. In 1982 alone, reductions in the Agriculture Department's child care food grants resulted in $20 million less to Head Start (Washington and Bailey, 1995).

A meaningful lesson I have learned over the years and often share with my students is that Head Start will have good periods when the administration in power believes in the program and cares about bettering it. Head Start will have bad times when the administration disagrees with the program's methods and goals and tries to turn it into something else. Head Start supporters must accept this as a reality and take the long view. In good periods we should work hard to maximize our gains, and during bad periods we must work even harder to keep Head Start's losses to a minimum. Realizing that progress comes in waves often followed by a period of backsliding, I remain optimistic that our nation will eventually accomplish what many other industrialized nations have already achieved to promote their children's well-being.

10

George H. W. Bush, the "Education President"

There was little in George H. W. Bush's past or during his 8-year tenure as vice president under Reagan that indicated a particular interest in education or early childhood intervention. Yet during the 1988 presidential campaign, Bush frequently voiced his intention to become the "education president" (as well the "environmental president"). The Republican party platform even contained a vow to increase Head Start funding "to help children get a fair chance at learning, right from the beginning" (Woolley and Peters, n.d.e). Candidates from both parties appeared to be in competition about who would do more for Head Start, promising to extend services to all eligible children and to ratchet up the money they would invest in the program. The momentum continued after the election, with the media carrying dazzling headlines like *Newsweek*'s "Everybody Likes Head Start" (Leslie, 1989) and Rovner's (1990) "Head Start Is One Program Everyone Wants to Help." It was as though policymakers had reunited with a long-lost friend and joined "a veritable lovefest" over Head Start (Chafel, 1992, p. 9).

What happened to make education the new domestic policy priority and to create such widespread support for Head Start? During Reagan's first term, the National Commission on Excellence in Education (1983) issued a shocking report on the status of America's education system entitled, *A Nation at Risk*. It detailed how poorly American students were doing in core academic competencies compared to children in many industrialized nations and indeed compared to their own achievement levels in past decades. High dropout rates and functional illiteracy, unqualified teachers, the lack of focus on higher-order thinking skills, and other major troubles imperiled not only our nation's economic and military strength but our democracy, which depends on a knowledgeable electorate. The Commission focused mainly on weaknesses in secondary education, as was its charge, but the connection to preschool learning was not hard to draw. In addition to reforming the public education system to make it more rigorous and effective, a natural step to address the crisis would be to assure that all young children are ready for school when they arrive.

As our nation's largest and most familiar preschool program, Head Start was rediscovered with a vengeance. Part of the reason is that by this time enough research evidence had accrued to prove that quality early intervention programs do benefit children when they enter school and likely beyond. Of course, the most publicized of this evidence was from the Perry Preschool. Their exciting finding that by age 19 every dollar spent on the program saved $3 in costs to society was widely (and wrongly) attributed to Head Start by reporters, policymakers, and candidates for federal, state, and local offices. The bandwagon effect was surely in play as well, as policymakers tried to outdo one another with praise and promises for Head Start. Either way, for the first time in a long while the Head Start community had high hopes that good things would come their way.

National Education Goals

George H. W. Bush's presidency followed that of the extremely conservative Ronald Reagan. Bush held conservative Republican principles as well, although he hoped "to put a 'kinder and gentler' face on his administration" (New York State Archives, 2006, p. 55). He planned to continue Reagan's work to reduce the size and power of the federal government, but this put him in something of a quandary when it came to his education reform initiatives. When President Johnson mounted the War on Poverty, he picked an outstanding leader (Shriver) to head the campaign, provided him with a huge new bureaucracy, and funded the effort with hundreds of millions of dollars. Bush had in place the Department of Education, but many conservatives in his party were eager to abolish it. To give credibility to his claim as "the education president," the Bush administration decided to create the post of Education Advisor to the President. They interviewed John Merrow, a well-known education expert, for the job. Merrow considered taking the position because it sounded as if it would have great importance and give him a real chance to influence national education policy. When he interviewed at the White House, however, he learned that the job would be half-time and that he would have no real authority. Instead he would have many superiors who would be making the actual decisions on education. Unsurprisingly, Merrow rejected the position because it was clear that he would be little more than a figurehead in President Bush's proclamations of being our education president. Matters at the Department of Education remained status quo.

In the Reagan tradition, President Bush's efforts to reform education would not be crafted and administered by Washington. Instead, the force for change would come from the states, private citizens, and concerned communities—the "thousand points of light" Bush frequently mentioned to describe his belief in grassroots rather than federal actions to move America forward. Many states were already working on ways to revamp their educational systems in response to the recommendations of the *Nation at Risk* exposé. Taking advantage of this interest, President Bush invited all the state governors to a national education summit in Charlottesville, VA in September 1989. In his opening remarks, "Bush made clear that the federal government was a supporting and coordinating partner, not a leader of the effort," warning, "we're going to work with you to help find answers, but I firmly believe that the key will be found at the State and local levels" (New York State Archives, 2006, pp. 55–56).

The governors discussed setting national education goals to "provide a common direction for educational improvement in all states, yet still allow states and local communities to determine for themselves how best to achieve desired results" (National Education Goals Panel, 1999, p. 1). The subsequent effort to articulate the goals was led by Arkansas Governor Bill Clinton, who also had a prominent role at the summit. Six goals were adopted, including having all children start school ready to learn, increasing high school graduation rates to at least 90%, raising adult literacy rates, achieving competence in challenging subject matter, enabling American students to be "first in the world in mathematics and science achievement," and assuring safe and disciplined schools (p. 1). (Two goals were later added by Congress, teacher education/professional development and parent participation, and the goals were codified in the Goals 2000: Educate America Act, signed into law in 1994 by President Bill Clinton.)

The governors were on a mission to improve education in America and wanted to put some teeth into the effort. They decided to adopt benchmarks for each goal so there would be a way to measure their progress. In 1990 President Bush issued an executive order creating the National Education Goals Panel, funded with a grant from the Department of Education. The panel created a task force for each goal to identify specific objectives and measurement tools.

Most relevant to our topic is Goal 1: "By the year 2000 all children in America will start school ready to learn." The Goal 1 Technical Planning Group identified five dimensions of school readiness: physical well-being and motor development, social and emotional development, approaches toward learning, language development, and cognition and general knowledge (Kagan, Moore, and Bredekamp, 1995). The overlap between Goal 1 and Head Start's objectives is clear. By supporting increased funding for Head Start, President Bush was fulfilling his commitment to the nation's governors.

Alas, the year 2000 has come and gone and not a single education goal of this effort was reached. The project's future looked bright when the goals were codified in 1994 and the panel received dedicated appropriations. Soon, however, a new Republican majority in the House greatly reduced that funding, and the panel itself was spared only through the efforts of Republican governors (Hoff, 2002). The panel admittedly experienced problems collecting timely data from vast numbers of school districts nationwide to use to assess movement toward the goals. As time went on, new leadership led Congress to approach educational reform from a different direction, and after 12 years, the National Education Goals Panel disbanded. The effort did succeed in focusing concerted attention on the nuts and bolts of education reform throughout the nation. Its lasting legacy was to define school readiness as a component of educational success and vital to system reform. The adoption of Goal 1 sparked a renewed interest in and commitment to Head Start, which had been trying for decades to help young children who live in poverty prepare for school. The program needed some help, however, and policymakers saw that it finally got some.

The Human Services Reauthorization Act of 1990

During their election campaigns, both George H. W. Bush and congressional candidates pledged "full funding" for Head Start. This in effect means enough money to provide Head Start services to all eligible children. After taking office they wasted no time trying to live up to their promise. In 1990 Head Start received one of its largest budget increases ever. Congress authorized an appropriation of $1.9 billion for 1991, with annual increases that would quadruple the budget in 4 years.

The competition between the executive and legislative branches had not subsided, with "President Bush and members of Congress ... waging something of a public relations battle over who is more supportive" (Rovner, 1990, p. 1191). Senators Christopher Dodd and Edward Kennedy, Head Start's most constant and effective supporters, introduced the School Readiness Act which would have made Head Start an entitlement for all poor children, providing $1 billion annual increases until the goal was met. Toward the end of his administration, President Bush proposed a $600 million increase for 1993, asserting he wanted to make Head Start available to all poor 4-year-olds, so that by the year 2000, all American children could start school ready to learn (an echo of the national education goals). The School Readiness Act did not pass, and actual sums given to Head Start fell far short of the authorized levels. Nevertheless, Head Start's budget nearly doubled, and there was a huge increase in the number of children served during President Bush's term in office.

Steps to Improve Quality

As detailed in Chapter 9, Head Start's quality problems had intensified during the Reagan years. In 1965 the staff–student ratio in Head Start classrooms was 1 to 5, but by 1989 it had risen to about 1 to 9. Although this is an acceptable level for preschool classrooms, practitioners knew that the at-risk children served by Head Start needed more individual attention. Teacher salaries were abysmal, with some teachers still being paid at or below the poverty level and with no benefits. This made it impossible to hire highly qualified teachers because they could easily obtain better-paying jobs elsewhere.

Central to the Head Start model are comprehensive services and parent involvement, which provide children with a spectrum of attention both in school and at home. By the George H. W. Bush years, caseloads for the health and social service staff had become unmanageable. The Department of Health and Human Services, where ACYF and the Head Start program were housed, recommended a caseload of 35 families per social service worker. Nationwide the average caseload was over 60 families (Chafel, 1992). The poster child of poor quality was one Head Start center where the caseload was a staggering 500 families. Bear in mind that these are families facing many problems associated with severe poverty. To make matters worse, there were no educational qualifications mandated for social service and parent-involvement staff.

The primary quality control mechanism in Head Start was the regional offices. Regional staff used to monitor each center for compliance with the Program Performance Standards and served as a resource to local programs to help them address problems and improve their service quality. In addition to annual reporting, centers were supposed to receive in-person site visits at least once every 3 years. The staff in the regional offices had been reduced so drastically in the Reagan years that by 1988 only 20% of Head Start programs were inspected (Chafel, 1992).

The deterioration in quality was by necessity silently tolerated during the Reagan years, when the critical goal was just to keep Head Start alive. Inspired by the change in administrations, Head Start advocates bombarded policy-makers with their quality concerns. In a landmark paper, education professor Judith Chafel (1992) thoroughly documented Head Start's quality shortcomings and offered reasoned solutions to the most urgent issues. Sally Styfco and I were asked to be peer reviewers of her piece after it was submitted to the *American Journal of Orthopsychiatry*, which follows a practice called "blind review" in which the author's name is removed from the manuscript. We were so impressed by Chafel's analysis that we begged the editors to reveal who had written it so we could immediately begin publicizing the ideas with proper citation. Dr. Chafel probably still wonders how so many references to her article began appearing in the literature months before it was published.

Many others argued the case for repairing Head Start quality. For example, in a May, 1990 *New York Times* op-ed column, David Weikart and Larry Schweinhart of Perry Preschool fame supported President Bush's desire to increase Head Start funding, but they argued the money should be spent to improve quality rather than to increase enrollment (Hacsi, 2002). They also noted that low pay kept teachers with college degrees away from jobs with Head Start and that research into the program's long-term effectiveness was badly needed. I testified before Congress that quality improvement must be the absolute top priority because program quality is the key determinant of the outcomes achieved by the children.

In 1990 the National Head Start Association (NHSA) convened a panel of experts to assess the status of Head Start on its twenty-fifth anniversary. The report by the Silver Ribbon Panel (1990) noted that the problems identified 10 years earlier by the fifteenth anniversary committee remained or had grown worse. They too pointed out the dire need to raise compensation to permit hiring more college-trained teachers. They also cited the needs for more training opportunities, better facilities and transportation, and reduced case-loads. The panel decried the lack of research effort, documenting that research, demonstration, and evaluation funds had fallen from 2.5% of the Head Start budget in 1974 to just 0.11% in 1989. This drop in funding had severely hindered the program from keeping up with the times in terms of best practices and the changing needs of its constituent population.

This time Congress was paying attention. Senator Kennedy spearheaded the Human Services Reauthorization Act of 1990, which gave Head Start huge budget increases and targeted some of the new money for quality improvements. I worked closely with both Senators Kennedy and Dodd and with George Miller, a leading Head Start champion in the House, to shape this legislation. The Act provided a 10% set-aside of new Head Start funds for program improvements in the first year, and 25% of new funds in following years for the same purpose. Half the set-aside was reserved for raising salaries and benefits. The other half was to upgrade facilities, training, transportation, and other facets of the program. Finally there was support to reverse the decline in the quality of Head Start services and begin what would be a long but welcome effort to make the program better.

Some years later Gregg Powell, once NHSA's research director, asked me to serve on his PhD dissertation committee at the University of California, Davis. Powell investigated the results of the quality set-aside in the 1990 Act on Head Start services. He articulated the need for and importance of these targeted funds: "After 10 years of neglect and dwindling investment during the 1980s, the quality of the program was at an all-time low while enrollment levels were approaching all-time highs" (1998, p. iii). Powell examined national data on a wide array of features such as education and staff turnover. He found the fiscal investments made in quality improvements significantly raised quality as measured by all these indicators. Further, he discovered the poorer quality centers displayed the greatest improvements. In a similar survey of the first 5 years of the set-aside, NHSA also reported positive results including reduced caseloads and higher compliance rates on annual monitoring reports (Verzaro-O'Brien, Powell, and Sakamoto, 1996). This work proved to Congress that their investment in quality was money well spent.

Rampant Expansion

All of the testimony, op-ed pieces, and reports pleading that quality improvement was essential to Head Start were not taken very seriously by President Bush. Although Congress attempted to address Head Start's quality issues in the Reauthorization Act, the Bush administration actually tried to block expenditures for the set-aside. The legislation provided that 25% of the 1991 increase be earmarked for quality improvements, but the administration only permitted 7% of the proposed increase to be used for this purpose.

During the presidential campaign Bush had promised full funding for Head Start. This campaign promise became his guiding light. His interpretation of "full," however, seemed to mean full enrollment, not that every participating child receive the full Head Start experience. The focus of the Bush administration was on the percentage of eligible children who could be squeezed into the program. By one account, Head Start only served 20% of children who lived below the poverty line when Bush took office (Rovner, 1990). The administration hoped the $500 million budget increase the president requested for 1991 "could allow us to serve up to 70% of eligible children for at least 1 year and bring within reach our goal of a universal Head Start program" (Rovner, 1990, p. 1194).

To increase enrollment and stay within budget, the administration planned to limit services to 4-year-olds for a single year and to restrict programs to half-days to allow double sessions. Yet Head Start had always served 3- and some 5-year-olds, and some very high-risk children stayed for 2 years. Further, some centers offered full-day programs to help poor, working mothers who needed child care outside of preschool hours. Granted, the percentage of such cases was relatively small, but it was important that these options be available to individual students and families who could be helped by them.

There was an absolutely driven quality and fervor in the momentum within the Bush administration to increase the number of children attending Head Start. Centers were pressured to boost enrollment whether they had the ability to handle more children effectively or not. The frenzied pace of growth left many program directors frantically searching for facilities, qualified staff, and indeed, children and families to enroll. (Impressed by the Perry Preschool findings, some states and cities were beginning their own preschool programs. As a result, nearby Head Start centers had to compete for staff as well as for students.) Often centers were ordered to open up large numbers of additional slots without adequate preparation time, leaving them short on everything from furniture to toys. Growth without a plan further eroded quality in many fragile centers that had been struggling to improve. Despite the attention Congress had given to quality in the 1990 Reauthorization Act, toward the end of the Bush administration, the Office of Inspector General (1993) concluded that expansion was not proceeding very smoothly and was straining the delivery of mandated services.

Rekindling Research and Demonstration

The call by social scientists for more and better research might seem self-serving in that annotated bibliographies of Head Start research contained 1,600 citations of empirical studies and articles that appeared in the literature between 1965 and 1984, and 600 more were added by 1996 (Ellsworth Associates, 1996). The problem is that much of this work was conducted in isolation, with investigators pursuing their own topics of interest, using whatever methodology each preferred, and studying children in Head Start centers convenient to the location of the researchers. Thus the results were not easily compared or nationally representative, nor could they produce a sturdy knowledge base.

In 1989 the Head Start Bureau convened the Advisory Panel for the Head Start Evaluation Design Project. The panel members were an illustrious group of experts in early intervention, empirical science, and social policy. Their charge was to recommend specific courses of research to address pressing questions about Head Start's effectiveness. The group decided that, given Head Start's diversity in thousands of classrooms and home-based programs in urban and rural sites across the nation, they would do better to create an overall strategy or set of guiding principles to direct future investigations. They concluded that research and evaluation planning should be organized around the questions of "Which Head Start practices maximize benefits for children and families with different characteristics under what types of circumstances?" and "how the benefits are sustained after pre-school?" (Advisory Panel, 1990, p. 4). The panel dismissed the usefulness of conducting a large-scale national study because Head Start was not a uniform treatment and the population it served was not homogeneous. They instead recommended a series of many smaller, coordinated studies that together would focus on the questions of which Head Start practices work, for whom, under what conditions, and for how long. The value of the "blueprint," as the panel's work came to be known, is that it was a thorough analysis of Head Start's research needs and pinpointed what information was required to guide the program's future direction.

As much as I admired the panel members—particularly Shep White, who was a leader in the area of applied developmental psychology, and Donald Campbell, an icon in the evaluation field—I could not endorse the group's recommendations. I learned from my stint in Washington that policymakers are a practical bunch. Whereas scientists may care about who and why a program helps, members of Congress simply want to know if the program helps enough to justify the continued expenditure of tax dollars. The Advisory Panel was embedded in the Head Start Bureau and approached their charge from the premise that Head Start had already been proven to work. That is why they focused on the finer details such as for whom Head Start works and what brings about the benefits. They were two steps ahead of Congress, which only wanted direct evidence proving Head Start's effectiveness.

Instead of envisioning a series of coordinated small studies to drill down the details, the panel should have endorsed a longitudinal study like that put into place by the Educational Testing Service (ETS; see Chapter 7). To improve on ETS, the study sample should have been enlarged to become representative of the entire Head Start population and the treatment and control groups formed through random assignment, the gold standard for social science evidence.

Looking back, I realize this was probably our last chance to conduct a study comparing Head Start participants with a "pure" control group of children who received no special services before school entry. Over time, preschool has become more accessible, and more children of working parents attend formal child-care settings. Today, studies can only assess whether an intervention experience adds value over other types of experience. In the final analysis, I thought the Advisory Panel had a lot of good ideas, and their blueprint was hailed by the scientific community, but it simply was not what Congress wanted. Here again we see the disconnect between academia and the world of policymaking.

Congress said what it wanted in the 1990 Reauthorization Act. The act acknowledged the research imperative and mandated a 20-year longitudinal study of Head Start participants as well as smaller studies of different service approaches and individual programs. In deference to the Advisory Panel, the legislation permitted the longitudinal evaluation to be conducted through a series of investigations rather than one huge project. Although Congress authorized $2 million a year to carry out the research mandate, the actual appropriations fell short of what was needed so the long-term follow-up was never conducted. The need for longitudinal research was finally addressed during the Clinton administration, which launched the National Head Start Impact Study (discussed in Chapter 13).

The Head Start Transition Project

In addition to renewing an interest in research, the Reauthorization Act revived to an extent my earlier efforts to situate Head Start as a national laboratory. The most serious criticism of Head Start over the years has been that its effects appear to fade out over time. (In point of fact, longer-term benefits of Head Start, such as lower criminality, have now been found.) A commonly advanced reason for the fade-out phenomenon is that elementary schools fail to protect and build on the gains children made in preschool. I worked with Senator Kennedy during the 1990 reauthorization to put into place the Head Start–Public School Transition Demonstration Project (Kennedy, 1993). As members of Congress often do, Senator Kennedy had sent me a draft of the reauthorization bill for my review and input. I took the opportunity to insert the idea of extending intervention services into the primary grades. When I was at OCD I had conceptualized Project Developmental Continuity precisely for this purpose (Chapter 5), and this was my chance to resurrect the idea. Senator Kennedy was immediately supportive and drafted language for a demonstration into the bill.

The goal was to stop the erosion of the gains made in preschool as children progressed through the elementary grades as well as to make public schools more responsive to the needs of poor children and their families by building teamwork between local Head Start and elementary school educators. Extending services into the primary grades has long been a goal of Head Start, beginning with Follow Through initiated in 1967 (see Chapter 5). When Follow Through became an experiment in curriculum variation rather than an older version of Head Start, several smaller pilots (including Project Developmental Continuity) were tried to continue services and ease the transition to school.

The Transition Project employed a rigorous experimental evaluation design and initially involved about 32 programs, 450 schools, and 85 school districts in 30 states. The hypothesis tested was that continued comprehensive services, developmentally appropriate curriculum, and a strong focus on parent involvement would prevent Head Start graduates from losing the advantage they had gained in preschool. For schools to incorporate the Head Start model necessitated whole-school reform. The clash between the philosophies of Head Start, which emphasizes both academic and social support services and parent participation, and the public schools attended by poor children has been apparent since the program began. This clash was in evidence when the Transition Project was implemented, witnessed by the large number of meetings and amount of training needed to "bring even receptive school systems to understand and accommodate Head Start's way of operating and to help Head Start programs learn how to work best with the schools" (Mills, 1998, p. 248). The huge disconnect between Head Start policies concerning parents and the practices of schools in poor neighborhoods was a particular obstacle. As Mills observed, "Some teachers see parents in the classroom as distractions, not helpers" (p. 247).

The evaluation of the Transition Project produced the seemingly disappointing finding that there were no differences in academic performance between children in the transition sites and comparison schools (Ramey et al., 2000). Yet our reading of the findings is that they were anything but disappointing. True, the children in the transition schools did not achieve more than children with similar backgrounds who attended schools that were not assigned to the extended intervention. What happened, however, was that when the teachers and administrators were trained to participate in the transition, their counterparts in schools that were not chosen to be transition sites became just as interested. Ramey et al. (2000) observed that they incorporated the supports, academic enhancements, and parent involvement policies of the pilots, and as a result, their students (the control group) performed better as well. In fact, the transition practices were so eagerly accepted that some comparison schools collected money from outside sources to fund the new services, and both project and comparison schools shared ideas and training opportunities. Thus the failure to find differences between the experimental and control groups was likely caused by what behavioral scientists call diffusion effects, that is, the practices that constituted the intervention were diffused to the control schools.

The finding of no difference masked the amazing result that not only did the gains children made in Head Start *not* fade out during the transition period but that their performance continued to improve. By the end of second and third grades, their reading and math achievement *was at the national average*. The comparison group, who were not supposed to but did receive a similar program, evidenced the same progress. This is one of the very few studies in which children who live in poverty achieved the same level of academic competence as middle-class children. (The more typical finding in early intervention research is that participants perform better than other poor children who did not receive services, but their absolute level of performance remains well below national averages.) The fact that there was no significant difference in the performance of program and comparison groups is significant in itself: with the right guidance, support, and motivation, and a willingness to involve parents, schools *can* boost academic achievement among at-risk children. The key is to get everyone on board and commit to delivering supports for a long enough time to make a difference (Reynolds, 2003; Zigler and Styfco, 1993b).

There are several possible reasons why the results of the Transition Project did not receive the attention they deserved. One is simply that a finding of "no difference" does not generate the same level of interest as one that shows large effects. Another possibility is that the investigators have long been actively involved in their own early intervention program (the Abecedarian project) and therefore did not pursue publicizing the Transition Project results very aggressively. Perhaps the overriding reason is that the attainment of national norms was only achieved after a multiyear effort, not after the more common single year of intervention available in programs like Head Start and state preschools. The fact is that programs of longer duration are more effective with high-risk children than more limited efforts (Reynolds, 2003). Decision makers appear to have some difficulty accepting this commonsensical proposal, probably because multiyear programs cost more. As much as policymakers yearn for one, there is no silver bullet. It is unrealistic to assume that a single year of even the highest quality intervention can offset the ravages of poverty that poor children experience before, during, and after that blink of time when they receive special attention in preschool.

Head Start National Research Conference

The federal official primarily responsible for implementing the Bush administration's policies was Wade Horn, Commissioner of ACYF. Horn was a welltrained clinical psychologist who had good political connections to the Republican Party. He was a very amiable young man who was a strange mix of competent child psychologist and political ideologue, with a penchant for right-wing causes. The Head Start community was relieved when early in his watch he made the very wise decision to keep the effective and knowledgeable Clennie Murphy in a central role at the Head Start Bureau.

Horn and I connected early in his tenure, and we became tentative friends. The fact that I was once in the Republican Nixon administration has always made me more acceptable to Republican leaders without costing me too much in trust from the Democrats. Even though Horn often pursued courses of action with which I disagreed or counseled him against, I found it hard to interact with him without liking him.

Horn had a respect for research and experimentation and mounted some non–Head Start pilots reminiscent of my own innovation efforts during the Nixon years. One of my favorite demonstrations from those days was the Child and Family Resource Program (CFRP), which provided a cafeteria of support services to poor parents with children from conception to age 8 (see Chapter 5). Horn liked the idea too and established a small network of family service centers that embodied some aspects of the CFRP.

Horn's biggest contribution to the research enterprise was to mount the Head Start National Research Conference, which is still in place. There has always been tension between the Head Start practitioners who actually deliver the program in the field and the research and evaluation scientists whose job is to expand our knowledge of child development and effective interventions, as well as to assess the efficacy of Head Start services. The practitioners complain that they get no useful feedback from the results of the studies, which admittedly are often couched in academic terms and written for scientists. Evaluators, for their part, complain about what they perceive as a lack of cooperation from center personnel, who don't always welcome the disruption in their daily classroom routine with open arms.

With Horn's absolutely necessary support, Esther Kresch in Head Start's research shop mounted a biennial conference to assemble practitioners, research scholars, administrators, and policymakers "to share research that promotes positive development in young children" (Administration for Children and Families, 2008). Participants are not only from the Head Start camp but include child care, health care, and related disciplines. In recent years these meetings have been organized through a collaboration among the Administration for Children and Families and scholars at Columbia University and the Society for Research in Child Development. The conferences are held in Washington, DC and draw hundreds of participants from around the country. Considered an unnecessary frill in the Reagan years, with nudging from Wade Horn, the research enterprise sprung to life during the Bush administration.

Intent versus Reality

On the surface, the increased attention to research and evaluation, the hikes in Head Start's budget and enrollment, and the dedication of funds to improve quality all suggest that Head Start fared very well under the George H. W. Bush administration. Yet although the president's rhetoric and legislative actions appeared very promising for reversing the slide Head Start suffered during the Reagan years, the view from the trenches was not as rosy.

Certainly Head Start received a great deal of additional money during President Bush's term, but actual appropriations never came close to meeting the goals inherent in the amounts authorized. In the debate over whether the new money being poured into Head Start should be spent on serving more children or shoring up quality, President Bush strongly sided with expansion. Head Start enrollment grew from roughly 450,000 children when he took office to over 700,000 children when he left. However, we never got close to fulfilling the president's promise (or that of Congress) to serve all eligible children. Not only was the full funding of Head Start not achieved by 2000, it has not been achieved by 2008 when about 50% of eligible children attend. Further, the drive to expand greatly exacerbated the program's quality shortcomings, which had a direct affect on the experiences of participating children and families.

Efforts to grow and to fix quality were working against one another. What was needed was a plan to proceed on both fronts in a more thoughtful fashion so one goal did not cancel out the progress of the other. George H. W. Bush's intense focus on expansion likely would have thwarted the development of such a plan. Indeed, in his bid for reelection, the president continued to promise full funding for Head Start so every eligible child could be served with no mention of the content of the child's experiences in the program. The pleas of the Head Start community were heard by the incoming Clinton administration, which quickly moved to make a bigger Head Start better.

II

Head Start's Golden Years under the Clinton Administration

During the 1992 presidential campaign, both George H. W. Bush and Arkansas Governor William Clinton pledged strong support for Head Start. In a last-minute effort to showcase his determination to be the education president, Bush signed the Higher Education Act of 1992 and again promised full funding for Head Start. Clinton called him on his promise, stating that under Bush's leadership only one in three eligible preschoolers was being served by the program and that funding for education had not even kept up with inflation. Chiding his opponent, Clinton said, "America needs an education President who shows up for class every day, not just once every four years" (1992, p. 6). The voters did not give President Bush another 4 years to make good on his campaign pledge. His defeat was widely attributed to his reneging on his famous declaration during his first run for president: "Read my lips: No new taxes." In the face of soaring budget deficits ignited during the Reagan years, the president reluctantly agreed with Congress to hike taxes. He was punished at the polls and did not have further opportunity to shape his desired legacy as America's education president.

Advocates of education and of Head Start were heartened by the election of President Bill Clinton, who set expectations that children's issues would be high on his list of priorities. Unlike his predecessor, Clinton had a long and strong history of support for education. Further, First Lady Hillary Rodham Clinton had a distinguished record of work to improve the lives of children and families. Before the election the important role that Hillary would play in a Clinton White House was signaled by her husband's frequent quip that Americans would be getting "two presidents for the price of one." In fact,

Hillary's credentials figured so prominently during the campaign that President Bush used some of her old legal writings to warn that if the Clintons won, children would be encouraged to sue their parents and public schools would be free to dispense birth control devices to students without parental consent (Rosenthal, 1992). (The writings were actually legal analyses about the rights of abused and neglected children.) Later, Hillary's influence was acknowledged by the fact that the Clinton administration was often referred to as headed by "Billary." This strong team of education advocates in the White House gave the Head Start community high hopes that their program would fare very well in the coming years.

A Commitment to Children and Learning

Judging from their past efforts, the Clintons' intentions on the education front were serious, major, and would be relentlessly pursued. Bill Clinton's passion for education was rooted in his childhood, as was his sensitivity to the plight of the poor. His past was surprisingly similar to the life conditions of many of the children served by Head Start. His father had died a few months before he was born, making him the son of a single mother. His grandparents helped raise him so his mother could return to school to study nursing. Clinton's stepfather was an alcoholic and was abusive. This pattern of a number of risk factors characterizes many children who live in poverty. Out of this barren childhood emerged a Rhodes Scholar whose success in life was enabled by a good education. Unsurprisingly, Clinton became a champion of educational improvement in all the posts he would hold in government.

Besides growing up poor, living in the South elicited Clinton's genuine compassion for racial minorities. Since its birth Head Start has been intertwined with the civil rights movement. Black children are overrepresented in Head Start, which is one reason why the program has long been favored by the Congressional Black Caucus. Bill Clinton had such a positive relationship with black citizens he was the first white to be included in the Arkansas Black Hall of Fame. His acceptance by the Head Start community seemed assured.

Clinton's sensitivity to educational and racial disparities was evident during his five terms as governor of Arkansas. With his wife Hillary as chair of the Arkansas Education Standards Committee, the Clintons worked tirelessly to improve education in the state. Their efforts resulted in more spending for the schools, smaller class sizes, expanded course offerings and vocational education, higher graduation requirements, and increases in teacher qualifications and pay. The transformation of the public school system had visible results, such as dropout rates falling below the national average and more students attending college. Hillary brought the home visiting program called HIPPY (originally started in Israel) to Arkansas. This program is directed toward helping parents become better socializers and teachers of their children. She also worked diligently to champion preschool education and to make kindergarten available in all school districts.

Governor Clinton's participation in national education policy evolved through leadership roles he held with the National Governors Association. In 1989, President George H. W. Bush convened the nation's governors to establish national education goals (Chapter 10). Clinton represented the Democratic governors at this gathering. The effort reached fruition after he became president, added two goals and funding, and along with Richard Riley, his Secretary of Education, presented to Congress the Goals 2000: Educate America Act. The law passed Congress with bipartisan support. Two of the goals have special relevance for Head Start. Goal 1 was the implicit purpose of the Head Start intervention since its inception: "All children in America will start school ready to learn." This essentially means that all children will be ready to profit from the opportunities they encounter in the classroom at the point of school entry—usually kindergarten. The nation's Head Start program was an obvious resource to aid in attaining Goal 1.

The eighth goal was new since the governors' summit but had always been part of Head Start: "Every school will promote partnerships that will increase parental involvement and participation in promoting the social, emotional, and academic growth of children." Two pillars of Head Start are comprehensive services (improving all facets of the child's development, including family life) and forming close partnerships with parents and inviting their participation. The fact is that our nation's schools have been slow in modeling practices that Head Start put in place decades ago, the value of which did not escape Hillary Clinton.

Hillary's Devotion to Children's Causes

Hillary's path to becoming a champion of children and families was markedly different than her husband's. She spent her childhood in a politically conservative, middle-class home, where her mother was more liberal than her right-wing Republican father. One of her early forays into politics was working the 1964 campaign for Senator Barry Goldwater, an important figure in the American conservative movement who held libertarian views.

I first heard of Hillary Clinton from my close friend and colleague Dr. Al Solnit, the director of Yale's Child Study Center. He and my friend Joe Goldstein were working on what would become a landmark book, *Beyond the Best Interests of the Child*, with their colleague Anna Freud. (This daughter of Sigmund Freud was then a visiting professor at Yale's Law School.) The book (Goldstein, Freud, and Solnit, 1973) urged gauging the implications of legal decisions affecting children through the lens of knowledge about child development and became must reading for juvenile and family court judges everywhere. The authors' thesis was expanded in a trilogy with *Before the Best Interests of the Child* and *In the Best Interests of the Child* (Goldstein et al., 1979, 1986).

Goldstein was a professor at Yale's Law School when he met Hillary Rodham, a bright young law student who had decided to concentrate on how the law affected children. He suggested to Hillary that she take a course of study at the Yale Child Study Center to learn more about child development. I have been at the Center for 50 years now, and I do not remember another law student who became as immersed in the group's work as did Hillary. In addition to doing research for Goldstein and Solnit on their book, she worked with my colleague Sally Provence, one of the world's greatest authorities on early child development and the problems associated with this stage of life. She also studied with Jim Comer and became conversant with his whole-school reform model called the School Development Program. This intervention champions both the whole-child approach and the importance of involving parents, particularly mothers, in the schools.

Hillary proved to be an indefectible Yale scholar. While at the Child Study Center she consulted with the medical staff at Yale–New Haven Hospital and helped draft the legal procedures for the hospital to employ with suspected child abuse cases. She also worked at a New Haven legal services office where she focused on legal situations involving abuse and neglect. These activities led to Hillary's first scholarly article titled, "Children Under the Law," which appeared in the prestigious *Harvard Educational Review* (Rodham, 1973). The paper explored the difficult decisions judges must make about whether or not to remove an abused or neglected child from the home and place him or her in foster care. The foster care system itself is plagued by myriad difficulties, and in due time Hillary's interests were extended to foster care and to the topic of adoption. These connected issues of child abuse and neglect, foster care, and adoption were for years closely monitored by our nation's Children's Bureau, where I was once chief. Thus Hillary and I had many common interests, and I only regret that I did not get to know her while she was a law student at Yale. I do know that she could not have gotten better tutoring than from Joe Goldstein, Al Solnit, Sally Provence, and Jim Comer.

Hillary's first job after law school was as an attorney for the Children's Defense Fund, where she was mentored by one of our nation's best known child advocates, Marian Wright Edelman. Eventually Hillary became chair of the Fund's Board of Directors. The ties between the Clintons and Edelmans were further strengthened when Marian's husband, Peter, was asked to serve as counselor to the Secretary in the Clinton administration's Department of Health and Human Services. Peter was a Harvard-trained lawyer with extensive experience in the judicial branch of government.

When Mrs. Clinton served as First Lady of Arkansas, she was not only involved in the important educational efforts noted above but was a visible advocate for children, joining the boards of many organizations dedicated to improving the lives of children and families. She worked hard in Arkansas on the issues of child abuse and neglect, foster care, and adoptions. Later in the White House she played a role in the passage of major legislation in these areas.

Hillary Clinton learned her lessons at Yale well. She internalized the theme of the three "interests of the child" books, which applied understanding of child development to legal issues affecting children in the juvenile and family courts. Doug Besharov, who reviewed her later book, *It Takes a Village* (Clinton, 1996), summed up her basic argument: "We learned a great deal about child develop-ment and . . . we need to do a better job of applying that knowledge" (1996, p. WBK1). Indeed, this has been the authors' view for many years and is consistent with the very important book from the National Academy of Sciences, *From Neurons to Neighborhoods* (Shonkoff and Phillips, 2000). Hillary's work with Sally Provence convinced her that the early years of life are critical to a child's developmental course, another theme she emphasized in her book. Even Besharov, who is also an expert on children's issues but is a solid conservative, concurred with her basic point that "Children need a good start in life and too many aren't getting one" (Besharov, 1996, p. WBK10). She said she chose the title, *It Takes a Village*, because "children will thrive only if their families thrive and if the whole of society cares enough to provide for them" (in Besharov, 1996, p. WBK1). Considering her emphasis on children needing a good start, it is not coincidental that Early Head Start was launched during the Clinton years. During those years I personally found Bill Clinton to be quite knowledgeable about children's issues, but he could not match Hillary's deep understanding about child development and the type of social policies that would enhance their chances in life.

A Strong Beginning

President Clinton's deeply felt concern for children and their families was made evident shortly after his inauguration. Earlier I had worked closely with

Senator Dodd to draft the Family and Medical Leave Act (FMLA), which provides a 12-week unpaid leave to either parent upon the birth or adoption of a child or in the event of a serious illness in the family. The Chamber of Commerce and the National Association of Manufacturers, among other groups of employers, opposed this bill vigorously, and as a result the measure was unacceptable to President George H. W. Bush. Dodd passionately pursued the cause for years, steering the act through Congress and once all the way to the president's desk and veto pen. In a tribute to Dodd's perseverance, the FMLA was the first piece of legislation that Clinton signed into law, just 2 weeks after becoming president. The signing ceremony was a clear signal that the new president's frequently voiced commitment to children and families would be more than just rhetoric.

The Head Start program was also prominent in President Clinton's beginning agenda. A piece in the *New York Times* shortly after he assumed office reported that he "extolled the program as an example of Government at its best and is asking Congress to increase financing by more than $9 billion over the next five years" (DeParle, 1993). In his first State of the Union address he called Head Start a "success story" and vowed to expand the program so there would be room for every eligible child. Unfortunately, in this nationally televised speech the president repeated an egregious error that has been all too common through the years. He informed Congress and the viewing public that every dollar spent on Head Start results in $3 of future cost savings. The $3 figure came not from Head Start but from the first cost–benefit analysis of the outcomes of the Perry Preschool graduates, an "arithmetic" error the *Times* reporter corrected. The hypothesis that investment in early childhood intervention yields savings in the future may be true, but any specific dollar amounts should be taken with a grain of salt. Not only are cost–benefit analyses premised on many debatable assumptions, but promising big returns on investment leads to an overly optimistic view of what preschool programs can accomplish without changing other negative aspects of poor children's environments, such as health care, housing, violence, and family status and income. I would like to think the president's gaffe was caused by a misinformed speech writer because, as I saw it, Clinton was assembling the best and brightest team ever to run and steer Head Start.

Building a Strong Team

I have worked with the Head Start decision makers in every administration since that of Lyndon Johnson. Since my views and those of the Clintons were so parallel, I had every expectation that I would work closely with the new administration on children's issues. I started shortly after the election when I was asked to join the Transition Team on Education, where I served with Al Shanker and numerous other luminaries in the education field.

I have witnessed many administrations in Washington come and go and have observed that presidents typically select top-level appointees for one of two reasons: their expertise and ability to do the job, or as payment for political favors made on the party's or president's behalf. President Clinton, like Richard Nixon, tended to ignore politics and appoint the most knowledgeable person who could be found for a particular leadership position.

I am honored to have been considered a candidate for Clinton's select team. During the transition period I had a couple of early talks about taking a post in the administration. I discussed this possibility with my senior staff at Yale, who were excited about this opportunity for me to again have a direct say in national policies affecting children (or about getting me to a distant city and out of their hair). Despite their enthusiasm, I decided against it. I remembered my experience as a Washington bureaucrat as similar to my stint in the Army during the Korean War. Both were interesting, and I learned a great deal about things I had known nothing about, but neither experience was one that I yearned to repeat. Further, I am a scholar well-known for my candor and outspokenness. This style cannot be practiced in Washington where you have many superiors who have to clear everything you say and do. I thought I could better help Head Start and the nation's children by staying politically neutral, free to preach what I wanted from my academic podium. Although I did not become an insider, I had a productive working relationship with the Clinton administration for the 8 years they were in office.

The people Clinton appointed to key positions in Head Start and child care were the most impressive group of leaders ever to have responsibilities for these programs. At the time the day-to-day responsibility for Head Start was the province of the Chief of the Head Start Bureau, who answered to the head of the Administration on Children, Youth and Families (ACYF), who in turn answered to the Assistant Secretary, whose superior was the Secretary of Health and Human Services (HHS), who answered to the president. Although this administrative structure has since changed, it is relevant to introducing Clinton's chain of command.

I did not personally know the Secretary of HHS, Donna Shalala, when she was appointed, but I was aware of her impressive career in higher education. (She came to her Clinton post from the chancellorship at the University of Wisconsin and after the Clinton years became the president of the University of Miami.) Over the years we had several opportunities to interact and came to admire each other. Her Assistant Secretary was a fine scholar and friend, Mary Jo Bane from Harvard. She and I had worked together awarding grants on the board of the Smith Richardson Foundation. As a scholar she was stronger on welfare issues than on children's issues, but she possessed more knowledge about children's growth and development than most bureaucrats I've known. Taking my old position at ACYF (the former OCD) was an absolute jewel, Olivia Golden. Olivia had a doctorate in public policy and, like Hillary, had worked at the Children's Defense Fund where she was mentored by children's advocate, Marian Wright Edelman.

Running the Head Start Bureau was an old friend, Helen Taylor, who had spent many years of her life working across the fields of early childhood education and child care. Unusual for practitioners, she understood and was sympathetic toward the research enterprise and appreciative of how important research is to the evaluation and accountability of a public institution such as Head Start. I have known many excellent Head Start Bureau chiefs, but I still consider Helen Taylor the finest of them all. She died too young when she was still heading the Bureau. In spite of suffering a serious illness, she insisted on working hard for Head Start right up until her death. Some days she was too ill to travel, and I remember pinch hitting for her on a couple of occasions to give addresses about Head Start to audiences who were expecting the top official.

Not all of these competent leaders stayed on the Clinton team for the duration of his presidency. Clinton had vowed "to end welfare as we know it" by imposing work requirements and strict time limits on the receipt of welfare checks. These proposals angered and frightened many advocates for children and the poor, who predicted inhumane consequences of hunger and homelessness should the safety net be withdrawn. After vetoing two earlier, more draconian versions of welfare reform, President Clinton signed the Personal Responsibility and Work Opportunity Act of 1996. In protest, a number of high-level administration officials resigned. Among them were Assistant Secretary Mary Jo Bane, Peter Edelman, and others at HHS who were in favor of a gentler approach to moving recipients off of welfare support

The Clinton administration wisely elevated Olivia Golden from the head of ACYF to become Assistant Secretary. The Secretary of HHS has a budget that is larger than that of many nations and a huge number of efforts to manage, so as Assistant Secretary Golden really had the day-to-day responsibility for running the programs under her, including Head Start. Golden's vacated position at ACYF was filled by the extremely competent Jim Harrell. Harrell was a close friend of Peggy Pizzo, and to be a close friend of Peggy one must own enlightened and proactive views about improving the lives of children. Jim of course had much more on his plate than Head Start. He also had to oversee the

National Center on Child Abuse and Neglect, the child care program which oversaw the large Child Care and Development Block Fund, and child adoption reform.

The Clinton group included one more highly notable individual, Joan Lombardi, a well-known early childhood educator and a longtime friend of mine. Joan worked closely with Taylor, Golden, and Harrell and took the lead in the administration's new effort to improve child care in America, the Child Care Bureau. We will have more to say on this important agency, and its close connection with Head Start's mission, below.

Focus on Head Start Quality

The presence of Bill and Hillary Clinton in the White House, both of whom were strong supporters of Head Start, freed advocates to expose Head Start's weaknesses and needs without fear that their criticisms would endanger the program's existence. The frenzied increase in the number of children served during the George H. W. Bush years had damaged the quality of Head Start services, which in many places were not that good even before the expansion. Yet Head Start would be judged a success or failure to the extent that it achieved the goals that had been set for it. This could only be accomplished if the program delivered the true services it was supposed to deliver, a feat that was hindered by burgeoning enrollment and strained quality controls.

After the Clinton victory, I felt brave enough to air my frustration from observing Head Start's quality deteriorate during the Bush years. Without foreseeing the shock effect I would have on the Head Start community, I asserted in a public address that "only about half the nation's 1,400 Head Start programs are of high quality, while about a quarter are 'marginal' and the rest are so poorly run they are doing virtually nothing to help children." After this was reported in the New York Times (DeParle, 1993), the phones in my office began ringing off the hook. Reporters, congressional staffers, colleagues, friends, and enemies all wanted to know if Head Start's most loyal friend had actually said such a thing. I was still on the road, and my staff were as shocked as everyone else that I would be so daring (or foolish) to deliver such a harsh remark in public. My co-author Sally Styfco, to whom many of these calls were referred, actually denied that I said what the first few callers quoted me as saying. After the reality became apparent, she instructed my secretary to stop directing the calls to her and instead take messages and promise that I personally would get back to them. I had a lot of explaining to do when I returned to the office, beginning with Sally.

My motivation was not to harm but to help Head Start, and my speech was delivered in the spirit of constructive criticism. My motives were at least apparent to noted journalist, Jason Deparle (1993), who wrote the article in the *Times* entitled, "Sharp Criticisms for Head Start, Even by Friends." DeParle explained, "Mr. Zigler's frank remarks are intended to bring more support to the program, in the form of higher teacher salaries and more intensive social services." As I had been saying for years, I warned that we not expect more from the Head Start program than it could possibly deliver. Lest Head Start shoulder all the blame, I noted the considerable data indicating that a major problem for poor children, Head Start graduates or not, is that they typically attend elementary schools of low quality. Thus in my public statement I added that even if the quality of Head Start is improved, I thought the advantage children gain in preschool is destined to fade away unless the quality of the public school system is also upgraded.

DeParle exonerated me a bit by describing other reports of weaknesses in the Head Start program. He noted that several government and academic reports had shown Head Start suffered from considerable management problems. For example, after a comprehensive study the Inspector General at HHS reported that only 43% of the children in Head Start had complete immunizations (a program requirement) and that only 28% of the families received most or all of the mandated social services. Program officials responded that these numbers did not reflect missed immunizations or services, but a failure in record keeping as result of the rapid growth in enrollment. A second government report noted by Deparle questioned the ability of the system to accommodate a sudden large expansion, saying "40 percent of the programs had recently experienced problems in hiring qualified staff, more than a quarter had been unable to enroll eligible children and a third had major problems in finding enough space for an expanded program." In response, Head Start administrators went on the defensive and stated, "It is our feeling that this overstates the problem." However, officials at HHS did acknowledge "there are problems in terms of uneven quality in the delivery of services."

I guess I opened the floodgates. In the same year, *Time* magazine had a piece that questioned whether Head Start should be considered a success or not. (I forgot about the interview, but fortunately Hacsi has written about it, and I quote him here.) The *Time* reporter also noted the investigation by the Department of Health and Human Services, which found that a good number of Head Start programs were poorly run. *Time* then quoted me as estimating that "'at best' only 40 percent of Head Start centers were 'high-quality'" (in Hacsi, 2002, p. 50). This was probably a better estimate than my 50% figure, which I had roughly rounded up. I also told *Time* that closing down

30% of Head Start centers "would be no great loss." After the article was published, I heard from a Head Start worker in the regional office in Atlanta, which covers more Head Start sites than any other region in the country. She had worked with me during my years in Washington and was comfortable enough to scold me for being too generous. Her view was that many more than 30% of the Head Start sites in her region were of poor quality. Like the *Time* magazine article, she noted the major culprit in low-quality centers was the very low pay for teachers.

Quality problems in Head Start were of course not new, but they had been exacerbated by the Reagan and George H.W. Bush administrations' actions to increase enrollment and cut overhead costs like quality controls. Although President Clinton acknowledged the concerns about quality and promised to address them, he too was talking about a major expansion.

Advisory Committee on Head Start Quality and Expansion

A battle was shaping up between those who wanted to expand Head Start to allow every eligible child to attend and those who wanted to slow down a bit and work on improving the quality of the services children received. A typical governmental approach to addressing concerns about programs and policies is to appoint a committee to study the issues, give their recommendations 15 minutes of fame in a press release, and relegate the report to some hidden archive where it will gather dust along with a million other committee reports on a million other topics.

I have seen this happen so many times I was not terribly optimistic when the Clinton administration formed the Advisory Committee on Head Start Quality and Expansion. This bipartisan group was charged with addressing the conflicting forces of growth and quality improvement. The committee was officially headed by Secretary of HHS, Donna Shalala, who made several appearances before the group. Olivia Golden chaired the meetings for Secretary Shalala. Members included several high-ranking representatives of the administration, and Congress was represented by staff members from both sides of the political aisle. There were leaders from relevant organizations like the National Head Start Association, the Children's Defense Fund, and the National Association for the Education of Young Children. Some Head Start veterans including Harley Frankel, Julius Richmond, and I also joined. In a reach outside of the Head Start fan club, the well-known critic and conservative thinker, Doug Besharov of the American Enterprise Institute, was also appointed. In the tradition of Head Start, parents' views were solicited by the advisory committee.

The need for a better quality Head Start program was validated by the committee. The group underscored the importance of excellence in every Head Start center and recommended not only fixing deficiencies but renewing the program by making it more responsive to the needs of its constituents, starting services earlier in a child's life, and forming stronger partnerships with communities, states, and the federal government (Advisory Committee, 1993). This is one of the few committee reports in memory that was not quickly shelved and forgotten. In a tribute to the Clinton administration's commitment to helping Head Start, the report became a roadmap for plans to make the program better. "Shalala saw the report as a blueprint that recognized the program's strengths, recommended adjustments to modern circumstances, and would help Head Start improve in the future" (Hacsi, 2002, p. 54).

Congress too was somewhat receptive to the committee's recommendations. Head Start was due to be reauthorized in 1994, and policymakers literally used the Advisory Committee's report as a guideline. I remember when Douglas Besharov and I testified at the Senate hearing for the reauthorization. Unsurprisingly, we gave two opposing views of the value of the committee's work. I applauded the committee and the Clinton administration's responsivity to their recommendations, saying this is exactly the outcome I had hoped for in my criticisms of the quality of Head Start over the years. Besharov's evaluation was essentially negative, asserting that the committee had prepared "a wish list of expensive 'quality enhancements' to the program" that would only make "Head Start too expensive for its own good'" (Mills, 1998, p. 306).

In his testimony, Besharov proposed sending Head Start to the states, a position he has championed ever since. Since the main issue for me has always been the quality of the program delivered, I have no vested interest in who delivers the high-quality program, the federal government or the states. I told the Senators their focus should be on improving Head Start services so the money being spent on the program would have a better chance of yielding the outcomes they desired.

The final legislation clearly reflected the influence of the Advisory Committee's recommendations. The Human Services Reauthorization Act of 1994 continued the set-aside for quality improvements, clarifying that the prescribed funding level of 25% of any budget increase was the minimum amount to be reserved for quality initiatives. The wording also emphasized that half of the set-aside was to be used to increase staff salaries. The legislation continued pressure on local programs to improve teacher qualifications by extending to 1996 the deadline put into place by the 1990 reauthorization for all classroom teachers to have at least a Child Development Associate credential, and maintained scholarship funding so the goal could be met.

New Program Performance Standards

The major instrument of quality control in Head Start is the Program Performance Standards. I had put these into place in the early 1970s, and all programs were required to comply by 1975. They had not been revised since. Certainly the characteristics, risks, and needs of poor children and families had changed over nearly 2 decades, and best practices in early childhood intervention and education had evolved. The Advisory Committee recommended that the standards be updated. The reauthorization act directed the Secretary to revise the regulations with respect to both daily classroom practices and administration. The new performance standards, which became effective in 1998, contained comprehensive policies and procedures governing early childhood development and health services, family and community partnerships, program design and management, and implementation and enforcement. The standards addressed services for children with disabilities as well as those younger than preschool age. The creation of written standards for birth to age 3 programs was long overdue. The Parent and Child Centers had been operating since 1968 without any guidance, and it was hard to ascertain more or less evaluate what the separate centers were doing or accomplishing.

The new performance standards held clear directions about the steps that would be taken with programs found to be out of compliance. Programs with deficiencies would be given a timetable to submit quality improvement plans, and the Head Start regional offices would provide the necessary training and technical assistance to help them meet their goals. If improvements did not occur within the timetable, their grants would be terminated. This was not an empty threat.

By 1996, 40 programs were actually terminated (Linehan and Schwarz, 1996). Defunding centers was a new precedent and a rude awakening for many Head Start grantees, some of whom had been funded since the first summer of 1965. Helen Taylor, Chief of the Head Start Bureau, noted that these centers "didn't believe we'd do anything. We did it. We defunded them" (in Mills, 1998, p. 230). Taylor emphasized that a great deal of assistance had been offered to these centers, but they had refused it and continued to do what they wanted. Termination cases involved a range of causes from financial malfeasance to downright incompetence to child endangerment. Olivia Golden, who herself headed the investigation of a large grantee in Denver, pointed out that the Head Start community itself approved of revoking the grants of inadequate programs. "They feel that having a few bad centers endangers the rest of them" (in Mills, 1998, p. 231).

So for the first time in the history of Head Start, the Clinton people did indeed close a considerable number of Head Start programs and awarded the grants to others who could do a better job. This took a great deal of courage on the part of Secretary Shalala since invariably when a Head Start site is threatened with defunding, its constituents mobilize their Representatives and Senators to pressure HHS to reverse the decision. With new money for quality improvements, revised performance standards, and new methods of enforcement with real teeth, the Clinton administration and Congress demonstrated their commitment to improving Head Start and, by so doing, their belief that the program was worth this effort.

Broadening Head Start Practices

The Advisory Committee advanced several proposals to modernize Head Start services, based as they were on the needs of the poor population in the 1960s, to better address the needs of poor families in the 1990s. The 1994 reauthorization act supported these changes. Policymakers recognized that to improve the academic outcomes of children raised in poverty, intervention must last longer than the 9 months before school entry. They therefore legislated transition-to-school services and a major new initiative for children from birth to age 3. To meet the needs of the increasing number of working parents, a section of the law authorized the use of Head Start funds to provide and/or collaborate with providers of full-day, year-long child care services. These changes had been proffered by the groups charged with plotting Head Start's future on its fifteenth and twenty-fifth anniversaries (Chapter 8). Now that there was authorizing legislation and a strong group of leaders in charge of the program, Head Start had the support needed to begin constructing that future.

Early Head Start

Just a few weeks after President Clinton was elected, his transition team approached me with a request that brought joy to my heart. Our new leader wanted a position paper on the wisdom of providing Head Start services to children before they reached preschool age. This idea had emerged early in the program's history when it became obvious that many of the 3- to 5-year-olds arriving at Head Start's door already showed delays in learning and social–emotional development. One Head Start demonstration project, the Parent and Child Centers, was started back in 1968 to serve families and children from birth to age 3 to try to prevent the incremental developmental damage of living in poverty. Two and a half decades later, we were about to have a president interested in taking the idea mainstream.

I instantly agreed to write the paper, and my co-author cleared her schedule and desk so we could tackle the assignment. The only problem was that we would not be able to use our desks. Recent oil embargos and the Gulf War had put Yale on a mission to conserve energy. Because most of the students and faculty deserted the campus over the December holiday break, university officials decided to call a general recess so they would not have to heat their nearly empty buildings. So Sally and I carted home our files and books, and at 8 a.m. the day after Christmas she drove to my house to begin the project. We thought and wrote, and wrote and thought, all week and had a brief to deliver to the president when we returned to our thawed offices on January 2. The piece, which we still call our "What I Did Over Christmas Vacation" paper, was published later that year in *Zero to Three* (Zigler and Styfco, 1993a).

A catalyst for Clinton's interest in an earlier Head Start program was likely the Carnegie Task Force on Meeting the Needs of Young Children. The group was convened in 1991 to review the scientific knowledge and create an action agenda for promoting the healthy development of all children from before birth to age 3 years. There were 30 members, including Richard Riley (who would become Clinton's Secretary of Education), Head Start veterans Julius Richmond and I, and leaders in science, law, business, education, and other fields, as well as the outstanding staff at the Carnegie Foundation.

The Carnegie Task Force's (1994) report, entitled *Starting Points*, offered a half dozen specific suggestions, such as improving the health care of pregnant mothers and young children, raising the quality of child care for infants and toddlers, and securing parental leave benefits. The members were surprised when the media essentially ignored most of the recommendations and instead became fixated on their discussion of early brain development, which represented less than two pages of the entire report. This work concerned molecular biology studies of the very rapid brain development during the first 3 years of life, when connections among brain cells multiply and undergo orderly pruning. The topic generated a huge media response, with cover stories about early brain development in national publications like *Time* and *Newsweek*. The media reports emphasized the important role of the environment in determining permanent brain structures and all but ignored the potent genetic component. It was as if we had returned to the 1960s when the false belief prevailed that intelligence was mostly determined by the environment, so the more environmental stimulation young children could get the better.

The more sensible approach, and the one the Carnegie group used to advocate for supports for the first 3 years of life, is that during this period the foundations for the child's later behavioral, emotional, social, and cognitive status are formed (Shonkoff and Phillips, 2000; Zigler et al., 2002). Without question, rightly or wrongly the early brain development work buried in the Carnegie report provided traction for getting Early Head Start established. Also without question, President Clinton's interest in creating intervention services for very young children predated the hype surrounding this work. Senator Kennedy led the way in Congress, and the Early Head Start program became a reality in the 1994 Head Start reauthorization.

In our brief to the transition team, Sally and I discussed not only the need for and possible content of intervention services for very young children but gave suggestions about planning and implementing such a program. We wanted to avoid the problems that have long haunted Head Start, which had been hurriedly planned and ended up with some systemic flaws. Our proposals were utilized by the knowledgeable people at ACYF, who were given the task of developing and launching Early Head Start. A big plus is that there was a great deal more expertise and a much larger knowledge base available than at the time of Head Start's inception. A planning committee representing many disciplines was put into place. Its members included some of the pioneers on the original Head Start planning committee, grateful for a second chance to get it right this time.

In our brief we underscored that the harshest lesson learned from the first Head Start is that it is unwise to begin very quickly and on a national scale because quality control cannot keep pace (Zigler and Styfco, 1993a). We recommended a gradual expansion of Early Head Start, guided by continuing evaluation. This is exactly what ACYF did. The launch began with 17 carefully selected sites, and a random assignment study was immediately put into place. I remember the first expansion when 600 applications were received. Unlike the frenzied assembly line where applications to run Head Start were glanced over and rubber stamped "approved," each Early Head Start application was carefully reviewed by a group of experts. Only 60 of the best proposals were selected. Today there are 650 programs serving some 62,000 children, about the same as there were when Clinton left office. After 15 years, Early Head Start serves only a minute percentage of eligible children and families. This number may at last grow with the infusion of money from the 2009 federal stimulus package.

Early Head Start was actually the newest effort in Head Start's national laboratory, which already included a zero to 3 program called the Parent and Child Centers. These centers were somewhat like "loose cannons" in the Head Start armamentarium. They were a heterogeneous group of about 30 sites and had never been covered by the performance standards so their practices and quality were essentially unknown. Senator Kennedy and I wanted to throw the application process for Early Head Start grants open to any group that had experience and expertise in working with infants and toddlers as well as their parents. The Parent and Child Center grantees would be welcome to apply, but so would others.

Whenever Congress reauthorizes Head Start, the views of the National Head Start Association (NHSA) are invariably solicited. I have worked closely with NHSA for decades, and its leadership and I are usually in agreement on policy issues. We parted company on Early Head Start. NHSA's membership consists largely of Head Start employees and the parents of Head Start children. It seemed to me that NHSA abandoned their characteristic concern about what is best for children and behaved like a union protecting the employment of its members. NHSA insisted on giving the Parent and Child Centers a monopoly on who could apply for Early Head Start grants. I remember Senator Kennedy contacting me, frustrated about NHSA's stance. He asked if I would intercede with their power structure to convince them to endorse the open application process that both of us preferred. I made an effort to resolve this conflict with NHSA but was unsuccessful. This is all now history, and NHSA has become a strong supporter of Early Head Start.

Transition to School

The Clinton administration endorsed the themes of easing the transition to school for children and their families as well as continuing intervention services beyond the preschool year. The revised performance standards required all Head Start providers to establish procedures to support successful transitions from other child care programs to Early Head Start, and from Head Start to the schools the children will attend. The 1994 reauthorization act extended the Head Start Transition Project for 4 years and provided funds for further evaluation. When the results of the project were released, they appeared to be a disappointment because the control group equaled the performance of the transition students. As explained in Chapter 10, in reality the comparison schools had adopted the practices of the demonstration sites, and both groups of students attained national achievement norms. Evidently decision makers in the Department of Education did not look further into these results, not recognizing this was the best evidence ever collected on how to reduce or even eliminate the achievement gap between poor and more affluent children.

The Transition Project represented a course of action that has long made sense to me, namely that in the early grades of public school poor children and their families should have Head Start-like experiences that center on education, comprehensive services, and strong parental involvement. The authors went so far as to suggest a plan for how schools in high-poverty districts could finance a Head Start-like program from kindergarten through third grade (Zigler and Styfco, 1993b). We proposed converting the massive Title I program that provides funds to the majority of the nation's schools to mount just about any type of intervention for any age to try to boost the educational performance of poor children. In our view, the huge amount of Title I money ($13.8 billion) is spread too thin on efforts of unknown effectiveness to have much of an impact on the achievement gap. We proposed transforming Title I into a Transition Project concentrated on grades kindergarten through three. The Nobel Laureate James Heckman (2000) has now presented empirical evidence that society gets a bigger return on its intervention investment by serving younger compared to older children and adults. He recommends expanding early intervention programming, but we do not believe this is the best use of Title I funds. While a small percentage of Title I's budget is spent on preschool-aged children, between Head Start and the state programs preschool education for poor children in America is already fairly well-funded. We would prefer to apply Title I funds to the early grades of elementary school, when cognitive skills and academic behaviors are still being shaped.

Attention to Child Care

In addition to strengthening Head Start, child care was also on my wish list when President Clinton took office. He had spoken about child care often during his campaign, and I was further encouraged knowing that Hillary Clinton had been pursuing the issue of child care quality for years. She had worked on the child care front as First Lady of Arkansas and was a member of the Board of Directors of the Child Care Action campaign, a highly visible and important advocacy group. However, like the Child Development and Child Care Council of America, the organization could not obtain the funds to stay in existence and had to close its doors.

With their history, I had high hopes the Clintons would address the huge policy vacuum in Washington on the child care issue, which represents a broader and more complex problem than Head Start. Following President Nixon's veto of the 1971 Comprehensive Child Development Act, the topic of child care was avoided by policymakers, who feared the wrath of the vocal right-wing opposition responsible for the popular legislation's demise. The need for child care became so pressing during the George H. W. Bush administration that a child care bill finally passed into law, some 2 decades after the Nixon veto. The Child Care and Development Block Grant Act of 1990 provided the states with federal money to help subsidize care for poor and near-poor families. Unfortunately, there were few assurances that the care purchased would meet even minimal quality standards.

In early 1995 the Clinton administration established the Child Care Bureau within ACYF and gave it responsibility for administering the block grants. I welcomed the new bureau as an extremely important step forward. It represented not just an awareness at the highest level of government of the child care problems confronting American families but hope that finally something would be done to address the crisis. As long ago as 1970 the delegates to the White House Conference on Children designated affordable, quality child care as the chief problem of our nation's children and families (Chapter 6). At that time I established an Office of Child Care in ACYF's predecessor, OCD. The office was not an official administration effort but just an idea I implemented with the approval of Secretary Richardson. I thought the office was needed because at that time OCD was working on both the Comprehensive Child Development Act, which would have created a national child care system, and the large child care component in President Nixon's welfare reform plan. However, the Office of Child Care was primarily symbolic and was staffed by only two people, Sam Granato and a part-time secretary. Clinton's Child Care Bureau was a substantial agency that would have a real say in policy.

I believe the Clintons genuinely hoped to improve the quality of child care experienced by American children, but their plans were stymied by the 1996 welfare reform act. The new limits on public assistance forced huge numbers of poor mothers into job training or the workforce. With the demand for child care exploding, the imperative to expand the number of slots available trumped concerns about quality. What little improvement we saw was primarily attributable to the efforts mounted by the Child Care Bureau, first under Joan Lombardi during the Clinton years and then by Shannon Christian during the George W. Bush years. They simply did not have the funds to tackle the issue. When Head Start was confronted with quality problems, Senator Kennedy took the lead in providing a 25% set-aside for improvement efforts. In my view this is minimally what federal child care programs need to begin to boost quality.

After the passage of the 1996 welfare reform bill, Olivia Golden was under considerable pressure to provide full-day, full-year child care for Head Start mothers so they could get jobs. I had faced the same type of pressure during the early 1970s, another time when interest in reforming welfare was high. Olivia asked me to come to Washington to advise her on this issue. My view was the same one I had advanced 2 decades ago. Head Start's goal was to help children get ready to learn in school. Given the demographic changes in our society, if we were to reinvent Head Start today the planning committee would undoubtedly have created a combined Head Start–child care program. I pointed out to Golden that Head Start could readily add a child care component simply by expanding the length of the school day and year, and it could do so when and if Congress appropriated sufficient funds. With her current budget, she could either provide high-quality preschool intervention with the goal of school readiness or stretch the money for a large-scale child care program that would have to be of mediocre quality to be affordable. I emphasized that Head Start was only accountable for children's school readiness and would receive no credit for providing child care so that poor parents could work.

Olivia and I then discussed whether there was any way we could do both. I knew of an innovative program in Kansas City that used Head Start money for the preschool component and federal and state child care money to wrap extended day services around the typical Head Start hours. Golden and I agreed that Head Start should give future funding priority to centers that proposed to augment the Head Start schedule with funds from other child care resources. In 1997 Secretary Shalala announced that some Head Start expansion funds would be used to create partnerships with child care providers, and guidance on this topic was included in the 1998 performance standards.

A basic tenet of Head Start has always been that providers do all they can to meet the various needs of participating families. To keep this promise to poor parents whose need for child care was becoming evermore desperate meant that Head Start had to respond. However, this is not the optimal way to run a Head Start program. To provide child care services, administrators often have to jump through hoops to meld two or more funding streams, each having its own purpose and restrictions. That this has been done to the extent it has is a tribute to the commitment of Head Start workers to serving their constituents.

The Clinton administration's desire to improve the child care situation in America was better evidenced by the after-school program known as the 21st Century Community Learning Centers. Clinton enlarged this program and increased its budget to approximately $1 billion a year. The Learning Centers provided enrichment programs to keep children engaged and safe during after-school hours. The least costly and easiest part of the child care puzzle is care for school-age children. Compared to younger children, they can be served in larger groups and, because they are in school during the day, for fewer hours. Parents and many entities have championed the availability of before- and after-school care. For example, the business community has advocated for after-school care because parents are not always effective workers in the late afternoons if they are worried about the safety and well-being of their children. Research on the millions of latchkey children in this country has demonstrated the proclivity of unsupervised children to use drugs and engage in other risky activities. The momentum to establish after-school care programs was increased when the Washington-based advocacy group, Fight Crime: Invest in Kids, reported more juvenile crimes occur between 3 p.m. and 6 p.m. than at other times (Newman, Fox, Flynn, and Christeson, 2000). This organization, composed of law enforcement professionals and crime victims, has words that carry great weight with Congress.

Despite all the new federal dollars for child care and the creation of the Child Care Bureau, child care in America today is little different than it was when the Clintons entered the White House in 1993. Welfare reform is the historical culprit, because it concentrates attention on reducing welfare cases instead of on children's needs. In 2006 President George W. Bush combined the Child Care Bureau with the Office of Family Assistance (which administers Temporary Assistance for Needy Families), cementing the federal approach to child care as a welfare issue instead of a support for working parents and healthy child development. From this perspective, quality care is considered a discretionary expense instead of a necessity.

New Agendas for Research and Evaluation

The leaders responsible for Head Start in the Clinton administration were quite sophisticated in their understanding of the importance of research efforts, efforts that could inform ways to make the program stronger as well as those that could measure its effectiveness. Helen Taylor, Director of the Head Start Bureau, took a much greater interest in the research enterprise than did most of the directors she succeeded. There has long been a tension and somewhat abrasive relationship between Head Start practitioners and researchers, neither group fully appreciating what the other has to offer. Taylor would not hear of it. She would give research a place of value and expect practitioners to cooperate.

In keeping with Clinton's practice of seeking the most qualified people to run the government, Head Start's research needs were put into the hands of national experts. In 1994 the administration put into place the Round Table on Head Start Research under the imprimatur of the prestigious National Research Council and the Institute of Medicine (both parts of the National Academy of Sciences). Chairing the Round Table was Sheldon White of Harvard. The staff work was directed by Deborah Phillips, then of the National Research Council. Many leading scholars knowledgeable about Head Start and early intervention served on the panel. I served both as a representative of the Institute of Medicine (of which I am a member) and as a scholar in the field.

The panel tackled the issue of how well Head Start meets the needs of its client families. The group's final report laid out a broad array of actions and research projects to pursue (Phillips and Cabrera, 1996). The report noted the increasing need of Head Start parents for full-time, full-year care for their children. The panel called for the continuation and expansion of the national laboratory approach I had taken in the 1970s and emphasized the need to disseminate the results. Oftentimes innovative and successful efforts implemented at one center were unknown to other centers grappling with the same issues, so Head Start needed to do a better job of sharing good ideas throughout the system. The work of the Round Table influenced the 1996 Research to Practice conference where some dissemination and collaboration took place. These included an asthma education project in Boston and an alliance among the Texas Instruments Foundation, two universities, and Head Start of Dallas centered on improving children's behavior.

The Round Table had many ideas for research. The panel called for a greater evaluation of Head Start's impact on other community services such as health delivery. They also wanted research on how the program could alleviate the negative emotional aftermath of experiencing violence, a growing problem for Head Start children. The panel's report once again emphasized that the most pressing research issue was achieving some definitive answer to the basic question of whether Head Start works. The group lamented that too many assessments have been limited to the program's impact on cognitive development. While Head Start also strives to nurture social and emotional development and strengthen families, studies of its results in these areas have been handicapped by the lack of good measurement tools. Although some measures do exist, they have not achieved the high-quality psychometric properties of measures of cognitive development such as standardized IQ and achievement tests. The panel called for Head Start to fund the development of such measures.

Helen Taylor attended the Round Table's meetings religiously and immediately began to put the recommendations to work. Most notably, she became the first director of the Head Start Bureau to tackle the question of whether Head Start was efficacious or not. (Her motivation came not just from the deliberations of the Round Table but from the passage of the Government Performance and Results Act of 1993, which required all federally funded programs to take steps to improve their performance and accountability.) Helen initiated several efforts to develop valid and reliable measures that could be used to collect empirical evidence of changes in children's behavior and performance as a result of attending Head Start. In 1995, ACYF funded four Quality Research Centers whose goals included developing new data collection instruments for Head Start. The agency also established the Performance Measures Center to begin collecting data with these instruments through an initiative called the Family and Child Experiences Survey, or FACES. The effort is funded through 2010 as of this writing and is gathering information on the relationship among family and program characteristics and child outcomes (Administration for Children and Families, December 2006).

Head Start Child Outcomes Framework

In collaboration with the research community as well as the community of practitioners, Taylor also undertook her own effort to inform the measurement of Head Start children's performance. She chose not to recommend specific measures of outcomes but instead developed a framework of the types of results Head Start programs should use to evaluate their progress. The Head Start Child Outcomes Framework was comprised of eight general domains: language development, literacy, mathematics, science, creative arts, social and emotional development, approaches to learning, and physical health and development. Elements of each domain and indicators of children's relevant abilities were illustrated for field personnel. For example, under language development, the elements included "listening and understanding" and "speaking and communicating," with listed indicators such as progress in following simple and multi-step directions and initiating conversations.

Respectful of Head Start's tradition of local control, Helen wanted local Head Start administrators to have ownership of the performance-based outcomes system. Rather than dictating specific measures for each domain, she allowed directors to select their assessment tools. This permitted them to keep instruments they were already using and their staff were familiar with if they chose. The results of the self-assessments were to be used to improve curricula and alter practices that did not show they were working as well as they could be.

Helen apparently did not fully appreciate that putting evaluation into the hands of practitioners was not a scientifically sound procedure because they have such a vested interest in demonstrating positive outcomes. Nonetheless, she was courageous to insist that every Head Start center undergo periodic assessments of its program's impact in specific domains. Understandably, the people who run Head Start classrooms believe with all their hearts that the program works and there is no need for time-consuming evaluation to prove it. Head Start parents feel exactly the same way. Taylor's release of the performance-based outcomes framework conveyed the message to staff that they would ultimately be judged by objective evidence of their students' progress rather than by their convictions that the program was successful. Helen Taylor was a heroic and much loved figure in the Head Start community, so staff accepted the task of assessing child outcomes rather than voicing their usual unhappiness with any sort of evaluation. Helen understood, and tried to help practitioners understand, that Head Start is ultimately accountable to decision makers in Congress who decide whether and how much to fund the program. We will see in the next chapter that when the George W. Bush administration imposed its National Reporting System (NRS), practitioners again became negative about evaluation. Displaying what Taylor had taught them, this time they were not disagreeable to accountability but to the duplication of effort they were already putting into measuring outcomes.

Head Start Impact Study

Prior to the 1998 reauthorization of Head Start, Congress charged the Government Accounting Office with the huge task of examining all the existing evidence to determine whether Head Start worked or not. The final report gave the disappointing but honest conclusion that despite the enormous amount of research that had been done, it was impossible to give Congress a clear yes or no about Head Start's effectiveness (U.S. GAO, 1997). The authors gave two main reasons the evidence was inconclusive: (1) Many studies had been conducted so long ago they could not shed light on Head Start's current degree of success, and (2) the methodologies employed in many of the studies were too weak to allow for firm conclusions or were incomparable, so the results could not be generalized.

I had been meeting with congressional staffers from both sides of the aisle weeks before the reauthorization hearings, and I also was a consultant to the GAO for their research synthesis. Thus I knew pretty well where Congress was heading, and I was aware of the GAO conclusions prior to the release of their report. I do not believe it was accidental that I was scheduled to give my testimony right after that of the GAO representative. I tried to stay positive and, without attempting to negate the GAO's opinion, told the committee the strongest and clearest evidence we had on the impact of Head Start was in a comprehensive review by economist Steven Barnett, who essentially came down on the side that Head Start was proven to work. Of course, I also made clear that as an expert in evaluation I could not take exception to the conclusion reached by the GAO.

With the GAO's report of no definitive findings as a catalyst, the 1998 reauthorization included an order by Congress that the Secretary of HHS Donna Shalala form an expert committee on evaluation to design a national impact study assessing Head Start's effectiveness. Again, the heavy lifting for this task was passed to Olivia Golden, who chaired the committee's delibera-tions. The committee was bipartisan and included several of our nation's very best evaluation experts. An important member was Wade Horn, who had been the federal official responsible for Head Start in the George H. W. Bush administration and would assume the same role for George W. Bush. The entire history of Head Start evaluation has been colored by debates about the value of using a nationwide sample in such a diverse program, appropriate design and methodology, and the most basic question of what outcomes to assess. The debates were ongoing so needless to say, the committee meetings were somewhat contentious, with the arguments becoming shrill from time to time.

I was in close discussion with Olivia Golden during the life of this com-mittee, and I sat beside her throughout the proceedings. Between the two of us we kept the meetings on course and moving toward the goal we both agreed Congress had in mind, namely a nationwide evaluation of Head Start. My own discussions with policymakers made it clear to me that we had little leeway as a committee. What Congress wanted was a study that would employ the gold standard of evaluation research, random assignment. In such a design children would be randomly assigned to either an experimental group who would receive the Head Start program or to a control group who would not. It was much too late in the preschool intervention movement to even think about doing a study comparing Head Start children with those being reared at home with no preschool experience. Instead of a treatment versus no treatment study, we were forced to conduct what is called a value-added study. Thus we would compare the effects of attending Head Start to the effects of attending what was available in the community, for example, state prekindergarten, a variety of types of child care, and private preschool settings.

One of the first arguments among committee members was that a random assignment study would be unethical in that we would be denying eligible children whose parents wanted to send them to Head Start the opportunity to participate. We solved this problem by deciding to use only Head Start centers that had large waiting lists. Since these centers could not serve all of the families who applied, the wait-listed children would not be receiving the Head Start program anyway. Thus we could solve our ethical issue by randomly assigning children at sites with long waiting lists to the Head Start and the control groups.

Unforeseen were the very strong feelings of the mothers of children who were placed in the control group. These mothers wanted their children to have Head Start and they could care less about the validity of the experiment in which they were participating. (All children and families were periodically assessed.) Thus many of them simply enrolled their children in other nearby Head Start programs. Since thousands of control children ended up receiving Head Start, their progress could match that of children in the official Head Start group, making it look as if Head Start did not convey any value. Even with the problems that arose, the authors believe that the National Impact Study is the best possible evaluation that the expertise of the nation could provide and that Head Start has ever had.

The scope and cost of this study were so large that it took a consortium of research groups to join together to bid to conduct the project. Later, a small subset of the planning group members was established to be an oversight committee to the project during the George W. Bush years. The results from the first stage of the longitudinal study, covering the effects accruing in a single year of Head Start either at age 3 or age 4, have been compiled (see Chapter 13). We still await the results on the effects of a 2-year program as well as a longitudinal portion that assessed first-grade performance. Our hope is that the study participants will be followed for many years, not only for the short term that is currently planned.

The Golden Years Wind Down

The Clinton administration's failure to fulfill its own goals for Head Start was partly due to the fact that Congress was not as enthusiastic about the program and its potential as was the president. Only 2 years into Clinton's presidency, both the House and Senate went to Republican majorities for the first time in 40 years. Foreshadowing the George W. Bush administration, Congress appeared to want a preschool education program that concentrated on academic skills instead of on the whole child. Although congressional members acknowledged the importance of comprehensive services to both the child and the family, they endorsed a cognitive approach that they reduced essentially to improving the child's literacy and math abilities. The tension between the Clinton administration and Congress concerning the nature of Head Start and appropriate goals was seen vividly during the deliberations for the 1998 reauthorization. Draft legislation imposed the specific goals that, by the end of the Head Start program, each graduating child would know 10 letters of the alphabet and 10 numbers. The numbers requirement was eventually dropped but the 10 letters mandate stood, although Congress never enumerated *which* letters children should know (The ones in their names might make sense.)

The 1998 reauthorization set a precedent that would be followed in subsequent Head Start legislation. Congress for the first time clearly attempted to micromanage the activities in every Head Start classroom across the nation, regardless of the needs of the children or preferred pedagogy of the center's constituents. This approach undercut decades of effort in which the national Head Start office has tried to give parents and communities a sense of ownership of their local Head Start programs. Congress's misunderstanding both of Head Start and of school readiness was obvious in the 10-letters and 10-numbers requirement. Rote learning of such items has little to do with a child's multifaceted literacy abilities or true understanding of the concepts of numbers and ordinality. Further, researchers have discovered that when kindergarten teachers were asked the major facets of school readiness, knowing letters and numbers was of little importance. Instead they listed physical well-being and the abilities to follow instructions and to behave appropriately with peers and adults.

Perhaps the 10-letters and 10-numbers requirement was a way for some policymakers to express their ire over reports that some children were graduating from Head Start without knowing *any* letters of the alphabet. Of course, policymakers found it was not so easy to impose their will on local centers, especially when staff and parents knew more about child development than most of them did. More alphabet cards and counting songs may have appeared in Head Start classrooms, but these activities did not replace the regular curricula until the NRS tested children's mastery in these subject areas (see Chapter 12).

Congress did make a positive and significant move forward in the 1998 reauthorization. After over 30 years of Head Start's existence, policymakers designated school readiness as the program's goal. Head Start has had at least three goals over its lifetime. The first was increases in IQ, a goal never advanced by program administrators but imposed by the research community during Head Start's early years. The second goal was everyday social competence, which OCD proclaimed in the early 1970s but was never able to operationalize (Chapter 5). The goal of school readiness was clear and readily understood, although it too lacked consensual definition and agreement on how it could be measured. This problem could be relatively easy to overcome because broad scholarship and a great deal of expert thought had been committed to defining the construct. The work group tracking progress toward Goal 1 of the Educate America Act issued a clear five-factor definition of school readiness (Chapter 10). This definition had much in common with both the Zigler and Trickett (1978) four-factor definition of social competence at school entry and Helen Taylor's eight performance domains. For example, all three approaches emphasized the importance of physical and mental health. One need not be a rocket scientist to understand that a child who is ill or depressed cannot fully utilize the learning environment provided in school.

In legislating the goal of school readiness, Congress may have awakened some debate over the concept but freed Head Start from the burden of unrealistic goals that had shadowed the program since its inception. No longer was Head Start to be judged by its success in eliminating poverty, making children smarter, or single-handedly closing the achievement gap. If the program's benefits eventually faded away in school, Head Start could no longer be blamed if it sent the children to school ready to learn. Although making the school readiness goal official has not stopped the flow of surreal expectations, it has helped Head Start concentrate on what it can and should be doing—preparing children and families for school.

Ridiculous hopes for what Head Start could achieve fed the far-right and libertarian organizations, who constantly attacked the program. As a case in point, the Cato Institute referred to Head Start supporters as hucksters in a paper titled, "The Head Start Scam" (Hood, 2004). Coloring Head Start a failure took on symbolic value for this group. Hacsi observed that "if they could show that Head Start, . . . run by the federal government, was a failure, it would be a major blow against all such efforts by the federal government" (2002, p. 52). Indeed, in 1993 *Newsweek* summed up the rising tide of attacks against Head Start in an article entitled, "Head Start Has Become a Free-fire Zone." Thus the Clintons' affection and advocacy for our nation's Head Start program required a certain amount of independent thought and courage.

President Clinton was just as strong a supporter of Head Start at the end of his administration as he was at the beginning. The president stood his ground on Head Start until the very end. His last budget agreement with Congress included an increase of $1 billion for Head Start (bringing funding up to $6.2 billion). As praiseworthy as this was, this amount would still fall far short of Clinton's promise that the program would have the funds to serve every eligible child. Regardless of whether his goals were too lofty or Congress not cooperative enough, the Head Start community continues to look back on the Clinton years as the golden age of Head Start. Hasci captured this impression in his statement, "President Clinton was probably the strongest supporter of Head Start to occupy the White House since its founder, Lyndon Johnson" (2002, p. 55). President Clinton continued a strong focus on improving quality and extended services to younger children with Early Head Start. He set into motion a sound longitudinal study of Head Start's effects. As this chapter should make clear, the Head Start heroes in the Clinton administration extended beyond Bill and Hillary to some of the most effective public servants who have ever managed the program. It is said that all good things must come to an end, and this era of progress ended with the election of George W. Bush, who had a very different vision of what Head Start should be.

12

George W. Bush versus Head Start

Head Start advocates feared the program would be in trouble if George W. Bush was elected president. During the 2000 campaign the Texas Governor gave many subtle and not-so-subtle indications that he thought Head Start was a disappointment and needed an extreme makeover. One hint was that Bush campaigned as a "compassionate conservative" and appealed directly to the religious right. These were the same groups who prompted Richard Nixon to veto the Comprehensive Child Development Act of 1971 and put enough of the fear of God into policymakers that they would not raise a serious child care bill for 2 decades. The conservative Christian philosophy was that mothers should stay at home to rear their children. Preschool programs like Head Start were therefore unnecessary at best and an intrusion of big government into private family life.

Another clue that George W. Bush would not befriend Head Start was his selection of Richard Cheney for Vice President. Cheney had a long history of enmity toward Head Start. I witnessed this posture myself in the early 1970s when he was deputy to Donald Rumsfeld, who was then Director of the Office of Economic Opportunity (OEO) and my nominal supervisor. The two of them nixed every idea I gave them about improving Head Start until I just stopped sharing my plans with OEO (see Chapter 4).

Throughout the campaign Bush's remarks about Head Start made it obvious he really did not understand the program. For example, he derogatorily referred to it as a "social program," implying either that it fostered socialization at the expense of preschool education or that social skills have little to do with school readiness. Hacsi notes another misconception Bush had when he stated Head Start "was originally intended as a literacy program" (2002, p. 57). He clearly had no familiarity at all with the program's history and philosophy. Nor did he appear to understand child development since most 3- and 4-year-olds (the age group served by Head Start) have not yet reached the stage of cognitive development when the processes required for reading emerge. To promote literacy training in Head Start, he proposed moving the program into the Department of Education (DOE), apparently ignorant of President Carter's failed attempt to do the same thing and the reasons why such a move would be detrimental to Head Start's goals. The mere mention of giving DOE responsibility for Head Start alerted advocates to the fact the program's unique federal-to-local funding structure would be threatened.

The balloting fiasco in Florida delayed the results of the national election for a suspenseful and long month. Head Start would either have a supportive Gore–Lieberman team steering its course or a disapproving Bush–Cheney team changing its course. The streets near Senator Lieberman's home here in New Haven were filled with "Go Joe!" signs and an imposing security detail. After the U.S. Supreme Court weighed in, the signs came down, the Secret Service disappeared, and George W. Bush became America's forty-third president. I knew I would have to change paths from trying to strengthen and grow Head Start to battling to save it.

A Different Kind of "Education President"

As governor, Bush felt he had made considerable progress revamping the education system in Texas and, like his father before him, now wanted to be seen as the nation's "education president." Early in his term he championed two major education efforts: high-stakes testing and school vouchers. Although Congress eventually agreed to the academic testing, they were firmly opposed to vouchers. These would be given to parents of children in "failing" public schools to help them pay the cost of private school tuition. Since the majority of private K–12 schools are run by religious groups, this school choice proposal was clearly an offering to Bush's conservative right-wing supporters. Another was the Office of Faith-based and Community Initiatives, which he established by executive order during his first month in office. The office was to expand the capacity of local and religious groups to provide social services, including those supported by federal funds. Soon the door was opened for faith-based organizations to apply for Head Start grants. We will have more to say about the controversy this created below.

Focus on Literacy

The new administration took a strictly academic approach to education, demanding that schools concentrate on literacy and cognitive development.

In his first State of the Union address President Bush declared, "Reading is the foundation of all learning" and proposed adding "$5 billion to help every child in America learn to read." He announced that First Lady Laura Bush would launch a new effort "to promote sound teaching practices and early reading skills in our schools and in programs such as Head Start" (Woolley and Peters, n.d.a). One part of this initiative was the White House Summit on Early Childhood Cognitive Development, convened in July of 2001.

The conference was chaired by Mrs. Bush, who had been a second-grade teacher and later a librarian. Others involved had backgrounds that assured the spotlight would be on literacy. One featured speaker was the Bushes' old friend from Texas, Susan Landry, now director of the Center for Improving the Readiness of Children for Learning and Education (CIRCLE). The center is known for its work in early literacy, and eventually the CIRCLE curriculum was placed into Head Start programs. Landry is a competent developmental psychologist as well as a professor at the University of Texas Hill Science Center in Houston. She was an important force in policymaking concerning children's programs in the state while Bush was governor. Further, she had been a college classmate of Laura Bush.

Another prominent participant in the conference was a civil servant, G. Reid Lyon, who held a post at the National Institute of Child Health and Human Development. Lyon's scientific credentials were in literacy development. A strong champion of phonemic instruction as opposed to the whole-language approach, he served as policy advisor to President Bush from 2001 to 2005. He was also an advisor to Margaret Spellings during part of her tenure as Bush's Secretary of the Department of Education. The department had another well-known expert in literacy development, Grover "Russ" Whitehurst, who was appointed Assistant Secretary for Education Research and Improvement.

I had worked closely with Whitehurst for several years and thought highly of him, but Lyon and I had had our share of disagreements. He had opposed funding the NICHD longitudinal child care study, which is a huge study of the effects of substitute care on child development. Lyon objected to the study on the grounds that it did not have sufficiently rigorous methodology. While he preferred a random assignment design, there are many instances when this is not possible. You certainly cannot randomly assign children into child care against the wishes of their parents.

The White House conference signaled that the Bush administration would press hard to shift the goal of Head Start from developing the whole child to developing cognitive skills, with an emphasis on literacy and numeracy. This approach would be reflected in the NRS discussed below and in the CIRCLE curriculum. That this was Bush's agenda is apparent in the fact that this was the only White House conference on children held during the 8 years of his presidency. During the Clinton years there were five such conferences chaired either by First Lady Hillary Clinton or by both the President and Mrs. Clinton. The five conferences were on: child care (1997); early childhood development and learning (1997), which covered the importance of the accelerated brain development during the early years of life; philanthropy and its relation to children's services (1999); children and adolescents (2000); and the White House Conference on Teenagers (2000).

As a known champion of the whole-child approach, I was clearly persona non grata and was not invited to the Bush conference. That of course did not stop me from publicly commenting on the proceedings. I reiterated my position that cognitive skills do not develop independently of the rest of the child, so it is foolish to focus on nurturing cognition without attending to other systems such as physical and mental health and social–emotional development. I also critiqued the conference title, the White House Summit on Early Childhood Cognitive Development, as a misnomer. The focus was almost exclusively on literacy, which is just one part of cognition. Even standard IQ tests, which are designed to measure intellectual development and were originally created to predict success in school, assess much more than verbal abilities. I argued that if the summit had been more appropriately named a conference on literacy, it still fell short because it centered on phonemic instruction alone. This instruction targets the ability to decode words on the written page but does not help much when it comes to comprehending what the words mean. That requires vocabulary knowledge, which is highly related to the child's everyday experiences. Curiosity and motivation also play a role in the acquisition of reading skills.

A Senate committee decided to hold hearings on the Bush administration's approach to literacy and early learning. Mrs. Bush herself would be a witness. Since her testimony would be written, it would certainly reflect the views of her husband's administration as well as her own belief in the primacy of literacy training over and above other developmental tasks. I too was invited to testify. Appearing before the Senate is always an honor to me, and having a First Lady present adds a tinge of excitement to the proceedings. That day turned out to have more excitement than anyone would ever care to experience.

On the morning of September 11, 2001, I went to the Senate Office Building and was invited to await the start of the hearings in Senator Kennedy's suite. I sat in the waiting room drinking coffee and going over my prepared testimony. I absentmindedly looked up at the TV long enough to see a plane crash into a World Trade Center tower. Soon Mrs. Bush and Senator

Kennedy appeared together on the screen, consoling the American people. A short time later an announcement rang throughout the building that everyone inside should evacuate. It was obvious there were be no hearings, so I hailed a cab and asked to be taken to the airport, thinking I could catch a flight back to New Haven. At that time I had no idea the other tower and the nearby Pentagon had also been targeted by terrorists. The driver told me there would be no flights anywhere in the United States, so I told him to take me to the train station instead. There I found that train service was also halted. I spent the day on a sidewalk bench in front of the train station, not knowing when or how I would ever get home.

Back at Yale, at first my staff were not too worried about me, My administrative assistant thought I was with Senator Kennedy when the first plane hit in New York, so she assumed I was whisked to a safe bunker alongside him. As the day wore on and no one heard from me, my staff and my typically unshakeable wife Bernice grew more and more concerned. It was late afternoon in Washington when an announcement came that finally a train would be leaving. The elderly and people with children got first seats, and for once in my life I was glad I was old. I will never forget the train going through New York City and seeing the smoke still rising from the World Trade Center. I arrived in New Haven late at night and was shocked to see my wife waiting for me at the station. Apparently one of Senator Kennedy's staff traced my ticket purchase through my credit card and called to tell her which train I would be arriving on. The very next day Bernice bought me a cell phone and patiently taught me how to use it.

The Senate hearings were rescheduled several months later. Evidently the White House had rethought having Mrs. Bush serve as a witness on a panel of experts. Instead of a live appearance she sent a statement. The witnesses were Jack Shonkoff, a pediatrician and old friend with whom I had ridden the train the night of September 11; Dorothy Strickland, a scholar with a well-deserved reputation as an expert in literacy; and I. Strickland had been offered the Head Start Bureau chief job by the Bush administration but had declined. The three of us all advanced the broad ecological approach to literacy development instead of the more narrow academic approach championed by the Bush administration. I remember one point the experts brought up that the underpinnings of a child's learning, including literacy, are broad and include good nutrition. Federal policy recognizes this and provides programs such as the Special Supplemental Nutrition Program for Women, Infants and Children (better known as WIC) as well as free and reduced-price breakfast and lunch programs in schools. Unconvinced, the Bush administration continued to treat reading as a function that develops independent from the rest of the child. Promote reading, they seemed to reason, and all other pieces of development will follow. The experts saw it the other way around.

No Child Left Behind

Eager to chisel his place as America's education president, in his first year in office George W. Bush changed the familiar name of the 1965 Elementary and Secondary Education Act to the No Child Left Behind Act (wording plagiarized from the Children's Defense Fund's mission statement to "leave no child behind"). The legislation gave the federal government a stronger say in local education than it had had in the centuries of public schooling in America. Although federal support of elementary and secondary schools amounts to less than 10% of their budgets, Washington would now demand greater accountability for those federal dollars. All schools would have to improve student performance, and if they did not improve it enough they would have to pay for tutoring and eventually give their student body the opportunity to go to better schools. Student achievement would be measured against benchmarks set by each state. Every year students would take standardized tests to assess their progress as well as that of their schools.

With the stakes so high, much classroom time is now spent coaching children for the tests, taking the tests, and reviewing test scores. Since the tests focus on reading and math, more time is devoted to instruction in these areas. To fit these lessons into the schedule, many schools have dropped courses in music, art, and/or gym. Some teachers have reduced playtime in kindergarten and eliminated recess for older children. The emphasis on testing has unquestionably weakened the bond students have with their schools because many of their favorite activities are gone, and there is no break from the stress of unrelenting academics.

Many criticisms have been leveled at NCLB, particularly the overemphasis on standardized tests as the only measure of a child's or a school's progress. The money that had originally been promised to help children with poor test scores was never forthcoming. Policymakers seemed to think that repeated testing alone would solve the problem, which is akin to saying if we keep taking the patient's temperature the patient will get well.

There is also no way the overarching goal of NCLB can be achieved. Supposedly by 2014 all children will be reading at grade level in third grade, and there will be no differences in educational performance between rich and poor or minority and mainstream children. This mandate includes special education students, as if teachers can miraculously make their special needs go away. Neither the president nor Congress has in their authority the power to repeal the biological law of human variability. Testing and teaching simply cannot erase individual differences in ability. Although NCLB has probably done more harm than good, it does have two commendable features: (1) prodding educators to set high expectations for all children, and (2) holding schools accountable for their students' learning.

Included in NCLB at the president's insistence was the Reading First program. This effort was to put "proven methods" of reading instruction into schools, along with testing to monitor children's progress. The program eventually became a point of controversy between the Bush administration and Congress. One issue was whether Reading First was actually proven to work. Congress demanded that the DOE conduct an evaluation assessing the program's impact on children's reading ability in the early years. The results showed it did not improve reading comprehension in the first, second, or third grade, which are nearly all the grades it targets. Secretary of Education Margaret Spellings, who had been a cheerleader for the program, had "no comment" on the study, but her spokesperson said the secretary often heard from educators extolling its effectiveness (Dillon, 2008a).

As if disappointing results from a study conducted by President Bush's own DOE were not bad enough, federal investigators uncovered questionable ties between some federal education officials and the publishers of Reading First materials. This conflict of interest led to accusations of cronyism at the expense of America's young readers.

Managing from the Top Down

The Bush administration's emphasis on literacy in NCLB was quickly extended to Head Start, an institution which the president himself had signaled that he would turn into a literacy program. To carry out his wishes he had to appoint like-minded individuals to administer the program. The key federal official responsible for Head Start in the early Bush years was Wade Horn, who had managed the program as head of ACYF during the George H. W. Bush administration. For the George W. Bush administration, he was promoted to Assistant Secretary for Children and Families at the Department of Health and Human Services (HHS), where Head Start was housed. Horn was trained as a clinical child psychologist and did not have special expertise in children's learning and development. He and I became friends during his earlier stint in government and had considerable respect for each other. Because of our relationship, I hoped I would be able to have some impact on Head Start matters during the George W. Bush years.

The key post of Head Start Bureau chief was filled by Windy Hill. Granted, she had big shoes to fill. The much beloved Helen Taylor, who had been chief in the Clinton administration, had died just a few months earlier. Hill was pretty much an unknown, and her appointment stunned the Head Start community. She had been director of a relatively small Head Start program in Texas, and her selection appeared to be based on little more than being from Bush's home state. Former Bureau chiefs, such as Clennie Murphy in a Republican administration and Helen Taylor in a Democratic administration, displayed considerable autonomy. While staying in step with each administration's policy decisions, they did their best to keep Head Start true to its roots and to improve services. This was not the case for Windy Hill, who automatically endorsed whatever policies Wade Horn and his superiors wanted.

Although not officially a member of the administration, an important player in Bush's literary emphasis in Head Start was Susan Landry. Unfortunately, many of her activities, especially her role in the CIRCLE curriculum, lead to the impression that she believed early childhood programs like Head Start should focus exclusively on the development of literacy skills. In point of fact, Landry's own writings (e.g., 2005) make clear that she champions the whole-child approach to early intervention. Her roots in Texas, where she took the lead in Governor and Mrs. Bush's initiative to promote language and literacy in early childhood programs, undoubtedly colored perceptions about her views as identical to those of the president even though they were not.

Wade Horn moved quickly to push Head Start practices toward literacy skills. He wanted Head Start directors to enhance the literacy component of whatever curriculum they were using and to enrich the general literacy environment in Head Start classrooms. The national office contracted with Susan Landry at CIRCLE to train representatives from each Head Start program in what was called the CIRCLE curriculum. It was not so much a complete curriculum as it was the inculcation of practices to beef up instruction in language and literacy. The idea here was that the representatives would be taught these new mechanisms and would return home to train the other staff. This approach is referred to as the "train the trainer" model. There is no way of knowing what impact this training had on the actual experiences of Head Start children, but we do know the impact on the Head Start community. Practitioners were shocked and threatened about having specific practices imposed from above. Local Head Start centers have always enjoyed a certain degree of autonomy and had never been micromanaged by the national office. The Bush administration thus signaled clearly that the Head Start Bureau would govern differently than it had in the past.

The difference was palpable. Head Start had always prided itself on being as much a bottom-up program as a top-down program. The ideal was that the federal and regional personnel worked closely and in cooperation with local staff in the trenches. This friendly relationship turned adversarial during the Bush years. This shift was painfully evident in the training and technical assistance (TTA) function, which has long been an important resource to local centers, helping staff correct deficiencies or address unique needs of their participants. Under Horn's direction, the Bush administration dismantled Head Start's entire TTA unit. Staff with decades of tenure were fired in an impersonal e-mail. Further, these experienced individuals were excluded from the selected group of 30 organizations that were allowed to bid for the funds in the TTA budget. The contracts went to organizations that were friendly to the Bush administration rather than to those with demonstrated competence in providing the services needed by Head Start centers. Unsurprisingly, TTA would now help with literacy initiatives instead of all aspects of practice.

Dismantling TTA was obviously an attempt to break with tradition by severing ties with those who were schooled in Head Start's whole-child approach and stacking the deck with new faces who would carry out Bush's plan to reinvent Head Start as a literacy program. In another break with the past, the Bush administration made clear at the outset that they had little use for the National Head Start Association (NHSA), the organization representing the Head Start community in Washington. For example, in prior administrations the first step in implementing the CIRCLE curriculum nationwide would have been to call in NHSA's executive director to solicit the group's advice. Then NHSA would have been made a player in promoting these new literacy practices in Head Start centers. Now, however, NHSA was treated as a foe. This attitude in turn caused the Bush administration to have to work with an equally hostile Head Start community. Previous administrations had also insisted on changes in Head Start but never incurred the hostility in evidence during the George W. Bush presidency. Practitioners not only resented the national Head Start office micromanaging their daily activities but felt they had been thrown off the team. Morale fell to an all-time low.

The National Reporting System

In the last chapter we discussed the Clinton administration's efforts to develop a new accountability system for Head Start. The FACES study was piloting measures of child outcomes and program quality. Helen Taylor had created a performance-based outcome system in which each Head Start program was to assess children's developmental progress in the eight domains services were meant to impact. Instead of building on this conceptual framework and trying to make it a more rigorous approach to evaluation, the Bush administration decided to ignore all of this work, which had been an effort of the entire Head Start community, and moved in an entirely different direction.

Accountability in Head Start would now be conducted through the National Reporting System (NRS), which was hastily constructed and thrust on Head Start personnel with little lead time. In keeping with the president's love of literacy and testing, the NRS consisted of five academic tests to be given to every 4- and 5-year-old child in Head Start at the beginning of the school year and again at the end. Instead of using recognized measures with proven psychometric properties, the Bush administration contracted Nicholas Zill of WestEd (apparently outside the usual government bidding process) to design some measures. Zill is an expert in evaluation, but he had an impossible timeframe and ended up using samplings of items from existing tests as well as some untried ones. There was no time to establish reliability and validity, so he "borrowed" these metrics from the full versions of the original tests. That this strategy was less than ideal is exemplified by two items in the first version of the NRS. In a picture vocabulary test, children were asked to identify the word "horrified," a term well beyond the range of 4-year-olds. Another item asked children to point to the "swamp." An inner-city Head Start director told me not one of his students got that one right, while a director in a rural area said her children had no problem with it. Zill obviously had no time to screen the items for culture fairness.

Administration of the NRS was also problematic. The tests were given by hastily trained testers, many of whom had to learn to administer them in two languages, and sometimes by the children's teachers. This is a particularly bad idea because especially at the start of a new school year, it is important for children to get to know their teacher as a supportive adult and develop trust and attachment. In the test situation, examiners cannot be supportive and must be careful to give no cues that would help the child with the answer. Having the teacher be the examiner undermines the development of a good relationship between teacher and student.

Another huge problem is that Head Start staff were never told the purpose of the tests, something that would have been explained to them by the NHSA if it had been invited into the planning. Program staff were only told the results would be used by the national office to target TTA to centers that needed more help. By this time the Head Start community had lost trust in the Head Start Bureau and did not buy this explanation. It was easy for personnel to instead jump to the conclusion that if their center did not measure up on these assessments, it would be closed. Since the staff were often the ones doing the testing, and they perceived their own salaries were at stake, they might consciously or unconsciously abandon protocol to see that their children got high scores. Wade Horn was a trained clinical child psychologist and had to be aware of such problems introduced by the testing procedure he had implemented.

Head Start directors soon complained that the money allocated to the field to conduct the testing did not begin to meet the actual costs they incurred. Many millions of dollars meant for core services such as teaching and health had to be redirected to defray the costs of the testing. To make matters worse, the Bush administration never instructed local sites to discontinue the performance-based outcome system, so they were doing both assessments simultaneously. The immensity of this task did not seem to be fully appreciated by those who ordered it done. Never before in the long history of the testing movement had some half-million young children been tested at once. As a scientific endeavor it was faulty on its face. Head Start staff were negative and angry about the whole procedure. As one Head Start trainer stated, "This is the first time that the Head Start Bureau has directed us to do something that could really do damage to children" (Meisels and Atkins-Burnett, 2004, p. 3).

A leading critic of the NRS was Sam Meisels, President of the Erikson Institute, a graduate school in child development. He drafted a letter pointing out the problems that was signed by 300 experts and sent it to the Bush administration and the media. He and Sally Atkins-Burnett (2004) wrote an article for *Young Children* (the primary journal of the National Association for the Education of Young Children) in which they exposed the inadequacies of the tests (culture bias, inappropriate items, etc.) and their lack of predictive power. A second article in the same journal issue that Cybele Raver and I wrote (2004) emphasized the inappropriateness of using only assessments of language, literacy, and math knowledge to evaluate a multifaceted program like Head Start. The program does not deliver preschool education alone but addresses parent involvement, health and social services, and emotional and social development—all of which are as important as and contribute to the acquisition of literacy and numeracy. Another widespread criticism of the NRS concerned the wisdom of testing such young children. A 4-year-old child's performance, willingness to comply, and attention span can vary from day to day and even hour to hour. For this reason it is widely recommended that standardized testing not be done until about 8 years of age. Even the NCLB, with its emphasis on testing, does not require it until the third grade when children are 8 or 9 years old.

The volume of complaints about the NRS by respected scholars eventually convinced Wade Horn to put into place a scientific advisory committee to oversee the endeavor. The committee was chaired by Craig Ramey, the founder of the Abecedarian project, and included Sam Meisels and several other scholars whose critiques of the NRS had become public. However, none of the members' criticisms or advice got past Craig Ramey, who relentlessly defended the soundness of the NRS philosophy and procedures. Since the chairman's views were at such odds with those of the individual committee members, rumors spread that Ramey, a famed scholar and senior investigator, had been co-opted by Wade Horn and the Bush administration.

The outcry by scholars and the complaints of local Head Start staff struggling with the burden of an NRS they did not quite understand finally reached the Bush White House. I received a call from a member of the White House Domestic Policy Council who asked if I would come to the Executive Office Building and share my concerns regarding the NRS with her at a meeting that would include others. I agreed to attend, assuming other critics would also be present and we could discuss the problems and suggest a corrective course of action. I was therefore surprised to discover that in addition to the White House person chairing the meeting, the only other participants were Wade Horn, Windy Hill, Nick Zill, who had constructed the measures, and Craig Ramey, who had made clear which side he was on at the earlier committee. With the exception of Windy Hill, I had worked with all of these people in the past and knew them very well.

The chairperson opened the meeting by telling me the Bush White House would like my advice about how to make the NRS more acceptable to the Head Start community and to the nation. I made a number of suggestions, beginning with my view that the Head Start Bureau should announce that the NRS was a "work in progress" and that the results of the first year of testing would be ignored. The pilot year would be used as a learning experience to help refine the tests and the testing procedure. I also said the many public criticisms of the tests should be taken seriously and recommended that the task of selecting specific measures of Head Start children's performance be given to our nation's premier organization on scientific endeavors, the National Research Council of the National Academy of Sciences. I emphasized that the tests employed were too narrow to measure the multiple facets of children's development involved in achieving school readiness. I pointed out that any assessment of Head Start should minimally include a measure of children's health, an area critical to learning and one where the program has had great success. I also emphasized that Head Start's whole-child approach demanded that any credible battery of tests include an assessment of socioemotional functioning.

Probably due to pride of ownership, Nick Zill defended the NRS, insisting that it was close to perfect the way it was. The White House official chairing the meeting had the authority to impose on Wade Horn any of the recommendations I had presented. Clearly she did not, so the response to my criticisms was left up to Wade. He liked the idea of selling the NRS as a work in progress and did adopt that stance. He also tried to add a socioemotional test to the battery. Nevertheless, the NRS continued in place pretty much as it was.

Horn later told me he was against having the National Research Council (NRC) critique the NRS and propose alternative measures because he would have little input into the process. He preferred that these tasks be given to an advisory committee at the HHS Secretary's level. I told him that as long as the committee was composed of nationally visible scholars whose credentials gave them credibility, then his idea had merit. I also thought the appointment of such a committee would give credence to his selling the NRS as a work in progress. Shortly thereafter Wade asked me to chair this committee.

I had worked with Horn over the years, and a considerable store of trust and respect existed between us. Given this, I agreed to chair the committee providing two conditions were met: (1) I could name the members, and (2) the committee would have complete autonomy in reaching any recommendations. Horn agreed to these conditions, so I made a list of names and started calling people to invite them to serve. I was pleased when every single one agreed to get on board. Matters were moving forward, and Horn sent me a copy of a press release that would be issued after he and I finalized the committee membership. I remember the draft emphasized my credibility with Congress.

I was pragmatic in my selection of the committee members and did not include people who had been particularly shrill in their criticisms of the NRS. Thus I did not invite the NRS's most visible critic, Sam Meisels. Sam was a friend and respected scholar, but I knew that having his name on my list would be akin to waving a red cape at a bull. I did include one public critic whose remarks against the NRS had been more timid than Sam's. She was a distinguished scholar who was a past president of the National Association for the Education of Young Children. I thought this umbrella organization for the field of early childhood education should be represented to enhance the committee's credibility. When Horn objected to this person being invited, I quoted a remark I once heard President Johnson make: "It's better to have your enemies inside the tent pissing out than outside the tent pissing in."

Things went downhill from there. Out of about 10 proposed committee members, Horn decided that four were unacceptable and he could not recommend them to the Secretary, whose committee this nominally was. His explanations were based on extremely thin grounds in my opinion. Then I learned that the nominees would have to *apply* to serve. I have served on many federal committees, and it is unprecedented to ask busy scholars to apply to put aside their work and professional responsibilities to donate their expertise to their government. Realizing I would not be the one approving the applications led me to recompute my involvement with this effort. I had been promised autonomy, but now I could not even choose my own team. Sensing there would be more than a little political interference, I told Horn I would not serve as chairman or a participant.

The Bush administration decided to move ahead with a different chairperson and different committee members. Only one of my proposed names was seated, a world-rank statistician and methodologist. To chair the committee, Horn turned to an ally and a person who was indebted to him for the contracts she received to train Head Start staff in literacy practices, Susan Landry. I thought that Landry had a number of contributions to her credit, but by no stretch of the imagination would she come to mind as an expert in evaluation. The committee took months to do its work, and I consider their final report an acceptable and helpful product. However, it fell far short of making the NRS a better evaluation so far as the Head Start or scientific communities were concerned.

My views were evidently shared by Congress. Heeding the experts' advice, policymakers turned to the NRC to study the assessment of Head Start-aged children and to recommend appropriate outcome measures. The person heading the effort at the NRC contacted me early in the process, and I was able to place some of the experts I had selected for my aborted NRS committee on the panel. The NRC committee recommended that assessments of preschoolers cover more than the language and cognitive skills that defined the NRS but include measures of physical and mental health, social–emotional development, and approaches toward learning (Snow and VanHemel, 2008). The group emphasized the imperatives for clarity as to the purpose of testing and for the use of psychometrically sound measures. All of the above were weaknesses of the NRS. After considering the prolonged controversy, Congress abolished the NRS in 2007. Without a doubt, the NRS story was a sorry episode in the Bush administration's stewardship of our nation's Head Start program, but it was not the only one.

Death by a Thousand Cuts

The Bush administration did much more to undermine Head Start than its public efforts to turn the program into an academic preschool with an emphasis on literacy and impose an unpopular testing regimen. We could fill another book with the "little things" that transpired during the Bush presidency to erode congressional and popular support for the program and to break the spirit of Head Start staff and families. Perhaps none was more blatant than a deliberate attempt to misinterpret the evidence regarding Head Start's effectiveness.

In June 2003, the U.S. Department of Health and Human Services issued a report criticizing the *improvements* found in children's school readiness as a result of Head Start. The complaints focused on the repeated finding that Head Start graduates do not have the same level of skills and knowledge as middle-class children. Of course they don't. This type of thinking is a throwback to the early years of Head Start when policymakers wanted to believe that a brief period of intervention could inoculate children against all of the ravages of poverty experienced before, during, and after the small slice of life spent in preschool. The report went on to describe programs that presumably do work, including model projects like the Perry Preschool and state efforts including Landry's project in Texas. The publication could be seen as just another sign that the Bush administration never fully understood the nature of the complex Head Start program or what goals it could reasonably be expected to accomplish. On the other hand, the report could be interpreted as a ploy to discredit Head Start, a hunch supported by the fact that the civil servant who essentially had been compelled to write it apologized to one of my close colleagues for its contents.

Once the report was released, one of the early intervention field's finest scholars, Jeanne Brooks-Gunn, was asked to provide a briefing to the House Ways and Means Committee. She reviewed the conclusions that could honestly be drawn from the evidentiary base on the effects of early childhood intervention, emphasizing that our expectations for programs like Head Start should be realistic. She concluded that the evidence shows children do benefit from high-quality preschool programs, and it is up to elementary schools to maintain and build upon these gains. She weakened the administration's position with one blunt statement: "If policymakers believe offering early childhood intervention for two years will permanently and totally reduce [socioeconomic class] disparities in children's achievement, they must be engaged in magical thinking" (Brooks-Gunn, 2003, p. 9).

A Den of Thieves

Scandals in federal programs are nothing new, and usually only the most egregious cases are given a full public airing. Instead of dealing with Head Start scandals from the inside, the Bush administration sometimes joined the fray. In 2005 the Government Accountability Office (GAO) released a study purportedly showing that three-quarters of Head Start grantees reviewed in a single year were out of compliance with financial management standards. The report, combined with leaks about dishonesty among some local Head Start providers, fed the perception that Head Start was poorly managed and served to cast a negative light over the entire program.

This was not the first alleged attempt by HHS to cast a pall over its own Head Start program. Earlier the agency had issued a report compiling centers' monitoring data. Instead of following the reporting categories used in previous reports, the agency changed them in a way that made it look as though large numbers of centers were not meeting quality standards (a classic example of manipulating data to support a conclusion instead of the other way around). In a press release titled "Uncooking the Books," the National Head Start Association (2004, p. 1) quoted Rep. George Miller's scathing comment: "It is alarming that the Bush administration's political agenda for changing Head Start is influencing its reporting of what is supposed to be an objective monitoring of the Head Start program. . . . [The administration] has chosen to distort the independent findings of its own evaluators." NHSA's president Sarah Greene added, "When you untangle the numbers . . . the new data puts the lie to those who have been trying in vain to cook up some kind of a case that there are widespread problems at Head Start programs that need to be fixed." Both Miller and Greene concluded that the vast majority of Head Start programs are properly managed.

The Kansas City scandal discussed in Chapter 5 illustrates the negative waves the Bush administration allowed to wash over Head Start. A prominent, long-time director of a large program in Kansas City, MO, was discovered to have a suspiciously high salary. There was also evidence that this director had inappropriately charged personal expenses and merchandise to his Head Start budget. The *Kansas City Star* ran a series of investigatory stories on the program and reported that one member of its grantee organization had been found guilty of embezzlement and had been jailed. A Republican Senator from neighboring Kansas, Pat Roberts, brought the articles to the attention of Congress and the executive branch, The Bush administration pounced and defunded the grantee. Particularly vociferous in her condemnation of financial misappropriations was the Head Start Bureau chief, Windy Hill. She demanded that every Head Start center provide the national office with voluminous details on the salaries of every single employee. Fearing it was a malicious attempt to create a scandal, NHSA unsuccessfully attempted to delay the survey in federal court. The amount of time that Head Start directors spent on this mountain of paperwork probably cost the federal government many times the amount of the misappropriated funds in Kansas City.

Windy Hill's attack on her own program raised the ire of the National Head Start Association. Thus, an interesting postscript developed to the Kansas City scandal: NHSA investigated Hill's prior record as director of a Head Start program in Texas and very publicly accused her of a number of fiscal irregularities. Shortly thereafter, Hill was allowed to submit her resignation, but HHS took the step of having the charges investigated for possible criminal action. The investigation disclosed considerable support for the charges NHSA had made, but HHS decided not to have the case prosecuted. This is understandable since such action would reflect badly on the Bush administration and the way it filled key positions. A possible reason for Hill's initial appointment was exposed by Mencimer, who reported that Hill had evidently been picked because she was a "Texas woman who had been tangentially involved with Laura Bush's literacy promotion efforts in Texas" (2008, p. 21)—hardly the qualifications needed for running a multibillion dollar program serving a million children and families each year across the nation and its territories. Noting that Hill had spent much of her 3-year tenure as Head Start's chief focused on mismanagement, Mencimer went on to disclose what the federal investigation had uncovered. According to this source, Hill had given thousands of dollars in contracts to family members and "dubious reimbursements" to herself. "She'd even written herself a $7,000 bonus from the Texas program's coffers after she took the helm of Head Start in Washington" (p. 22).

With stories of financial disgrace in Head Start in every newspaper, the Republican-controlled House wanted to find a culprit in this whole matter. They appeared to come to the conclusion that these problems resulted from the failure of Head Start's parent-dominated Policy Councils to be whistle blowers when they found evidence of financial malfeasance. The House then tried to reduce the power of the Policy Councils by making their decisions only advisory to the real power in Head Start, which would rest with the board of directors of the grantee agency.

While all of this was going on, a GAO investigation found occasions when Policy Councils had indeed brought to light financial wrongdoing in their respective Head Start centers. This truth did not sway the House, which passed a bill to diminish their power. This change would undercut the commitment to parent involvement that was a pillar of Head Start. I received an "off the record" call from Wade Horn, who told me he thought the Policy Councils were one of Head Start's greatest assets. He asked me to do all I could to preserve the integrity of this body. I sent letters to several key Senators spelling out the value of the Policy Councils and asking that they be maintained in the Senate bill. This evidently helped, and the reconciliation process between the Senate and House bills eventuated in the Policy Councils losing relatively little of their authority.

Withdrawing Support for Training

If local management of Head Start programs was seen as weak, one would think the central office would do what it could to strengthen it. One effort to do so was the Head Start director's Management Fellows Program conducted at UCLA. This intensive course had been jointly funded by the Head Start Bureau and Johnson & Johnson since 1991. Head Start directors often have backgrounds in social services and early childhood education. Many lack training in the management aspects of running a Head Start center, which is not unlike running a small business. The UCLA course was designed to provide directors with skills in human resources, finance, information systems, operations, and other areas germane to managing a Head Start program. Classes were small and admissions selective, so graduating from the course became something of a status symbol. Many leaders in Head Start, including Helen Taylor, went through the program. All the Head Start directors I have spoken to over the years who took the course invariably told me of the great value it had for their own growth as executives.

The course was a bargain for the federal government because Johnson & Johnson defrayed half of the cost. During the Bush administration, Wade Horn decided that the Head Start Bureau would no longer financially support the program. I heard many complaints from the Head Start community, so I asked Horn directly why he made this decision. His response was that there was no empirical evidence to prove the program was successful. Although I doubted this was the real reason, I suggested that it would be relatively simple to assess the efficacy of the training and offered to personally take the lead in an objective evaluation of the UCLA program. Horn did not take me up on my offer. Thanks to the generous support of Johnson & Johnson and the ingenuity of Head Start directors in balancing their budgets and finding travel money, this helpful and much needed course has continued in place.

Another withdrawal of support came in the form of reduced travel money to NHSA's annual training conference. It was as if the Head Start Bureau preferred to complain about directors and staff lacking skills rather than to help them acquire the skills they needed. Even the tone of external reviews, in which outside experts visit centers at least every 3 years, changed under the Bush administration. Prior to this administration, these reviews had been collegial, with the visitors trying to be supportive and helping staff correct any deficiencies that were found. In the Bush years these reviews became adversarial and abrasive, emphasizing program weaknesses instead of strengths.

The withdrawal of resources to enable Head Start staff to better do their jobs was a thinly veiled ploy to weaken the program and induce its failure. This undermining was apparent not only at the center and grantee levels but also at the federal level. The strength of leadership responsible for each of Head Start's components at the Bureau had deteriorated in the Reagan years and continued through the Bush administration. For example, for many years Head Start had an outstanding pediatrician to head the health component and an expert in early childhood education to head the education component. These jobs were typically civil service jobs that went to competent and well-qualified individuals. The pediatrician in Head Start today is not permanent but serves on a yearly contract. This situation is not conducive to the development of long-range plans to modernize or raise the quality of services. It is hard to commit to change when you know you might not be around to oversee it. I complained about this problem to Wade Horn, giving special emphasis to Head Start's need for a permanent medical director. He justified the situation by telling me that if you made a permanent hire, you were pretty much stuck with that person even if his or her performance proved unsatisfactory. I refrained from telling him the same could be said for certain presidents and assistant secretaries. With the change in administrations, I intend to suggest that Congress legislate the credentials required for key staff members in Head Start and make these positions permanent and not contractual.

The Long, Long Road to Reauthorizing Head Start

George W. Bush's disdain for Head Start is obvious in the fact that the program missed an entire reauthorization cycle during his presidency. Head Start's last reauthorization in 1998 was due to be renewed in 2003, but the legislation was not enacted until December of 2007. The reauthorization process typically tweaks program operations and sets the budget for the next 4 or 5 years. Without reauthorization, Congress passes what is called a "continuing resolu-tion" to keep the program running for a year at a time. The program gets essentially the same money as the previous year, but with inflation this meant Head Start received less purchasing power. The longer there is no reauthoriza-tion, the further Head Start falls behind because of inflation. Indeed, although the program's budget inched up during the resolution years, the number of children served in 2007 was lower than enrollment in 2002.

The delay was caused by Bush's determination to dismantle the program in its historical form and by a fiercely partisan Congress where Republicans did not dare disagree with the president and Democrats refused to agree with him. When Bush could not get his way with Congress, he used executive orders, backdoor approaches, and the loyal people he had appointed to HHS and the

Head Start Bureau to do what he wanted done. Looking back over the 8 years of his term, it is surprising that there was a Head Start program left to reauthorize.

Attempts to Gift Head Start to the States

President George W. Bush came to Washington with the intention of moving Head Start from HHS to the DOE. This in effect meant that Head Start would be block-granted to the management of the 50 states since unlike HHS, the DOE does not itself run programs the size of Head Start. In early 2003 the president proposed not only to move the program to DOE but to give states the option of receiving their Head Start grants and deciding how to spend the money. However, he quickly learned there was no enthusiasm for such a move, even by a Republican Congress. The administration needed a different approach and moved quickly to develop one.

I have it on good authority that Ron Haskins was invited to the White House to draft a change in Head Start's administrative structure that would be more palatable to Congress. Haskins and I had been friends since the time he was Associate Director of the University of North Carolina's Bush Center in Child Development and Social Policy, a sibling of the Bush Center here at Yale (now the Zigler Center). Later he served as a staff member of a major committee in the House of Representatives. Haskins was well-grounded in developmental scholarship and was quite conversant with intervention programs for young children. He was one of the first scholars to correctly point out that because of core differences in the programs, the outcome results of the Perry Preschool project should not be generalized to Head Start. This stance, plus his basic conservative ideology, made him a logical person for the Bush administration to turn to for ideas on giving Head Start to the states.

Haskins came up with a plan to allow just eight states to run their Head Start programs in a pilot project. These states would be chosen from those that applied on the basis of which had the best plans to coordinate Head Start with state preschool programs and to develop better transitions between Head Start and the public schools. The Bush administration was clever to frame their proposal as no huge change in Head Start but, rather, just an experiment in keeping with the program's long history as a national laboratory. Of course, once the eight-state proposal was included in the reauthorization bill in the Republican-controlled House of Representatives, advocates immediately saw it as a slippery slope that would eventually slide the entire Head Start program into state control.

As a scholar, I was primarily concerned with the quality of the Head Start program that was being delivered. It made little difference to me whether Head

Start was managed by the federal government or by the states. At least I thought so, but about this time my students and I were engaged in studies comparing the quality of Head Start to that of various state preschool programs (Gilliam and Ripple, 2004; Gilliam and Zigler, 2001). We discovered that state programs were generally superior to Head Start in two ways. First, the eligibility criterion for admission was more liberal in state prekindergartens so classrooms were more socioeconomically integrated. Second, state preschools were more likely to have better-trained teachers. However, Head Start was much stronger on several other factors such as parental involvement and providing comprehensive services to the high-risk children and families enrolled. This evidence, coupled with the fact that the eight states that would run Head Start would not be required to adhere to the Program Performance Standards (the primary mechanism of quality control), convinced me to oppose the eight-state plan.

My opposition took many forms. I debated Haskins on the issue at a forum in Washington. Another debate took place at the Brookings Institute between Mike Castle, sponsor of the reauthorization bill in the House, and George Miller, the Democratic Minority Leader on the House Education Committee. I was on a panel of scientists who participated in the event. Although I agreed that the goals of better coordination and better transition of Head Start children to elementary school were worthwhile, I pointed out that there were much less draconian ways to accomplish them. The Brookings event was packed with reporters and many staffers from the Hill. Also in attendance was Wade Horn, the key federal official responsible for Head Start. A representative from the media asked him whether my alternative approach to achieving the goals of the eight-state plan would be considered. Paraphrasing a popular advertisement of the time, Horn said, "When Ed Zigler speaks, we all listen." In point of fact, I had little impact on the Bush administration in regard to the eight-state plan or much of anything else.

To publicize our opposition to the plan, the authors wrote a guest editorial entitled "Moving Head Start to the States: One Experiment Too Many," which appeared in a widely read scientific journal (Zigler and Styfco, 2004). Our analysis and recommendations were circulated throughout Congress, but they were clearly more appealing to the minority Democrats than to the Republicans. Sarah Greene, President of the National Head Start Association, and I were invited to give our views on the reauthorization before the House Democratic Caucus, which was akin to preaching to the choir. During the Bush years, Head Start had become a much more partisan issue than previously. In all prior reauthorizations I spoke routinely with both parties in Congress. After all, I had once served in a Republican administration. Even Republicans who disagreed with my views typically found something of value in what I had to say about Head Start. This time I was stunned by the partisanship that characterized the division in Congress over Head Start's future. Only Democrats invited my input, but they really needed little convincing to vote against this bill. Most saw through the Bush language about an "experiment" and were fully aware that if this reauthorization passed it would end Head Start as we have always known it.

Adding to my angst was that my own Governor, John Rowland, decided that Connecticut would apply to be one of the eight states to run their Head Start programs. Rowland sent a high-level emissary from his staff to meet with me in my office at Yale. He told me the governor would like to collaborate with me in overseeing the Connecticut Head Start program. I guess they thought that if I was involved, the Head Start community and wary policymakers would go along. I pointed out my opposition to the eight-state plan but that did not deter my visitor. He went on and announced that the Governor planned to come to New Haven and hold a press conference with me to launch the idea. To the best of my knowledge, Head Start programs in Connecticut were functioning quite well, and I saw little reason to take a chance with the quality that was in place and try a system headed by the state. The meeting ended awkwardly when I simply said I did not care to participate.

When the reauthorization came up to its first vote in the House, it was apparent the vote was going to be tight. It was indeed tight, passing by a single vote after Republican Rep. John Sullivan, who was healing from a serious automobile accident, returned to Washington in the middle of the night and was rolled into the room in a wheelchair to cast the tie-breaking vote (CNN.com, 2003). This was a bitter kind of loss. However, there is no law until there is a counterpart bill in the Senate, so I began working with my Senator friends from both parties. I was happy to discover there was little enthusiasm for the eight-state plan even among Republican Senators, and Democrats were dead set against it. With the two chambers so far apart, there was no reauthorization emanating from this Republican-led Congress.

The next Congress again took up the reauthorization of Head Start. The one-vote margin of victory in the previous Congress proved to be a sobering experience for the Republican majority leadership. It was certainly clear there was no great mandate for the controversial eight-state proposal. Further, during this second reauthorization attempt the Republican leadership on the bill moved from Mike Castle to John Boehner. Boehner decided to reach out for my counsel, and I was happy to meet with a combined group of his key staffers and a number of other Republicans. We quickly reached agreement that the eight-state proposal would be dropped. Even without this section, Congress was still unable to pass a bill. After the next election, the Democrats took control of both the House and Senate, and this Congress finally produced the 2007 Head Start reauthorization entitled, Improving Head Start for School Readiness Act of 2007.

Defining Deficient Head Start Programs

In the reauthorization, Congress addressed the wisdom of the long-standing practice of automatically funding Head Start programs every 5 years. Some charged that this made Head Start a monopoly in that current grantees had a lock on funding. Unless they did something seriously wrong, they were assured their money. To give other agencies who might do a better job a chance, some voices argued for a competitive process in which grantees would have to compete for their grants every time they came up for renewal. This would create a huge amount of work. There are currently 1,600 Head Start grantees and many of them subcontract to delegates, all of which would have to write grant proposals. This would not only take an inordinate amount of time, but the federal government would have to have a larger staff to review the applications.

The recompetition issue aside, no one—including the Head Start community—wants to see programs funded that fall beneath the quality threshold defined by the performance standards. One way to avoid this is to develop an objective and reliable procedure for determining when a program is so poor as to fall below an acceptable level of quality. Earlier versions of the reauthorization bill would require programs to set their own (largely academic and literacy) goals and face competition for their grants if they did not measure up. It appeared that the Secretary of HHS would have the final judgment on which programs passed and failed. With the current Secretary a Bush appointee, many feared an inordinate number of programs would be deemed deficient. The raw materials for determining what constitutes an acceptable quality threshold have been in place for many years and include an annual self-evaluation by each program and a 3-year review by an outside group of experts. In the reauthorization bill, Congress used the term "a systematic or substantial material failure . . . in an area of performance" to define deficiency. Being designated as deficient did not mean that the program's grant would automatically be redirected but rather that the grantee would have to compete with other applicants for the Head Start funds. Programs considered not deficient would not have to compete for their grants.

While this debate was occurring, I went to the Executive Director of the National Head Start Association and pointed out that they had been outspoken in their desire to terminate poor quality centers and that they knew better than anyone else what poor quality looks like. I suggested that rather than having a system imposed upon them by the federal government, they should take the lead and develop clear criteria by which we could judge a center deficient. Policymakers have no idea how to objectively define a deficient center, so they could use NHSA's criteria as a starting point in their deliberations. If Congress did not agree, for example finding the NHSA definition too lenient, they could tweak the details, but the final definition would likely be built from NHSA's recommendations. Although I had several discussions with NHSA about pursuing this task, they took no action. With little to go on, during the reauthorization process policymakers had difficulty coming up with a way to determine which Head Start programs were so poor they would have to compete for their grants. Unsurprisingly, they decided to punt and have the Department of Health and Human Services determine the criteria on the basis of the advice of an expert panel. Congress instructed that the panel consist of seven members with expertise in specific areas.

Shortly after the reauthorization passed, I received a phone call from a member of the HHS Secretary's staff. The Bush administration wanted me to help them form the committee that was to develop some sort of scoring system to identify deficient Head Start programs. The staffer actually asked me to nominate myself, but I told her I never nominate myself for anything. Her response was that she would see to it that I was seated on the committee. I sent her the names of outstanding experts in each of the designated areas of expertise, including two prominent authorities in the measurement of quality of preschool education settings. Mindful of my earlier exercise in futility in naming an advisory committee for the NRS, I was not surprised when the expert panel was named and did not include a single person I recommended. Needless to say, neither I nor any representative of NHSA was included.

In hindsight, the new Democratic Congress that took the lead in drafting this reauthorization should have been cognizant of a possible upcoming change in administrations and simply assigned the quality threshold measurement task to the Government Accountability Office. The GAO is an arm of Congress and already has or can recruit all of the experts needed to carry out the project. While Bush was still in power, Congress was relying on an administration that displayed considerable hostility toward Head Start and displeasure with the reauthorization itself. Given the administration's track record, the Head Start community feared HHS would set the threshold for a quality center too high and thus force the reapplication of many relatively good Head Start programs. Their concerns seemed founded after none other than Craig Ramey was named chairman of the committee—the same Craig Ramey who could find nothing wrong with the National Reporting System when he chaired the group of scientific advisors who voiced some criticisms of the tests. Ramey's appoint-ment did not go unnoticed by Congress. Three leading champions of Head Start in both the Senate and the House wrote the Secretary of HHS a personal letter objecting to Ramey serving as the panel's chairman. Evidently Ramey was uninvited, but the Bush administration's intent was still evident in that the panel did not contain members in some of the expertise areas mandated by Congress.

Ideas to Raise Quality

In keeping with the time-honored practice of honing and improving federal programs through the reauthorization process, Congress mandated a number of changes to strengthen Head Start in the 2007 Act. Wisely, the legislation ordered HHS to develop new Program Performance Standards and gave the Secretary considerable direction in what to include. I believe the standards should be revised periodically to reflect new knowledge and direction, unlike the first set of standards I helped develop that became stale after staying in place for 2 decades. Congress also ruled that the new standards involve recommen-dations then being developed by the National Academy of Sciences regarding outcome assessments for Head Start children.

Congress's emphasis on improving Head Start can be seen in the quality set-aside they provided. Some of this money will be used by Head Start managers to help programs address weaknesses identified by the monitoring system. This is an important step forward in providing support services to Head Start centers. Forty percent of new funds will be used for quality enhance-ments, including increases in teacher salaries and professional training for staff. A central factor in determining the quality of a preschool center is the qualifications of the lead teacher. There is a growing consensus that a lead teacher should possess a BA in early childhood education (Bowman, Donovan, and Burns, 2000). In the reauthorization Congress mandated that by 2013, half of Head Start teachers and all education coordinators will have a BA degree. Assistant teachers must have at least a CDA credential and be enrolled in an Associate or Bachelor degree program by 2011. Of course, Congress has mandated these qualifications before, and they almost concede the issue in the new law, stating "the Secretary of HHS cannot impose any penalties or sanctions on an individual agency . . . for not meeting these goals." Evidently the BA requirement is a "goal" but not a hard requirement. Today more than 50% of Head Start lead teachers do have an AA degree, which is an improve-ment from the recent past and an indication that prior mandates, however weak or unfunded, have had some impact.

Congress also addressed strengthening the skills of parents on the Policy Councils so they could better govern their programs. The Act requires Head Start to provide technical assistance for members of the governing bodies at the grantee level and members of the Policy Councils. This training was once routine, and renewing it supports and respects the principle of parent involvement in Head Start. Relieving the Policy Councils of the responsibility to judge fair executive pay, Congress bowed to the scandals noted above by legislating that no person working for Head Start can be paid more than the salary received by the Secretary of HHS ($162,000 at this writing).

In the years I was involved with this Head Start reauthorization, I began working with Senator Lamar Alexander of Tennessee. He was a former Secretary of the Department of Education and had a long history of trying to improve children's educational performance. Senator Alexander proposed that 200 of the most outstanding Head Start centers across the country be designated as "Centers of Excellence." These centers would be nominated by the governors in their states and would serve as models for programs in their geographical area. They would be designated for a 5-year term and would receive approximately $200,000 per year in extra support. This idea acknowledges that all Head Start wisdom does not reside in Washington or the regional offices.

Over the years, individual Head Start centers have been instituting innovative and successful activities. Prior to the reauthorization, NHSA had designated a number of these Head Start centers as models. I was working with NHSA to launch an evaluation of these programs to discover whether their outcomes were indeed superior to those of the average Head Start center. NHSA would have liked to have done this research but could not raise the funds to support it. Likewise, missing in the reauthorization is the requirement that the Centers of Excellence be subject to outcome evaluation. The Office of Head Start should use its general research budget to assess these centers. They could use the same measures employed in the National Impact Study of Head Start and compare that study's outcomes with those achieved by children in the Centers of Excellence.

Congress did mandate one study in the name of quality and accountability that, in my opinion, is unnecessary. The legislation officially terminates the National Reporting System and hopefully asserts that the National Academy of Sciences assessment effort will be employed by the HHS Secretary in developing a new national assessment. This struck the authors as odd since Head Start has just carried out a national longitudinal study that employs a broad array of acceptable measures for the various facets of Head Start intervention such as cognitive, emotional, and health. We only have the first year of findings of this study and await further reports that should continue until the children finish third grade. This is exactly the evaluation Head Start has needed for decades, and there is little sense in requesting new evaluations until this huge and expensive study runs its course.

Expansion and Paying for It All

The reauthorization guides Head Start toward specific types of expansion. A fairly large kitty of money will be available for expanding Head Start, half of it going to the preschool program and half to increase the number of Early Head Start programs. Head Start managers are to help local centers work with the Child Care and Development Block Grant service providers to create more full-day, full-year Head Start programming. To further meet the needs of Head Start parents, the reauthorization provides that local centers may apply to the Secretary to convert part-day sessions into full working-day sessions. Congress also displayed sensitivity about the complaint that the poverty level is so low that many children who could profit from Head Start participation are ineligible. The reauthorization act permits 35% of Head Start enrollment to be between 100% and 130% of the poverty level, with the caveat that families below the poverty line must be served first.

This brief overview of the 2007 Head Start reauthorization should make clear that the new mandates imposed upon the program require a higher budget. Congress was aware of this, and their authorization amounts for the first fiscal year included an increase of approximately $400 million, with further increases in subsequent years. However, an authorization is not an appropriation. The Head Start budget was included in an omnibus appropriations bill and was sent to the president for his signature. President Bush issued another blow to the Head Start community by vetoing the entire bill.

In preparing a budget bill the president would sign into law, Congress proposed a Head Start budget that was $11 million less than the program received in the previous year. Thus, Head Start was once again thrust into a financial crisis. For a number of years Head Start was operating under continuing resolutions because of the inability of Congress to pass a reauthorization, resulting in fewer real dollars to spend after the effects of inflation. To add insult to injury, ACYF instructed grantees to review their expenses, including staffing positions, salaries, benefits, and even enrollment size, to find places to economize. To meet the new mandates, programs would be forced to take the costs out of their already decimated budgets. The decision by Congress to allow children above the poverty line to enter the program meant that many more children would become eligible. With no money to serve them, these children would simply be added to already long waiting lists. Early Head Start would stay the same size it has held for years. The quality set-aside, derived as it is from funding increases, was empty. The 2007 reauthorization was certainly filled with good intentions, but it was unlikely they could unfurl. It remains to be seen whether an infusion of funds from the 2009 stimulus package enables the intentions of the reauthorization to be realized.

George W. Bush's Parting Shots

President Bush was very critical about the reauthorization since it mostly ignored his own recommendations. However, he did sign this bill into law. In his signing statement, he praised the NRS and lamented its termination, apparently oblivious to all the controversy and criticism that led to its demise. He also complained that Congress authorized a higher Head Start budget than he had proposed, never acknowledging the underfunding that had reduced enrollment and dented quality during his watch. Finally, the president expressed his disappointment that Congress did not go along with his proposal to allow faith-based Head Start grantees to discriminate in their hiring practices.

The political base for President George W. Bush's election was the religious right. This, combined with his own religious faith, led his administration to make a special effort to see that religiously affiliated organizations were given the opportunity to provide federally funded social services, including Head Start. To manage this effort, he created an office within the White House to move forward on his commitment. It should be noted there is no evidence that faith-based social service organizations provide better services than secular groups. The president just wanted to include them—and to make it known he was doing so.

Each year the Office of Head Start publishes a Head Start Program Fact Sheet that lists facts and figures about program operations. During the Bush administration a new line appeared in the format showing how many Head Start sites were affiliated with religious groups. (Interestingly, this number decreased by 25% during Bush's presidency.) Consistent with the Bush administration's philosophy, two Republican-led Congresses wrote into versions of the reauthorization bill that religiously affiliated Head Start centers could discriminate in their employment practices and only hire staff members who shared their faith. This was quite a blow to the tenets of a program that was founded as part of a political and social movement to advance civil rights and social integration. Discriminating on the basis of race, religion, or anything else was counter to all Head Start stood for. The Democratic Congress that finally produced the reauthorization act eliminated the discriminatory hiring proposal. This angered President Bush and left him without a parting gift to the religious conservatives who had elected him, although even their support had dwindled as his term progressed.

The Head Start George W. Bush left behind was in a state of disarray. The Bush administration had torn down the supportive relationship between the field and the national and regional offices and suffered its own leadership voids. Wade Horn decided not to stick it out until the end of Bush's term and resigned from his post. Temporary appointments were made for both the Assistant Secretary slot and the Head Start leader slot. One of Horn's acts before leaving was to pull the Head Start Bureau out of ACYF, rename it the Office of Head Start, and place it directly under the Assistant Secretary for Children and Families. He left ACYF in a weakened condition. The Children's Bureau is a shell of its former self and no longer has a real chief. Horn also pulled the Child Care Bureau out of ACYF, placed it in his own office, and altered its goal from improving the quality of care for all children to making child care a tool to move poor mothers from welfare to work.

The Bush administration's stewardship of Head Start and several other children's programs including child care and health halted and even erased some of the progress it has taken many years to achieve. The 2007 Head Start Act corrects some of the problems created by the administration and holds the intent to fix others and move the program forward again. At this writing, President Obama has just begun his term and has proposed large new investments in Head Start, which he defends as investments in America's future. With the pain and scars of the George W. Bush years behind them, and encouraged by Obama's friendly words, Head Start's supporters are looking to better days ahead.

13

Does Head Start Work? Does it Work Enough?

The preceding chapters brim with the variety of expectations that have been placed on Head Start over the decades. From President Johnson's naive hope that a few weeks of intervention would end poverty in America to George W. Bush's demand that Head Start close the achievement gap between rich and poor, policymakers have habitually wanted more than any finite program could deliver. Based on the criteria of eradicating poverty or eliminating the achievement gap, Head Start is clearly a failure. Judged by changes in the risk profiles and attainments of the children and families it has served, maybe not. Like all programs that receive taxpayers' hard-earned money, Head Start must be held accountable. A lack of clarity over exactly what it should be held accountable for has allowed the controversy over whether the program works or not to rage without answer even after all these years.

As a member of Head Start's planning committee, I admit to being one of the guilty parties who set the stage for this endless debate because we did not present to Sargent Shriver or to the nation a clear program goal. Instead we waxed on with a litany of many different child and family objectives. The matter was obfuscated further by Sarge himself, who was enamored with the possibility that children's IQ scores could actually be raised but only attached this goal to Head Start when it was politically expedient to do so. There is no doubt in my mind that Shriver and the planning committee were in agreement that Head Start's overarching goal was to prepare young children so they would be more capable at the time of school entry. Yet he kept making the point that Susan Gray had been able to raise the IQs of children with borderline mental retardation (Chapter 1), so Head Start should be able to raise the IQs of poor children with normal intellect. In the 1960s people were not yet using the term "school readiness," which probably did not enter the public lexicon until the 1994 Educate America Act, so it was only natural that they focused on the IQ part of Shriver's statements instead of the mumbo jumbo about preparing children for school entry.

Early assessments of Head Start proved the folly of using IQ increases as the benchmark of the program's success. Immediate improvements in IQ scores were found, but this benefit appeared to fade over time as children who did not attend the program caught up to the preschool graduates, or the graduates lost their momentum. So what did this mean? First, it confirmed that the IQ is probably the most stable measure psychologists ever created. It is next to impossible to raise an individual's innate intelligence, although a child's cognitive functioning can be improved and show itself as a higher score on an IQ test. Second, while there is no denying that a child's preschool IQ is related to later school performance, the IQ's predictive ability is limited to only about half of the variation seen in children's progress in school. Obviously factors unrelated to IQ scores, such as a child's health status and social skills, also influence school success. In recent years the field has developed measures of emotional intelligence, and these too have been found to be related to school performance.

When I ran Head Start at the Office of Child Development, I tried to end the practice of using IQ increases to determine the program's success by officially declaring that Head Start's goal was to enhance children's everyday social competence. Although this helped forgive Head Start for delivering a broad base of services instead of academic programming alone, the concept of social competence was no clearer to policymakers and the public than the laundry list of program objectives the planners handed to Sargent Shriver.

The 1998 reauthorization of Head Start finally rescued the program from the ambiguity concerning its mission. The act clearly stated that the goal of Head Start is to improve children's school readiness. However, this still left open the questions of just what children need to be deemed ready for school and what degree of readiness is necessary to deem Head Start a success. The Bush administration interpreted school readiness as having strong literacy and math skills and thought the program was worthwhile only if graduates were just as school ready as middle-class children. Certainly Head Start never had and never will have the power to equalize the incomes of poor and middle-class parents, provide the health care and social services that poor children may need for all their growing years, clean up the drug- and crime-infested neighborhoods where many families in poverty live, or ameliorate the litany of privations that affect children in low-income families. Thus even with the comparatively clear goal of school readiness, there is still a tendency to expect more from Head Start than it can realistically deliver.

Judgments of Bias

One would think that hard scientific data could supply all the answers we need to determine if Head Start works or not. What one finds in the data, however, depends on what one is looking for. Someone sifting through the evidence to see if Head Start increases, say, church going, will find none and write a scathing critique of the program. Therefore, when reading reviews of early intervention in general or Head Start in particular, it is important to separate ideological views from conclusions built upon a thorough and objective evaluation of findings. For example, right-wing and libertarian think tanks invariably favor young children remaining in the care of their mothers rather than attending any sort of out-of-home program or allowing interference from home visitors. They also share the view that government programs simply do not work and, rather than solving problems, actually make them worse. Knowing this ideology, it is not surprising that conservative think tanks like the Goldwater Foundation and the Cato Institute have produced "scientific" reviews proclaiming Head Start and other early intervention programs a dismal failure.

As noted several times in this book, Douglas Besharov of the right-leaning Economic Enterprise Institute and a professor at the University of Maryland has been another outspoken critic of Head Start. His complaints arise not only from his perception that the evidence of the program's efficacy is weak but from his strong objections to its cost. He champions less expensive alternatives such as devolving Head Start to the states or distributing its budget to parents in the form of vouchers they can use to purchase their own (presumably cheaper and better) child care. True, Head Start is somewhat expensive, currently costing about $7 billion per year. However, this is much less than the amount spent on Title I, which has yet to produce clear evidence of its value. It is also less than the money spent on the Child Care and Development Block Grant (CCDBG), which subsidizes child care for poor and near-poor families. There is agreement among scholars that the general quality of care paid for by CCDBG is between poor and mediocre. Yet children and their healthy overall development have little to do with the goal of this program as perceived by Congress. The purpose is simply to enable poor mothers to buy child care so they can work and stay off welfare. Like Head Start, in the CCDBG too we can see that different expectations influence the goal we pick for a program, which in turn colors our interpretation of its effectiveness.

At the opposite end of the popularity spectrum, participants in Head Start invariably proclaim it a huge success. Parents volunteer in Head Start classrooms in large numbers, devote their time to administration, and tell hundreds of thousands of stories of changed lives. Millions of Head Start graduates are also fans of their alma mater and relate their own fond memories and personal success stories. Their ranks include many notable professionals such as California Rep. Loretta Sanchez (2004). In a customer satisfaction index, the U.S. Department of Health and Human Services (1999) found that Head Start received a higher customer satisfaction score than any government agency or private company, including even client-focused Mercedes-Benz and BMW.

Educators also endorse the broad category of preschool education and sometimes the specific case of Head Start. One of our nation's famous "educationists" is John Merrow, education editor for the nightly Lehrer Report on PBS. I know Merrow as a champion of preschool education for young children and was surprised when he wrote an article for a popular professional outlet entitled, "The 'Failure' of Head Start" (2002). In this piece he stated clearly that children who experience Head Start do profit from their attendance. The failure to which Merrow alluded was the fact that after more than 4 decades of existence, Head Start was serving only half of the children it could help. He used his provocative headline to draw attention to the failure of Congress to extend the benefits of Head Start to all eligible children.

Economists too have brought their perspective to the dialogue about the value of early childhood intervention. Their practice is to use cost–benefit analyses to assess the merits of all types of programs. If a program pays for itself in identifiable cost savings or turns a profit on the social investment, the effort is considered worthwhile. Investigators of the High/Scope Perry Preschool were the first to use cost–benefit analysis in the early intervention field. Their famous findings of substantial returns on investment swayed the support of policymakers, scholars, and the public for early childhood programming.

Later cost–benefit analyses of the Abecedarian Project, the Chicago Child–Parent Centers, and the Nurse Home Visiting program also found the benefits that accrued as a result of participating in the programs far outdistanced their costs. Impressed by these results, economists such as Nobel Laureate James Heckman and Arthur Rolnick at the Minnesota Federal Reserve Bank have become very effective advocates for early childhood programs. As economists, they see the wisdom of investing in human capital, particularly in the early years, and make their arguments in terms of the return on investment to society in the form of a more productive workforce and a stronger position in the competitive global economy.

A big part of the savings attributed to early intervention programs is in reduced delinquency and crime. This rationale is enunciated by the Chief of Police of Seattle, who stated, "Head Start, like Perry Preschool, . . . reduces the chances that children grow up to become criminals by teaching them to get along with others and follow directions and cuts problem behaviors" (Kerlikowske, 2005, p. A-12). Fight Crime: Invest in Kids (2004), an organization of law enforcement officials and crime victims, has also chosen to support preschool education because of its potential to reduce crime.

Personal and professional bias obviously has much to do with judgments of the return on investment of Head Start and other early intervention programs. For example, if one looks at their value in providing child care for working parents, as Besharov does, it is easy to find less costly alternatives than Head Start. If one looks instead at the cost of compromised school readiness resulting from poor quality child care, which is unquestionably an unexamined cost of the CCDBG, Head Start is by far more economical. Janet Currie (2001) is one of very few scholars who include in Head Start's cost–benefit analysis the value to children and parents of the child care the program provides. The evidence is clear that the school readiness achieved by Head Start children is greater than that achieved by children attending more typical child care centers or family day care homes.

With policymakers, scholars, and laypersons coming from so many different directions in deciding whether Head Start is worth the effort, it is wise to turn to traditionally less biased empirical science to provide objective evidence of whether Head Start works.

Quality Matters

In evaluating Head Start, a distinction must be drawn between the program's potential accomplishments as opposed to the outcomes it is currently producing. We saw this difference in the discussion of the Cornell Consortium (Chapter 7), which showed that model preschool education programs had clear and impressive outcomes. Today Head Start's *potential* is typically extrapolated from the findings of three model programs, namely the Perry Preschool, the Abecedarian Project, and the Chicago Child–Parent Centers. All three have demonstrated convincing, long-term positive effects. As this book has made clear, Head Start does not have the funding and quality of these programs, and it is wrong to generalize their results to Head Start. The Head Start program can only be fairly evaluated by comparing the outcomes of its graduates to those of a peer group of poor children who did not attend the program.

Quality is the keyword in scientific assessments of the value of early childhood education programs. For example, the leading organization for evaluation scholars, the American Educational Research Association, concluded there is "Strong evidence pointing to the benefits of high-quality early childhood education and how to achieve them" (Resnick and Zurawsky, 2005, p. 1). This same sentiment is expressed in a review by Brooks-Gunn, one of the field's leading workers. She makes four general points summarizing what we know about the outcomes of high-quality preschool programs:

- High-quality center-based programs enhance vulnerable children's school-related achievement and behavior.
- These effects are strongest for poor children and for children whose parents have little education.
- These positive benefits continue into the late elementary school and high school years, although effects are smaller than they were at the beginning of elementary school.
- Programs that are continued into elementary school and that offer high "doses" of early intervention have the most sustained long-term effects. (2003, p. 1)

The impact of any program depends in large part on how well the program model is implemented and on the overall quality features of the services delivered. Head Start was launched too quickly and grants were approved too freely to assure quality in the program's early years. Perhaps Head Start had to suffer these growing pains, but stepping off on the wrong foot made it very hard to change course. Since that time the Program Performance Standards were implemented, a quality control system of annual self-reports and periodic external reviews was put into place, training and technical assistance was developed for center personnel, and a sometimes-funded quality set-aside has been legislated—all of which have resulted in continuous improvement in the program. A weak spot remains the educational component, which is slowly being remedied as more and more lead teachers have BAs in early childhood education.

Employing a standard measure used to assess preschool education settings, two large studies (FACES and the National Impact Study) found the average quality of Head Start centers to be good. Although education services are weaker than the model programs, Head Start is superior in the broad array of services it provides both to the child and to the family as well as in its degree of parent involvement. Thus, even with the comparatively poorer quality education component, it is not surprising that Head Start programs have been found to produce some of the very same benefits that have been reported to accrue from the model programs.

The distinguished Federation of Behavioral, Psychological, and Cognitive Sciences invited W. Steven Barnett to make a presentation at a congressional Science and Public Policy briefing. Barnett is an economist and the scientist responsible for the famous cost–benefit analyses of the Perry Preschool. In his presentation he unequivocally stated the evidence is clear that Head Start children have increased achievement test scores and that the program has favorable long-term effects on grade repetition, special education, and high school graduation (2002). He too noted that the majority of Head Start classrooms are good when evaluated in terms of developmentally appropriate practices. Targeting preschool education as the program's weakness, Barnett argued that Head Start teachers should be better trained and better paid. Noting that the minority of Head Start teachers have 4-year college degrees, he pointed out the barrier to hiring better qualified preschool educators is the low salaries Head Start is able to pay them. The average Head Start teacher compensation is "less than the average secretary and little more than half what the average kindergarten teacher earns" (2002, p. 2).

Barnett also spoke of the futility of the George W. Bush administration's attempts to force the literacy-oriented CIRCLE curriculum on Head Start teachers. Referring to a consensus reached by the National Research Council (Bowman, Donovan, and Burns, 2000), Barnett concluded, "Research offers no hope that specialized training in teaching methods alone, no matter how 'teacher-proof' the design, is a substitute for well-educated and reasonably compensated professional teachers" (p. 2). Barnett estimated that if every Head Start lead teacher had a BA and was paid parity with teachers in public schools, the program's annual cost (which is currently about $7 billion) would increase by approximately $1 billion. He believes strongly that this increase is needed to improve the preschool education Head Start children receive and recommends the added expense be phased in over time.

Congress has tried to be responsive to the pleas for better qualified teachers made by Barnett and many others. In the 2007 reauthorization act, they legislated that at least half of Head Start teachers have a BA within a few years. Unfortunately, they ignored Barnett's price tag for this initiative and did not provide sufficient funds to fulfill the mandate. Congress must master the simple dictum that quality costs money, and if they sincerely want Head Start to be a high-quality program that delivers good results, they must appropriate the support to make this happen.

A study by Gormley, Phillips, and Gayer (2008) provides Congress with robust evidence that an investment in qualified Head Start teaching staff results in better child outcomes. In this study, the Tulsa, Oklahoma universal preschool program conducted in public schools was compared with the same program conducted in Head Start centers. Unsurprisingly, the outcomes for children in the public schools were better than those found for Head Start children. This should be expected since the Head Start centers served poor neighborhoods, and the children were likely more economically disadvantaged than those in the public schools.

What made the study unique was the insight it provided about the value of teacher qualifications. For the Tulsa Head Start agencies to receive funds from the state universal preschool budget, every lead teacher had to have a BA degree and be certified in early childhood education. Thus we can compare the findings of the National Impact Study, which sampled representative Head Start programs nationwide, with the Tulsa Head Start program, which had only highly qualified teachers. The Tulsa findings were much more impressive than those reported in the Impact Study. After only a 1-year program, Tulsa's Head Start children displayed a 6-month advantage on a preliteracy measure, a 3-month advantage on a spelling measure, and a 5-month advantage in early math skills. This study provides evidence that an investment in qualified Head Start teachers raises student outcomes and should prod Congress to fund its BA mandate. (We should note that the Gormley et al. findings are in contrast to those of Currie and Neidell, 2007, who found that child outcomes were not affected by whether their teachers had AA or BA degrees.)

Research Expands to Other Outcomes and Newer Methods

Over a decade ago the U.S. General Accounting Office (1997) examined hundreds of studies of Head Start and found that the majority were too old, methodologically weak, narrowly focused, or statistically problematic to support a conclusion about the program's effectiveness. Since that time, some larger, sounder studies have been conducted and later syntheses performed that build a relatively strong case that Head Start is indeed effective in preparing poor children for school. Comprehensive reviews of this work have been published (e.g., Love, Tarullo, Raikes, and Chazan-Cohen, 2006), and I will not repeat the efforts here. Instead, I will briefly look at some new or novel research approaches that contribute to the literature on Head Start's efficacy. Of course, such evidence may not be strong enough to satisfy the critics because most of the studies did not employ random assignment. Although outstanding methodologists have noted some inadequacies in this design, it has become the gold standard among policymakers. (This may be more a bandwagon effect than a preference grounded in a solid understanding of the application of research methods.)

Economists Garces, Thomas, and Currie (2002) used an interesting research design in which they compared children who attended Head Start with their siblings who did or did not attend. This design has the strength of controlling for the possible differences between families who select themselves into Head Start and those who do not care to or bother to apply. The investigators found there were diffusion effects to younger siblings when an older child had attended Head Start. Because of the program's emphasis on parent education and involvement, it makes sense that if a mother learned better parenting skills while her older child was in preschool she would employ these practices in raising her younger children. Seitz and Apfel (1994) found the same phenomenon from a program for teenage mothers. The benefits Garces et al. (2002) found for younger siblings suggest that Head Start's positive effects are greater than what is reported in more typical studies that assess only Head Start children and a control group of agemates.

Looking at longer-term outcomes, Garces et al. (2002) found less grade repetition, greater educational achievements, and less criminal behavior among Head Start graduates when they were young adults. Consistent with other studies, Head Start was not powerful enough to bring poor children up to the achievement level of children from wealthier families. A surprising finding was that although black and white children showed the same benefits when they graduated from Head Start, the black children did not maintain the advantage beyond the early grades of school. Currie and Neidell (2007) attributed this to the poorer schools blacks generally attended, finding that those who went to schools in higher-spending districts after they left Head Start continued to do better on academic assessments. Another benefit for blacks was that Head Start participation was associated with a reduction in the chance of being arrested by around 12 percentage points. The authors concluded that schooling effects for whites were quite large, while the crime effects for blacks were also meaningful.

A rigorous methodology that has been gaining respect in recent years is the regression–discontinuity design. There is a general consensus that this design produces findings that closely approximate those found with a random assignment experiment. Unlike random assignment, children are assigned to treatment and control groups because of pre-program differences. Sophisticated statistical manipulations are used to uncover the sources of discontinuities in child outcomes. Ludwig and Miller (2007) conducted a regression–discontinuity design evaluation and found that Head Start had long-term educational benefits for both blacks and whites. They also found that Head Start attendance resulted in increased school attainment of about half a year, and the likelihood of attending college increased by about 15%.

They concluded that the cost–benefit of Head Start is similar to the model programs that reported a savings of some $7 for each $1 invested.

A weakness in the Ludwig and Miller study was that it only assessed children who had participated in Head Start during the 1960s and 1970s. The results therefore are not generalizable to students who attended at later dates. With the quality improvements that were put into place in the early 1970s and built on over the ensuing years, the logical conclusion is that as positive as the Ludwig and Miller findings are, they are a conservative test of the value of Head Start.

A very dramatic finding of the Ludwig and Miller study was reduced mortality rates for children aged 5 through 9 years from causes that could be ameliorated through Head Start's health services (i.e., anemia, meningitis, and respiratory problems) but not other mortality causes. The health benefits of Head Start have essentially been ignored over the program's entire lifetime. In the closing plenary session of Head Start's Eighth National Research Conference, John Love (2006) reflected on 40 years of Head Start research and pointed out that the health-related effects found by Ludwig and Miller should have been expected. Love recounted that in the first 2 years of Head Start, 98,000 children had eye defects diagnosed and treated, 900,000 dental problems were discovered with an average of five cavities per child, and immunizations were given to 740,000 children who had not previously been vaccinated against polio and to 1 million children who not previously been vaccinated against measles. Decreased mortality has not been examined in the famous model programs since they generally did not have an ongoing health component.

Head Start has never received sufficient credit for improvements in children's physical health, which we know impacts school readiness. The area of health actually should be hard to overlook. Health activities have been included in the Program Performance Standards since 1975, and about 12% of participants are children with disabilities who often have special health needs. A major reason why health outcomes go pretty much unexamined is that most studies of Head Start are conducted by behavioral scientists who feel medical outcomes are the domain of pediatricians or public health experts. The relatively little work in this area that has been done reveals an impressive success story. For example, O'Brien, Connell, and Griffin (2004) and Zigler, Piotrkowski, and Collins (1994) document the many accomplishments of Head Start in regard to physical health, dental health, and nutrition.

An empirical study of Head Start's health services discovered that Head Start children were more likely than middle-class children to receive age-appropriate health screenings and dental examinations and that the health care benefits extended to siblings (Hale, Seitz, and Zigler, 1990). David Frisvold, a health policy scholar, studied the impact of Head Start on obesity. Children in Head Start manifested less obesity than a comparable demographic group, an outcome attributable to the program's nutrition component. One of our nation's leading authorities on obesity, Kelly Brownell, commented on these findings by saying, "It looks like being in Head Start might be a more powerful means of reducing obesity than any other program specifically designed for that purpose" (personal communication, May 7, 2008). This is not surprising inasmuch as Head Start models good nutrition during the school day and also works with parents to use healthful nutrition practices at home.

This finding and those of Garces et al. (2002) bring up another of Head Start's accomplishments that has been unappreciated in the literature. Many longitudinal studies have now been done containing data on parent outcomes. Pizzo and Tufankjain (2004) reviewed 41 of these studies and found that Head Start experience resulted in more parental participation in their children's later schooling and improved the quality of parent–child interactions. Both of these phenomena directly impact a child's school readiness and later educational performance. Further, Head Start has provided jobs for tens of thousands of poor parents. These jobs often lead to career development and further education, eventually boosting the family's economic status and overall quality of life. Although such facts escape scientific scrutiny, these contributions by Head Start certainly have a positive impact on our society.

In sum, as investigators expand their horizons and methodology, broad evidence is accruing that Head Start has positive, lasting effect on children's academic and life success as well as family and personal benefits that tend not to be included in formal assessments.

The Head Start National Impact Study

In the current atmosphere, it is guaranteed that only the most rigorous methodological study designs will be taken seriously by decision makers. This means random assignment. The study that will take center stage in Washington will be the congressionally ordered National Impact Study, the largest and most thorough evaluation of Head Start that has ever been conducted. The purpose is to gauge Head Start's impact in a design using 84 nationally representative Head Start agencies and almost 5,000 children. Approximately half were 3 years, and half were 4 years old when the study began. Their families all applied for Head Start admission. Children were randomly assigned to Head Start or to a control group who were not admitted to Head Start but were free to take advantage of other community services. Thus the study essentially assessed the value added by Head Start over other available programs.

The data collected came from interviews with parents, direct child assessments, and ratings of the children by care providers. Observations of the quality of the centers Head Start and control children attended were also made. The investigators were fully aware that a child's school readiness is made up of many factors and took the whole-child approach to choosing their measures. The battery included assessments of cognitive development, general knowledge, social and emotional development, fine and gross motor skills, and physical well-being. The evaluators also adopted Head Start's fundamental belief that parents' behavior has a strong influence on school readiness and examined parenting practices.

Positive findings were obtained for Head Start attendees across a wide array of measures, although these benefits were in the small to modest range (U.S. Department of Health and Human Services, 2005). A Head Start FACES report indicated that the early literacy skills of Head Start children have begun to improve (U.S. Department of Health and Human Services, May 2003), perhaps in response to the Bush administration's push to focus on reading in Head Start classrooms. This finding was substantiated by the National Impact Study, where the gap in reading skills between Head Start students and the national norm was only half as great as that for the control group. More benefits were found for 3-year-olds than for 4-year-olds. In addition to cognitive measures, the younger children were superior on social–emotional variables such as frequency and severity of problem behaviors. Compared to control group parents, Head Start parents engaged in significantly more behaviors conducive to school readiness such as reading to the child and also displayed better parenting practices such as less spanking. Further, better health status and dental care were found for the Head Start compared to the control group. Although this outcome is to be expected because of the program's health component and the performance standards, it was based primarily on parent reports. One would like more objective, verified evidence of health outcomes.

On the numeracy measure, the average scores of Head Start children were higher than those of the comparison children, but the difference did not reach an acceptable level of statistical significance. This finding highlights a value of the Impact Study beyond its scientifically strong assessment of Head Start's effects. A good evaluation study provides more than the accountability required for any program receiving tax dollars. It also gives those implementing the program insights into what needs to be improved. Reminiscent of what I have called the Head Start national laboratory, Zaslow (2008) refers to the long history of Head Start as a learning community that continually learns from its failures. She notes a body of relatively recent work shown to improve preschool children's numeracy skills and explains how easily these teaching methods could be incorporated into Head Start classrooms. Whereas naysayers may focus on Head Start's poor showing in mathematics, I believe Zaslow is correct in expecting that this information will be used to institute more effective ways to present this academic content.

The magnitude of the effects reported in the National Impact Study are about what one would expect from the brief, 9-month intervention. I have long felt that poor children burdened by multiple developmental risks need 2 years of Head Start rather than just 1 year. At this writing the study's second-year findings have not yet been released, but they should provide evidence about the comparative value of 1 versus 2 years of Head Start. They will also show whether there are program effects as the children progress through the early grades of elementary school.

Despite its sophistication, the design of the National Impact Study guarantees an underestimate of the full value of Head Start. In a standard evaluation study, one compares the benefits of the program being assessed versus no treatment. The Impact Study compared the value of Head Start with other types of programming children in the control group experienced, including parent care. Some 60% of the control group attended center-based programs. Thus the Impact Study does not assess the absolute value of Head Start, but rather the added value of experiencing Head Start rather than something else. This design did allow the evaluators to compare the quality of Head Start centers with that of the other settings attended by the control group. Head Start was found to have better quality, a finding that mirrors other studies.

In addition to the value-added nature of the study, other weaknesses in the design could have compounded the underestimation of Head Start's benefits. Zaslow (2008) points out that a peculiar characteristic of the random-assignment experimental design used in the Impact Study is that children who were placed into the Head Start and no Head Start groups did not all follow-up on their position. Some families who were assigned to the Head Start group ended up not enrolling, but for the purposes of the study they remained in this group. On the other hand, many parents who were disappointed when their children were assigned to the control group simply enrolled at another Head Start site where the study was not being conducted. Zaslow points out that a "substantial minority of the control group found their way into other Head Start programs" (2008, p. 6). In essence, the initial random assignment placed children in "intent to treat" or "not treat" groups, and they remained there even if the intention was betrayed. The Impact Study scientists report that these "cross-overs" diluted the strength of their findings because so many children who were not supposed to experience Head Start actually did, perhaps raising the performance of the comparison group, while some children who were supposed to have experienced Head Start did not, perhaps dragging down the program group's performance. It is a simple matter to correct for this problem by forming purer groups. This is exactly what Ludwig and Phillips (2007) did, as will be discussed below.

Are the Benefits Big Enough?

Controversy over the results of the Impact Study has swirled around whether the size of the positive effects was large enough to prove that Head Start is a success and worth the cost. In her well-balanced scholarly analysis of the first-year results, Zaslow steps back from the individual domains of development that were assessed and underlines "a noteworthy pattern is the breadth of impacts" (2008, p. 11), noting that this pattern was more marked for the 3-year-olds than the 4-year-olds. Following McCartney and Rosenthal (2000), who emphasized the possible importance of effects of small size, Zaslow points out that even small improvements can later result in meaningful educational benefits. Every child displays a developmental growth trajectory. If early in life you can place a child further along on that trajectory, over time the difference between that child and one who received no acceleration will grow. This is what we have seen in model programs where the benefits compound over time.

The authors of the National Impact Study also defend the value of effects that are small in magnitude. They cite scholars who have asserted that effect sizes (a statistic that indicates how large the difference is between the treatment group and the control group on a particular measure) derived from a given study should be interpreted within the context of the findings from comparable interventions designed to produce similar effects. They explain that the effect sizes found in the Impact Study across various measures were higher than the effects obtained when examining poor versus good quality child care centers and were about the same as the effects found as a result of reducing class size in the early school grades.

Nevertheless, in the public arena the findings of relatively small effects have disappointed and led some to wonder if the popular Head Start program is actually a failure. In the wake of the controversy, our nation's leading scientific organization in the field of human development, the Society for Research in Child Development (SRCD), released a one-page statement to objectively interpret the Impact Study's findings. The brief was prepared by Hirokazu

Yoshikawa (2005), a professor at Harvard's Graduate School in Education who served on the national advisory committee that planned the Impact Study. Because of the importance of this study and the fact that the brief carried the prestigious SRCD imprimatur, Yoshikawa developed the statement in consultation with no fewer than 15 experts in the fields of early intervention, methodology, and statistics.

The SRCD report comes down firmly on the side of interpreting the Impact Study findings as indicating that Head Start is successful. The brief notes that all significant results of Head Start were consistently positive (increases in "good" outcomes, decreases in "bad" outcomes). Yoshikawa lists the broad range of positive effects in the cognitive, social, emotional, and health areas while noting that no impact of Head Start was found in the sub-areas of oral comprehension, phonological awareness, early math, aggressive or withdrawn behaviors, social skills, or parenting safety practices. He stated, "Research in child development suggests that when positive effects of early childhood programs accumulate across important health and developmental areas, success in the longer term is also more likely" (2005, p. 1). Placing the magnitude of the benefits in context, he argues that the size of the effects found for 9 months of Head Start is "comparable to or larger than" that of other large programs.

Yoshikawa emphasizes that the Impact Study findings were "particularly impressive" since the Head Start children were being compared not to others who had no intervention, but rather to children the bulk of whom were in other types of center-based programs (including some in Head Start). SRCD attributes the wide-ranging positive effects to the performance standards that require services targeting a broad swath of developmental areas. The report also underlines the finding that "classroom quality in Head Start is substantially better than that in other preschool and child care settings for low-income children" (p. 1). This can be partly explained by one of the study's findings that Head Start teachers are more likely than teachers in other child care settings to use a curriculum.

The final word to date on the appropriate interpretation of the findings of the National Impact Study was presented in a paper written by two scholars with impeccable scientific credentials, economist Jens Ludwig and developmental psychologist Deborah Phillips. These authors write that in spite of the high hopes, the study has not yet resolved the question of whether Head Start should be considered a success or a failure because of "confusion about how to judge the magnitude of program impacts" (2007, p. 3). Ludwig and Phillips creatively decided to reconceptualize the problem and employ a simple and clear criterion of success, namely whether "the program is likely to generate benefits to participants and society as a whole that are larger than program costs" (p. 1). As we can see in the well-publicized evaluations of famous model programs like the Perry Preschool, the field of evaluation is moving away from significance levels and effect sizes and is embracing the cost–benefit measure. Insisting on a commonsensical approach, Ludwig and Phillips employed a sophisticated statistical procedure for translating the intent-to-treat effects of the Impact Study into "effect of treatment on the treated" (p. 8).

These scholars concluded that small positive effects like those found in the Impact Study would be "large enough to generate long-term dollar-value benefits that outweigh program costs" (p. 6). They note that their judgment is consistent with the findings of Currie and her colleagues and of Ludwig and Miller, all discussed above. As Yoshikawa did, Ludwig and Phillips compared the effects found in the Impact Study with those found in other programs and concluded, "the ratio of benefits to costs for Head Start . . . may compare favorably with most other educational interventions" (p. 3). They attributed the broad range of positive impacts for Head Start to its comprehensive services "focused on nutrition, physical and mental health, parenting and social services, as well as education" (p. 11). They pointed out the huge impact of crime reduction in the cost–benefit analyses of early intervention efforts and concluded that Head Start's comprehensive approach is necessary for this effect because crime eventuates from developmental pathways that have both cognitive and social–emotional roots.

It is very important to recognize that the first-year findings of the National Impact Study are actually limited in their usefulness. All they reflect are the comparative benefits to poor children of experiencing the Head Start program for a 9-month period, either at age 3 years or age 4 years. More will be revealed in future reports of children's progress through the third grade of school. The third grade is a particularly critical year since most future educational accomplishments have been found to be related to third-grade performance, which in turn should be related to a child's school readiness. Thus it may be too early to engage the results of the Impact Study in any definitive conclusions about the value of Head Start.

Conflicting Interpretations or Conflicting Agendas

The charge of the National Impact Study was to provide evidence on how well Head Start achieves its goal of improving school readiness and whether its influence carries through the early grades of elementary school. Inherent here is the accompanying question of just how much improvement in school readiness is necessary to decide if Head Start succeeds. I'm afraid the first-year findings of the Impact Study have become something of a Rorschach test.

People have looked at the findings through different lenses and have come to quite different conclusions.

Public debate over the initial Impact Study findings may have been ignited by President George W. Bush when he signed the 2007 Head Start reauthorization into law. In his signing statement he first praised Head Start by stating, "Because of the National Reporting System, we know that more Head Start programs are helping children gain early reading and math skills" (Woolley and Peters, n.d.b). Not only did Bush ignore the new data from the sounder Impact Study but also all the methodological criticisms that had been made of the NRS. After this reference to the NRS evidence, which was flawed but positive in regard to Head Start's success, the president took his usual anti-Head Start stance by saying, "But we must take steps to improve Head Start to ensure that low-income children arrive at school ready to learn." This statement was in keeping with that made by his senior lieutenant on Head Start matters, Wade Horn. Horn explicitly asserted that the weak findings of the National Impact Study proved Head Start needed much more work to be successful.

Doug Besharov, a constant critic of Head Start who has espoused devolving the program to the states, also publicly proclaimed that the small positive findings obtained in the Impact Study proved that Head Start did not work. In a statement on the website of the American Enterprise Institute titled, "Head Start's Broken Promise," Besharov (2005) called the positive findings of the Impact Study "disappointingly small." Ludwig and Phillips contrast this negative spin with a positive interpretation of the exact same findings by Yoshikawa (2005), who judged the results were consistently positive and impressive.

Besharov used the findings of the Impact Study to condemn Head Start because participation did not eliminate the large gap between the educational achievements of rich and poor children. Reflecting the views of the George W. Bush administration, Besharov insists that Head Start only warrants further taxpayer support if its graduates achieve the same degree of school readiness as more affluent children. Ludwig and Phillips counter that it is unfair to require that a "program generates miraculous benefits and totally eliminates a complicated social problem" to deem it worthy of public support (2007, p. 3).

Perhaps the best antidote to unrealistically optimistic views of the potential of preschool intervention is the book, *Class and Schools*, by Richard Rothstein (2004). Rothstein describes the broad array of social and economic reforms that would be necessary to equalize the chances of lower- and middle-class children by the time of school entry. It is true that many western democracies have engaged in the types of reform that Rothstein recommends, but citizens of these nations pay a large share of their income in taxes and give up free choice. This is not in keeping with the American ethos.

We must give up the magical thinking that Head Start or any preschool intervention program can put poor and middle-class children on a level playing field. Nor should we waste our time in deciding just how much improvement in poor children's school readiness must be achieved to proclaim Head Start's success. Head Start provides both hope and promise to the poor segment of our society, and evidence is now conclusive that participants leave the program better off than when they arrived. Policymakers would be very wise to leave it up to hard-core trained scientists, not ideologues or voices with an agenda, to determine just how much better.

14

Deploying the Lessons in Head Start's History

In terms of size and national and international impact, Head Start is one of the most important children's programs mounted in America during the twentieth century. It remains unique in that it is managed directly by the federal government, which sends funding to local grantees throughout the nation. These grantees include Community Action Agencies, nonprofit and for-profit organizations, schools, Indian tribes, and a variety of groups serving migrant workers This broad coverage, and the physical and spiritual support of Americans from all walks of life, give Head Start a huge family of friends. One must admire the foresight of Lyndon Johnson, Sargent Shriver, Julius Richmond, and Jule Sugarman, who insisted on opening Head Start on a giant scale so it blanketed the nation. This omnipresence guaranteed that the program would retain national visibility and concern and have the staying power it could not enjoy as a small experimental program (which the experts recommended) that could quietly vanish without so much as a parting headline.

After some 45 years of operations, Head Start's mark extends far beyond the 25 million children and families it has served, and the millions more who have become involved in a variety of capacities. The program's first associate director, Jule Sugarman, feels that Head Start has never received the credit it deserves for the "enormous impact [it] has had on public policy at local, state, and federal levels" (Richmond, 2004, p. 108). To prove his point, he writes that "Head Start connected millions of low-income children to health care, often for the first time since their birth." He believes the results of Head Start's health component were critical to spurring federal and state Medicaid financing for poor children. Related to the health initiative, Sugarman notes that Head Start centers served healthy breakfast and lunch meals, providing "many children with an enormous boost in the adequacy of their nutrition." He feels that these experiences "were important to the development of the federal child nutrition and school lunch programs." He could have easily added the school breakfast program.

Reflecting on his Community Action sympathies, Sugarman also emphasizes the fact that Head Start has given employment opportunities to throngs of low-income people who began with little experience or formal training. He praises Head Start for its role in the creation of a cadre of early childhood education personnel. Indeed, the Child Development Associate credential developed within Head Start is now recognized as an indicator of teaching competency in 49 states and the District of Columbia. Sugarman concludes, "The Head Start experience has been valuable in and of itself, but its impacts on other public policies and programs must be considered as part of its achievements" (Richmond, 2004, p. 109).

Preschool Pioneer and Leader

At the top of the list of Head Start's contributions is the fact that it was the trailblazer for our nation's huge investment in preschool education. Sugarman notes that at Head Start's debut in 1965, only 15 states had universal kindergarten and none served younger children. Today at least 38 states have followed Head Start's example and mounted preschool programs. Three of these (Florida, Georgia, and Oklahoma) offer universal access, while the rest mainly concentrate on at-risk children or economically disadvantaged neighborhoods. The nonuniversal programs generally serve only a limited percentage of their target populations, so much of the mission of providing preschool education to poor children is still carried out by local Head Start centers. In fact, some of the states that fund preschool services do so by augmenting their Head Start programs.

Besides inspiring so many states to mount preschool programs for poor children, Head Start has also had an impact on other nations. I regularly entertain visitors at Yale from as far away as China who are interested in the Head Start approach and how it might be adaptable to their cultures. Canada has mounted a Head Start-like program, and England's Sure Start is similar to our Early Head Start. In recent years some global regions such as Latin America and the Caribbean nations have been particularly active in mounting early childhood development efforts. Britto and Gilliam (2008) note how much these developing countries have relied on the Head Start model to inform the construction of their own initiatives. As was the case at Head Start's birth, many of these nations view their programs as hope for reducing the incidence of poverty by improving children's educational status. They have also adopted Head Start's whole-child approach to educational success and provide health, nutrition, and other services as well as preschool education.

There is one dramatic difference in the underpinnings of the Head Start program and those of the developing nations. They have adopted the United Nation's Convention for the Rights of Children, which contains the statement, "Children are born with a right to have their learning needs met through approaches that promote their holistic development" (Britto & Gilliam, 2008, p. 88). At the time of Head Start's birth there was a little of the flavor of this doctrine in the sense that by helping poor children be ready for school, the program would promote social justice. However, over the years the basic rationale for Head Start and the billions of dollars the program has cost has come to center on economics. Children's rights certainly are no longer part of arguments for continuing to fund Head Start. This is not particularly surprising inasmuch as the only two nations that have not signed onto the United Nation's CRC are the United States and Somalia. The American approach has been strengthened in recent years by the use of cost–benefit analyses that show the dividends of investing in early intervention. The dollar amount of savings, not necessarily the egalitarian motive, has been the impetus for expanded access to preschool in the United States.

Some of the states that have mounted prekindergartens hope eventually to move from targeted programs for poor children to universal preschool available to all. (New York, Illinois, and West Virginia have already passed such legislation.) The field is currently witnessing a serious debate between those who champion the targeted approach and those who favor universality. In addition to the fact that targeted programs are less expensive than universal ones, the targeted approach rests on the argument that poor as compared to more affluent children have been found to benefit more from preschool education. Advocates for universal preschool counter with considerable evidence that poor children perform better when they are in classrooms integrated across socioeconomic class lines. Further, findings from Oklahoma's universal program show that middle-class children also profit from preschool experience (Gormley, Grayer, Phillips, and Dawson, 2005). As discussed in Chapter 5, another plus for universal programs if that they have a broad constituency that has more political clout than poor parents alone. This bigger voter block has a better chance of gaining the ears of policymakers. Several foundations as well as national business organizations have become advocates for universal access.

The momentum toward universal preschool education is far enough along that some thinkers have raised the question of what will become of Head Start if preschool becomes universally available. We ruminate on the possibilities in a chapter written with Sally J. Styfco in Zigler, Gilliam, and Jones (2006). Given the facts that a number of states have made no commitment to prekindergarten and most of those that have run relatively small programs, Head Start will be needed for some time to come to meet the early education needs of our nation's poor children.

However, in the distant future when universal preschool education becomes a reality, Head Start could be reconceptualized to fill the gap in critical services not addressed by public preschools. One possibility is to turn the whole program into Early Head Start to serve the needs of poor families with children from conception to age 3 years. Another plan arises from the fact that the state preschools tend to have better quality educational services than Head Start, but they do not provide health and other ancillary services to the extent that Head Start does. Since the education establishment has been reluctant to adopt Head Start's comprehensive approach to preparing children for school, Head Start centers could concentrate on these services. In this scenario the schools will provide education, which is their area of comfort and expertise, while Head Start will provide the needed health and social services that likewise contribute to school readiness.

Another potential role for Head Start is to become a therapeutic nursery school to treat preschoolers from all socioeconomic groups who are exhibiting mental health and/or behavior problems. These groups are not always well-served by public educators, who are quick to suspend them from preschool programs or tell their parents to wait another year so their children can "mature." Head Start has long had a mental health component that could be strengthened and expanded so the program becomes a primary provider of early therapeutic treatments.

Impact on the Field of Child Development

Head Start has certainly had a huge influence on me and on the field of child development that goes beyond the generation of a large scientific literature on early intervention. As I detailed in the early chapters of this book, prior to my involvement with Head Start I was a scientist conducting basic research, generating theories, and testing hypotheses emanating from theory in a rigorous experimental fashion. When I started in the field of human development some 50 years ago, developmental influences were thought to emanate from the mother–child dyad in a single direction flowing from the mother to the child. We now know that infants influence mothers as much as mothers influence children, and we have learned much about this intricate interaction between the two. The determinants of the course of human development have also been found to be much broader than the mother alone. We now appreciate the importance of the father, siblings, and the extended family as well as peers. We have come to recognize the role of the neighborhood and community and can appreciate national circumstances in wide-ranging areas such as economics and the environment, and the almost daily decisions made about children's lives by federal and local policymakers. This bio-ecological model is now the leading paradigm in the field but was not fully formulated when Head Start was founded. It is not accidental that the father of this paradigm was Urie Bronfenbrenner, who was a member of Head Start's planning committee. Urie was fond of saying, "You never understand a phenomenon until you try to change it." That is what we are doing in Head Start, namely by attempting to improve the child's growth trajectory, scientists and practitioners have learned much about child development and about effective interventions.

Before Head Start there was a great distinction between basic and applied science in the field of child development, with basic scholars granted a much higher status than applied workers. I took a lot of heat for what I thought was service to my country—administering a large early intervention program that was founded without the benefit of much scientific evidence and was struggling for direction. Bronfenbrenner and I both learned that entering the sphere represented by efforts like Head Start led to knowledge that enriched our theoretical structures, just as sound theory enriched our everyday efforts to improve children's performance. Today, the basic and applied sides of science are viewed as synergistic rather than two discreetly different sets of activities—a transformation helped along by scientists' engagement in Head Start.

Just as I have had the privilege of working in Head Start for some 4 decades, I have had the honor of playing a role in the birth of a new subdiscipline within the general field of psychology called child development and social policy. Scholars in this area work at the intersection of the knowledge base in child development and the construction of social policy for children and families. When I joined this movement I had only two role models, Urie Bronfenbrenner and Julius Richmond, one a child psychologist and one a pediatrician. In my generation there were dozens of such workers, and in the next generation there were hundreds. This subdiscipline now has several journals, a handbook, and a division in the American Psychological Association centered on children's services.

The Archibald Granville Bush Foundation of St. Paul provided the support to move this field along in its early years. Shortly after I returned to Yale following my service in Washington, a foundation representative approached me and asked if I would be willing to construct some useable measures to assess children's motivation (one of my areas of expertise). I pointed out how many measures already existed and how many more were in progress. I suggested that the foundation do something more exciting and needed with their philanthropy. The timing of their visit was opportune because my exasperation with working in Washington was still fresh in my mind. I remained troubled by the fact that I took on a major federal position with little knowledge of the nature of government or of how the system worked. I remember my frustration at having to burn up so much of my time by learning what I could have learned in a good course in advanced civics. I suggested that the foundation seed a training program in child development and social policy for students working in disciplines related to child development who wanted to learn about policymaking or policymakers who wanted to learn about child development.

The foundation representative voiced some interest and took the idea back to his home office. A serious barrier was that the foundation was not national but limited its activities to states in the upper Midwest. However, the idea generated enough interest and approbation that I was asked to come to St. Paul to make my case directly before the Board of Directors. I brought with me renowned scholars who had already crossed the line into policy: Urie Bronfenbrenner of Cornell and Julius Richmond and Sheldon White, both of Harvard. Fortunately, one of the board members was Irving Harris, a well-known Chicago businessman who knew a great deal about child development and had become one of our nation's leading advocates for better social policies and programs for children. The foundation decided to engage in its first national effort and granted start-up money for the Bush Centers in Child Development and Social Policy.

The flagship center was at Yale University under my direction. Added soon after was the center at Michigan under my mentor Harold Stevenson. This was followed by the center at UCLA under the joint direction of educator John Goodlad and child psychologist Norma Feshbach. The final center was at the University of North Carolina under the directorship of Jim Gallagher, who had himself served in an important position in the federal government. The associate directors at each site were also to become leading figures in the field. For example, Sharon Lynn Kagan was the Associate Director at the Yale center, and Ron Haskins was the Associate Director at the North Carolina center. The centers graduated several hundred fellows, many of whom likewise went on to become famous contributors in the area of child development and social policy. Although three of the original four Bush centers are no longer operative, many other centers with similar missions have opened in universities around the country. (The Bush Center at Yale has been renamed the Zigler Center in Child Development and Social Policy.)

Just as Head Start inspired the creation of this subdiscipline, it has also led decision makers in Washington to have a more positive view about the value of the advice that could be offered by experts in the field of human development. Learning from scholars, policymakers and their staffs have become much more knowledgeable about the nature of evaluation in the accountability process so dear to their hearts. The call for rigorous evaluation and scientifically based practices in government programs has become standard both in Washington and in state capitals. Unlike the pre-Head Start days, members of Congress today are quite conversant with "cost–benefit analyses" and "logic models." By the same token, researchers today typically add policy implications to write-ups of their work.

How and Whom to Serve

Over its lifetime, Head Start has had the unique foundation pillars of parent involvement and comprehensive services. To keep the structure strong, these pillars must be constantly maintained and refurbished. In the early twenty-first century, the parent involvement pillar has been more challenging to maintain than it was in the twentieth century. With changing demographics as well as the welfare reform of 1996, more Head Start parents are working outside the home. This gives them less time to participate in Head Start classrooms and administration. Further, parents must sometimes choose programs other than Head Start because they need full-day child care while they work. Head Start providers must analyze barriers to parent involvement and develop efforts to overcome them. For example, some programs are scheduling parent activities on weekends and in the evenings when working parents can attend.

Head Start had never been charged with providing child care to meet the needs of working parents. Its mission has always been to prepare children for school. There is not enough money in the Head Start budget to provide a high-quality preschool program and high-quality child care. Some Head Start programs have accessed the federal Child Care and Development Block Grant and state funds available to low-income parents to provide all-day, full-year wraparound sessions. The Clinton administration gave priority to grantees who were working to create extended-day and year-long programs. This strategy has been remarkably successful. Today nearly half of Head Start centers are open all day, all year to provide the preschool and ancillary services that the children need as well as the child care their parents must have.

Perhaps someday our nation will revisit the Comprehensive Child Development Act of 1971, which proposed combining Head Start with child care. Head Start centers would provide two types of service: a school readiness program for children of the poor and child care for children from all income groups. This would permit the integration of children across socioeconomic groups that is known to enhance poor children's educational performance but is currently forbidden by Head Start policy. Absent a merger of the preschool and child care systems, the policy of giving higher funding priority to Head Start centers that access child care funds has important advantages for poor children. The average quality of child care in America today is poor to mediocre. Research to date has indicated that when child care is combined with the Head Start program, the quality of the child care improves (Zigler, Marsland, and Lord, 2009). The current policy that encourages providing Head Start families with child care as well as preschool education has therefore been a win-win situation even if it falls short of the ideal of making Head Start a full-day, full-year program.

Best Practices

Head Start's approach to preparing children for school has always been comprehensive, addressing the needs of the whole child across physical, cognitive, and socioemotional domains. Although this approach has now been validated, unrest remains about how to balance the amount of attention given to each of these areas. At the extremes are those who take a strictly cognitive approach to school readiness and believe activities should be limited to academics and those who champion the socioemotional approach, arguing that academic skills will fall into place when children are socially and physically ready for formal schooling. Over the years as one side or the other appeared to be winning the debate, Head Start was pressured to follow the leading position. In Chapter 12 we saw that George W. Bush demanded that Head Start emphasize cognitive development in general and literacy in particular. Not only did the Bush administration impose the CIRCLE curriculum onto Head Start classrooms, but teachers had little choice but to teach to the cognitive tests that comprised the NRS. These practices were the opposite of those encouraged in an earlier period, when there was almost an abhorrence for early literacy training and some Head Start workers refused to have alphabet letters up on the walls. They were following the lead of David Elkind, a national authority who was arguing that an emphasis on academic training in preschool produced "The Hurried Child" (1981) or constituted "Miseducation" (1987). Elkind's extreme view was matched by those who believed the entire purpose of preschool is to inculcate in the child a positive self-image. This presumably will enable the child to approach learning with an eagerness and "I can do it" attitude.

It is now clear that neither of these extreme positions is defensible. Head Start has weathered the push and pull from the opposing sides and should take the lead in the debate between those who insist on a cognitive focus and the "self-esteem" enthusiasts. Preschoolers of course need exposure to academics so they will hit the ground running when they begin elementary school. At the same time, they need to feel confident that they are capable learners and can meet the behavioral and social expectations present in the classroom environment. Some early childhood educators have long argued that we can intentionally teach preschool literacy and numeracy skills but should do so in a developmentally appropriate way. For example, Ann Epstein (2007) writes that preschool teachers should use knowledge, judgment, and expertise to organize learning experiences for preschoolers but should pay attention to teaching opportunities that arise and take advantage of these "teachable moments." Epstein's guide, published by NAEYC, provides specific teaching strategies for interacting intentionally with children in key subject areas (literacy, mathematics, scientific reasoning, social development, and social studies, as well as physical movement and visual art).

Needless to say, such teaching strategies are brought into an educator's repertoire through coursework and training. The findings of the FACES and the National Impact studies make clear that the quality of teaching in Head Start today is far superior than that found in Head Start classrooms in the early years, when it was not uncommon to find high school graduates as lead teachers. First Head Start moved to CDAs for this position, and today the bulk of Head Start's lead teachers have AA degrees. Employing better trained teachers and making sure the curricula used in Head Start is at the cutting edge of our knowledge base in preschool education should be Head Start's top priorities for the future. Congress must do its share by providing the program with the funds required to improve the quality of teaching in Head Start centers.

Target Population

Head Start has always been charged to serve the poorest of the poor. Very low income is certainly a risk factor, and the lower the income level, the more harmful the effects on the course of child development. Yet the artificial (and some say antiquated) poverty line used to define Head Start eligibility does not portray a homogeneous group of families. Poor families have very different strengths and needs. For example, considerable research has now been done to demonstrate how much more in need are families with incomes at half the poverty level than those who are just below the line. Further, a family's needs are not determined by income alone. Head Start workers have been trained to appreciate that some families need more services than others and have attempted to individualize the program for participants. However, this has never been done in any formal or systematic way by the national Office of Head Start. It is interesting that some state preschool programs determine eligibility not by income alone but by other risk factors as well, for example, the child being abused or homeless. It is time that Head Start eligibility be redefined to incorporate the knowledge base in determining which families to enroll.

Over recent decades a great deal of work has been done on demographic characteristics that are known as risk and protective factors. For example, having a high intelligence quotient is considered a protective factor, whereas low parental education and single parenthood are considered risk factors. The more risk factors a child is exposed to, the more prone he or she is toward a variety of developmental difficulties. The effects of these risk factors have proven to be multiplicative rather than additive. Having four risk factors results in more than twice the poor outcomes than is found in families with two risk factors. There is a limit, however, to the predictive power of the number of risk factors a child experiences. For example, in the evaluation of Early Head Start, families with very few risks or a great many risks were found not to profit much from the program (Administration for Children and Families, April 2006). Apparently those carrying few risks were able to provide for their children's physical and emotional needs without the services of Early Head Start. Those families burdened with many risks were not helped by the program because the negative consequences of their troubles basically swamped the benefits from participation.

The meaning of the number, types, and effects of risk factors is still being unraveled scientifically. For example, Wheeler (2002) conducted a study in a Head Start program in Austin, TX, where intake workers collected data on risk factors at the time of the family's enrollment. Services were then adjusted to meet the needs of each family, with riskier families receiving more effort than those with less risk. Wheeler discovered that the number of risks was not destiny. Children's school readiness was found to be unrelated to their risk burden, likely because the Austin program was tailored to addressing these developmental threats.

The promise inherent in taking an explicit risks approach in the delivery of Head Start was emphasized in a study by Foster and colleagues (2005). They investigated what factors determined Head Start children's school readiness in the two key areas of emergent literacy and social functioning. They discovered that a family's socioeconomic standing did indeed influence these school readiness measures. They also looked at specific risks including the child's exposure to violence and criminality, depression in the child's primary caregiver, and the family's lack of social support. These had more of an influence on the readiness measures than socioeconomic status. They also found that the quality of the home as a learning environment (e.g., presence of books and reading to the child) also influenced both outcome variables. Thus, they conceptualized a poor home learning environment as a circumscribed risk variable. The similar relationships between these risk factors and both literacy and social outcomes lead the investigators to interpret the child's cognitive literacy outcomes and the child's social ability outcomes not as opposites but as intertwined phenomena. This interpretation is in keeping with the whole-child approach Head Start has always taken.

Such accumulating evidence on the role of constellations of risk factors suggests ways Head Start can be more responsive to participants' needs. In addition to conducting a needs assessment of newly enrolled families as is currently done, staff should create individual risk profiles. Services can then be tailored to each child and family and modified as progress is recorded. This way Head Start can begin to fit itself to the families it serves instead of requiring families to fit the program.

The Quality Imperative

As this book has hopefully hammered home, Head Start can only achieve the goal Congress has set for it if the services provided are of high enough quality to deliver their intended impact. Beginning with quality in the classroom, during the 2007 reauthorization (Chapter 12) Congress demonstrated that it was well-aware of the centrality of improving teaching quality in Head Start by again setting a timeline for when at least half of lead teachers must have BA degrees. And once again, Congress failed to provide the money to achieve this goal.

Head Start teacher salaries must be commensurate with those of public school systems or the program will never be able to attract and retain teachers with BA degrees.

Congress has also failed to walk their talk in their support of needed research. Although policymakers have finally funded a national impact study, the program has never been given the money for the pointed practical research necessary to illuminate essential elements of quality and the most effective practices. This was not the case in Head Start's early years at the Office of Economic Opportunity when between 1% and 2% of the program's $340 million budget was spent on research and evaluation. If that same percentage were being spent today, approximately $100 million would be targeted to research (Love, 2006). This amount is certainly not unreasonable for a $7 billion-a-year program. Private industry spends much more than that on R & D because it is treated not as an unnecessary frill but as vital to a company's health and future.

The Government Accountability Office (GAO) has been concerned about Head Start quality not just in the classroom but in all program components for many years. An arm of Congress, the GAO plays a watchdog role over all programs funded by the federal government. The agency attempted to add to Head Start's quality control infrastructure by conceptualizing what they have chosen to call a "risk management plan." The plan calls for far greater coordination among local centers, the regional offices, and Head Start's training and technical assistance (TTA) arm. Unfortunately, during the George W. Bush years the TTA was limited to literacy pedagogy, and the relations between the regional offices and local sites took on a definite abrasive quality. A clear manifestation of this was hostility evident during the external 3-year reviews, which traditionally were supposed to help local centers correct problems and improve service delivery. Instead, the charge was made that the external reviewers displayed much more animus than was necessary toward center staff. With the Bush administration retired, a richer collegial relationship is being established in which local programs, the regional offices, and the TTA arm work closely together toward the mutual goal of improving quality.

The philosophy underlying this new risk management system is reminiscent of the original concept of the regional office in which knowledgeable staff from the region viewed themselves as partners with local personnel, both having the same goal of advancing quality. Thus, the joint planning for quality improvement by the regional offices, the training and technical assistance experts, and local sites is the resurrection of a very good idea. GAO is to be commended for coming up with this plan, as is the national Head Start office for quickly beginning to implement the system.

Leadership

The Office of Head Start should have a leadership role in advancing quality. The federal official responsible for the national Head Start program during the George W. Bush years was knowledgeable about child development, but these years witnessed a serious deterioration in the qualifications of the Washington Head Start staff. Experts were in short supply, and key positions were made into temporary contract jobs. What the program needed was the opposite, that is, trained professionals who had the job security to commit to long-range planning. For example, weaknesses in Head Start's preschool education component have long been known. That the problems were not fixed is hardly surprising since for many years the education component was directed by an excellent civil servant who herself did not have the training or credentials of an early childhood educator. The fact that the mental health component has been continuously criticized over Head Start's lifetime is also not surprising since with the exception of a couple of years in the early 1970s, this major component had no director at all. The job was given to the director of the health component, typically a pediatrician. It is unrealistic to think that a good pediatrician can also direct the mental health component, which requires a different set of skills and training. During the Bush years the pediatrician position in Head Start was made temporary. Someone who works on a 1-year contract simply cannot make a sufficient long-term investment in his or her assigned component. It is time for each of Head Start's components to get a committed director who has experience and can advocate for that particular service in Washington to assure that the activity gets the proper funds and direction.

Head Start is approximately a $7 billion a year program, and it is penny wise and pound foolish not to provide the positions necessary to permit this large sum of money to be spent as effectively as possible. A careful human resources inventory should be conducted, beginning with the clear need for wise officials at the top to implement, manage, and care about the Head Start program. The national Head Start office should assure that each component has a director with appropriate training and abilities. The qualifications of personnel in each of the 10 regional offices should also be reviewed. Head Start's quality control infrastructure is such that these federal workers are absolutely essential to optimizing quality at the local sites.

Under Assistant Secretary Wade Horn, the Bush years witnessed a case of empire building in the Administration for Children and Families (ACF) that I feel is injurious to children not only in the Head Start program but to children in general. When I headed what is today the Administration on Children, Youth and Families (a branch of ACF), I worked directly with the Secretary. This arrangement allowed both Head Start and the Children's Bureau to have a certain amount of influence with top decision makers. Although this has not been the case since I left Washington, even after my tenure, Head Start had a bureau with its own chief. This person was directed by a senior federal official, the head of ACYF, who was typically an expert on children. This expertise was helpful because in addition to Head Start, this person was also responsible for the Children's Bureau. The Head Start Bureau chief was typically a high-level civil servant with training in management rather than in children's development. Ideally, people with knowledge of children's issues should head both ACYF and the Office of Head Start, as was the case during the Clinton administration when Olivia Golden headed ACYF and Helen Taylor directed Head Start. The ACYF chief answered to the Assistant Secretary, who answered to the Secretary of HHS. However, under Assistant Secretary Wade Horn the leadership structure of ACYF became extremely truncated. The Head Start Bureau was taken out of ACYF and turned into the Office of Head Start in ACF.

The same fate befell another major bureau in ACYF, namely the Child Care Bureau, which had responsibility for improving the quality of child care for all children in the United States. It was moved to the Office of Family Assistance, and its charge was changed to supporting child care for poor working parents. There have been a good number of complaints about Horn's decisions about the Child Care Bureau. (Indeed, the very competent head of the Bureau resigned shortly after it was moved.) As I have argued elsewhere (Zigler et al., 2009), the Child Care Bureau should be returned to ACYF and its mission restored to the original purpose of improving the quality of child care for all children and families in the nation. Just as a human resources inventory for Head Start is necessary, the diminution in the authority of the director of ACYF should be closely examined and an effort made to determine an organizational structure in HHS that enables those federal officials responsible for both Head Start and child care to best perform their duties.

Early Head Start

Another problem in need of solution concerns the relation between Head Start and the Early Head Start program. Currently Early Head Start is viewed by decision makers as little more than an adjunct to the much larger Head Start program. Because of the difference in the size and familiarity of the two programs, Congress is much more interested and involved in Head Start than in its younger version. Using John Merrow's criterion, a program should be judged as a success or failure by the percentage of eligible recipients it serves. On this metric the difference between Head Start and Early Head Start is dramatic. Head Start serves approximately 60% of eligible children, although with the recent extension of eligibility raised to 130% of the poverty line, the percentage of eligible children attending will in all likelihood decrease. By contrast, Early Head Start serves only about 3% of those eligible.

States have been slower in following Head Start and mounting programs for birth to age 3 as compared to programs for at-risk 3- and 4-year-olds. The state preschool programs today serve almost as many children as the 900,000 served each year by Head Start. For the most part, the states have not mounted intervention programs for children from birth to age 3, with the exception of some state home-visiting programs that do not work directly with children but rather with parents. As a major scholar in the field of infants and toddlers recently noted, "Early Head Start is basically stuck, serving less than 3% of the eligible population," while no one is stepping up to fill the gap (Knitzer, 2008, p. 18). This lack of attention persists in spite of the evaluation of Early Head Start that employed rigorous methodology and resulted in some positive findings, as did the longitudinal follow-up (Administration for Children and Families, April 2006).

I worked with the late Senator Edward Kennedy and the Clinton administration in putting the Early Head Start program into place, and I know from personal experience that there is a great deal of enthusiasm for the program on the part of Congress. The way policymakers have chosen to expand the program, however, shows that they think of it as a unit of preschool Head Start. In the 2007 Head Start reauthorization, Congress allowed Head Start centers to use monies originally to be spent on preschool slots for Early Head Start slots. It is time to move toward seeing these programs as two equally important interventions for different periods in a child's life. Congress should treat each program as a ship with its own bottom and fund each separately.

Early Head Start does not have its own budget. Instead, its primary funding comes from a small percentage of the Head Start budget. This is a flagrant case of stealing from Peter to pay Paul. As Head Start's funds are transferred to Early Head Start, and as preschool slots become infant and toddler slots, Head Start has fewer resources to carry out its mission. Congress is adamant about improving the quality of Head Start, but quality costs money—money the program can ill-afford to give to Early Head Start. Given the scientific base and huge need, Early Head Start should be at least as large a program as Head Start. This will never happen if Congress continues to conceptualize Head Start and Early Head Start as conjoined programs.

The basic problem of course is that there is simply not enough money being allocated to bolster the early lives of children with experiences that we know impact school performance and later life success. Until recently, major advocates for Head Start and Early Head Start have been parents and professionals who have a special interest in children's well-being. This situation has changed dramatically in recent years. Today the most effective advocates for children's programs are economists who view them as wise investments. These scientists have made careful calculations and claim that early childhood programs have a 17% or 18% annual return on the investment society makes in them. James Heckman has argued that the younger the child receives intervention, the greater the payoff to society. Today policymakers are paying close attention to economists, and their endorsement of the mission of Head Start and Early Head Start may be what it takes for these programs to grow and improve.

Plausible Expectations

If there is one lesson to be gleaned from the history of Head Start presented in this book, it is the importance of not overselling what early intervention in general and Head Start in particular can deliver. We knew in the 1960s that growing up in poverty was detrimental to a child's development. In the years since, we have learned a great deal about the extent to which specific mechanisms of poverty can compromise a child's potential. Even before this evidence was in, Head Start's planners did not believe that a brief summer program, which is how Head Start began, would have any effect. We just did not do a good job convincing policymakers and the public.

Today, Head Start is a 1- or 2-year program, but decision makers still have grandiose expectations for what it can achieve. From time to time, analysts still voice disappointment that the program does not sustain big increases in IQ scores as graduates progress through elementary school. Using the same mindset, the George W. Bush administration still criticized Head Start on the grounds that poor children who attend do not attain the same degree of school readiness as more affluent children. Of course they don't. They are, however, more prepared for school than they would have been without the experience. This outcome is not very sensational, so it has been difficult to convince decision makers of its very real value.

Today's most vocal Head Start advocates are economists, and they strike me as a mixed blessing. Their approach is to quantify early intervention's monetary benefits. Their cost–benefit analyses support their argument that early childhood programs are a good investment for taxpayers and will eventually raise the quality of the American workforce and ensure our nation's productivity and competitiveness in global markets. It seems to me the economists have brought the field full circle back to Head Start's beginnings when the program was hurt by ridiculous promises that this little preschool gesture would end poverty in America. If the savings to society the economists are promising do not materialize or cannot be precisely quantified, Head Start will once again disappoint. State preschool programs, many of which were mounted on the hope of economic returns, will also be threatened or deemed failures.

The economists make their predictions and build their cost–benefit analyses mainly based on three model programs—the Perry Preschool, Abecedarian project, and Chicago Child–Parent Centers. Although I believe the Perry Preschool and Abecedarian projects are theoretically of great impor-tance, I think it is unwise to make predictions about future benefits based on these two small interventions, each done in only one location many years ago. In the early days of intervention there were close ties between preschool experiments and the desire to reduce the prevalence of mental retardation (see Chapter 1). Both Perry and Abecedarian recruited children who were lower in intelligence than most children who live in poverty, many of whom have superior intelligence. The truth is that the poor children selected for these two famous programs were not representative of the poor population, so we cannot generalize from these findings to poor children in general.

Another problem is that these programs were mounted decades ago, and their results would not be replicated today. When these studies were done it was still possible to compare the treatment group with controls who had had no alternative program. The differences between the groups reflected the poor performance of the controls as well as the enhanced performance of the program participants. Such controls no longer exist. Modern comparisons of treatment and no-treatment groups are essentially tests of whether the intervention adds value over other available services. Today the Perry control group would probably be attending Head Start or Michigan's state preschool program. The North Carolina children would be in Head Start or the state's Smart Start centers. Love stresses that "the very success of [the Perry] experiment has had a negative influence in that it holds up a standard for expected effects that represent 1960s conditions and not 21st century community realities" (2006, p. 8).

Another issue is that in absolute terms, the performance of the participants in both programs is not very good compared to that of more affluent children. Although intervention children do better than the comparison groups, they still remain far below middle-class children. For example, being arrested fewer than five times was an indicator of the success of the Perry intervention, but this would be taken as abject failure in a middle-class community. Economists must not oversell how much preschool intervention can accomplish in closing the achievement gap between low- and middle-income children or they will only hurt those efforts they are trying to advance. (The same warning should be heeded by advocates of Early Head Start, who too casually borrowed from the early brain development research to promote very early intervention as a way to increase cognitive growth.)

Advocates must face the fact that efficacy studies of interventions should not be used to justify rolling out programs in the real world. The question is how well will the intervention travel and how will it fare when run by workers who are not its inventors? There is no such effectiveness evidence on either the Perry or the Abecedarian projects. As a scholar, I admire the theoretical contributions of these studies, but as a one-time decision maker and an advisor to decision makers, I would ignore them in setting policy. Not only did the creators conceptualize and implement their models, they also evaluated them. One would like arms-length evaluations across many sites utilizing the model, which is what we have in the Head Start Impact study as well as in the Early Head Start evaluation.

At this point in time I do not believe we have the evidentiary base to support the promises the economists (with the exception of Barnett) are making to policymakers and the public. We should rely less on programs mounted decades ago and seek to expand the empirical research that will give us a sound base for predictions and cost–benefit analyses. I agree with Greg Duncan (personal communication) that the only program among the three models that can truly inform today's decision makers is the Chicago Child–Parent Centers. This modern-day intervention has been conducted with representative poor children across many sites for many years. I also think we should pay more attention to the Oklahoma universal preschool, a high-quality program that is being externally evaluated by Bill Gormley and his colleagues. The results to date have certainly been impressive.

The NIEER center and many others are currently providing us with other evidence we need to make a solid case for the benefits of early intervention. If we use the evidence we have judiciously and conservatively, I remain optimistic that we will eventually produce the knowledge adequate to the task of informing policymakers and program developers. If we continue to promise the moon, we will only hurt the cause—a fact painfully obvious from Head Start's history.

As this book has made clear, absolutely central to Head Start's funding and future is whether decision makers in Washington perceive Head Start as a program that works or not. Central to assessing Head Start's effectiveness is having a clear, realistic goal. In 1998 Congress decreed that improvement in children's school readiness is Head Start's goal. This is a worthy and achievable mission. Of course, when a child is better prepared for school it is not unreasonable to expect better academic performance beyond the point of school entry. Such progress is the responsibility of parents and schools together. A family's involvement in the Head Start program strengthens the adults' parenting skills—skills that do not end when Head Start does. A great deal of Head Start's services target parents, so it is incomplete to judge the program's merit on the basis of child outcomes alone. Head Start provides parents with a variety of social services, helps to acculturate immigrant families, and promotes career development. To the extent that Head Start helps families become more functional, children can be expected to benefit for the long term.

Although I am satisfied with Congress's goal for Head Start as school readiness, I recommend that we remain explicitly aware that a corollary of this goal is improved family functioning, be it in a parent's child-rearing abilities, mental health, or financial status. This is a corollary since these factors also directly impact the child's preparation for school. The school readiness goal plus this suggested corollary would then reflect the actual nature of Head Start's two-generation contributions.

With these suggestions for the future, I step back from my nearly half-century involvement with America's Head Start program. Its history has been bold, illuminating, agonizing, and filled with potholes. Events within and outside of the program's control have shaped its course for better and for worse. Head Start today is not perfect, but its quality continues to improve and its traditional adaptability will serve it well as it adjusts to fill its niche in a changing society. A grasp of the successes as well as failures of the past will hopefully guide the next generation of Head Start's supporters and leaders in building a stronger, continuously better program.

Afterword

As this book goes to press, it is early in the term of President Barack Obama, who was elected to succeed George W. Bush. There is no question that the actions of the Bush administration demoralized the Head Start community, a sense of dejection that drifted over the entire field of early care and education. Obama's campaign promises as well as the actions he has taken since becoming president portend a new drive to advance children's causes and invest the nation's resources in their futures.

Obama's words earn credence from the public actions of the "first parents" toward their two young daughters. Mrs. Obama told American parents that before getting to her duties as First Lady, she will focus on being "first mom" to ease the girls' transition to their new home and schools. Their father promised them a puppy as a reward for enduring his long absences while he was on the campaign trail. Despite having a White House full of domestic staff, the children must share puppy-care chores and make their own beds so they will learn responsibility. Their grandmother has moved into the White House to help with child care. The Obamas are openly striving to be good parents and in the process modeling good parenting behaviors and the value they place in children. These attitudes give children's advocates a sense of hope that the ground they lost during the previous administration can be quickly made up, and real progress can resume.

In developing his early childhood policies, Obama had some very knowledgeable mentors. One was my friend and colleague of some 40 years, Barbara Bowman, a founder of the Erikson Institute and still a faculty member there. Dillon quotes her saying, "I talked with him [Obama] a lot about these issues, but he understood it from the beginning. He was always on board. I don't think I was the person who convinced him" (2008b, p. A1). Credit for this may belong to another very old friend of mine, Irving Harris. Harris was a Chicago philanthropist and self-taught expert on children's development. He too was a founder of the Erikson Institute, which was started in 1966 to meet the booming need for early childhood educators sparked by the creation of Head

Start. (According to Sam Meisels [personal communication, June 19, 2009], Harris thought his old Yale roommate, Sargent Shriver, would supply the money to fund the teacher training program but had to support it himself when the money never came through.) Harris was instrumental in putting into place Zero to Three, a national nonprofit whose board includes some of our nation's finest scholars on the development of children during these early years. He also founded the Illinois-based Ounce of Prevention Fund, a nonprofit devoted to improving the life chances of young children living in poverty. The president of the fund, Harriet Meyer, said, "Irving could mesmerize you" and "Barack met with Irving many times" (in Dillon, 2008b, p. A1).

In her interview with Dillon, Meyer recalled a 2001 reception her group held in Springfield, Illinois to discuss prekindergarten programs. She remembered that the only lawmaker who attended was Barack Obama, then a state senator. Another of Obama's advisors was Arne Duncan, who headed the Chicago public school system and is a strong advocate for poor children and for preschool education. Now the Secretary of Education, Duncan helped write Obama's preschool education platform and made sure it was not limited to 3- and 4-year-olds but extended to infants and toddlers and their families.

The list of early childhood experts the Obama team reached out to is long. To cite one familiar example, during the campaign Barbara Bowman and I discussed co-chairing Obama's children's policy committee. Barbara declined because of family reasons. I turned down the invitation because of my historical stance of always being politically neutral. I never wanted to close any doors should the side I wasn't on win. After the election, I did serve as a member of the transition team on early childhood. I was encouraged that the members included Dr. George Askew, a pediatrician and former Head Start student, as well as Olivia Golden, who was the Assistant Secretary responsible for Head Start during the Clinton administration.

The transition period was closely followed by the Head Start community. This group had little access to policymaking during the George W. Bush years. Their representative organization, the National Head Start Association (NHSA), was essentially ostracized by the Bush administration. The group was not consulted when major changes to the program were dictated, and Head Start officials took aim by limiting the funds available to Head Start personnel to attend NHSA's training institutes, which hurt the association's finances. There was of course a mutual distaste, since NHSA constantly and outspokenly criticized the actions of the administration. Thus it was a very good sign to the Head Start community when Ronald Herndon, chair of NHSA's board, was asked to be a member of the Obama early childhood transition committee. At these meetings Herndon emphasized the slippage that had taken place in Head Start and the dire state of poor children in America. He told me, "The case that I made over and over is that if it's going to change, it's going to take the attention of the presidency" (personal communication, December 15, 2008). Herndon's very presence at the transition meetings indicated that a page has been turned in the relationship between NHSA and the federal government.

After the inauguration, the Obama administration's policies and proposals for children did not disappoint child and family advocates. In the words of Sam Dillon, the $10 billion annually Mr. Obama initially pledged for early childhood education "would amount to the largest new federal initiative for young children since Head Start began in 1965" (December 2008, p. A1). It promises to be the largest federal initiative in support of early childhood education since President Clinton put into place Early Head Start. Since then, what forward motion in early education we have seen has taken place at the state level. Some 38 states have now mounted preschool programs for children at risk, including some that either have in place or are planning preschool education for all children regardless of family income. The most visible weakness of these programs is that the majority serve only 4-year-old children rather than 3- and 4-year-olds as does Head Start. There is also wide variation in per-pupil spending for state prekindergartens, ranging from nothing in the 12 states that have no program, to less than $3,000 in five states, to nearly $11,000 in New Jersey (Barnett, Epstein, Friedman, Boyd, and Hustedt, 2008).

Obama specifically promised to quadruple Early Head Start, which at the time was serving only about 3% of eligible children. He also pledged to establish a presidential early learning council to coordinate federal, state, and local policies. Promising to make poor children a priority of his administration, his proposals include expanding home-visiting programs for low-income mothers. Dillon notes Obama has not ignored the dismal state of child care, which millions of young children attend, and proposed "federal challenge grants for states to use for early care and education programs" (2008b, p. A1). Some of these proposals have already been passed into law. Investments in children include $1 billion added to the Head Start budget and a little over a billion earmarked for Early Head Start. Two billion dollars were added for child care. These additions were dwarfed by the huge increase for Title I of the No Child Left Behind Act. I recommended against this increase because there is little evidence that the national hodge-podge of Title I programs results in measurable benefits to children (Zigler, 2009). I concede there was probably little choice on the part of education officials. With the states reeling from reduced tax revenues during the recession, Congress could not overtly reduce or redirect their education grants at this time.

The increases in federal spending for early childhood programs were expeditiously passed because they became part of the economic stimulus package. With the economic crisis and pervasive recession affecting our nation and the world, stimulating the economy became policymakers' top priority. Obama's proposed early childhood investments were incorporated into the stimulus package on the premise that they will produce both long-term and short-term impacts on the economy. Arguing the long-term case, Sara Mead concluded, "High-quality early education is an investment in our future economic growth" (2008, p. 1). Economists like the Nobel Laureate James Heckman have been claiming for some time that the best economic investment we can make is in human capital, with the largest payoff coming from investments in programs for very young children. Cornelia Grumman (2008) carried this reasoning a step further, arguing that spending on early childhood initiatives not only creates immediate jobs for those employed in the programs but also contributes to a better economic future. She quotes NHSA findings that for every billion dollars invested in Head Start, 22,000 new jobs are created, and there are considerable savings down the road as program graduates do better in school and become more productive citizens.

An important caveat has been issued in response to Obama's ambitious early childhood education plan. Mead cautioned that there was danger from making these investments too quickly. She pointed out that "if funding gets ahead of capacity to deliver high-quality programs—the results will not live up to the high expectations advocates have created" (2008, p. 1). She correctly notes that high-quality programs have demonstrated impressive payoffs, whereas poor-quality programs have not. As illustrated in earlier chapters of this book, there have been historic instances when large additions of money have been given to Head Start to quickly increase the number of children served, with little attention to the quality of the services that could be delivered.

Although Mead's concern is a legitimate one, I am not really worried that Head Start officials will permit program quality to slump. The president himself has emphasized the importance of high-quality services. Further, the new administration contains some leading experts on children who have repeatedly made the quality argument. I trust that they will steer Head Start on the path of continuous improvement. We already know which way to go, and I am confident these leaders will seize every opportunity to take us there.

References

Administration for Children and Families. (2006, April). *Research to practice. Preliminary findings from the Early Head Start prekindergarten followup.* Washington, DC: Author.

Administration for Children and Families. (2006, December). *FACES findings. New research on Head Start outcomes and program quality.* Washington, DC: Author.

Administration for Children and Families. (2008). *About Head Start's National Research Conference.* Retrieved from http://www.acf.hhs.gov/programs/opre/hsrc/about/index.html#one.

Administration on Children, Youth and Families. (1981, October 22). *Head Start: Directions for the next three years* (draft report). Washington, DC: Office of Human Development Services, Department of Health and Human Services.

Advisory Committee on Head Start Quality and Expansion. (1993). *Creating a 21st century Head Start.* Washington, DC: U.S. Department of Health and Human Services.

Advisory Panel for the Head Start Evaluation Design Project. (1990). *Head Start research and evaluation: A blueprint for the future.* Washington, DC: U.S. Department of Health and Human Services. ERIC Document ED325257.

Alinsky, S. (1946). *Reveille for radicals.* Chicago: University of Chicago Press.

Ames, L. J., and Ellsworth, J. (1997). *Women reformed, women empowered: Poor mothers and the endangered promise of Head Start.* Philadelphia: Temple University Press.

Barnett, W. S. (2002, September 13). *The battle over Head Start: What the research shows.* Presented at a congressional Science and Public Policy briefing, Washington, DC. Retrieved from http://nieer.org/resources/research/BattleHeadStart.pdf.

Barnett, W. S., Epstein, D. J., Friedman, A. H., Boyd, J., and Hustedt, J. (2008). *The state of preschool 2008. State preschool yearbook.* New Brunswick, NJ: National Institute for Early Education Research.

Beatty, B. (1995). *Preschool education in America: The culture of young children from the colonial era to the present.* New Haven, CT: Yale University Press.

Beatty, B. (2001). The politics of preschool advocacy: Lessons from three pioneering organizations. In C. J. DeVita and R. M. Williams (Eds.), *Who speaks for America's children?* (pp. 165–190). Washington, DC: Urban Institute Press.

Berrueta-Clement, J. R., Schweinhart, L. J., Barnett, W. S., Epstein, A. S., and Weikart, D. P. (1984). Changed lives: The effects of the Perry Preschool program on youths through age 19. *Monographs of the High/Scope Educational Research Foundation*, No. 8.

Besharov, D. J. (1996, January 28). First Lady knows best. *Washington Post*, pp. WBK 1, WBK 10.

Besharov, D. J. (2005, October). Head Start's broken promise. *On the Issues.* Retrieved from http://www.aei.org/publications/pubID.23373/pub_detail.asp.

Bloom, B. S. (1964). *Stability and change in human characteristics.* New York: Wiley.

Bowman, B. T., Donovan, M. S., and Burns, M. S. (Eds.) (2000). *Eager to learn: Educating our preschoolers.* Washington, DC: National Academies Press.

Britto, P. R., and Gilliam, W. (2008). Crossing borders with Head Start: An analysis of international early childhood programs. *Infants and Young Children, 21*, 82–91.

Bronfenbrenner, U. (1974). Is early intervention effective? *Teachers College Record, 76*, 279–303.

Bronfenbrenner, U. (1997). Head Start, a retrospective view: The founders. In E. Zigler and J. Valentine (Eds.), *Project Head Start: A legacy of the War on Poverty* (2nd ed., pp. 77–88). Alexandria, VA: National Head Start Association.

Brooks-Gunn, J. (2003). Do you believe in magic? What we can expect from early childhood intervention programs. *SRCD Social Policy Report, 17*(1), 3–14.

Brown, B. (1985, August 23). *Review of CSH Synthesis Study of Head Start impact.* Unpublished memorandum, Department of Health and Human Services, Office of Human Development Services.

Cahan, E. D. (1989). *Past caring: A history of U.S. preschool care and education for the poor, 1820–1965.* New York: National Center for Children in Poverty.

Caldwell, B. M., and Richmond, J. B. (1968). The Children's Center in Syracuse, New York. In C. A. Chandler, R. S. Louris, and A. D. Peters (L. L. Dittmann, Ed.), *Early child care: The new perspectives* (pp. 326–358). New York: Atherton Press.

Campbell, D. T. (1969). Reforms as experiments. *American Psychologist, 24*, 409–429.

Campbell, F. A., Pungello, E. P., Miller-Johnson, S., Burchinal, M., and Ramey, C. T. (2001). The development of cognitive and academic abilities: Growth curves from an early childhood educational experiment. *Developmental Psychology, 37*, 231–242.

Carnegie Task Force on Meeting the Needs of Young Children. (1994). *Starting points: Meeting the needs of our youngest children.* New York: Carnegie Corporation.

Chafel, J. A. (1992). Funding Head Start: What are the issues? *American Journal of Orthopsychiatry, 62*, 9–21.

Clark, K. B., and Clark, M. P. (1950). The Negro child in the American social order. *Journal of Negro Education, 19*, 341–350.

Clarke, A. D. B., and Clarke, A. M. (1977). Prospects for prevention and amelioration of mental retardation: A guest editorial. *American Journal of Mental Deficiency, 81*, 523–533.

Clinton, H. R. (1996). *It takes a village and other lessons children teach us.* New York: Simon & Schuster.

Clinton, W. J. (1992, May 14). *They are all our children.* Speech at East Los Angles College, Los Angeles, CA. Retrieved from http://campaigntrails.org/catalogs/1992-Clinton-FTP/educat.txt

CNN.com. (2003, July 25). *House passes Head Start changes.*

Cohen, S. (2001). *Championing child care.* New York: Columbia University Press.

Condry, S. (1983). History and background of preschool intervention programs and the Consortium for Longitudinal Studies. In Consortium for Longitudinal Studies, *As the twig is bent . . . Lasting effects of preschool programs.* (pp. 1–32). Hillsdale, NJ: Erlbaum.

Consortium for Longitudinal Studies. (1983). *As the twig is bent—lasting effects of preschool programs.* Hillsdale, NJ: Erlbaum.

Copple, C., Cline, M., and Smith, A. (1987). *Paths to the future: Long-term effects of Head Start in the Philadelphia school district.* Washington, DC: U.S. Department of Health and Human Services.

Council for Professional Recognition (2008). History and mission of the Council for Professional Recognition and CDA. Retrieved from http://www.cdacouncil.org/ab_his.htm.

Currie, J. (2001). Early childhood education programs. *Journal of Economic Perspectives, 15,* 213–238.

Currie, J., and Neidell, M. (2007). Getting inside the "black box" of Head Start quality: What matters and what doesn't. *Economics of Education Review, 26*(1), 83–99.

Darlington, R. B. (1981). The Consortium for Longitudinal Studies. *Educational Evaluation and Policy Analysis, 3*(6), 37–45.

Darlington, R. B., Royce, J. M., Snipper, A. S., Murray, H. W., and Lazar, I. (1980). Preschool programs and later school competence of children from low-income families. *Science, 208,* 202–204.

Datta, L. E. (1976). The impact of the Westinghouse/Ohio evaluation on the development of Project Head Start: An examination of the immediate and longer-term effects and how they came about. In C. C. Abt (Ed.), *The evaluation of social programs* (pp. 129–181). Beverly Hills, CA: Sage.

DeCoster, S. (2008, Fall). Eight members of the Connecticut College community reflect on what shaped their political character. *Connecticut College Magazine.* Retrieved from http://aspen.conncoll.edu/camelweb/index.cfm?fuseaction=publications&circuit=cconline&function=view&uid=32&id=201629974

DeParle, J. (1993, March 19). Sharp criticism for Head Start, even by friends. *New York Times.* Retrieved from http://query.nytimes.com/gst/fullpage.html?res=9F0CE4D81E3AF93AA25750C0A965958260.

Deutsch, M. (1967). *The disadvantaged child: Studies of the social environment and the learning process.* New York: BasicBooks.

Deutsch, M., Deutsch, C. P., Jordan, T. J., and Grallo, R. (1983). The IDS program: An experiment in early and sustained enrichment. In Consortium for Longitudinal Studies, *As the twig is bent . . . Lasting effects of preschool programs* (pp. 377–410). Hillsdale, NJ: Erlbaum.

Dillon, S. (2008a, May 2). An initiative on reading is rated ineffective. *New York Times.* Retrieved from http://www.nytimes.com/2008/05/02/education/02reading. html?_r=1&scp=1&sq=An%20Initiative%20on%20Reading%20is%20Rated%20 Ineffective&st=cse&oref=slogin.

Dillon, S. (2008b, December 17). Obama's $10 billion promise stirs hope in early education. *New York Times*, p. A1.

Doernberger, C., and Zigler, E. (1993). Project Follow Through: Intent and reality. In E. Zigler and S. J. Styfco (Eds.), *Head Start and beyond: A nation plan for extended childhood intervention* (pp. 43–72). New Haven, CT: Yale University Press.

Elkind, D. (1981). *The hurried child.* Reading, MA: Addison-Wesley.

Elkind, D. (1987). *Miseducation: Preschoolers at risk.* New York: Knopf.

Ellsworth Associates. (1996). *An annotated bibliography of Head Start research: 1985–1996.* Washington, DC: U.S. Department of Health and Human Services.

Ellsworth, J., and Ames, L. J. (Eds.) (1998). *Critical perspectives on Project Head Start: Revisioning the hope and challenge.* New York: State University of New York Press.

Epstein, A. (2007). *The intentional teacher: Choosing the best strategies for young children's learning.* Washington, DC: National Association for the Education of Young Children.

Fight Crime: Invest in Kids. (2004). *Quality pre-kindergarten: Key to crime prevention and school success.* Washington, DC: Author.

Finder, A. (2005, September 25.) As test scores jump, Raleigh credits integration. *New York Times*, p. 1.

Foster, M. A., Lambert, R., Abbott-Shim, M., McCarty, F., and Franze, S. (2005). A model of home learning environment and social risk factors in relation to children's emergent literacy and social outcomes. *Early Childhood Research Quarterly, 20,* 13–36.

Galbraith, J. K. (1958). *The affluent society.* Boston: Houghton Mifflin.

Gamble, T., and Zigler, E. (1989). The Head Start Synthesis Project: A critique. *Journal of Applied Developmental Psychology, 10,* 267–274.

Garces, E., Thomas, D., and Currie, J. (2002). Longer-term effects of Head Start. *American Economic Review, 92,* 999–1012.

Gilliam, W. S., and Ripple, C. H. (2004). What can be learned from state-funded prekindergarten initiatives? A data-based approach to the Head Start devolution debate. In E. Zigler and S. J. Styfco (Eds.), *The Head Start debates* (pp. 477–497). Baltimore, MD: Paul H. Brookes.

Gilliam, W. S., and Zigler, E. (2001). A critical meta-analysis of all evaluations of state-funded preschool from 1977 to 1998: Implications for policy, service delivery, and program evaluation. *Early Childhood Research Quarterly, 15,* 441–473.

Goffman, E. (1961). *Essays on the social situation of mental patients and other inmates.* New York: Anchor Books.

Goldstein, J., Freud, A., and Solnit, A. J. (1973). *Beyond the best interests of the child.* New York: Free Press.

Goldstein, J., Freud, A., and Solnit, A. J. (1979). *Before the best interests of the child.* New York: Free Press.

Goldstein, J., Freud, A., and Solnit, A. J. (1986). *In the best interests of the child*. New York: Free Press.

Gormley, W. T., Jr., Gayer, T., Phillips, D., and Dawson, B. (2005). The effects of universal pre-K on cognitive development. *Developmental Psychology, 41*, 872–884.

Gormley, W. T., Jr., Phillips, D., and Gayer, T. (2008). The early years: Preschool programs can boost school readiness. *Science, 320*, 1723–1724.

Government Accountability Office. (2005, February). *Head Start: Comprehensive approach to identifying and addressing risks could help prevent grantee financial management weaknesses* (Report No. GAO-05-176). Washington, DC: Author.

Gray, S. W., and Klaus, R. A. (1970). The Early Training Project: A seventh-year report. *Child Development, 41*, 909–924.

Greenberg, P. (1969). *The devil has slippery shoes: A biased biography of the Child Development Group of Mississippi*. Washington, DC: Youth Policy Institute.

Greenberg, P. (1998). The origins of Head Start and the two versions of parent involvement: How much parent participation in early childhood programs and services for poor children? In J. Ellsworth and L. J. Ames (Eds.), *Critical perspectives on Project Head Start: Revisioning the hope and challenge* (pp. 49–72). New York: State University of New York Press.

Greenberg, P. (2004). Three core concepts of the war on poverty: Their origins and significance in Head Start. In E. Zigler and S. J. Styfco (Eds.), *The Head Start debates* (pp. 61–84). Baltimore, MD: Paul H. Brookes.

Grotberg, E. H. (1983). A tribute to the Consortium. In Consortium for Longitudinal Studies, *As the twig is bent... Lasting effects of preschool programs* (pp. xi–xiii). Hillsdale, NJ: Erlbaum.

Grumman, C. (2008, December 4). The pigtail stimulus package. *Huffington Post*. Retrieved from http://www.huffingtonpost.com/cornelia-grumman/the-pigtail-stimulus-pack_b_147880.html.

Hacsi, T. A. (2002). *Children as pawns: The politics of educational reform*. Cambridge, MA: Harvard University Press.

Hale, B. A., Seitz, V., and Zigler, E. (1990). Health services and Head Start: A forgotten formula. *Journal of Applied Developmental Psychology, 11*, 447–458.

Harmon, C. (2004). Was Head Start a Community Action program? In E. Zigler and S. J. Styfco (Eds.), *The Head Start debates* (pp. 85–102). Baltimore, MD: Paul H. Brookes.

Harmon, C., and Hanley, E. J. (1997). Administrative aspects of the Head Start program. In E. Zigler and J. Valentine (Eds.), *Project Head Start: A legacy of the War on Poverty* (2nd ed., pp. 379–396). Alexandria, VA: National Head Start Association.

Harrington, M. (1962). *The other America*. New York: Simon & Schuster.

Haywood, H. C. (Ed.). (1970). *Social-cultural aspects of mental retardation*. New York: Appleton-Century-Crofts.

Head Start has become a fire-free zone. (1993, April 12). *Newsweek*, p. 57.

Heckman, J. J. (2000). Policies to foster human capital. *Research in Economics, 54*, 3–56.

Henrich, C. C. (2004). Head Start as a national laboratory. In E. Zigler and S. J. Styfco (Eds.), *The Head Start debates* (pp. 517–532). Baltimore, MD: Paul H. Brookes.

Henrich, C. C., and Blackman-Jones, R. (2006). Parent involvement in preschool. In E. Zigler, W. S. Gilliam, and S. M. Jones (Eds.), *A vision for universal preschool education* (pp. 149–168). New York: Cambridge University Press.

Herbers, J. (1970, June 27). Provocative child agency head. *New York Times.*

Herrnstein, R. J., and Murray, C. (1994). *The bell curve: Intelligence and class structure in American life.* New York: Free Press.

Hicks, N. (1970, March 15). Child experts find development of knowledge stressed at expense of social and emotional growth. *New York Times,* p. 37.

Hoff, D. J. (2002, January 9). Mission imponderable: Goals panel to disband. *Education Week, 21*(16), 21,24.

Hood, J. (2004). Caveat emptor: The Head Start scam. In E. Zigler and S. J. Styfco (Eds.), *The Head Start debates* (pp. 499–510). Baltimore, MD: Paul H. Brookes.

Humphrey, H. (1964). *War on poverty.* New York: McGraw-Hill.

Hunt, J. McV. (1961). *Intelligence and experience.* Oxford: Ronald Press.

Institute of Education Sciences. (2007, October). *National assessment of Title I. Final report* (NCEE 2007-4014). Washington, DC: U.S. Department of Education. Retrieved from http://ies.ed.gov/ncee/pdf/20084014_rev.pdf.

Jensen, A. R. (1969). How much can we boost IQ and scholastic achievement? *Harvard Educational Review, 39*(1), 1–123.

Johnson, Lady B. (1997). Head Start, a retrospective view: The founders. In E. Zigler and J. Valentine (Eds.), *Project Head Start: A legacy of the War on Poverty* (2nd ed., pp. 43–49). Alexandria, VA: National Head Start Association.

Johnson, Lyndon B. (1997). Head Start, a retrospective view: The founders. In E. Zigler and J. Valentine (Eds.), *Project Head Start: A legacy of the War on Poverty* (2nd ed., pp. 67–72). Alexandria, VA: National Head Start Association.

Jordan, T. J., Grallo, R., Deutsch, M., and Deutsch, C. P. (1985). Long-term effects of early enrichment: A 20-year perspective on persistence and change. *American Journal of Community Psychology, 13,* 393–415.

Kagan, S. L., Moore, E., and Bredekamp, S. (Eds.) (1995). *Goal 1 Technical Planning Group. Reconsidering children's early development and learning.* Washington, DC: U.S. Government Printing Office.

Kantrowitz, B. (2007, August 21). Trouble in toyland [Newsweek Web Exclusive]. Retrieved from http://www.newsweek.com/id/35413.

Kennedy, E. M. (1993). The Head Start Transition Project: Head Start goes to elementary school. In E. Zigler and S. J. Styfco (Eds.), *Head Start and beyond: A national plan for extended childhood intervention* (pp. 97–109). New Haven, CT: Yale University Press.

Kerlikowske, R. G. (2005, July 4). Reducing criminality [Letter to the editor]. *New York Times,* p. A-12.

Keyserling, M. D. (1972). *Windows on day care.* New York: National Council of Jewish Women.

Kirschner Associates. (1970, May). *A national survey of the impacts of Head Start centers on community institutions* (ED045195). Washington, DC: Office of Economic Opportunity.

Klaus, R. A., and Gray, S. W. (1968). The Early Training Project for disadvantaged children: A report after five years. *Monographs of the Society for Research in Child Development, 33,* No. 4.

Knitzer, J. (2008). Giving infants and toddlers a head start: Getting policies in sync with knowledge. *Infants and Young Children, 21,* 18–29.

Kuntz, K. R. (1998). A lost legacy: Head Start's origins in Community Action. In J. Ellsworth and L. J. Ames (Eds.), *Critical perspectives on project Head Start: Revisioning the hope and challenge* (pp. 1–48). New York: State University of New York Press.

Labov, W. (1966). *The social stratification of English in New York City.* Oxford: Center for Applied Linguistics.

Lally, J. R., Mangione, P. L., and Honig, A. S. (1988). The Syracuse University Family Development Research Program: Long-range impact of an early intervention with low-income children and their families. In D. R. Powell (Ed.), *Parent education as early childhood intervention: Emerging directions in theory, research and practice* (pp. 79–104). Norwood, NJ: Ablex.

Landry, S. (2005). *Effective early childhood programs: Turning knowledge into action.* Houston: University of Texas Health Science Center.

Lazar, I., Darlington, R., Murray, H., Royce, J., Snipper, A., and Ramey, C. T. (1982). Lasting effects of early education: A report from the Consortium for Longitudinal Studies. *Monographs of the Society for Research in Child Development, 47*(2/3).

Lee, V. E., Brooks-Gunn, J., and Schnur, E. (1988). Does Head Start work? A 1-year follow-up comparison of disadvantaged children attending Head Start, no preschool, and other preschool programs. *Developmental Psychology, 24,* 210–222.

Lee, V. E., Brooks-Gunn, J., Schnur, E., and Liaw, F. R. (1990). Are Head Start effects sustained? A longitudinal follow-up comparison of disadvantaged children attending Head Start, no preschool, and other preschool programs. *Child Development, 61,* 495–507.

Leslie, C. (1989, February 20). Everybody likes Head Start. *Newsweek,* pp. 49–50.

Linehan, A., and Schwarz, R. (1996, Fall). Monitoring grantee performance and quality. *National Head Start Bulletin, 1*(60), 16–17.

Love, J. M. (2006, June 23). *24 million and counting: Reflections on 40 years of Head Start research in support of children and families.* Presentation prepared for the closing plenary session of Head Start's Eighth National Research Conference, Washington, DC.

Love, J. M., Tarullo, L. B., Raikes, H., and Chazan-Cohen, R. (2006). Head Start: What do we know about its effectiveness? What do we need to know? In K. McCartney and D. Phillips (Eds.), *Blackwell's handbook of early childhood development* (pp. 550–575). Malden, MA: Blackwell Publishing.

Ludwig, J., and Miller, D. L. (2007). Does Head Start improve children's life chances? Evidence from a regression discontinuity design. *Quarterly Journal of Economics, 122,* 159–208.

Ludwig, J., and Phillips, D. A. (2007). The benefits and costs of Head Start. *Social Policy Report, 21*(3), 3–18.

Madow, W. G. (1969). Head Start: Methodological critique. *Britannica Review of American Education, 1,* 245–252.

Magat, R. (1979). *The Ford Foundation at work: Philanthropic choices, methods, and styles.* New York: Plenum Press.

McCartney, K., and Rosenthal, R. (2000). Effect size, practical importance, and social policy for children. *Child Development, 71,* 173–180.

McKey, R. H., Condelli, L., Ganson, H., Barrett, B., McConkey, C., and Plantz, M. (1985). *The impact of Head Start on children, families and communities: Head Start Synthesis Project* (DHHS Publication No. OHDS 85-31193). Washington, DC: U.S. Government Printing Office.

McNemar, Q. (1940). A critical examination of the University of Iowa studies of environmental influences upon the IQ. *Psychological Bulletin, 37,* 63–92.

Mead, S. (2008, December 28). Solutions/Mead: Obama's $10 billion early childhood education pledge. *Washington Times.* Retrieved from http://www.washingtontimes. com/news/2008/dec/28/solutions-mead-obama-10-billion-pledge/.

Mediax Associates. (1980). *Accept my profile! Perspectives for Head Start profiles of program effects on children.* Westport, CT: Author.

Meisels, S., and Atkins-Burnett, S. (2004). The Head Start National Reporting System: A critique. *Young Children, 59*(1), 64–66.

Mencimer, S. (2008, January 21). Crayons down! Babes in test land. *Mother Jones.* Retrieved from http://www.motherjones.com/news/outfront/2008/01/crayons-down.html.

Merrow, J. (2002, September 25). The 'failure' of Head Start. *Education Week,* p. 52.

Miller, L. B. (1997). Development of curriculum models in Head Start. In E. Zigler and J. Valentine (Eds.), *Project Head Start: A legacy of the War on Poverty* (2nd ed., pp. 195–220). Alexandria, VA: National Head Start Association.

Mills, K. (1998). *Something better for my children: How Head Start has changed the lives of millions of children.* New York: Plume.

Morgan, G. G. (1981). The politics of day care. *Early Childhood Education Journal, 9*(2), 33–36.

Murray, C. (1984). *Losing ground: American social policy 1950–1980.* New York: BasicBooks.

National Commission on Excellence in Education. (1983). *A nation at risk: The imperative for educational reform.* Washington, DC: U.S. Government Printing

National Council of Jewish Women. (1999). *Opening a new window on child care: A report on the status of child care in the nation today.* New York: Author.

National Education Goals Panel. (1999). *The National Education Goals report: Building a nation of learners, 1999.* Washington, DC: U.S. Government Printing Office.

National Head Start Association. (2004, March 18). *Uncooking the books: Head Start grantees did better in 2001–2002 than in 2000, according to unpublicized HHS data.* Alexandria, VA: Author.

New York State Archives, States' Impact on Federal Education Policy Project. (2006). *Federal education policy and the states, 1945–2004: A brief synopsis.* Albany: New York State Education Department. Retrieved from http://www.archives.nysed.gov/ edpolicy/altformats/ed_background_overview_essay.pdf.

Newman, S. A., Fox, J. A., Flynn, E. A., and Christeson, W. (2000). *America's after-school choice: The prime time for juvenile crime, or youth enrichment and achievement.* Washington, DC: Fight Crime: Invest in Kids.

NICHD. (2007). Establishment and history. Retrieved from http://www.nichd.nih.gov/about/overview/history/index.cfm.

O'Brien, R. W., Connell, D. B., and Griffin, J. (2004). Head Start's efforts to improve child health. In E. Zigler and S. J. Styfco (Eds.), *The Head Start Debates* (pp. 161–178). Baltimore, MD: Paul H. Brookes.

Office of Head Start. (2007, February). *Head Start program fact sheet.* Washington, DC: Author.

Office of Inspector General. (1993). *Head Start expansion: Grantee experiences* (OEI-09-91-00760). Washington, DC: U.S. Department of Health and Human Services.

Omwake, E. B. (1997). Assessment of the Head Start preschool education effort. In E. Zigler and J. Valentine (Eds.), *Project Head Start: A legacy of the War on Poverty* (2nd ed., pp. 221–228). Alexandria, VA: National Head Start Association.

Palmer, F. H., and Andersen, L. W. (1997). Long-term gains from early intervention: Findings from longitudinal studies. In E. Zigler and J. Valentine (Eds.), *Project Head Start: A legacy of the War on Poverty* (2nd ed., pp. 433–466). Alexandria, VA: National Head Start Association.

Phillips, D. A., and Cabrera, N. J. (Eds.) (1996). *Beyond the blueprint: Directions for research on Head Start's families.* Washington, DC: National Academy Press.

Pizzo, P. D., and E. E. Tufankjian. (2004). A persistent pattern of progress: Parent outcomes in longitudinal studies of Head Start children and families. In E. Zigler and S. J. Styfco (Eds.), *The Head Start debates* (pp. 193–214). Baltimore, MD: Paul H. Brookes.

Powell, C. G. (1998). *Targeted fiscal investment and quality in preschool intervention programs: Policy lessons learned from the Head Start Expansion and Improvement Act of 1990.* Ann Arbor, MI: UMI Dissertation Services.

Ramey, S. L., Ramey, C. T., Phillips, M. M., Lanzi, R. G., Brezausek, C., Katholi, C. R., and Snyder, S. (2000). *Head Start children's entry into public school: A report on the National Head Start/Public School Early Childhood Transition Demonstration Study.* Washington, DC: U.S. Department of Health and Human Services.

Raver, C. C., and Zigler, E. (1991). Three steps forward, two steps back: Head Start and the measurement of social competence. *Young Children, 46(4),* 3–8.

Raver, C. C., and Zigler, E. (2004). Another step back? Assessing readiness in Head Start. *Young Children, 59(1),* 58–63.

Recommendations for a Head Start program by a panel of experts. (1965, February 19). Washington, DC: U.S. Department of Health, Education and Welfare.

Resnick, L. B. and Zurawsky, C. (Eds.) (2005, Fall). Early childhood education: Investing in quality makes sense. *AERA Research Points, 3(2),* 1–4.

Reynolds, A. J. (1995). One year of preschool or two: Does it matter? *Early Childhood Research Quarterly, 10,* 1–31.

Reynolds, A. J. (2003). The added value of continuing early intervention into the primary grades. In A. J. Reynolds, M. C. Wang, and H. J. Walberg (Eds.), *Early childhood programs for a new century* (pp. 163–196). Washington, DC: CWLA Press.

Richardson, E. (1976). *The creative balance.* London: Hamish Hamilton.

Richmond, J. B. (1997). Head Start, a retrospective view: Section 3, The early administrators. In E. Zigler and J. Valentine (Eds.), *Project Head Start: A legacy of the War on Poverty* (2nd ed., pp. 120–128). Alexandria, VA: National Head Start Association.

Richmond, J. B., with J. Sugarman. (2004). An early administrator's perspective on Head Start. In E. Zigler and S. J. Styfco (Eds.), *The Head Start debates* (pp. 103–109). Baltimore, MD: Paul H. Brookes.

Riessman, F. (1962). *The culturally deprived child.* New York: Harper.

Riessman, F. (1976). *The inner-city child.* New York: Harper & Row.

Rioux, J. W. (1967). The disadvantaged child in school. In J. Hellmuth (Ed.), *Disadvantaged child* (Vol. 1, pp. 77–120). Seattle, WA: Special Child Publications.

Rodham, H. (1973). Children under the law. *Harvard Educational Review, 41,* 487–514.

Rosenbaum, D. E. (1981, March 17). Reagan's "safety net" proposal: Who will land, who will fall. *New York Times.* Retrieved from http://query.nytimes.com/gst/fullpage. html?res=9E05EEDC1239F934A25750C0A967948260&sec=health&spon=&page wanted=all.

Rosenthal, A. (1992, July 23). The 1992 campaign; Bush on the attack but charges against Clinton and Gore could raise his own negative image. *New York Times.* Retrieved from http://query.nytimes.com/gst/fullpage.html?res=9E0CEEDC153 DF930A15754C0A964958260&n=Top/Reference/Times%20Topics/People/R/ Rosenthal,%20Andrew&scp=20&sq=andrew%20+%20rosenthal%20+%201992& st=cse#

Rosenthal, R., and Jacobson, L. (1968). *Pygmalion in the classroom.* New York: Holt, Rinehart & Winston.

Ross, C. J. (1997). Early skirmishes with poverty: The historical roots of Head Start. In E. Zigler and J. Valentine (Eds.), *Project Head Start: A legacy of the War on Poverty* (2nd ed., pp. 21–42). Alexandria, VA: National Head Start Association.

Rothstein, R. (2004). *Class and schools: Using social, economic, and educational reform to close the black–white achievement gap.* Washington, DC: Economic Policy Institute.

Rovner, J. (1990). Head Start is one program everyone wants to help. *Congressional Quarterly, 48,* 1191–1195.

Rusk, D. (2006). Housing policy is school policy. In N. F. Watt, C. Ayoub, R. H. Bradley, J. E. Puma, and W. A. LeBoeuf (Eds.), *The crisis in youth mental health. Vol. 4: Early intervention programs and policies* (pp. 53–80). Westport, CT: Praeger.

Sale, J. S. (1997). Implementation of a Head Start preschool education program: Los Angeles, 1965–1967. In E. Zigler and J. Valentine (Eds.), *Project Head Start: A legacy of the War on Poverty* (2nd ed., pp. 175–194). Alexandria, VA: National Head Start Association.

Sanchez, L. (2004). A former Head Start student's views. In E. Zigler and S. J. Styfco (Eds.), *The Head Start Debates* (pp. 219–220). Baltimore, MD: Paul H. Brookes.

Schemo, D. J. (2004, April 16). Chief of Head Start is accused of mismanaging a center. *New York Times*, p. A17.

Schlafly, P. (1988a, January 21). Anti-religious provisions of child care bill, S.1885. *Daily Spectrum*, p. 53.

Schlafly, P. (1988b, January 21). A plan to "sovietize" the American family. *Daily Spectrum*, p. 12.

Schweinhart, L. J., and Weikart, D. P. (1980). Young children grow up: The effects of the Perry Preschool Program on youths through age 15. *Monographs of the High/Scope Educational Research Foundation*, No. 7.

Sears, R. R., and Maccoby, E. E. (1957). *Patterns of child rearing*. Palo Alto, CA: Stanford University Press.

Segal, A. (1989, May 31). *Quality in child care: What it is and how it can be encouraged*. Retrieved from http://aspe.hhs.gov/daltcp/reports/ccqual.htm.

Seitz, V., and Apfel, N. H. (1994). Parent-focused intervention: Diffusion effects on siblings. *Child Development, 65*, 677–683.

Shelton, E. (1970, May 7). Don't crucify child on cross of IQ. *Des Moines Register*, p. 11.

Shonkoff, J., and Phillips, D. A. (Eds.). (2000). *From neurons to neighborhoods*. Washington, DC: National Academy of Sciences.

Shriver, S. (1997). Head Start, a retrospective view: The founders. In E. Zigler and J. Valentine (Eds.), *Project Head Start: A legacy of the War on Poverty* (2nd ed., pp. 49–67). Alexandria, VA: National Head Start Association.

Silver Ribbon Panel. (1990). *Head Start: The nation's pride. A nation's challenge*. Alexandria, VA: National Head Start Association.

Silver, H., and Silver, P. (1991). *An educational war on poverty: American and British policy-making 1960–1980*. New York: Cambridge University Press.

Skeels, H. M. (1966). Adult status of children with contrasting early life experiences: A follow-up study. *Monographs of the Society for Research in Child Development, 31*(3). Serial No. 105.

Smuts, A. B. (2006). *Science in the service of children 1893–1935*. New Haven, CT: Yale University Press.

Snow, C. E., and VanHemel, S. B. (Eds.). (2008). *Early childhood assessment: Why, what, and how*. Washington, DC: National Academies Press.

Spatig, L., Parrott, L., Dillon, A., and Conrad, K. (1998). Beyond busywork: Crafting a powerful role for low-income mothers in schools or sustaining inequalities? In J. Ellsworth and L. J. Ames (Eds.), *Critical perspectives on project Head Start: Revisioning the hope and challenge* (pp. 73–110). New York: State University of New York Press.

Special Olympics. (2007). From backyard camp to global movement: The beginnings of Special Olympics. Retrieved from http://www.specialolympics.org/Special+Olympics+Public+Website/English/About_Us/History/default.htm.

Spitz, H. (1986). *Raising of intelligence: A selected history of attempts to raise retarded intelligence*. Hillsdale, NJ: Erlbaum.

Social Security Administration (SSA). (n.d.). Social Security Online. History: The Children's Bureau. Retrieved from http://www.ssa.gov/history/childb1.html.

Stendler-Lavatelli, C. B. (1968). Environmental intervention in infancy and early childhood. In M. Deutsch, I. Katz, and A. R. Jensen (Eds.), *Social class, race, and psychological development* (pp. 347–380). New York: Holt, Rinehart & Winston.

Stone, J. G. (1997). General philosophy: Preschool education within Head Start. In E. Zigler and J. Valentine (Eds.), *Project Head Start: A legacy of the War on Poverty* (2nd ed., pp. 163–174). Alexandria, VA: National Head Start Association.

Stossel, S. (2004). *Sarge: The life and times of Sargent Shriver.* Washington, DC: Smithsonian Books.

Sugarman, J. M. (1997). Head Start, A retrospective view: The early administrators. In E. Zigler and J. Valentine (Eds.), *Project Head Start: A legacy of the War on Poverty* (2nd ed., pp. 114–120). Alexandria, VA: National Head Start Association.

Towns, E. L. (Ed.). (1975). *A history of religious educators.* Grand Rapids, MI: Baker Book House.

U.S. Department of Health and Human Services, Administration for Children and Families (2005, May). *Head Start Impact Study: First year findings.* Washington, DC: Author.

U.S. Department of Health and Human Services. (1980). *Head Start in the 1980s. Review and recommendations.* Washington, DC: Author.

U.S. Department of Health and Human Services. (1999, December 13). *HHS News. Head Start bests Mercedes and BMW in customer satisfaction.* Washington, DC: Author.

U.S. Department of Health and Human Services. (2003). *Biennial report to Congress: The status of children in Head Start programs.* Washington, DC: Author.

U.S. Department of Health and Human Services. (2003, May). *Head Start FACES 2000: A whole-child perspective on program performance.* Fourth Progress Report. Washington, DC: Author.

U.S. Department of Health and Human Services. (2003, June). *Strengthening Head Start: What the evidence shows.* Washington, DC: Author

U.S. General Accounting Office. (1997, April). *Head Start. Research provides little information on impact of current program* (Report GAO/HEHS-97-59). Washington, DC: Author.

Valentine, J. (1997). Program development in Head Start: A multifaceted approach to meeting the needs of families and children. In E. Zigler and J. Valentine (Eds.), *Project Head Start: A legacy of the War on Poverty* (2nd ed., pp. 349–365). Alexandria, VA: National Head Start Association.

Verzaro-O'Brien, M., Powell, G., and Sakamoto, L. (1996). *Investing in quality revisited.* Alexandria, VA: National Head Start Association.

Vinovskis, M. A. (1999). *History and educational policymaking.* New Haven: Yale University Press.

Vinovskis, M. A. (2002). *The Carter Administration's attempt to transfer Head Start into the U.S. Department of Education in the late 1970's.* Unpublished manuscript, University of Michigan.

Vinovskis, M. A. (2005). *The birth of Head Start: Preschool education policies in the Kennedy and Johnson administrations.* Chicago: University of Chicago Press.

Washington, V., and Bailey, U. J. O. (1995). *Project Head Start: Models and strategies for the twenty-first century*. New York: Garland.

Watt, N. F., and Bradley, R. H. (2006). Introduction: Transforming the village that raises our children. In N. F. Watt, C. Ayoub, R. H. Bradley, J. Puma, and W. LeBoeuf (Eds.) *The crisis in youth mental health. Vol. 4: Early intervention programs and policies* (pp. xvii–xxxv). Westport, CT: Praeger.

Wegman, M. E. (1997). Head Start, a retrospective view: The founders. In E. Zigler and J. Valentine (Eds.), *Project Head Start: A legacy of the War on Poverty* (2nd ed., pp. 109–112). Alexandria, VA: National Head Start Association.

Westinghouse Learning Corp. (1969). *The impact of Head Start: An evaluation of the effects of Head Start on children's cognitive and affective development*. Ohio University report to the Office of Economic Opportunity. Washington, DC: Clearinghouse for Federal Scientific and Technical Information (ED036321).

Wexler, J. G. (1997). Head Start, a retrospective view: The founders. In E. Zigler and J. Valentine (Eds.), *Project Head Start: A legacy of the War on Poverty* (2nd ed., pp. 112–114). Alexandria, VA: National Head Start Association.

Wheeler, C. M. (2002). A longitudinal investigation of preschoolers' Head Start experience and subsequent school readiness (Doctoral dissertation, Yale University). *Dissertation Abstracts International, 63*(03), 1592B.

White, S. H. (1970). The National Impact Study of Head Start. In J. Hellmuth (Ed.), *Disadvantaged child. Vol. 3: Compensatory education: A national debate* (pp. 163–184). New York: Brunner/Mazel.

Wolff, M., and Stein, A. (1966). Study I: Six months later, a comparison of children who had Head Start, Summer 1965, with their classmates in kindergarten. Washington, DC: Research and Evaluation Office, Project Head Start, OEO.

Woods, R. B. (2006). *LBJ: Architect of American ambition*. New York: Free Press.

Woolley, J. T., and Peters, G. (n.d.a). George W. Bush address before a joint session of the Congress on administration goals, February 27, 2001. *The American presidency project* [online]. Santa Barbara: University of California (hosted). Retrieved from http://www.presidency.ucsb.edu/ws/?pid=29643.

Woolley, J. T., and Peters, G. (n.d.b). George W. Bush statement on signing the Improving Head Start for School Readiness Act of 2007, December 12, 2007. *The American presidency project (online)*. Santa Barbara, University of California. Retrieved from http://www.presidency.ucsb.edu/ws/index.php?pid=76124.

Woolley, J., and Peters, G. (n.d.c). Lyndon B. Johnson remarks at the swearing in of Frederick DelliQuadri Chief of the Children's Bureau. *The American presidency project* [online]. Santa Barbara: University of California. Retrieved from http://www.presidency.ucsb.edu/ws/index.php?pid=28948&st=&st1=

Woolley, J. T., and Peters, G. (n.d.d). Republican party platform of 1980. *The American presidency project [online]*. Santa Barbara: University of California. Retrieved from http://www.presidency.ucsb.edu/ws/?pid=25844.

Woolley, J. T., and Peters, G. (n.d.e). Republican party platform of 1988. An American vision: For our children and our future. *The American presidency project [online]*.

Santa Barbara: University of California. Retrieved from http://www.presidency. ucsb.edu/ws/?pid=25844.

Woolley, J. T., and Peters, G. (n.d.f). Richard Nixon. Veto of the Economic Opportunity Amendments of 1971. *The American presidency project [online]*. Retrieved from http://www.presidency.ucsb.edu/ws/?pid=3251.

Woolley, J. T., and Peters, G. (n.d.g). Ronald Reagan 1981 inaugural address. *The American presidency project [online]*. Santa Barbara: University of California. Retrieved from http://www.presidency.ucsb.edu/ws/print.php?pid=43130.

Yando, R., Seitz, V., and Zigler, E. (1979). *Intellectual and personality characteristics of children: Social class and ethnic group differences*. Hillsdale, NJ: Erlbaum.

Yoshikawa, H. (2005). *Placing the first-year findings of the National Head Start Impact Study in context*. Washington, DC: Society for Research in Child Development.

Zaslow, M. (2008). Issues for the learning community. *Infants and Young Children, 21*(1), 4–17.

Zigler, E. (1970). The nature–nurture issue reconsidered. In H. C. Haywood (Ed.), *Social-cultural aspects of mental retardation* (pp. 81–106). New York: Appleton-Century-Crofts.

Zigler, E. (1997). Head Start: Not a program but an evolving concept. In E. Zigler and J. Valentine (Eds.), *Project Head Start: A legacy of the War on Poverty* (2nd ed., pp. 367–378). Alexandria, VA: National Head Start Association.

Zigler, E. (1998). A place of value for applied and policy studies. *Child Development, 69*, 532–542.

Zigler, E. (2009, February 4). A new Title I: From a "hodgepodge of efforts" to a targeted K-3 program. *Education Week, 28*(20), 26,34.

Zigler, E., and Anderson, K. (1997). An idea whose time had come: The intellectual and political climate for Head Start. In E. Zigler and J. Valentine (Eds.), *Project Head Start: A legacy of the War on Poverty* (2nd ed., pp. 163–174). Alexandria, VA: National Head Start Association.

Zigler, E., and Cascione, R. (1977). Head Start has little to do with mental retardation: A reply to Clarke and Clarke. *American Journal of Mental Deficiency, 82*, 246–249.

Zigler, E., Finn-Stevenson, M., and Hall, N. W. (2002). *The first three years and beyond: Brain development and social policy*. New Haven, CT: Yale University Press.

Zigler, E., Gilliam, W. S., and Jones, S. M., with Styfco, S. J. (2006). A place for Head Start in a world of universal preschool. In E. Zigler, W. Gilliam, and S. M. Jones, *A vision for universal preschool education* (pp. 216–240). New York: Cambridge University Press.

Zigler, E., Gordic, B., and Styfco, S. J. (2007). What is the goal of Head Start? Four decades of confusion and debate. *NHSA Dialog, 10*, 83–97.

Zigler, E., and Hodapp, R. M. (1986). *Understanding mental retardation*. New York: Cambridge University Press.

Zigler, E., and Lang, M. (1991). *Child care choices: Balancing the needs of children, families, and society*. New York: Free Press.

Zigler, E., Marsland, K., and Lord, H. (2009). *The tragedy of child care in America*. New Haven, CT: Yale University Press.

Zigler, E., and Muenchow, S. (1992). *Head Start: The inside story of America's most successful educational experiment.* New York: Basic Books.

Zigler, E., Piotrkowski, C. S., and Collins, R. (1994). Health services in Head Start. *Annual Review of Public Health, 15,* 511–534.

Zigler, E., and Styfco, S. J. (1993a). An earlier Head Start: Planning an intervention program for economically disadvantaged families and children ages zero to three, *Zero to Three, 14*(2), 25–28.

Zigler, E., and Styfco, S. J. (1993b). Strength in unity: Consolidating federal education programs for young children. In E. Zigler and S. J. Styfco (Eds.), *Head Start and beyond: A national plan for extended childhood intervention* (pp. 111–145). New Haven, CT: Yale University Press.

Zigler, E., and Styfco, S. J. (1994). Is the Perry Preschool better than Head Start? Yes and no. *Early Childhood Research Quarterly, 9,* 269–287.

Zigler, E., and Styfco, S. J. (2004). Moving Head Start to the states: One experiment too many. *Applied Developmental Science, 8,* 51–55.

Zigler, E., and Trickett, P. (1978). IQ, social competence, and evaluation of early childhood intervention programs. *American Psychologist, 33,* 789–798.

Zigler, E., and Valentine, J. (Eds.). (1997). *Project Head Start: A legacy of the War on Poverty* (2nd ed.). Alexandria, VA: National Head Start Association.

Index